PAUL AND THE NEW PERSPECTIVE

Paul and the New Perspective

SECOND THOUGHTS
ON THE ORIGIN OF PAUL'S GOSPEL

SEYOON KIM

WILLIAM B. EERDMANS PUBLISHING COMPANY
GRAND RAPIDS, MICHIGAN / CAMBRIDGE, U.K.

Published 2002 by Wm. B. Eerdmans Publishing Co.
255 Jefferson Ave. S.E., Grand Rapids, Michigan 49503 /
P.O. Box 163, Cambridge CB3 9PU U.K.
www.eerdmans.com

A parallel edition has been published by
J. C. B. Mohr (Paul Siebeck) Tübingen
Wilhelmstraße 18
D-72074 Tübingen
www.mohr.de

Printed in the United States of America

07 06 05 04 03   7 6 5 4 3 2

Library of Congress Cataloging-in-Publication Data

Kim, Seyoon.
Paul and the new perspective : second thoughts
On the origin of Paul's gospel / by Seyoon Kim.
       p.   cm.
Includes bibliographical references.
ISBN 0-8028-4974-1 (pbk.)
1. Bible. N.T. Epistles of Paul — Theology.
2. Paul, the Apostle, Saint. I. Kim, Seyoon.
On the origin of Paul's Gospel.
BS2651.K555 2002
227'.06 — dc21

2001040538

For Otto and Isolde Betz
Saints, Mentors, and Friends

Contents

CONTENTS

Contents

CONTENTS

Preface

It is a pleasant duty to acknowledge my debt to the many persons and institutions that have helped me in writing this book. I would like to thank Fuller Theological Seminary for granting me a sabbatical quarter during the fall of 1999, the *Alexander von Humboldt-Stiftung*, Bonn, Germany, for enabling me to concentrate on my research during the sabbatical with its generous fellowship, and the University of Tübingen for hosting me. I owe a debt of gratitude to my former teachers in Tübingen, Professors O. Betz, M. Hengel, and P. Stuhlmacher for their friendship and encouragement. During my stay at Tübingen, Professor Stuhlmacher put his office at my disposal, and it was a great help for my work. My old friend Professor Herrmann Lichtenberger was a generous host to me, and his secretary, Frau Monika Merkle (another old friend!), and his other *Mitarbeiter* in the Evangelisch-theologischen Seminar lent me many helping hands in practical matters. I have a fond and grateful memory of my stay at Wilhelmsstift, the Catholic convent, in Tübingen. I would like to thank Professor Hengel also for recommending this work to J. C. B. Mohr (Paul Siebeck) for publication. I am grateful to Bill Eerdmans, his son, Sam, and Georg Siebeck for undertaking to publish this book, and to their staff for their dedicated labor.

I would like to thank Susan Carlson Wood of Faculty Publications Services, School of Theology, Fuller Theological Seminary, for improving my style and editing the book, and Jin Ki Hwang and Scott Mackie, Ph.D. students at Fuller, for help with compiling the bibliography and indices. Finally, I record my appreciation of the loving support that my wife, Yea Sun, and our two daughters, Eunice Songi and Hahni, have provided me.

I affectionately dedicate this book to Professor and Mrs. Otto Betz. As I (*d.v.*) expect to have the honor of having my name associated with the great name of my British teacher, the late Professor F. F. Bruce, in my next work, and I hope to dedicate that work to his memory, I think it is appropriate for me to dedicate this work to my German teacher and his dear wife for their matchless care over all these years.

Pasadena, California,   Seyoon Kim
Thanksgiving 2000

Introduction

In 1977 I submitted my doctoral dissertation to the University of Manchester; it was published in 1981 by J. C. B. Mohr (Paul Siebeck) of Tübingen, Germany, as *The Origin of Paul's Gospel*, volume 4 in the second series of *Wissenschaftliche Untersuchungen zum Neuen Testament*. In the following year, Wm. B. Eerdmans of Grand Rapids, Michigan, U.S.A., published its American edition. In 1984 J. C. B. Mohr (Paul Siebeck) published its second edition with a postscript in which I interacted with some of the reviewers of the book and also with Heikki Räisänen. As the American edition has been out of print since the mid-1980s, my friends at Wm. B. Eerdmans have several times expressed their desire to reprint the book. Each time I told them to wait until I revised the book or at least added another postscript interacting with the new developments in Pauline scholarship, especially the revolution of the New Perspective on Paul that had been initiated by Ed P. Sanders's *Paul and Palestinian Judaism*, which was published in the year I submitted my dissertation. However, my eight-year stint of service in Korea was not conducive to the work of serious research and writing, and my subsequent relocation in 1995 to an entirely foreign setting, namely Fuller Theological Seminary, in Pasadena, California, required much time for adjustment. When I began to feel better settled into the life and work at Fuller, I was given a sabbatical quarter during the fall of 1999, and the Alexander von Humboldt-Stiftung of Germany was kind enough again to invite me over to Tübingen for a research stay during the period. I decided that the work was to consist of merely adding a new chapter because I saw the content in need of supplementing in the light of new discussions rather than of thoroughgoing revision. But I soon realized that with one chapter I could not do justice to the discussions that have taken place in Pauline scholarship during the twenty-three years since the book was written. Therefore, the publishers and I agreed to publish a new book as a sequel to *The Origin of Paul's Gospel.* J. C. B. Mohr (Paul Siebeck), the original publisher of my first book, has joined in publishing this sequel as well.

For this new book, I have written five new essays, chapters 1 to 5. Of them, three (chs. 1, 2, and 4) are directly concerned with the New Perspective on Paul, and one (ch. 3) is also partly or indirectly concerned with it. The fact that in my renewed discussion of the origin of Paul's gospel I should devote more than half of the space to an interaction with the New Perspective must be self-explanatory. Since the Reformation, I think no school of thought, not even the Bultmannian School, has exerted a greater influence upon Pauline scholarship than the school of the New Perspective. With its radical reinterpretation of Paul's gospel, especially his doctrine of justification, on the basis of Ed P. Sanders's definition of Second Temple Judaism as covenantal nomism, the New Perspective School is in many respects overturning the Reformation interpretation of Paul's gospel. The potential significance of the school for the whole Christian faith can hardly be exaggerated. Some representatives of the school are so confident about the correctness of their perspective and about its epoch-making significance that they deride as out of date those who have not adopted their perspective, and they divide scholarship in terms of pre- or post-Sanders.

In the debate with the New Perspective School, the question of the origin of Paul's justification doctrine, when and how it originated, is a vital element. It is not possible to address all the issues raised by the New Perspective in this book, but from this angle I try to cover at least some of the major ones. Furthermore, since James D. G. Dunn has tied the New Perspective closely to the question of the origin of Paul's justification doctrine and has repeatedly denied the role of Paul's Damascus experience in this, my debate with the New Perspective School takes in part the form of a critical discussion with him as a most prominent representative of the school.

Besides the New Perspective, there has been another important development in Pauline scholarship that is relevant to my thesis, namely the interpretation of Paul in the light of the Old Testament-Jewish apocalyptic-mystical vision tradition of Ezek 1. Although the influence of this interpretation cannot be compared with that of the New Perspective, Alan F. Segal and others have made it more acceptable at least to some quarters of New Testament scholarship. This lends great support to the thesis that I propounded about Paul's Image-, Adam- and Wisdom-christology in the light of the *merkabah*-vision tradition of Ezek 1 as well as other epiphany visions of Old Testament and Jewish literature. Therefore, one chapter (5) is devoted to a reexamination of the thesis in an interaction with Segal and others.

As the grip of the Bultmannian existentialist interpretation over New

Testament scholarship is loosened, there is now more willingness to see continuity as well as discontinuity between the historical Jesus and Paul. To be sure, there are still those hypercritics who maintain extreme scepticism about Paul's knowledge and use of the Jesus tradition. But I think it is fair to say that now an attempt to see a measure of the historical as well as the theological continuity between Jesus and Paul is no longer rejected out of hand. My work on the Jesus tradition in Paul's letters has convinced me that Paul used various elements of it extensively and that it played a vital role in the development of his gospel. Therefore, concerning the origin of Paul's gospel, we can now contemplate the hypothesis of a double origin: the Damascus revelation and the Jesus tradition. Together with Paul's use of the Old Testament, this raises the question of his method of theologizing. Therefore, I have my essay on the Jesus tradition in Paul reprinted here (ch. 8), and I try to see whether the Jesus tradition plays any role with regard to the theological topics dealt with in this book (especially in ch. 5).

The book reprints two more essays that I have already published, one on Paul's concept of "reconciliation" and the other on the "mystery" of Rom 11:25-26, as they substantiate further my theses on their origin from the Damascus experience. Both of them are at least indirectly relevant to the question of the New Perspective as well.

Thus, in this book with essays old and new, I reconsider the question of the origin of Paul's gospel and I do it especially in *Auseinandersetzung* with the New Perspective School.

CHAPTER 1

Paul's Conversion/Call, James D. G. Dunn, and the New Perspective on Paul

James D. G. Dunn is certainly the most tireless, if not the most prominent, proponent of the "New Perspective on Paul." The "New Perspective on Paul" is in fact the phrase that he himself coined for the new approach to the interpretation of Paul[1] based on Ed P. Sanders's definition of Second Temple Judaism as covenantal nomism.[2] To my knowledge, in recent years no scholar has treated Paul's conversion and call more often than Dunn; he has repeated basically the same interpretation of the event in his numerous writings.[3] Apparently he has done so because it is a cornerstone of his "New Perspective on Paul."[4] These facts alone should be sufficient to justify my concentration here

---

1. J. D. G. Dunn, "The New Perspective on Paul," originally in *BJRL* 65 (1983), reprinted in J. D. G. Dunn, *Jesus, Paul and the Law* (Louisville: Westminster/Knox, 1990), 183-214.

2. E. P. Sanders, *Paul and Palestinian Judaism* (London: SCM; Philadelphia: Fortress, 1977).

3. E.g., J. D. G. Dunn, " 'A Light to the Gentiles,' or 'The End of the Law'? The Significance of the Damascus Road Christophany for Paul," originally in *The Glory of Christ in the New Testament* (ed. L. D. Hurst and N. T. Wright; Oxford: Clarendon, 1987), reprinted in Dunn, *Jesus, Paul and the Law*, 89-107; *The Partings of the Ways between Christianity and Judaism* (Philadelphia: Trinity, 1991), 119-39; "Paul and Justification by Faith," in *The Road from Damascus* (ed. R. N. Longenecker; McMaster New Testament Studies; Grand Rapids: Eerdmans, 1997), 85-101; "Paul's Conversion — A Light to Twentieth Century Disputes," in *Evangelium, Schriftauslegung, Kirche* (P. Stuhlmacher Festschrift; ed. J. Adna, S. J. Hafemann and O. Hofius; Göttingen: Vandenhoeck, 1997), 77-93; *The Theology of Paul the Apostle* (Grand Rapids: Eerdmans, 1998), 346-89; see also his *The Epistle to the Galatians* (BNTC; London: Black; Peabody: Hendrickson, 1993), 51-71.

4. In his essay, "Paul's Conversion," 77, Dunn calls "Paul's conversion" "a good test passage" for the "New Perspective on Paul"; cf. also Dunn, *The Theology of Paul*, 345-56. For Dunn, Gal

on a critical examination of his interpretation of the Damascus event.[5] However, the fact that Dunn has repeatedly advanced his view in opposition to my own interpretation adds further justification.

Dunn's Interpretation

According to Dunn, Paul's autobiographical statement that he was a Pharisee with "zeal" for the law in "Judaism" (Phil 3:5; Gal 1:13-14) indicates that the pre-conversion Paul was a "zealot" who, after the model of the Maccabees (1 Macc 2) and Phinehas (Num 25:6-13), devoted himself to maintaining the integrity of the Jewish religion over against the syncretistic corruption of Hellenism and to safeguarding Israel's distinctive national identity from the pressures of the gentiles.[6] So Paul persecuted the Hellenist Jewish Christians not for their preaching of the crucified Jesus as the Messiah nor for their breaking the law but for their preaching the gospel to the gentiles and accepting gentile converts without requiring their circumcision. He perceived the latter as a serious threat to "Israel's integrity and purity."[7] But then at the Christophany on the Damascus road he was called to be an apostle to the gentiles. Therefore he converted "from *this zeal,* and from 'Judaism' as it called forth this zeal," to a mission "to the Gentiles,"[8] "*from* a zealous determination to defend Israel's Torah-defined boundaries . . . *to* fulfil[ling] Israel's eschatological mission to the nations."[9] Thus, the primary significance of the Damascus Christophany is that it was a divine call or commission which also involved such a conversion on his part. In order to stress this point, Dunn has repeatedly criticized those who, like myself, try to see the significance of the Damascus event also in terms of Paul's obtaining new convictions about

---

3:10-14 is another test passage for the New Perspective: see his "Works of the Law and the Curse of the Law (Gal 3:10-14)," in *Jesus, Paul and the Law,* 225-30. We shall deal with this "test case" (ibid., 225) in ch. 4 below.

5. In the postscript to the second edition of Seyoon Kim, *The Origin of Paul's Gospel* (WUNT 2/4; Tübingen: Mohr-Siebeck, 1984), 345-58, I have countered the views of H. Räisänen, *Paul and the Law* (WUNT 29; Tübingen: Mohr-Siebeck, 1983; Philadelphia: Fortress, 1986), and, to a lesser extent, also the views of E. P. Sanders, *Paul and Palestinian Judaism* and *Paul, the Law, and the Jewish People* (Philadelphia: Fortress, 1983), which are in many ways similar to Dunn's.

6. Dunn, *Partings,* 119-22; "Paul and Justification by Faith," 93; "Paul's Conversion," 87-89; *The Theology of Paul,* 347-54.

7. Dunn, "Paul's Conversion," 90; similarly also *Partings,* 121-22; *The Theology of Paul,* 352.

8. Dunn, "Paul's Conversion," 90 (his italics).

9. Ibid., 92 (his italics).

christology and soteriology and new insights about the law.[10] Whereas, for Dunn, God's call for Paul to the gentile mission had *"immediacy"* and so was the *"primary* feature" of Paul's Damascus experience, "the implications for the law and its bearing on the gospel [were] more the *corollary,* worked out with increasing sharpness over the early years of his work as a missionary to the church at Antioch."[11]

This interpretation of the Damascus event leads Dunn to see the distinctive Pauline doctrine of justification as developing late in the wake of the Antiochian incident, and to understand it mainly in terms of defending against Jewish nationalism the gentile converts' right to be included within the people of God without works of the law.[12] In this context, the phrase "works of the law" is concerned not with general deeds of law observance but specifically with the deeds of obedience to those commandments that mark the covenant people of Israel off from the nations, namely circumcision, food laws, and sabbath.[13] So Dunn concludes

> that the law became a primary concern for Paul precisely in its boundary-defining role (separating Jew from Gentile); that justification through faith emerged in Paul's theology as Paul's attempt to explain why and how Gentiles are accepted by God and should be accepted by their Jewish fellow believers; and that the works of the law . . . were precisely those practices which had most clearly defined Judaism and most sharply distinguished Jew from Gentile since the time of the Maccabees (circumcision, food laws and feast days/sabbath).[14]

This, of course, represents a new understanding of Paul's doctrine of justification. This new understanding of the doctrine, ultimately based on Ed P. Sanders's notion of Judaism as covenantal nomism constitutes the heart of the New Perspective that Dunn has enunciated.[15] Insofar as the doctrine is understood in the narrow sense of its function of defending Paul's gentile mission, it is characteristic of the New Perspective School as a whole.[16] As it

10. Dunn, "A Light to the Gentiles," 91-98; "Paul's Conversion," 80-84.
11. Dunn, "A Light to the Gentiles," 92 (his italics).
12. Dunn, *Partings,* 130-39; "Paul and Justification," 90-100; *The Theology of Paul,* 359-79.
13. Dunn, *Partings,* 135-37; "Paul and Justification," 95-99; *The Theology of Paul,* 354-66.
14. Dunn, "Paul's Conversion," 92.
15. See J. D. G. Dunn, "The New Perspective on Paul," *BJRL* 65 (1983), reprinted in *Jesus, Paul and the Law,* 183-214.
16. Cf. e.g., E. P. Sanders, *Paul, the Law, and the Jewish People;* H. Räisänen, *Paul and the Law;* T. L. Donaldson, *Paul and the Gentiles: Remapping the Apostle's Convictional World* (Minneapolis: Fortress, 1997); N. T. Wright, *What Saint Paul Really Said* (Grand Rapids: Eerdmans;

leads Dunn to such an understanding of the doctrine, Dunn's interpretation of Paul's Damascus experience is a cornerstone at least for his version of the New Perspective.

Dunn's Critique of My Thesis

Dunn criticizes me for deriving directly from Paul's experience of the Damascus Christophany his doctrine of justification through faith without works of the law as well as his εἰκών-christology, from which I argued his Adam- and Wisdom-christology, in turn, developed.[17] I grant that sometimes my unguarded language gave readers an impression that I was claiming Paul obtained all these christological and soteriological doctrines immediately from the Damascus Christophany.[18] However, anybody who reads my book carefully would note not only how my youthful enthusiasm gave way to such unguarded language at many places, but also how I made efforts to show the _process_ by which Paul developed those doctrines from the Damascus revelation of Christ through reflections on the primitive church's kerygma, the relevant texts of the Old Testament, the Jewish tradition, and partly also the Jesus tradition. By its very nature, the process could not be completed instantly at the moment of the Damascus Christophany but did take time. I still hold that the process did not take a long time and that the main features of Paul's gospel took firm shape within the first few years, although they continued to be refined through his biblical reflection, his controversies with his opponents, and his other experiences in the mission fields, eventually reaching the state in which they are now found in his epistles. I base my conjecture on an appreciation of Paul as a trained theologian, the circumstances of his conversion, the nature of the Damascus revelation, his experience of the Holy Spirit, and, of course, his call to the gentile mission and his immediate experiences in it. I have attempted to set as a _terminus ad quem_ for the "mystery" of Rom 11:25-26 Paul's first visit to Jerusalem "to get to know Peter" (Gal 1:18), that is, A.D. 33-36. Paul's doctrine of justification is related to his gentile mission, no mat-

---

Cincinnati: Forward Movement Publications, 1997). Dunn, _Partings_, 305 n. 31, traces the insight of the New Perspective to W. Wrede, _Paul_ (London: Philip Green, 1907), 122-28, and K. Stendahl, "The Apostle Paul and the Introspective Conscience of the West," _HTR_ 56 (1963), reprinted in _Paul among Jews and Gentiles_ (London: SCM, 1973), 1-7.

17. Dunn, "A Light to the Gentiles," 93-98; _Partings_, 119-24; "Paul and Justification by Faith," 85; "Paul's Conversion," 81-85; _The Theology of Paul_, 346. See Kim, _Origin_, 193-311.

18. But surely it does not give D. J-S. Chae (_Paul as Apostle to the Gentiles_ [Carlisle: Paternoster, 1997], 302-5) the right to distort my thesis to such an absurd extent.

ter whether it developed out of the latter as Dunn claims or originated together with the latter as I claim. This being so, if my dating the "mystery" is plausible, it should be reasonable to believe that the doctrine of justification also took a firm shape by that time. Nevertheless, in my book I was concerned to show *how* the main lines of Paul's theology originated from the Damascus revelation rather than *when* they did so, let alone when the mature formulations of various christological and soteriological doctrines came into being. I still stand by my main thesis that Paul's gospel is basically an unfolding of the revelation of Jesus Christ on the Damascus road.

In chapter 5 I will reply to Dunn's critique of my deriving Paul's christology from the Damascus Christophany. This chapter is concerned with the origin of the doctrine of justification. But before taking up that question, I will address Dunn's criticism that I did not properly observe the "immediacy" of the call to the gentile mission and failed to show adequately the correlation of Paul's christological and soteriological affirmations with his gentile mission.[19] This is a strange criticism because in my book I discussed the Damascus event as "the Apostolic Commission"[20] even before discussing it as "the Revelation of the Gospel."[21] Dunn himself quotes my sentence from the former section: "for Paul the Christophany on the Damascus road constituted [both his gospel and] his apostolic commission for the gentile mission."[22] Furthermore, Dunn refers even to my thesis that Paul obtained the "mystery" of Romans 11:25-26 by interpreting the Damascus Christophany in the light of Isaiah 6 and 49:1-6.[23] So there is no question of my failing to observe the "immediacy" of the divine call for Paul to the gentile mission. Dunn complains that I did not show adequately how my affirmation of Paul's call to the gentile mission ties in to my "main christological and soteriological thesis."[24] In fact, I showed how Paul's soteriology of justification through faith alone and his christology of the universal lordship of Jesus Christ correlate to his gentile mission, and concluded the discussion as follows:

> Now we can see the inner unity of Paul's gospel and his apostleship to the Gentiles, both of which he received on the Damascus road. On the one hand, the gospel that proclaims God's institution of Jesus Christ as the Son of God

19. Dunn, "A Light to the Gentiles," 94-95.

20. Kim, *Origin,* 56-66.

21. Ibid., 67ff.

22. Kim, *Origin,* 57, quoted by Dunn, "A Light to the Gentiles," 95. Significantly Dunn quotes the sentence, leaving out the phrase "both his gospel."

23. Dunn, "A Light to the Gentiles," 95.

24. Ibid., 95.

in power, the universal Lord, *spells an imperative* for Paul to go to the Gentiles, proclaim him to them, and bring about the "obedience of faith" among them (Rom 1.5; 15.16-18). On the other hand, the gospel which is at the same time "God's power for salvation to every one who has faith, to the Jew first and also to the Greek" *justifies* Paul's mission to the Gentiles now. Only because Paul saw Christ's death and resurrection as God's redemptive act for our justification *sola gratia* and *sola fide,* could he so freely go to the Gentiles and proclaim the gospel of God's grace to them, while the Jewish Christians, failing to see the principle of *sola fide* so clearly as he, hesitated to do the same but rather criticized him for his law-free Gentile mission. The Letter to the Galatians is an eloquent testimony to this contrast as well as to the unity of Paul's gospel and apostleship.[25]

In another place I hinted also at the correlation of Paul's Adam-christology and its related new creation-soteriology with Paul's universal mission.[26] Showing such a correlation was natural for me, because a thesis of mine was that the call for Paul to the gentile mission, the revelation of the christo-logical/soteriological gospel, and the revelation of the divine *Heilsplan* em-bodied in the "mystery" of Rom 11:25-26 were rooted together in the event of the Damascus Christophany, and therefore the three elements belonged to-gether. It is true that I devoted more pages to expounding Paul's christo-logical/soteriological gospel than to discussing Paul's gentile apostleship. It was not because I neglected the latter, but rather because the former is much more complicated and so requires a much longer explanation. In spite of his emphasis on Paul's gentile apostleship as an *Ansatzpunkt* for his theological thinking, in his book *The Theology of Paul the Apostle,* Dunn himself devotes incomparably more pages to an exposition of Paul's soteriological gospel than to a discussion of Paul's gentile apostleship.

When I stated that Paul's christology of the universal lordship of Christ spelled a universal mission, while his soteriology of justification *sola gratia/fide* justified it, I did not mean that he developed his sense of a call to the gentile mission only as a *corollary* of his christology/soteriology. I only meant to show how the two components of the Damascus event — the revelation of the gospel and the call to gentile apostleship — were *logi-cally* related to each other. Since I believe that the revelation of the gospel and the apostolic commission to the gentiles coincided at the Damascus Christophany, I had no reason to be concerned about the *chronological* or-der of the two elements. Apparently Dunn is ignoring this fact because he

---

25. Kim, *Origin,* 308-11 (quotation from pp. 310-11; italics in the original).

26. Ibid., 268; Dunn, "A Light to the Gentiles," 95, recognizes this.

has determined that the proper correlation between Paul's gentile mission and his theology should show the former determining the latter, or the latter developing as a (chronological as well as logical) corollary of the former. I suspect so because in all his writings on the Damascus event he argues for this form of their correlation. No doubt Paul's experience in his actual missionary work among the gentiles and especially his controversies with the Judaizers about the gentile mission contributed to sharpening his doctrine of justification *sola gratia/fide,* and I acknowledged this.[27] However, the form of their correlation that Dunn proposes cannot be substantiated exegetically, as the following will demonstrate.

Only an Apostolic Call for the Gentiles?

It should first be pointed out, however, that Dunn's singling out Paul's call to the gentile mission as the primary significance to the exclusion of the revelation of the christological and soteriological insights makes him unable to fulfill his own promise to show how the "different aspects of Paul's response to and understanding of the Damascus road Christophany . . . all hang together or tie up in Paul's thinking."[28] In fact, it makes Dunn self-contradictory at a couple of points. He strongly disputes my thesis that Paul saw the exalted Christ appearing as the "εἰκών of God" on the Damascus road and that from that revelation both Paul's Adam-christology and Wisdom-christology originated.[29] But then in the concluding section of his article, without any demonstration of his own, he strangely adopts my main thesis: at the Damascus Christophany, "[Paul] saw Christ as the 'image of God.' "[30] Well then, in the end, Dunn appears to differ with me only on the second part of my thesis: whereas I think that both Paul's Adam-christology and Wisdom-christology originated from the εἰκών-christology, Dunn would like to see only the former as originating from it.[31] While his tacit acceptance of my thesis that Paul's Adam-christology is rooted in the Damascus Christophany[32] is welcome, his denial of Paul's Wisdom-christology developing at least partly from

27. Kim, *Origin,* 334-35.

28. Dunn, "A Light to the Gentiles," 95.

29. Ibid., 95-97. For my reply to this, see ch. 5 below.

30. Ibid., 100.

31. Ibid., 97, 100

32. Cf. J. D. G. Dunn, *Christology in the Making* (London: SCM, 1980; Grand Rapids: Eerdmans, 1996), 98-128, where his extensive discussion on Paul's Adam-christology does not contain this explanation of its origin.

his εἰκών-christology is wrong, and I will show that in chapter 5 below. However, for the moment, let us see how Dunn develops his view:

> if indeed the εἰκὼν τοῦ θεοῦ in 2 Corinthians 4.4 speaks primarily of Christ as Adam, then the immediate *corollary* is that in 2 Corinthians 3–4 Paul deliberately transforms the matrix of salvation-history from Israel and Sinai to man and creation. The rationale of Paul's thought would then have been more direct: if with Christ now raised from the dead God's purpose for man (and not simply Israel) has been realized, it must follow that the object of his concern is mankind as a whole and not merely the Jews; God's purpose (not least in stopping Paul short in his full flight as a persecutor on behalf of Israel's prerogatives and law) must be to realize through Christ his purpose of creation and not simply election. The puzzling "therefore to the Gentiles" thus becomes a more immediate *deduction* from the Damascus road Christophany than even Kim allows.[33]

In the conclusion, Dunn says similarly,

> [at the Damascus Christophany . . . Paul] saw Christ as the "image of God," as the risen embodiment and therefore eschatological fulfillment of God's plan from the beginning to share his glory with the human kind he had created. And he understood this glorious vindication as a reversal of the curse of Deuteronomy 21.23, and therefore as implying God's covenant concern to embrace both outsider and insider, sinner as well as blameless, Gentile as well as Jew.[34]

How can Dunn say that his correlation of Paul's Adam-christology with his gentile mission shows the gentile mission to be "a more immediate deduction from the Damascus road Christophany than even Kim allows"? I do not find in his explanation anything different from what I suggested, his explanation being at most an unfolding of my suggestion.[35] Be that as it may, I am particularly interested in Dunn's favorite term "corollary" (and also "deduction") here. Having specifically complained about my listing Paul's "conviction of universal mission as a corollary of the 'new creation' corollary of his Adam Christology, itself derived from the Damascus Christophany,"[36] Dunn is do-

---

33. Dunn, "A Light to the Gentiles," 97-98 (my emphasis).
34. Ibid., 100.
35. See above n. 25.
36. Dunn, "A Light to the Gentiles," 95. See also p. 89 for his emphatic denial: "What is even more striking, however, is the fact that he understood his commissioning from the first as having the Gentiles in view. This is not presented as a <u>deduction</u> or a <u>corollary</u> which Paul drew from some *other* conviction given to him in or brought home to him by the encounter on the Damascus road" (Dunn's italics and my underlines).

ing exactly the same! He says that this way of explaining the correlation between Paul's christology and gentile mission fails to bring out the "immediacy" of the latter.[37] In his eagerness to affirm only the "immediacy" of Paul's call to the gentile mission, he largely neglects to inquire of the christological component of the Damascus revelation, only to tacitly adopt part of my thesis which he ostensibly seeks to criticize. But then once he begins to reflect on the possible correlation between Paul's christology and gentile mission, he cannot help but use the language of the latter being a "corollary" of the former. Thus, in spite of his strong desire to affirm only the "immediacy" of Paul's call to the gentile mission, he cannot help but find himself in the same situation as myself.[38]

The same self-contradiction appears again in Dunn's correlation of Paul's christology/soteriology of the "crucified Christ" with his gentile mission. Dunn says:

> [F]or Paul the loyal Jew, the curse of Deuteronomy 21.23 was the opposite of the blessings of the covenant (particularly Deut. 27–28); to be cursed by God was to have the covenant revoked, to be put out of the covenant (28.58-68) — that is, to be put in the position of the Gentile sinner. The crucifixion of Jesus meant that God had rejected him, numbered him with the Gentiles, reckoned him as outside the covenant. The Damascus road Christophany must obviously have turned such a line of reasoning completely on its head, for it indicated clearly that God had accepted and vindicated this one precisely as the crucified. The *immediate* corollary for Paul would be that God must therefore favor the cursed one, the sinner outside the covenant, the Gentile. And thus it can be easily seen how the conclusion "therefore to the Gentiles" could follow directly from the Damascus road Christophany and not at some further remove as a corollary to more elaborate Christological and soteriological schemes.[39]

How Paul can be said to have derived his gentile mission as an "immediate" corollary from such a "tortuous" interpretation of the crucified Christ[40] is a baffling question in itself. Be that as it may, here we are interested only in Dunn's explanation of Paul's gentile mission as a "corollary" of his christology/soteriology! Has he not specifically written: "[Paul's apostolic commis-

37. Ibid., 95.
38. See above, p. 6.
39. Dunn, "A Light to the Gentiles," 99-100 (Dunn's italics and my underline).
40. So N. T. Wright, "Curse and Covenant: Galatians 3:10-14," in *The Climax of the Covenant* (Edinburgh: T & T Clark, 1991), 153; also C. E. B. Cranfield, " 'The Works of the Law' in the Epistle to the Romans," *JSNT* 43 (1991): 92.

sion for the gentiles] is not presented as a deduction or a corollary which Paul drew from some *other* conviction given to him in or brought home to him by the encounter on the Damascus road"?[41] It is also not easy to understand how Dunn can claim that his way of explaining the correlation between Paul's christology/soteriology and gentile mission connects the latter more directly to the Damascus Christophany than the more traditional explanation of their correlation on the assumption of the insight of the "crucified" Christ as "the end of the law."

Dunn would avoid the charge of confusion and self-contradiction here if he admitted that both Paul's call to the gentile mission and his christology/soteriology are rooted in the Damascus Christophany and that we use the language of "corollary" here only in explication of their logical, rather than chronological, connection with each other.

All this trouble with Dunn's interpretation of the Damascus event stems from his arbitrary disjunction of the different components of the event, the revelation of the gospel which Paul formulates both christologically and soteriologically, the apostolic commission to the gentile mission, and the revelation of the divine *Heilsplan* involving the mission to the gentiles prior to the Jews (Rom 11:25-26). Rather than trying to see how they all belong together, Dunn insists on seeing only the call to the gentile mission as the immediate significance of the event and neglects the rest, treating them sometimes at most as a secondary (chronological as well as logical) "corollary" of the former.[42] The cases of self-contradiction above clearly prove his thesis wrong.

However, Dunn repeatedly bases his thesis on Paul's testimony in Gal 1:13-17.[43] But it is beyond my comprehension how he can read the text to deny the immediacy of the revelation of the gospel and to affirm only the immediacy of Paul's apostolic commission to the gentiles, or how he can separate ἐν τοῖς ἔθνεσιν from ἀποκαλύψαι τὸν υἱὸν αὐτοῦ ἐν ἐμοί, ἵνα εὐαγγελίζωμαι αὐτὸν in Gal 1:16 and put all the stress on the former while virtually ignoring the latter.[44] Paul's testimony in Gal 1:13-17 makes it clear

41. Dunn, "A Light to the Gentiles," 89.

42. So he explains the rise of the soteriology of justification through faith without works of the law. See above, pp. 2-3.

43. Dunn, "A Light to the Gentiles," 89-107; "Paul and Justification by Faith," 85-101; "Paul's Conversion," 80-93; *The Theology of Paul*, 346-54, although in the last-mentioned work Dunn avoids setting up an antithesis between the call to the gentile mission and the revelation of the law-free gospel by passing quietly over the latter.

44. Those who, like Dunn, insist that Paul's justification doctrine with its contrast between faith in Christ and works of the law originated for the first time in the wake of his conflict with

10

that the revelation of the gospel and the apostolic commission for the gentiles
were the two components of the Damascus Christophany and that they were
inseparably bound up together. However, in Gal 1–2 Paul's primary concern
is to defend his gospel, the gospel that he had preached to the Galatians but
was now doubted by them because of his opponents' contrary teaching (1:6-
9); his main emphasis is not his gentile apostleship or mission.[45] That is why
Paul prefaces the whole autobiographical section in these terms: "For I would
have you know, brethren, that the gospel which was preached by me is not according to a human being. For I did not receive it from a human being, nor
was I taught it, but it came through a revelation of Jesus Christ" (1:11-12).
That is why Paul says that he "laid before [the Jerusalem apostles] the gospel
which I preach among the gentiles" (2:2) and that they recognized his gospel
to the gentiles, adding nothing to it (2:1-10). And that is also why Paul says
that he rebuked Peter at Antioch when he saw him not walking straightfor-
wardly according to the truth of the gospel (2:11-21). In this defense of his
gospel, it is vital for Paul to show that the gospel that he had preached has divine origin. That is why he reports his Damascus experience in Gal 1:13-17.
And that is why he prefaces his report with the summary heading: "I received
[the gospel] . . . through a revelation of Jesus Christ" (1:12). Thus, in Gal 1–2
Paul's primary concern is to demonstrate that his law-free gospel[46] that has

---

the Judaizers in Antioch have the task of explaining why then Paul traces the doctrine to his experience of the Damascus revelation of Christ in both Gal 1:11-17 and Phil 3:3-11. "Unless this
contrast [between faith in Christ and works of the law] had been a real element in his experience of conversion/call, why is it necessary for him to start the defence of his position in Gal.
from his Jewish background and his revelation experience, and not simply from the Antiochian
incident?" (Kim, *Origin*, 352). Is Dunn turning a blind eye to the element of the gospel revealed
at the Damascus event in order to avoid the inconvenient task of explaining this question?

45. Cf. Kim, *Origin*, 68-69; B. Lategan, "Is Paul Defending His Apostleship in Galatians?"
NTS 34 (1988): 411-30; B. Witherington, *God's Grace in Galatia: A Commentary on St. Paul's
Letter to the Galatians* (Grand Rapids: Eerdmans, 1998), 25, 38, citing J. H. Schütz, *Paul and the
Anatomy of Apostolic Authority* (SNTSMS 26; Cambridge: Cambridge University Press, 1975),
128ff.

46. Some critics argue that "the gospel which was preached by me [Paul]" in Gal 1:11 cannot simply be assumed to be the same as the law-free gospel that Paul expounds and defends in
the rest of Galatians. The latter may be a version of Paul's gospel which is more refined with more
biblical substantiation and theological argumentation in the face of the challenge of the
Judaizers. Nevertheless, it must be essentially the same as the gospel which Paul originally
preached to the Galatians. Otherwise Paul's whole argument in Galatians would fall down. The
original gospel must have been a "law-free" gospel *at least* in the sense that Paul preached the
good news of salvation through faith in Christ without any requirement of the law observance
(cf. 1 Thess and 1 Cor 6:9-11 — below, pp. 67-70, and ch. 2). In Gal 1:11-17 Paul is claiming that
this "law-free" gospel was revealed to him at the Damascus Christophany, i.e., that from that rev-

met with controversy at Galatia was the gospel that he received through the revelation of God's Son, Jesus Christ, on the Damascus road. Paul mentions his apostolic call to the gentiles together with the revelation of the gospel in Gal 1:13-17 and speaks of his apostleship to the gentiles together with his

elation of the gospel he learned he should offer the gentiles salvation in Christ without any requirement of the works of the law. Then, in Gal 2:1-10 he is claiming that the Jerusalem apostles
approved of this "law-free" gospel. Below, pp. 47-48. B. R. Gaventa, "Galatians 1 and 2: Autobiography as Paradigm," *NovT* 28 (1986): 309-26, argues against me that in Gal 1 and 2 Paul is not arguing that he received the gospel from the Damascus revelation but rather he is presenting himself as a paradigm for his readers. G. Lyons argues similarly: *Pauline Autobiography: Toward a
New Understanding* (SBLDS 73; Atlanta: Scholars Press, 1985), 123-76. But they have been rightly
criticized for their strange neglect or denial of the primary apologetic purpose of Paul in
Galatians in favor of the paradigmatic purpose, which is at most secondary. See, e.g., M. Silva, "Is
the Law against the Promises? Galatians 3:21 for Covenant Continuity," in *Theonomy: A Re-
formed Critique* (ed. W. S. Barker and W. R. Godfrey; Grand Rapids: Academie, 1990), 157 n. 10;
K. O. Sandness, *Paul — One of the Prophets* (WUNT 2/43; Tübingen: Mohr-Siebeck, 1991), 51;
M. A. Seifrid, *Justification by Faith: The Origin and Development of a Central Pauline Theme*
(NovTSup 68; Leiden: Brill, 1992), 140-42; L. W. Hurtado, "Convert, Apostate or Apostle to the
Nations: The 'Conversion' of Paul in Recent Scholarship," in *Studies in Religion/Sciences
Religieuses* 22 (1993): 278 n. 22. Against the view that takes Paul's testimony in Gal 1:11-17 at its
face value, Gaventa asserts: "Indeed, the reverse is true. It is Paul's understanding of the gospel
that brings about a re-construction or re-imagining of his past" (op. cit., 313). Thus she boldly
turns Paul's own testimony in Gal 1:11-17 upside down, but without providing an adequate basis
for it. P. Fredricksen, "Paul and Augustine: Conversion Narratives, Orthodox Traditions, and the
Retrospective Self," *JTS* 37 (1986): 3-34, argues for basically the same view as Gaventa's: "the conversion account is both anachronistic and apologetic . . . anachronistic, because the account rendered in the conversion narrative is so shaped by later concerns. The conversion account, never
disinterested, is a condensed, or disguised, description of the convert's *present,* which he legiti-
mates through his retrospective creation of a past and a self" (p. 33, her italics). Fredricksen seeks
to provide a basis for this view from an analogy drawn from Augustine's various accounts of his
conversion. Thus she raises a fundamental methodological problem of making the conversion
narrative more or less fictional and so any attempt of its historical reconstruction impossible.
But, for such a radical conclusion, one wishes that she had studied Paul's various references to his
conversion/call at least as closely as she examines Augustine's accounts, instead of devoting so
much space to her largely irrelevant criticism of Luke's accounts in Acts. No doubt, Paul must
have interpreted his conversion experience ever more deeply at least in the initial few years of his
Christian life, and he varies in emphasizing one or another element of his conversion/call experience according to the needs of the different contexts: e.g., his apostolic call through the appearance of the risen Christ in 1 Cor 9:1-2; 15: 8-10; the revelation of the exalted Christ as the image
of God and as the inaugurator of the new covenant of the Spirit over against the Sinai covenant
of the law in 2 Cor 3:1–4:6; a new understanding of Christ and an experience of reconciliation to
God and of new creation as well as the apostolic call in 2 Cor 5:11-21; the revelation of the gospel
of justification *sola gratia/fide* and his apostolic call to the gentiles in Gal 1:11-17; the doctrine of
justification *sola gratia/fide* in Phil 3:3-10. However, there is enough constancy in these various
references to his conversion/call: e.g., the revelation of Jesus as Christ, Lord, Son, and Image of

gospel for the gentiles in Gal 2:1-10 only because his gospel and his apostle-ship are inseparably bound up together.

When the context demands, Paul can indeed refer to the Damascus event primarily in terms of his apostolic commission (1 Cor 9:1; 15:8-11). Equally, however, when the context demands, he can refer to it exclusively in terms of his conversion to the law-free gospel (Phil 3:2-11).[47] The First Corinthians passages and the Philippians passage do not mean that the Damascus event was only this or that. Rather, because of the needs of the context, each refers only to one of the two components of the Damascus event, one to the revela-tion of the gospel, and the other to the apostolic call to the gentiles. Therefore it is wrong to interpret the Damascus event only in terms of Paul's apostolic commission to the gentiles. Neither Phil 3:4-11 nor Gal 1:11-17 allows this.

The Christological Component Not Essential?

Dunn's zeal for seeing the Damascus event only in terms of Paul's apostolic call to the gentiles leads him to advance quite unrealistic and incredible argu-ments against those who see the new christological insights as essential parts of the Damascus revelation.[48]

Dunn grants that from 1 Cor 1:23 it can fairly be inferred that the pre-conversion Paul was offended by the Christian proclamation of the "crucified Messiah," and from Gal 3:13 that on the basis of Deut 21:23 he persecuted the

---

God; an emphasis on God's grace and a reassessment of the law; justification and reconciliation; and his apostolic call to the gentiles. All these accounts complement one another very well. If we have to declare Paul's account of his conversion from a zealous Pharisee to an apostle to the gen-tiles a mere retrojection of his gospel or his present self-understanding, how can we account for his distinctive gospel and his present peculiar self-understanding in the first place? Where did he obtain them? How did a "zealot" for the law become an apostle to the gentiles in A.D. 32-34? Is his testimony that he "immediately" went away to Arabia after his experience of conversion/call (Gal 1:16-17) also a retrojection of his present self-understanding or gospel? See ch. 3, n. 12. Cf. also Hurtado, op. cit., 280-81, against the indiscriminate use of analogies drawn from sociological studies of conversion in modern religious groups for understanding Paul's conversion; also C. C. Newman, *Paul's Glory-Christology* (Leiden: E. J. Brill, 1992), 181.

47. In "Paul and Justification by Faith," 93, Dunn admits that in Phil 3:4-11 the gentile mission "is not to the fore," but the fact does not restrain him from advancing his one-sided thesis.

48. Before the New Perspective revolution, Dunn himself appreciated the formative signif-icance of Paul's "religious experience" on the Damascus road for his life and theology as a whole (*Jesus and the Spirit* [London: SCM, 1975], 4), and I cited his judgment on this in support of my thesis in my *Origin*, 334 n. 1.

Christians who proclaimed the crucified Jesus as God's Messiah.[49] So Dunn recognizes that Paul was converted to "Christ crucified," which "was part of the base-rock faith of the first Christians."[50] Dunn seems to be prepared even to acknowledge in view of 1 Cor 15:3 and Acts 9:22 that at conversion Paul accepted their belief in Christ's death as a sin-offering.[51] He further grants that "a christological revelation is clearly indicated in Gal 1.16" and that "Phil 3.7-8 certainly indicates a complete transformation of life-centre with personal piety now focused in an all-absorbing way on Christ."[52] So Dunn acknowledges that H. G. Wood and Philippe Menoud are right in their interpretation of the significance of the Damascus event in terms of Paul's christological conversion.[53]

However, Dunn disapproves of my attempts to see in the Damascus revelation more christological insights in connection with the εἰκών-christology beyond that basic insight. He argues that Paul's more elaborate christology is the result of reflection over time on his Damascus experience, the Jesus tradition, and the Scriptures.[54]

I have no quarrel with Dunn's argument as far as Paul's Adam-christology and Wisdom-christology are concerned. For I also recognize that it must have taken some time before Paul derived them from his εἰκών-christology through reflection on the Jesus tradition and the Scriptures. However, I believe that his εἰκών-christology is directly rooted in the Damascus Christophany as it arose, as I argued, out of his experience of seeing the exalted Christ appearing in divine δόξα and in the likeness of God.[55] As shown earlier, Dunn himself once accepted (albeit only tacitly and self-contradictorily) this thesis of mine and even went on to claim that Paul's Adam-christology was also directly rooted in the Damascus Christophany, although his Wisdom-christology was a later development.[56] But ten years later Dunn apparently changed his mind on this point.[57] Regardless of the reason for such a change, there are also some other christological insights involved in the Damascus revelation, which Paul

49. Dunn, "Paul's Conversion," 80.
50. Dunn, "A Light to the Gentiles," 91.
51. Dunn, "Paul's Conversion," 80.
52. Ibid., 81.
53. Ibid., 81. Cf. H. G. Wood, "The Conversion of Paul: Its Nature, Antecedents and Consequences," NTS 1 (1954-55): 276-82; P. H. Menoud, "Revelation and Tradition: The Influence of Paul's Conversion on His Theology," Int 7 (1953): 131-41.
54. Dunn, "Paul's Conversion," 81.
55. Kim, The Origin of Paul's Gospel, 193-233; and ch. 5 in this book.
56. Dunn, "A Light to the Gentiles," 100.
57. Compare Dunn, "Paul's Conversion," 81.

expresses in connection with the titles "Lord" (cf. 1 Cor 9:1) and "Son (of God)" (Gal 1:16; 2:20; Acts 9:20), although those insights were later developed into the elaborate *Kyrios*-christology and Son-christology through further reflections.

The real problem with Dunn's interpretation is that even the minimum christological insight that he allows as from the Damascus revelation plays little role in his overall interpretation of the significance of the Damascus event or in his overall reconstruction of Paul's theological and missionary development. In fact, he is eager to minimize the importance of even this minimum christological insight. Indeed, on page 82 of his essay "Paul's Conversion — A Light to Twentieth Century Disputes," he even withdraws what he granted as an "entirely plausible" deduction from various Pauline statements on page 80 of the same essay. For he says, "It was evidently *not* the claim for Jesus' Messiahship which occasioned the persecution in which Paul was a leading player."[58] According to Dunn, "the claim that the crucified Jesus was Messiah was not in principle objectionable for a Jew to hold."[59] He supports this view with the remark that "after all, many devout and well-regarded Jews themselves had been crucified in the past."[60] What then becomes of his preceding observation from 1 Cor 1:23 that "the offence evidently lay in the juxtaposition of the two words — 'Messiah' and 'crucified' "?[61] Further, what becomes of his earlier inference from the citation of Deut 21:23 in Gal 3:13: "So the probability must be ranked as high that it had been used in the earliest Jewish polemic against the first expression of Christian faith in Jesus as Messiah — probably by Paul himself"?[62]

According to Dunn's latest interpretation, 1 Cor 1:23 and Gal 3:13 indicate that what was offensive was not so much the Christian claim itself that the crucified Jesus was the Messiah, as that claim coupled with the demand for other Jews to accept him as the Messiah.[63] To me, this appears another fine but arbitrary distinction. One may wonder whether "the claim for Jesus' Messiahship" ever existed in the primitive church without such a demand implicitly or explicitly made. Evidently Luke or his sources did not think so: see

58. Ibid., 82 (Dunn's italics).
59. Ibid., 82.
60. Ibid., 82.
61. Ibid., 80.
62. Dunn, "A Light to the Gentiles," 99. Cf. also his remark on p. 101: "Paul the persecutor would presumably have regarded the cross as the inevitable outworking and consequence of Jesus' disregard for the rules of the covenant during his ministry (particularly his association with 'sinners' — Mark 2.15-17; Matt. 11.19//Luke 7.34)."
63. Dunn, "Paul's Conversion," 82.

15

Luke 24:44-48; Acts 1:8; 2:22-36; 3:12-26; 4:8-12, 17-20; 5:30-32; and so on. Nor did the other Evangelists (or their sources): see, for example, Matt 28:18-20; Mark 13:10; John 20:30-31. The kerygma "Jesus is the Messiah" is inherently missionary and demands a response from its hearers. In the first-century Jewish context, it must have been so all the more clearly.

In support of his unrealistic view, Dunn advances three more arguments. Let us take them in reverse order.

First, Dunn observes that the Jewish believers in Messiah Jesus seem to have been left in Jerusalem "undisturbed" as the persecution in the wake of Stephen's execution was directed mainly against the Hellenists.[64] But this observation is quite futile. For Luke, to whom Dunn appeals for it, shows that the Hebrew Christians were also very much "disturbed" and persecuted by the Jews for their preaching of Jesus as the Messiah (Acts 4:1-31; 5:17-42; 12:1-19), although they were not driven out of Jerusalem like the Hellenists.

Second, arguing on the basis of what he considers to be "a surprising fact that [in Paul's letters] the claim regarding Jesus as Messiah is on the whole uncontentious," Dunn maintains that "if the claim that Jesus was Messiah was indeed at the heart of Paul's earlier persecution and continued to be a major issue between Jews and Christians we would have expected more echoes and indications than we find — echoes such as we find with regard to the law."[65]

It is difficult to understand why Dunn finds it "a surprising fact" that in the letters addressed to Christians, those who were believing in Jesus as Messiah, Jesus' messiahship does not appear contentious. To me, it appears only very natural. Certainly in Paul's letters there are no such extended arguments to prove Jesus' messiahship as those concerning the law. It is because the letters were not addressed to the unbelieving Jews who required such arguments. However, some of the churches to which Paul sent his letters had Jewish Christians in their midst or were under the influence of the Jewish Christians who were advocating the observance of the law. This necessitated Paul's development of his extended arguments concerning the law in those letters. Nevertheless, numerous passages (Rom 10:1-21; 1 Cor 1:23; 12:3; 2 Cor 3:14-18; 4:4-6; Gal 3:13; 5:11; 6:12-14; Phil 3:18-19) more than "echo" the Jewish rejection of the crucified Messiah which stands in the background of those letters, that is, the controversies which Paul had with the Jews in synagogues and elsewhere in the course of his mission. Some of the references probably echo also the shyness of even the Jewish Christians about the crucified Messiah.

---

64. Ibid., 82.
65. Ibid., 81-82.

In order to deny the Hellenists any substantial breach with the law and to claim Paul as the first creator of the real tension between law and gospel, Dunn appeals to the Jewish Christian tradition which portrays Paul as the chief arch-heretic and apostate (*Epistula Petri* 2.3; Clem. *Hom.* 17.18-19).[66] One wonders why Dunn does not employ the same kind of argument in connection with the Jewish rejection of Jesus' messiahship. Should we not take, for example, Celsus's rejection of Jesus' messiahship on account of his crucifixion (Origen, *Contra Celsum* 2.33-37) as evidence as to how problematic the messiahship of the crucified Jesus was to the Jews? In this connection, it is not to be forgotten that John 7–10, especially 9:13-41, provides clear evidence that the messiahship of Jesus was a major issue between Jews and Christians and that Christians were persecuted by Jews for their belief in it.

The third argument that Dunn advances to deny the central significance of the christological conversion at Paul's Damascus experience is that "in his most explicit recollections of his conversion Paul does not mention such a transformation in his beliefs about Jesus (Gal. 1.13-14 and Phil. 3)."[67] This is a most incredible argument. For, as we have seen, in Gal 1:11-17 Paul does recall his Damascus experience first and foremost in terms of "the revelation of Jesus Christ" or God's "revealing his Son" to him. This is also supported by Luke's account in Acts 9:20-22, as Dunn himself recognizes.[68] Dunn's argument is all the more strange because only a few sentences before that problematic sentence Dunn himself correctly wrote:

> It is hard to see what Paul's conversion (from persecutor to apostle) could have meant had it not at least included a radical "change of mind" on his part with regard to the first Christian claims regarding Jesus. A christological revelation is clearly indicated in Gal. 1.16 (God revealed his Son in Paul). And Phil. 3.7-8 certainly indicates a complete transformation of life-centre with personal piety now focused in an all-absorbing way on Christ.[69]

Having written these sentences, how can Dunn say that "in his most explicit recollections of his conversion Paul does not mention such a transformation in his beliefs about Jesus (Gal 1:13-14; Phil. 3)"?[70] To me, this appears to be another case of Dunn's self-contradiction. Further, it is curious to know why Dunn passes silently over 1 Cor 9:1 and 15:8, where "in his most explicit rec-

66. Dunn, "A Light to the Gentiles," 92.
67. Dunn, "Paul's Conversion," 81.
68. Ibid., 80.
69. Ibid., 81.
70. Ibid., 81.

ollections" of his Damascus experience Paul does refer to the appearance of (the crucified) Jesus as the risen Christ and Lord.[71]

In his essay "A Light to the Gentiles," Dunn has one further argument against seeing the christological revelation as part of the central significance of the Damascus event. Having recognized that there was a "radical rethink" on Paul's part about the crucified Jesus as the Messiah at the Damascus Christophany, Dunn says:

> But it is hardly enough to explain the rationale of Paul's commissioning: the conviction "Jesus is Messiah" hardly leads immediately to the corollary, "therefore to the Gentiles." More damaging is the fact that Paul himself never seems to trace out or imply such a progression of thought. The recognition of Jesus' Messiahship is insufficient explanation of Paul's apostolic self-understanding.[72]

However, a few pages later Dunn expounds the quotation of Deut 21:23 in Gal 3:13. Since his exposition is in direct contradiction to what he says in the above quotation, I cannot help but quote it here once more:

> The line of thought behind Galatians 3.13 was part of the reversal which Paul experienced in the Damascus road Christophany. The point is this: that for Paul the loyal Jew, the curse of Deuteronomy 21.23 was the opposite of the blessings of the covenant (particularly Deut. 27–28); to be cursed by God was to have the covenant revoked, to be put out of the covenant (28.58-68) — that is, to be put in the position of the Gentile sinner. The crucifixion of Jesus meant that God had rejected him, numbered him with the Gentiles, reckoned him as outside the covenant. The Damascus road Christophany must obviously have turned such a line of reasoning completely on its head, for it indicated clearly that God had accepted and vindicated this one precisely as the crucified. The *immediate* corollary for Paul would be that God must therefore favor the cursed one, the sinner outside the covenant, the Gentile. And thus it can be easily seen how the conclusion "therefore to the Gentiles" could follow directly from the Damascus road Christophany and not at some further remove as a corollary to more elaborate Christological and soteriological schemes.[73]

---

71. Just as in Gal 1:13-16, so also in 1 Cor 9:1 and 15:8, Dunn ("Paul's Conversion," 90) affirms only the reference to Paul's apostolic commission to the gentiles, completely ignoring the (logically) more fundamental reference to the revelation of Christ.

72. Dunn, "A Light to the Gentiles," 91.

73. Ibid., 99-100 (his italics).

Though I do not accept the substance of this exposition,[74] here I only point out Dunn's explanation of the ("immediate") progression of Paul's thought *from* the revelation of the crucified Jesus as the Messiah *to* "therefore to the Gentiles," which Dunn categorically denied in the earlier quotation.

Others avoid this sort of self-contradiction because they do not have to show the (chronological) progression of Paul's thought from the christological revelation to the gentile mission. The kind of argument represented in the first quotation above will be valid only against those who would deny that the Damascus Christophany involved God's call for Paul to the gentile mission as well as the revelation of Jesus Christ. There are, of course, some who do this, but it is rare for any of them to argue that Paul's gentile mission was a result of Paul's later deduction from his Damascus insight that Jesus was the Messiah. However, there are many like myself who insist on the simultaneous nature of the revelation of Jesus Christ and the call to the gentile mission on the Damascus road. To us Dunn's argument here has no force; it is only curious to watch how Dunn arbitrarily attempts to separate the two inseparable elements of the Damascus event and unjustifiably plays one off against the other in this manner.

"Paul himself never seems to trace out or imply such a progression of thought," yes, indeed, but it is because he does not have to do it, in the first place, as his apostolic call to the Gentiles and the revelation of the gospel of Jesus Christ took place together simultaneously at the Damascus Christophany.[75] If Dunn insists on splitting the two elements up and claims the immediacy only of Paul's call to the gentile mission, he himself has the responsibility to show where Paul does "trace out or imply such a progression of thought" *from his call to the gentile mission to his christology.* Does Paul do this anywhere? Or has Dunn ever shown Paul doing this? Ironically, Dunn ends up showing the progression of Paul's thought only *from the christological revelation to the gentile mission!*

As in many other cases, all these arguments of Dunn turn out, upon a close examination, to be marked by strange evidence-taking and serious self-contradiction. Thus, his repeated attempts to see only the immediacy of Paul's call to the gentile mission at the Damascus event, at the cost of neglecting the revelation of the christological/soteriological gospel, prove to be a failure.

---

74. See above, n. 40; below, pp. 132-34.

75. For the logical, though not chronological, connection between the two elements and Dunn's confusion and self-contradiction about it, see above, pp. 6-10.

The Crucified Christ Only for the Gentiles?

It is an amazing fact that Dunn's interpretation of Gal 3:13 completely loses sight of Israel. If the corollary that Paul drew from the revelation of the crucified Jesus as the vindicated Messiah at the Damascus Christophany was only that God was favoring the sinners outside the covenant, the gentiles, and therefore that the gospel had to be preached to the gentiles, did Paul have no thought of the benefit of Jesus the Messiah for those inside the covenant, the Jews? Is this credible? If a Messiah did not benefit Israel, what kind of messiah would he be? A Messiah who does not save Israel is an oxymoron! Yet in his book *The Partings of the Ways,* Dunn elaborates on his interpretation of Gal 3:13 along this line.[76] So he rejects the more traditional interpretation which I represent, namely, that the Damascus revelation of the crucified Jesus as the vindicated Messiah led Paul to reassess the law as the means of achieving one's justification. According to Dunn, that revelation led Paul to assess rather "the law's significance *for Gentiles,* as limiting God's grace to those *en nomo,* 'within the law,' and as excluding those *anomoi,* 'outside the law, not having the law.' " So Dunn concludes:

> It is simply to affirm that the *primary thrust and cutting edge of the doctrine of justification* as it emerges in Paul's writings is as an expression of his Damascus-road-given insight that *God's covenant grace is also for the Gentiles as Gentiles, that the eschatological fulfillment of the promise through Abraham does not require Gentiles to merge their ethnic identity into that of the Jewish people.*[77]

With this elaboration Dunn makes Christ even more clearly irrelevant to the Jews.

Now when Dunn says that the Damascus revelation led Paul to understand that God's grace cannot be limited to those within the law but that it is

---

76. Dunn, *Partings,* 123-24. Cf. also Dunn, "Works of the Law and the Curse of the Law," 225-32. Here, while giving the basically same interpretation, Dunn does say that Christ removed the "curse" that was on the Jews (p. 229). However, by interpreting the "curse" as "the curse of a wrong understanding of the law" or "the ill effects of the too narrow understanding of the covenant and law" which had limited God's grace only to themselves and prevented the gentiles from participating in it, Dunn again makes Christ's redemption really beneficial only to the gentiles. For, according to his interpretation, Christ's redemption benefits the Jews at most in correcting their "wrong understanding of the law," so that they may see that God's grace is not their national monopoly but is extended also to the gentiles! See below, pp. 132-34, regarding Dunn's confusion here. On Gal 3:14, see below, p. 142, n. 61.

77. All these quotations from Dunn, *Partings,* 124 (his italics).

"*also* for the Gentiles as Gentiles," does he mean that Paul continued even after his conversion to assume that the Jews were under God's grace by being within the covenant (of Sinai) and therefore that they would be saved by being faithful to the law of that covenant? Is he saying that since God's grace is already there for those within the law and since the Damascus Christophany revealed only that it is "*also* for the Gentiles as Gentiles," the Jews would not need to avail themselves of God's grace *in Christ* like the gentiles?[78] Or since the Jews already have God's grace available within the law and since Christ's having become a "curse" (Gal 3:13) was only to make God's grace *also* available to the gentiles, the Jews should not concern themselves about God's grace in Christ? So, feeling no need to preach the gospel to the Jews, Paul understood his apostolic call only in terms of mission to the gentiles? Raising such questions as these, Dunn's argument here appears to present Paul as assuming that the Jews would be saved by God's grace within the Sinai covenant. Then how different is this really from the "two-covenant-theory" that some advocate[79] but Dunn himself explicitly rejects elsewhere, the theory that the Jews are to be saved by the Sinai covenant while the gentiles by the new covenant in Christ?[80] Dunn's interpretation of Gal 3:13 is a far cry from Paul's claim that his gospel of God's Son Jesus Christ (Rom 1:3-4, 9) "is the power of God for salvation to every one who has faith, to the Jew first and also to the Greek. For in it the righteousness of God is revealed through faith for faith" (vv. 16-17).

78. See also Dunn, "Paul and Justification by Faith," 93. There, in connection with Paul's talk in Phil 3:4-6 of his own blameless righteousness in the law, Dunn argues that "evidently what Paul experienced [on the Damascus road] was not so much his acceptance as one who had previously been without acceptance by God, but primarily the shattering of his assumption that righteousness before God was Israel's peculiar privilege and his corollary assumption that those who threatened Israel's set-apartness to God, by preaching Messiah Jesus to Gentiles, had to be persecuted." If so, even after the Damascus experience Paul must have recognized that the Jews who were faithful to the law as he had been were accepted by God. Thus, *for their own acceptance by God* the Jews would not need to believe in Christ. If they only needed to develop a more liberal and less nationalistic view about righteousness, they needed faith in Christ at most for developing such a more tolerant attitude to the gentiles.

79. Cf. C. Plaq, *Israels Weg zum Heil: Eine Untersuchung zu Römer 9 bis 11* (Stuttgart: Calwer, 1969), 49-61; F. Mussner, " 'Ganz Israel wird gerettet werden' (Röm. 11,26). Versuch einer Auslegung," *Kairos* 18 (1976): 245-53; L. Gaston, *Paul and the Torah* (Vancouver: University of British Columbia, 1987), esp. 148-50; J. G. Gager, *The Origins of Anti-Semitism: Attitudes toward Judaism in Pagan and Christian Antiquity* (New York: Oxford University Press, 1983).

80. J. D. G. Dunn, *Romans 9–16* (WBC 38a; Waco: Word, 1988), 683.

The Problem of the Law

Dunn's zeal for seeing the Damascus event only in terms of Paul's apostolic call to the gentiles leads Dunn also to advance quite unrealistic and incredible arguments against those who see Paul's new insights into soteriology and into the problem of the law as essential parts of the Damascus revelation.

According to many upholders of the Old Perspective on Paul,[81] Paul the Pharisee and "zealot" for the law persecuted the Hellenists because with their faith in Jesus Christ they sat loose to the law. But seeing Jesus crucified under the curse of the law appearing as the Messiah and Lord vindicated by God on the Damascus road, Paul realized that Christ's death was indeed the eschato-logical atonement for us and therefore that Christ was "the end of the law" for salvation (Rom 10:4). Thus, Paul began to develop his distinctive soterio-logical formulation of the gospel in terms of justification through faith in Christ without works of the law. This new soteriology provided a theological basis for his gentile mission to which he was also called at the Damascus Christophany.

Dunn admits that there is at least some truth in this, and specifically re-fers to Gal 2:19-21 and Phil 3:5-9 as reflecting Paul's conversion from seeking (or remaining in) righteousness through observance of the law to obtaining God's righteousness in Christ.[82] But then Dunn promptly begins to attack this view[83] for the sake of his own thesis that at Damascus Paul received only God's call to the gentile mission and that coming to be aware of the problem of the law very slowly, he began to develop his doctrine of justification only in the wake of the Antiochian incident and the Galatian controversy.[84] As with his arguments in connection with the christological insights that Paul ob-tained at the Damascus Christophany, this manner of Dunn's argument again

---

81. For them, see Kim, *Origin*, 44-50, 269-75; C. Dietzfelbinger, *Die Berufung des Paulus als Ursprung seiner Theologie* (WMANT 58; Neukirchen: Neukirchener, 1985). Ever since his essay " 'Das Ende des Gesetzes': Über Ursprung und Ansatz der paulinischen Theologie," *ZThK* 67 (1970): 14-39, P. Stuhlmacher has consistently represented the Old Perspective in his numerous writings, including his latest *Biblische Theologie des Neuen Testaments*, vol. I, *Grundlegung von Jesus und Paulus* (Göttingen: Vandenhoeck, 1992), 234-68. See the most recent and comprehen-sive representation of this perspective in M. Hengel, "Der vorchristliche Paulus," *Paulus und das antike Judentum* (WUNT 58; Tübingen: Mohr-Siebeck, 1991), 268-91; M. Hengel and A. M. Schwemer, *Paul between Damascus and Antioch* (Louisville: Westminster/Knox, 1997), 98-105.

82. Dunn, "A Light to the Gentiles," 91-92; "Paul's Conversion," 82-83.

83. Dunn, "A Light to the Gentiles," 92-93; "Paul's Conversion," 83-84.

84. Dunn, "A Light to the Gentiles," 98-99; *Partings*, 119-39; "Paul and Justification by Faith," 91-100; "Paul's Conversion," 83-84; *The Theology of Paul*, 346-89.

fails to explain how the element of truth in the Old Perspective that he admits is integrated into his New Perspective.

Quite apart from this problem, there are many serious difficulties with Dunn's arguments.

(1) First of all, Dunn rejects the view that the Hellenists were critical of the law. According to Dunn, the testimony of Acts 6–7 shows that they were critical of the temple but not of the law. In Acts 7 Stephen is reported as having spoken most positively of Moses and the law and having charged the Jews with failing to keep the law (vv. 20-25, 35-38, 53), while criticizing the temple "made with hands" (vv. 47-49). In Acts 6:11-14, the Hellenists are represented as having criticized the law as well as the temple, but then this is attributed to the false witnesses. So for Dunn it is untenable that Paul persecuted the Hellenists for criticizing the law.[85]

However, here again I have great difficulty in comprehending Dunn's logic. He correctly recognizes that "since the Temple cult and its right ordering stands at the centre of the law and of the customs which Moses handed down, a hostile view of the Temple cult would be regarded as a threat to the law as well."[86] This should lead us to think that Paul must have perceived the Hellenists' attack on the temple as also an attack on the law. It is, therefore, reasonable to think that Paul persecuted them for threatening the law as well as the temple. Yet Dunn denies this even while making the correct recognition.

Luke does indeed present Stephen as having been loyal to the law and even presents him as having criticized his fellow Jews for failing to keep the law. But this should be understood from a New Testament perspective and especially in analogy to Jesus and Paul. In the Gospel of Matthew, for example, Jesus, who sets aside the laws concerning the sabbath, food, purity, and so on, claims to have come to fulfill the law and says that not an iota of the law is to be broken (Matt 5:17-19). He criticizes the Pharisees and the scribes for not keeping the law properly (15:1-20; 19:3-9; 23:1-36) and demands that his disciples have a better righteousness than that of the Pharisees (5:20). Paul also sets aside the laws concerning circumcision, food, festival days, and so on, and yet claims to fulfill the law (Rom 8:3-4; 1 Cor 9:21; Gal 6:2; etc.) and charges the Jews for failing to keep the law properly (Rom 2:1–3:20). Luke also portrays Paul as faithful to the law (Acts 21:17-26; 24:14-16). All these examples witness to the early Christians' consciousness that they were the true law-observing people of God, over against the Jews who disobeyed God and failed

---

85. Dunn, "A Light to the Gentiles," 98; *Partings*, 69, 119-20; "Paul's Conversion," 83.
86. Dunn, "Paul's Conversion," 83; a similar sentence also in his *Partings*, 119.

to keep his law properly. However, from the perspective of their Jewish opponents, they could not help but appear as law-breakers, indeed as posing real threats to the law and the ancestral customs.

Luke's description of the charge against Stephen as "false" (Acts 6:13) should also be understood in this context. From the opponents' point of view, the charge that Stephen criticized the temple and the law was literally true, insofar as he attacked the cult of the Jerusalem temple and thereby also the law that both required and regulated the cult. However, for Stephen, Luke, and other Christians who had come to believe that in Jesus Christ's atoning death the cult was fulfilled and superseded, faith in him and obedience to his way was the true way of observing the law as well as the true cult. So, from their point of view, they were not criticizing the cult and the law as such; they were only criticizing the existing cult system and the Jews' current practice of law observance as not according to God's will. In addition, with the criticism they were in fact trying to establish the right cult and the right observance of the law. Insofar as the Jewish charge against Stephen represented a failure to understand this, it was a "false" charge.[87]

(2) For his strenuous denial that Paul's persecution of the Hellenists involved the problem of the law, Dunn's second argument claims that Paul persecuted them only for their gentile mission. He exploits Paul's references to "Judaism" in Gal 1:13-14 and "zeal" in Gal 1:14 and Phil 3:6 to the fullest extent. From his survey of the use of the term "Judaism" in Second Temple Judaism (2 Macc 2:21; 8:1; 14:38; 4 Macc 4:26), Dunn concludes: "the term 'Judaism' seems to have been coined as a means of giving focus to the determination of the Maccabean patriots to defend the distinctive national identity given them by their ancestral religion." So it carried overtones of "a religion which identified itself by its determination to maintain its distinctiveness and to remain free from the corruption of other religions and peoples." "The term's function was evidently determined by its antithesis with 'Hellenism,' to denote Jewish identity over against other nations and peoples." And "this confrontation between Judaism and Hellenism came to particular focus in key test cases," such as the temple and the feasts, circumcision, and food laws.[88] "Zeal" was "a feature of being 'in Judaism,' " and as can be seen

---

87. Contra K. Haacker, *Paulus: Der Werdegang eines Apostels* (SBS 171; Stuttgart: Katholisches Bibelwerk, 1997), 90-91. If anybody wants to argue from Luke's description of the charge as "false" that the Hellenists criticized only the temple but not the law, he should be consistent and deny the Hellenists' attack on the temple as well. For Luke designates as false the charge, not just that Stephen speaks against the law, but rather that "he speaks against this holy place and the law" (Acts 6:13-14).

88. All these quotations from Dunn, "Paul's Conversion," 86-87.

from Israel's "heroes of zeal" such as Simeon and Levi (Gen 34; Jdt 9:2-4; *Jub.* 30), Phinehas (Num 25:6-13; Sir 45:23-24; 1 Macc 2:54; 4 Macc 18:12), Elijah (1 Kgs 18; Sir 48:2-3; 1 Macc 2:58), and the Maccabees (1 Macc 2), it had three features: (a) an unconditional commitment to maintain Israel's distinctiveness as God's covenant people; (b) a readiness to defend its religious and national boundaries by force; and (c) a targeting not only of gentiles but also of Jews who threatened Israel's boundaries.[89] With this survey on "Judaism" and "zeal," Dunn triumphantly declares:

> From this we gain a surprisingly clear picture of Paul's motivation as a persecutor, but one too little noted in contemporary discussion of Paul's conversion. His motivation was that of earlier heroes of zeal. It was directed against the Hellenist Christians because they were seen to threaten Israel's distinctiveness and boundaries. The deduction is unavoidable that this threat was constituted by the Hellenists taking the gospel of Messiah Jesus to the Gentiles. By opening the door of this particular expression of Jewish religion and tradition to the Gentiles they were in danger of compromising Israel's integrity and purity. By failing to require of such Gentile converts circumcision and the practice of the covenant distinctives on which the Maccabeans had founded "Judaism," the Hellenists were removing the boundary markers and tearing down the palisades and iron walls put up by Moses to hedge Israel in on all sides (*Aristeas* 139-42).[90]

This is a strange argument. For Paul, the "zealot" for the law and the ancestral traditions, "the gospel of Messiah Jesus" would have been no "gospel" but a blasphemous and heretical doctrine, because it claimed as its Messiah and Savior Jesus of Nazareth, who had been prosecuted by the defenders of "Judaism" for being a false messiah and false prophet and for his alleged threat to "Judaism," so as to be crucified by the Romans under the pronouncement of God's curse by the law (Deut 21:23; Gal 3:13). Yet Paul, the "zealot" for the law, was not concerned at all about the Hellenists' "gospel" itself nor about its negative implications for the law[91] but only about their taking this "gospel" to the gentiles! Why would he have been concerned about the heretics feeding the gentiles with their heretical doctrine about which he was not at all concerned? If Paul was incensed by the Hellenists' failure to require of their gentile converts "circumcision and the practice of the covenant distinctives," would Paul not have regarded this first and foremost as a breach of the law?

---

89. Ibid., 88-89; also Dunn, *Partings*, 120-22.
90. Dunn, "Paul's Conversion," 90.
91. See above, pp. 15-17.

Apparently those who were "zealous for the law" did not persecute only those Jews who consorted with the gentiles, but also those Jews who were perceived as undermining the law. For Philo speaks of "ζηλωταὶ νόμων, strictest guardians of the ancestral institutions, merciless to those who do anything to subvert them" (*Spec. Leg.* 2.253).[92] So it is quite incredible that Paul persecuted the Hellenists only because their preaching to the gentiles of a false messiah appeared to him as compromising the integrity and purity of Israel. It seems much more sensible to think that Paul persecuted them because in his eyes they were subverting the law by preaching the false messiah Jesus and by ignoring "circumcision and the practice of the covenant distinctives" in their dealings with the gentiles.

(3) In his third argument against the view that at his Damascus conversion Paul began to see the problem of the law as the means to obtaining (or remaining in) righteousness, Dunn points to the "remarkably positive view [Paul] continues to maintain in his letters regarding the law" (e.g., Rom 3:31; 8:4; 1 Cor 7:19; Gal 5:14). According to Dunn, it shows that Paul did not abandon the law completely at his Damascus conversion.[93] But no serious scholar claims that at his conversion Paul completely abandoned the law. Many upholders of the Old Perspective would claim that at his conversion Paul realized that for salvation observance of the law was not necessary, as it was obtained through faith in Christ. But they do not deny that Paul nevertheless thought that Christians should and could fulfill "the just requirements of the law" — probably centered around the double command of love — by the power of the Holy Spirit (Rom 8:4; 13:8-10; Gal 5:14; 6:2; cf. also 1 Cor 10:14–11:1).[94] At the same time they would point out the truly remarkable fact that Paul, an erstwhile "zealot" for the law, levels (at least implicit) criticism on the law — as in, for example, Rom 5:20; 7:5; 2 Cor 3:4-18; Gal 4:21-31; Phil 3:4-9 — beyond pointing out the limitation of the law in passages such as Rom 3:20; 8:3; Gal 3:21, 24. They would think that such a negative view of the law, which is unimaginable of a pious Jew, let alone a former "zealot" for the law, is best explained in terms of a new insight into the problem of the law that Paul obtained at his conversion. The dialectic of Paul's

92. Quoted according to the rendering of F. H. Colson in the Loeb edition of Philo, vol. 7. I owe this reference to Haacker, *Paulus*, 89.

93. Dunn, "Paul's Conversion," 83-84.

94. In 1 Cor 10:14–11:1 Paul summarizes and concludes his long and careful discussion of the problem of eating the meat offered to idols (1 Cor 8–10) in terms of the principles of Christian liberty and the double command of love, the wholehearted devotion to God which excludes idolatry, and the love to neighbors which demands giving up one's right for the sake of the weak brethren.

view of the law is indeed complex. However, it will not do to point only to its positive side and deny that at his conversion Paul began to doubt the law as the means of obtaining righteousness, regardless of whether in the sense of the Old Perspective or the New Perspective. Pointing to Gal 2:21, Dunn does acknowledge that there was "some reassessment of Paul's relation to the law" at his conversion, but he says, "Precisely what this amounted to has still to be clarified."[95] As far as I know, Dunn has clarified it nowhere in his numerous and voluminous writings on the subject of Paul's conversion and the law.

(4) Dunn's fourth argument against the view that Paul's conversion involved a devaluation of the law as the means of justification after the revelation of the crucified Jesus at Damascus is to point to the apostolic conference in Jerusalem (Gal 2:1-10) and the Antiochian controversy (Gal 2:11-14) and ask why the problems of circumcision of gentile converts and table-fellowship with them arose so late.[96] On this Dunn presents another difficult argument:

> What is of relevance for us here is the way in which this particular formulation, the antithesis between faith and works, seems to emerge from the incident at Antioch (Gal 2.11-14). Why had it not emerged earlier? Paul had been converted for perhaps as many as seventeen years. He had been active in missionary work among Gentiles for most of that period. And yet the issue of Jew and Gentile fellowship and integration within the new house groups had not been posed. Even at the Jerusalem consultation, when the issue of circumcision, a primary work of the law, had been resolved, the question of these (other) works that had traditionally marked out Israel's separateness from the nations had not been raised. It looks very much, therefore, as though it took the particular confrontation at Antioch to bring out this fundamental declaration of principle from Paul. What had been thus far a gray area — an issue not perceived, a question not posed — suddenly had the spotlight turned on it. And Paul, in one of the great defining moments in Christian theology, pronounced what was to become his most memorable and telling principle: no one is justified by works of the law, but only through faith in Christ.[97]

It is quite incredible that Paul did not perceive the issues of circumcision and food laws for his gentile converts until shortly before the Jerusalem confer-

95. Dunn, "Paul's Conversion," 84.
96. Dunn, "A Light to the Gentiles," 92, 98; *Partings,* 124-135; "Paul and Justification by Faith," 99.
97. Dunn, "Paul and Justification by Faith," 99.

ence of the apostles and until the Antioch conflict, respectively.[98] Dunn speculates at length why the former issue did not arise until around A.D. 50: (a) as the Lucan narrative of the Cornelius episode (Acts 10–11) indicates, perhaps the first Jewish Christians regarded the conversion of such God-fearers as Cornelius with evident manifestations of the Spirit's endowment as exceptions that posed "no real threat to the normal pattern of entry into the covenant people."[99] (b) Most, if not all, of the earliest converts were proselytes and God-fearers. Already "judaized" considerably, they "would presumably appear less threatening to most of the Jerusalem believers," and "the more traditional Jerusalem believers might also have been content for the time being to allow such Gentiles to remain in an anomalous status, as presumably the synagogues did with regard to their God-fearers."[100] Dunn asks, "Why then did the issue of circumcision arise when it did?" and gives three answers: (a) "The numbers of uncircumcised Gentile converts were increasing too rapidly"; (b) the success of the Christian mission to the Jews brought in a significant number of converts with their Pharisaic halakoth (Acts 15:1-5; Gal 2:4); and (c) the deteriorating political situation in Judea during the period from A.D. 40 on moved many Jewish Christians to defend their national identity more zealously. So arose the issue of circumcision for gentile converts in the late 40s.[101]

All these points may be granted as far as most of the non-"zealotic" or non-Pharisaic Jewish Christians are concerned. However, even in this scheme of Dunn's, the Jewish Christians with a Pharisaic background are supposed to have perceived the issue of circumcision for gentile converts. Then the question immediately arises regarding what Paul with not just a Pharisaic but "zealotic" background would have perceived of his gentile converts. If the Jewish Christians with a background in Pharisaic halakoth perceived the issue of circumcision for them, how much more would Paul, the "zealot" for the law, have seen it? Dunn has maximized the significance of the pre-conversion Paul's "zeal" for the defense of "Judaism." If Paul had been so "zealous" to defend the identity and purity of Israel from the gentile contami-

---

98. Dunn strictly separates the two issues from each other and claims that at the Jerusalem council only the issue of circumcision was dealt with and the issue of the food laws and table-fellowship with the gentile converts did not arise (ibid., 99; also *Partings*, 124-135). Although for this unrealistic view Dunn appeals to Acts 15, Acts 15 in fact quite properly implies that the issues of food and other laws were bound up with the central issue of circumcision (see esp. vv. 10, 20, 29).

99. Dunn, *Partings*, 124-25 (quotation from 125).

100. Ibid., 125-26 (quotations from 126).

101. Ibid., 126-27 (quotations from 126).

nation in the tradition of Phinehas and the Maccabees and was moved to persecute the Hellenists precisely for threatening this purity with their acceptance of their gentile converts without circumcision, how could Paul not have perceived the issue of circumcision for gentile converts when called to the gentile mission on the Damascus road?

Here the issue is primarily not what other early Jewish Christians thought or perceived but rather what *Paul,* the persecutor, convert and apostle, perceived or thought.[102] It is not credible that Paul — who was going to Damascus in order to persecute the Hellenists precisely for ignoring circumcision in their mission to the gentiles — decided to join in their mission without any consciousness of the issue of circumcision. It is inconceivable that Paul went about with his mission among the gentiles for as long as seventeen years without posing and resolving this issue theologically.[103] The Damascus event was certainly a conversion experience for Paul, and it is more likely that his conversion involved, among other things, a conscious reevaluation of the law of circumcision than that it involved his complete amnesia about that law. Or, to put it another way, the Damascus call to the gentile mission included a conversion of Paul on the issue of circumcision for gentile converts. It will not do to turn this genuine event of conversion into something like a modern-day car accident that resulted in Paul's partial memory loss.

These arguments are to be applied, *mutatis mutandis,* also against Dunn's claim that the problem of food laws and table-fellowship with gentile converts did not arise until the Antioch conflict. From the fact that Jewish and gentile Christians ate together at Antioch before "certain men came from James" (Gal 2:12), Dunn conjectures that "the basis of their table-fellowship was at least a modest observance of the food laws."[104] For the men from James, however, "the modest level of law-observance in the table-fellowship at Antioch was tantamount to abandoning the law altogether."[105] From Paul's

---

102. In order to strengthen his argument that other Jewish Christians did not regard the Hellenists' views as serious threats to the identity and integrity of Israel, Dunn emphasizes Paul's excessive zeal (Gal 1:14) and his being an exceptional case (ibid., 305 n. 33). But the more Dunn emphasizes Paul's exceptional zeal, the more serious my questions against him here become.

103. Dunn himself recognizes that "Gal 5.11 implies that circumcision became an issue as a result of Paul's own missionary work" (ibid., 305 n. 33). Why then in the face of such clear evidence does Dunn insist on such an unrealistic thesis that the issue did not arise until the Jerusalem conference? If other Jews could raise the issue of circumcision against Paul's gentile mission, could it have been possible that Paul the former "zealot" for the law failed to perceive the issue in connection with his gentile mission?

104. Dunn, *Partings,* 131.

105. Ibid., 132 (italics in the original).

29

charge that Peter and the other Jews "separated themselves" from the gentile Christians in Antioch (Gal 2:12), Dunn infers Paul's probable implication "that Peter and the other Jewish believers, by withdrawing from the table-fellowship of Antioch, were acting like Pharisees."[106]

Apparently Dunn is not aware that these observations really undermine his own position. If Peter's adopting a Pharisaic position meant his disapproval of the table-fellowship with the gentile Christians and if the men from James perceived "the modest level of law-observance in the table-fellowship at Antioch" as "tantamount to abandoning the law altogether," how would Paul, the former real Pharisee[107] who used to excel in zeal for the law over his peers, have thought of "the modest level of law-observance in the table-fellowship at Antioch"? From his Pharisaic and "zealotic" perspective, surely Paul would also have condemned it "as tantamount to abandoning the law altogether." Yet why did he happily participate in such table-fellowship with gentile Christians at Antioch? Did he fall into a long amnesia also about the food laws after his Damascus call? Was he awakened to the laws only when the men from James began to agitate in Antioch, and Peter, Barnabas, and other Jewish Christians withdrew from that table-fellowship? And then did he instantly work out his argument for justification through faith in Christ without works of the law for the first time?

To me, this whole scenario is incredible. It is much more reasonable to infer from Paul's participation in table-fellowship with gentile Christians at Antioch that he had thought through and theologically resolved the issue of the food laws and table-fellowship with gentile Christians. His Damascus call to the gentile mission must have also included a conversion on this issue. Again, our primary concern here need not be what other, theologically less astute Jewish Christians in the earliest church might have thought, but rather what Paul, the former Pharisee and "zealot" for the law, might have thought. Therefore, I cannot support Dunn's view that at the Antiochian conflict or in Gal 2:15-16 Paul for the first time formulated his doctrine of justification through faith in Christ without works of the law.[108]

As one who had persecuted the Hellenists in order to defend the integrity and purity of Israel against gentile defilement, Paul, the fresh convert to the

---

106. Ibid., 132.

107. On Dunn's premise, it would be more proper to speak of Paul simply as "the real Pharisee" rather than as "the *former* real Pharisee" here. For on Dunn's premise Paul would not have abandoned his Pharisaic position on the food laws until the Antioch conflict, as he had not yet thought them through.

108. J. D. G. Dunn, "The New Perspective on Paul," *BJRL* 65 (1983), now reprinted in *Jesus, Paul and the Law,* 198; "Paul and Justification by Faith," 99; *Partings,* 134.

faith in Jesus the Messiah, could not help but face the issues of circumcision of his gentile converts and table-fellowship with them from day one of his gentile mission. In the course of discharging his apostolic commission for the gentiles, he frequently used synagogues, aiming his gospel message at the God-fearers as well as at the Jews there (cf. 1 Cor 9:19-23). On many occasions he got into trouble with the Jews (cf. 2 Cor 11:24; Gal 4:29; 5:11; 1 Thess 2:14-16; also Acts 9:20-30; 13:44-50; 14:19; 17:5-7, 13; 18:12-17). At least on some occasions he seems to have been persecuted by the Jews for his mission to the gentiles without requiring law observance (cf. Gal 4:29; 5:11; 1 Thess 2:14-16; also Acts 13:38-39, 42-50; 15:1-2; 18:12-17; 21:20-21).[109] If not his former Pharisaic and "zealotic" convictions nor his theological astuteness, then at least these persecutions must have kept the issues of circumcision and food laws before him. In this situation, is it conceivable that at least in his mind the issue of "Jew and Gentile fellowship and integration within the new house groups had not been posed" until the Antioch conflict?[110] Is it credible that until that conflict he had not thought through the issue of whether the gentiles were "justified" only through faith in Christ or whether they had to keep the law as well?

Apparently Dunn himself finds it not quite credible, for he tries to mitigate the force of his argument by saying:

---

109. So also Dunn, *Partings*, 305 n. 33, 320 n. 42. It would be perverse to try to argue from the absence of the material in Acts that Paul experienced Jewish persecution for his gentile mission beginning only shortly before the Jerusalem council and after. The simple fact is that before Acts 13 Luke does not report much of the details of Paul's gentile mission. If we consider together Paul's own persecution of the Hellenists and the Jewish persecution of Paul as reported in Acts 13 onward, it seems more reasonable to suppose that even during the earlier period of his mission Paul was persecuted by the Jews for his preaching to the gentiles without requiring observance of the law.

110. Actually Dunn contradicts himself here again. In his "A Light to the Gentiles," 101, he writes: "Paul the persecutor would presumably have regarded the cross as the inevitable outworking and consequence of Jesus' disregard for the rules of the covenant during his ministry (particularly his association with 'sinners' — Mark 2.15-17; Matt. 11.19//Luke 7.34). The reversal of the Damascus road would then carry with it a radical revision in attitude to this feature of Jesus' ministry: God accepts sinners, including 'Gentile sinners,' as did Jesus when on earth (an echo of this may be implicit in Gal 2.17)." If so, Paul *did* pose the problems of the food/purity laws and the Jew-Gentile table-fellowship and *did* have them resolved through the insight obtained from the Damascus revelation. Incidentally, this statement of Dunn's also contradicts his denial that Paul persecuted Christians because he perceived in their preaching of the crucified Christ an antithesis between the law and Christ. Finally, it makes Dunn's view odd that the Damascus reversal led Paul only to the conclusion of God's acceptance of gentiles but did not make him think about the problem of the law.

That is not to say, however, that this was a wholly new principle for Paul, first discovered, as it were, in and through the Antioch incident. It would be more accurate to say that the principle was implicit in the "revelation" made to him on the Damascus road. For that revelation, if we are right, came to focus in the realization that the God of Israel was also the God of the nations — that the good news of God's Son was not to be restricted to Israel, but was also for the Gentiles as freely as for the Jews (Gal 1:12-16); that the promise of Abraham was also of blessing for the nations (3:6-14). What his years of initial missionary work, climaxing in the Jerusalem consultation and the Antioch incident, brought home to him were the ramifications of this basic revelation. The controversies that his preaching of Christ among the nations provoked forced him to think through and to articulate in sharper and anti-thetical terms what that revelation amounted to — that is, what was at stake in the gospel itself. And he summed it up in the classic slogan: justification from faith and not from works.[111]

I am content with this statement as far as it goes, although it falls short of re-flecting on the factor of Paul's Pharisaic and "zealotic" background which must have made Paul immediately and powerfully aware of "the principle im-plicit" in the Damascus revelation and call. As we have repeatedly tried to point out above, *it is a fundamental problem of Dunn's that he emphasizes or indeed maximizes the significance of Paul's "zeal" for "Judaism" up to the mo-ment of the Damascus event only to refuse to consider it as a factor in the devel-opment of Paul's theology and missionary practice after that moment.*[112] Never-theless, I am glad that Dunn now recognizes that the principle of justification through faith without works of the law was at least "implicit" in the Damas-cus revelation/call and that the controversies provoked by his preaching of the gospel among the gentiles forced him to think it through and articulate it in sharper and antithetical terms.

However, did those controversies erupt for the first time only shortly be-fore the Jerusalem conference of the apostles and at the Antioch incident? To be consistent with his earlier insistence that the issues of circumcision and the

111. Dunn, "Paul and Justification by Faith," 99-100.
112. T. L. Donaldson, "Zealot and Convert: The Origin of Paul's Christ-Torah Antithesis," *CBQ* 51 (1989): 662, rightly criticizes Räisänen for ignoring Paul's pre-conversion "zeal" for the law in his argument that Paul's doctrine of justification without works of the law developed only in the wake of the Judaizing controversies in Antioch and Galatia (Räisänen, *Paul and the Law,* 251-63; "Paul's Conversion and the Development of His View of the Law," *NTS* 33 [1987]: 404-19). In the light of this criticism of one New Perspectivist by another New Perspectivist, Dunn's failure to consider the factor of Paul's "zeal" for the law in his post-conversion theologizing appears even more strange.

food laws were not perceived or posed until the Jerusalem conference and the Antioch incident,[113] Dunn would have to answer this question affirmatively. But, again, is this not incredible?[114] In any case, the debate over whether the controversies arose for the first time only after fifteen to seventeen years of Paul's missionary work among the gentiles is really an idle one. The violent controversies that right up to the moment of the Damascus event Paul had had with the Hellenist Christians about welcoming gentiles into the fold of the people of God without requiring circumcision and the food laws must have operated in Paul's mind no less powerfully than any subsequent controversies.[115] Paul's epistles show him to have been possessed of a perspicacious and acute mind. When having received the revelation of the gospel of Jesus Christ and the apostolic call to the gentiles on the Damascus road he had to abandon his previous arguments about circumcision and food laws and go over to his opponents' position, he would not have done so without thinking through the principle of justification through faith in Christ without works of the law.

According to Dunn, "the more significance one reads back into the Damascus road event (Christ at once seen as the end of the law), the less easy it is to understand why the confrontations of Galatians 2 did not take place earlier."[116] This is not necessarily so. We have already implied that even before the confrontations referred to in Gal 2 Paul's mission to the gentiles provoked controversies with and persecutions from the Jews.[117] It is much easier to explain such controversies and persecutions with the presupposition that Paul had worked out his principle of salvation through faith in Christ without works of the law soon after the Damascus revelation and call and before embarking on his gentile mission, than without it. The Jerusalem council clearly was not an impromptu event but a well-prepared consultation necessitated by the controversies which had been building up for some time in both Judea

113. See above, pp. 27-28.

114. It is all the more incredible in view of the fact that apparently Jesus himself was critical of the food/purity law, at least as it was interpreted by the Pharisees (Mark 2:15-17 pars.; Matt 11:19/Luke 7:34; Mark 7:1-23/Matt 15:1-20), something Dunn himself recognizes ("A Light to the Gentiles," 92, 101; "Jesus and Ritual Purity: A Study of the Tradition-History of Mark 7.15," in *Jesus, Paul and the Law*, 37-60).

115. 1 Cor 15:9-10; Gal 1:13, 23; and Phil 3:6 (cf. Eph 3:7; 1 Tim 1:13) make it clear that Paul carried with him the consciousness of his past persecution of the church for a long time, allowing it to shape his self-understanding, missionary practice and theology (cf. Hengel and Schwemer, *Paul between Damascus and Antioch*, 96-97; Kim, *Origin*, 295; see ch. 6). While being so conscious of his past persecution of the church, would he not have also been conscious of *why* he persecuted the church?

116. Dunn, "A Light to the Gentiles," 98.

117. See above p. 31.

and Antioch about the issue of circumcision for gentile converts. Probably we are to see the Antioch incident also not as an abrupt happening but rather as the climax of a series of confrontations about the issue of the food laws and table-fellowship. Considering the circumstances of the ancient world, where there were no telephones or cars, as well as the circumstances of the primitive church, where doctrinal definitions and institutional organizations were only gradually emerging, the period of fifteen to seventeen years between Paul's call and the Jerusalem council was not so long a delay.[118]

The following scenario is the more realistic: right after receiving his gospel and apostolic call at Damascus, Paul began to preach the gospel to the gentiles (as well as the Jews) without requiring observance of the law. The Jews often persecuted Paul for this. Feeling uneasy about his teaching and about eating with gentile Christians in house churches, some Jewish Christians would also initially raise controversies about them. Paul would persuade them theologically, so that in places like Antioch Jewish Christians and gentile Christians shared table-fellowship, even if with some tension between them. Over some length of time, the Jerusalem church heard of the practices of the Antioch church. Some of its members with a Pharisaic background became alarmed, especially under the pressure of the zealotic fervor rising in Judea during the 40s. Some of them took the trouble of traveling to Antioch to enforce the requirements of the law there. This aggravated the tension between Jewish and gentile Christians in Antioch, the tension that had been contained only by Paul's persuasive teaching. So Paul and Barnabas sent a message to the Jerusalem apostles to have a consultation. Thus came about the Jerusalem consultation. Strengthened in his theological position through the endorsement of the Jerusalem apostles, Paul happily went about with his preaching of the gospel of salvation through faith in Christ without works of the law. But the "Judaizers" were not happy with the outcome of the apostolic consultation. So they started a kind of anti-Pauline mission in Paul's churches, first in Antioch, then in Galatia, and so on. Thus came about the Antioch conflict and the Galatian crisis. I have little difficulty imagining that it took years for these events.

With this response to Dunn's summarizing argument, "the more signifi-

---

118. Would it be too far-fetched to compare this time interval with the more than eleven years that it took in our age of the global village and the electronic revolution for the Durham-Tübingen-Symposium on Paul and Judaism/the Law to begin (September 26-29, 1988–September 20-25, 1999) after the lively debate had been touched off on the New Perspective on Paul by the publication of E. P. Sanders's *Paul and Palestinian Judaism* (London: SCM; Philadelphia: Fortress, 1977)? Cf. M. Hengel and U. Heckel, eds., *Paulus und das antike Judentum* (WUNT 58; Tübingen: Mohr-Siebeck, 1991).

cance one reads back into the Damascus road event (Christ at once seen as the end of the law), the less easy it is to understand why the confrontations of Galatians 2 did not take place earlier," I would suggest that in fact the opposite is truer: *the more Dunn emphasizes the pre-conversion Paul's zeal for the law and the "immediacy" of Paul's call to the gentile mission at Damascus, the less credible Dunn's thesis about the late development of Paul's doctrine of justification through faith without works of the law becomes.*

Excursus: Terence L. Donaldson's Theory

T. L. Donaldson is a New Perspectivist. Like Dunn, he bases his theory on E. P. Sanders's notion of Judaism as covenantal nomism.[119] For him also Paul's doctrine of justification through faith without works of the law was formulated secondarily to defend the more fundamental conviction of the gentile mission, and the "works of the law" refer primarily to the elements of the Torah that serve to distinguish Jew from gentile.[120] With such a fundamental understanding, Donaldson has written *Paul and the Gentiles: Remapping the Apostle's Convictional World*, to inquire into the origin of Paul's convictions about the gentiles.[121]

Although Donaldson thus stands on the shoulders of the pioneers of the New Perspective like K. Stendahl and E. P. Sanders, he criticizes them for accounting for Paul's gentile mission by a simple appeal to the "call" on the Damascus road. According to Donaldson,

> it either begs the question or renders Paul's convictional shift arbitrary and inexplicable — or both. Prior to the Damascus experience, Paul was, in his own terms, a zealot for the law and a persecutor of the church (Gal 1:13-14; Phil 3:5-6). Before his experience could have been understood, then, as a call "to proclaim God's Son among the Gentiles" (Gal 1:15-16) . . . it must have been an experience in which he became convinced that the crucified Jesus was even so and after all the "Messiah" and "Son of God." Further, since his persecution of those who proclaimed the message of the crucified Messiah was linked to his zeal for Israel's law and ancestral tradition, any revision of his estimation of Jesus would necessarily entail a reassessment of these other fundamental convictions as well. Moreover, since each of these convictions (about Israel, the Torah, messianic salvation, and so on) carried with it implications for the situation and status of the Gentiles, Paul could not have arrived at the conviction that he was to proclaim a Christ-

---

119. Donaldson, *Paul*, 8ff.

120. Ibid., 113, 161.

121. Donaldson has presented a summary of the book in his article, "Israelite, Convert, Apostle to the Gentiles: The Origin of Paul's Gentile Mission," in *The Road from Damascus* (ed. R. N. Longenecker; Grand Rapids: Eerdmans, 1997), 62-83.

centered message of salvation to the Gentiles without the situation and status of the Gentiles becoming part of this convictional assessment. Kim's assumption of an explicitly verbal call . . . would have made no sense to him at all, unless it fit into a framework where Jew, Gentile, and God's message about Christ made coherent sense. In other words, a perceived call to a Gentile mission could not have been Paul's starting point. There must have been a first stage in which a Christ-centered mission to the Gentiles made sense before there could be a second-stage perception that he himself was called to play a central role in such a situation.[122]

I cite Donaldson's criticism here at length because it is essentially the same as the criticism that I have been making of Dunn. But I do not understand why Donaldson includes me in the company of Stendahl and Sanders here. Dunn criticizes me for making Paul's call to the gentile mission a corollary of his christological and soteriological insights obtained on the Damascus road.[123] But Donaldson criticizes me for not doing that! Donaldson may disagree with me in the way I connect Paul's christological, soteriological and salvation-historical convictions with his sense of call to the gentile mission, but he cannot say that I have not done it. I believe that Donaldson's criticism is applicable to Dunn rather than to me. For it is Dunn who strenuously isolates Paul's Damascus call to the gentile mission from his christological, soteriological and salvation-historical convictions obtained from the Damascus Christophany.

As I said above, however, it is questionable whether we can really speak like Donaldson of the two (chronological) stages, one for Paul's obtaining his new christological/soteriological convictions and their bearings on Israel and the gentiles, and the other for his perceiving his own call to the gentile mission. If with his talk of the "two stages" Donaldson means that Paul's conviction about his call to the gentile mission was a (not only logical but also chronological) corollary of the prior process of reassessment of Jesus and his messianic salvation, of the Torah, of Israel and the gentiles, and so on,[124] Dunn's criticism will apply to him for failing to appreciate the "immediacy" of Paul's apostolic call to the gentiles. Thus, it seems that Dunn and

---

122. Donaldson, *Paul,* 250, similarly also 18, 259-60; "Israelite, Convert, Apostle to the Gentiles," 70.

123. See above, pp. 4-7.

124. With his skepticism about the possibility of Paul's hearing a "verbal call" to the gentile mission at the Damascus Christophany ("Israelite, Convert, Apostle to the Gentiles," 63; *Paul,* 249-50), Donaldson apparently thinks he can conceive of the emergence of Paul's sense of call only as the consequence of the reassessment process of those elements. Even if we discount the possibility of Paul's hearing the call — but on what ground do we have the right to discount it completely (cf. 2 Cor 12:4, 9)? — we can see that not only his experience of the reversal of his views involved in his persecution of the Hellenists for their gentile mission but also his experience of the endowment of the Spirit on the Damascus road would have helped him to develop such a sense of call quite quickly. The latter seems to have led him to Isa 42, where the Servant is called to be a bearer of light and salvation to the gentiles and is endowed with the Spirit for the mission. See pp. 115-23 below.

Donaldson cancel out each other's extreme views. So, for me, it is best to affirm that the revelation of the gospel and the apostolic call (and also the "mystery" of Rom 11:25-26 — the salvation of the gentiles and the Jews) were rooted together in the Damascus Christophany and the insights and convictions about them developed together.

According to Donaldson, Paul's conviction about gentile mission can be accounted for only under the assumption that before the Damascus event he was actively engaged in proselytizing gentiles. Paul, a covenantal nomist, persecuted the church because he perceived the "Christ-Torah" antithesis in the church's preaching, in that Christ was presented as a means for membership in the people of God rivaling the Torah. To Paul with such a mindset, Christ appeared on the Damascus road. This "experience convinced him that God had raised Jesus and that Jesus was indeed Messiah and Savior. This experience necessitated a fundamental reconfiguration of his set of world-structuring convictions, with Christ replacing the Torah as the means by which membership in the people of God was to be determined." So now with the gospel of Christ replacing the Torah and with a new energy he continued his proselytizing activities for the gentiles.[125]

Donaldson's thesis is vulnerable at many points. But to point out only the most crucial one, on his premise, Paul, the "zealot" for the law and Judaism, did not need to become an apostle *to the gentiles*. It would have been more logical if he had become an apostle to the Jews with openness to a law-free gentile mission. If Paul's conviction about his call to the gentile mission is to be derived from his pre-conversion activities of proselytism, the latter would have to be something Paul pursued with a compelling perception of its salvation-historical necessity, with an absolute commitment and concentration equal to those with which he now pursues his gentile apostleship. But that sort of phenomenon is difficult to envisage within the Judaism of New Testament times. Since in New Testament times Judaism had no real mission to the gentiles,[126] Donaldson has to qualify his claim about Paul "play[ing] some active role in the making of proselytes," with the denial: "This is not to say that he was involved in any full-

---

125. Donaldson, *Paul,* esp. 203-305; "Israelite, Convert, Apostle to the Gentiles," esp. 81-83 (the quotation from 82). Thus, unlike Dunn, Donaldson does recognize that Paul saw the "Christ-Torah" antithesis already in the post-Easter church's preaching. However, true to the fundamental assumption of the New Perspective School, Donaldson also insists that Paul saw the antithesis not as a rival means of obtaining righteousness, but rather "as a rival means of determining membership in the people of God" ("Zealot and Convert," 682; *Paul,* 296-97). Yet Donaldson also writes: "Since it was necessary even for a conscientious Torah observer such as himself to believe in Jesus in order to be eligible for salvation, Paul perceived the message as implying that the Torah was not enough" (*Paul,* 296). If so, why does Donaldson insist that Paul saw the "Christ-Torah" antithesis only in terms of Christ replacing the Torah as a requirement for membership in the people of God, but not also (or even more) as the means of salvation?

126. This is almost a consensus in scholarship. Cf. esp. S. McKnight, *A Light among the Gentiles* (Minneapolis: Fortress, 1991); M. Goodman, *Mission and Conversion: Proselytizing in the Religious History of the Roman Empire* (Oxford: Clarendon, 1994).

scale 'mission,' " and he can do no more than refer to the analogy of the at-most-occasional proselytizing activities of Eleazar, the Pharisaic adviser to King Izates (Josephus, *Ant.* 20.34-48).[127] But for a man with only that much of commitment to the gentiles, how could the "paradigm shift"[128] brought about by the replacement of the Torah by Christ, in itself, have meant a call to commit his whole life to the gentile mission? How could it alone have caused him to devote the best part of his intellectual acumen to the defense of the gentile mission? Would it not have been more natural if Paul had just continued his former occasional efforts of proselytism, of urging, like Eleazar, gentiles attracted to Judaism to become "full proselytes," now, of course, not by accepting the yoke of the Torah, but by believing in Christ? Furthermore, we should not forget that Paul was a "zealot" for the law and Judaism, an extreme nationalist. In fact, Donaldson has been one of those who have emphasized the significance of this element of Paul's background.[129] Donaldson emphasizes also how Paul in spite of his conversion remained an Israel-centered thinker.[130] Then, for such a Paul, would not the paradigm shift on the Damascus road have meant first and foremost a call to preach Christ to his compatriots and have them confirmed as the members of the true people of God by their faith in their Messiah?[131] Why would such a Paul have seen it more urgent to bring the gentiles into the fold of the people of God?

127. Donaldson, *Paul,* 275-84; "Israelite, Convert, Apostle to the Gentiles," 82 (quotations from the latter).

128. Donaldson, *Paul,* esp. 43-47, interprets Paul's Damascus experience in terms of Thomas Kuhn's concept of "paradigm shift."

129. Donaldson, "Zealot and Convert," 655-82; *Paul,* 284-92. Not only the absence of mission in Second Temple Judaism but also the "zealotic" background of Paul should restrain us from seeing the pre-conversion Paul as an active proselytizer who went about with his work of proselytizing out of his positive concern for the gentiles' salvation. Given his "zealotic" background, his proselytizing activity must have been motivated more by his desire to protect the integrity and purity of Israel than to make God's grace available to the gentiles. Donaldson, *Paul,* 277-78, tries to present Paul as having been concerned both about protecting the integrity of the covenant and Israel and about the salvation of the gentiles. But for the latter he can only appeal to Paul's use of the word "preached" in Gal 5:11. However, the word can hardly bear the weight of the noble thesis. To make his thesis convincing, Donaldson would need to provide us with examples where some Jewish "zealots" for the law in the first century were also concerned about the salvation of the gentiles and so went about trying to proselytize them.

130. Donaldson, *Paul,* 251-59.

131. Donaldson actually recognizes this when he says that "the most immediate" consequence of the paradigm shift concerned Israel: "Since Christ identifies first with Israel, the saving benefits made possible in his death and resurrection pertain in the first instance to Israel. Thus, it is quite to be expected that we should find the Jewish Christian remnant perceived as the primary beneficiary of Christ's ministry, and the means by which those benefits are extended to the Gentiles" (ibid., 245). This being so, to account for Paul's sense of call to the gentiles rather than to the Jews, we need another explanation than merely pointing to the paradigm shift which occurred to a former "zealot" who had occasionally sought to ensure a proper proselytization of some pro-Judaism gentiles for the sake of the integrity of Israel.

Thus, on Donaldson's premise, Paul should have become an apostle *to the Jews*, who would occasionally also preach Christ to the gentiles. There is no reason why Paul had to become specifically an apostle to the gentiles. Donaldson's thesis cannot account for Paul's sense of his personal call to the gentile mission (Gal 1:15-16; 2:7-9; Rom 1:5; 15:15-16), let alone his sense of it as his *Schicksal* (Rom 1:14-15; 1 Cor 9:16).[132] It can hardly explain Paul's understanding of God's *Heilsplan* in terms of the full number of the gentiles entering the kingdom of God before the salvation of the Jews (Rom 11:25-26), which is closely tied to his gentile apostleship. Although he devotes his large book to the task of answering the question why Paul became a gentiles' apostle, criticizing others for failing to provide a satisfactory explanation of it, his explanation appears to me to be far less satisfactory than the explanation that I have represented.

Although Donaldson's main thesis thus fails to be convincing, his views that Paul perceived the "Christ-Torah" antithesis in the Hellenists' preaching to the gentiles, that therefore the Damascus revelation directly led to the "paradigm shift" or the doctrine of justification through faith in Christ without works of the law, and that this paradigm shift accompanied his sense of call to the gentile mission, confirm the thesis that I have represented.[133] So his arguments for these views may be cited to counter his fellow New Perspectivist Dunn's unrealistic views.

(5) Dunn's fifth and last argument, that I can identify, for the late development of the doctrine of justification through faith in Christ without works of the law, takes the form of opposing the attempt to see "the Damascus road experience itself" as having "posed the sharpness of the antithesis to Paul." Dunn summarizes the attempt in its two varieties:[134]

> Either we could say that Paul's own experience of grace in that encounter (accepted by Christ despite his persecution inspired by zeal for the law) brought home to him "the bankruptcy of the law and the all-sufficiency of Christ"[135] there and then, and therefore the accessibility of that grace to Gentile as well as Jew (compare 1 Cor. 15.10). Or we could argue that Paul's confrontation with a Jesus crucified and cursed by the law (Gal. 3.13), but

132. See Kim, *Origin*, 288-96.
133. Of course, there is still the basic disagreement between Donaldson and me concerning the meaning of "works of the law" as well as the meaning and status of the doctrine of justification within Paul's theology.
134. Dunn, "A Light to the Gentiles," 92-93.
135. This quotation comes from F. F. Bruce, *The Epistle to the Galatians* (NIGTC; Grand Rapids: Eerdmans, 1982), 93-94.

now obviously vindicated by God, convinced him there and then that the law could no longer function as God's instrument of salvation, and that therefore the gospel of this Jesus should go to Gentile as well as to Jew.[136]

Having conceded that this attempt "can also claim some support," Dunn again somewhat self-contradictorily but still summarily declares that "nowhere does Paul himself develop or even hint at this line of argument."[137] Of course, there have been many who have seen this line of thinking embedded especially in Gal 1–4, but also in Rom 9:30–10:4; 1 Cor 2:8; Phil 3:3-11, and their exegesis of these passages appears to me more convincing than Dunn's.[138] It is a well-recognized fact that there is almost an explosion of the religion-historically rather new concept of "grace" in Paul's references to his Damascus experience (Rom 1:5; 12:3; 15:15; 1 Cor 3:10; 15:9-10; Gal 1:15; 2:9, 21; cf. also Eph 3:2, 7, 8; 1 Cor 7:25; 2 Cor 4:1; 5:14). This fact has led Joachim Jeremias and Klaus Haacker to view this distinctive Pauline theologoumenon as Paul's own innovation out of his Damascus experience.[139] Thus, Paul's contrast of grace with the law in connection with his doctrine of justification (Rom 3:21-26; 5:20; 6:14; Gal 2:20-21)[140] may be seen as a reflection of his own Damascus experience. Paul's recognition of Christ as "the end of the law" and his experience of the divine grace of forgiveness for his opposition to him in the name of the law belonged together. Therefore, together they led Paul to formulate his doctrine of justification by God's grace apart from the law.

Dunn tries to buttress his opposition to such a view by pointing to the fact that the pre-Pauline Jewish Christians did not develop such a negative view of the law, although like Paul they also faced the charge that Jesus was

136. E.g., Bruce, *Galatians*, 93-94; R. Y. K. Fung, *The Epistle to the Galatians* (NICNT; Grand Rapids: Eerdmans, 1988), 66-67; R. N. Longenecker, *Galatians* (WBC; Dallas: Word, 1990), 31-32; Witherington, *Grace in Galatia*, 114-15; Stuhlmacher, *Biblische Theologie I*, 262-68; Hengel and Schwemer, *Paul between Damascus and Antioch*, 98-101; J. C. Beker, *Paul the Apostle* (Philadelphia: Fortress, 1980), 185-86; Dietzfelbinger, *Berufung*, 95-102; cf. also Donaldson, *Paul*, 293-307; S. Westerholm, "Sinai as Viewed from Damascus: Paul's Reevaluation of the Mosaic Law," in *The Road from Damascus* (ed. R. N. Longenecker; Grand Rapids: Eerdmans, 1997), 163-64. See also ch. 4, n. 109.

137. Dunn, "A Light to the Gentiles," 92-93.

138. This is shown at several places in this book.

139. J. Jeremias, *Der Schlüssel zur Theologie des Paulus* (Stuttgart: Calwer, 1971), 22ff.; K. Haacker, "Die Berufung des Verfolgers und die Rechtfertigung des Gottlosen," *Theologische Beiträge* 6 (1975): 12.

140. Cf. Paul's contrast between grace and "works" (Rom 4:4; 11:6; cf. also Rom 3:24; 9:12; Eph 2:8-10; 2 Tim 1:9; Tit 3:4-7); I. H. Marshall, "Salvation, Grace and Works in the Later Writings in the Pauline Corpus," *NTS* 42 (1996): 350-57.

crucified under the curse of the law (Deut 21:23) and recognized that he was vindicated by God.[141] Why did Paul develop such a negative view of the law whereas other Jewish Christians had not? This is a fair question and an important one. No matter whether Paul derived his negative view of the law from his recognition of the crucified Jesus as the vindicated Christ or not, there is no question that alongside his positive statements, Paul makes some seriously negative statements on the law that few Jewish Christians would have dared to make. The law that has been given cannot give us life, so that righteousness cannot be by the law (Gal 3:21). On the contrary, it is a mere "letter" that brings only condemnation and death (2 Cor 3:6, 7, 9; also Rom 7:9-11, 13) because it is weakened by the flesh (Rom 8:3) and exploited by sin to arouse our sinful passions (Rom 7:5, 8-10, 13; also 6:14). It "came in to increase the trespass" (Rom 5:20), and it is "the power of sin" (1 Cor 15:56). So God had to send his Son to redeem those who were under the law (Gal 4:4-5).[142]

Therefore the question of why Paul developed such a negative view of the law while other Jewish Christians had not, faces not only those who like me try to trace the Christ-law contrast to Paul's Damascus experience but also those who like Dunn want to see it develop late. Since it is Dunn's thesis that Paul developed his doctrine of justification through faith in Christ without works of the law only in the wake of the Antiochian and Galatian controversies, and that the "works of the law" in this case refer mainly to the observance of Israelite identity-markers such as circumcision, food laws, and the sabbath, I suppose that Dunn can explain how Paul's very negative judgments of the law originated from his gentile mission or from his controversies with the Judaizers on the issues of circumcision, food laws, and the sabbath. However, I am not aware that Dunn has ever explained this. To me, it would be an amazing feat if he can account for Paul's associating the law with sin and death with his view that the issues of the law outstanding between Paul and the Judaizers were focused only on circumcision, food laws, and the sabbath, rather than concerned with the general and fundamental problems of the law.

Nevertheless, for me the difference between Paul and other Jewish Christians in their attitude to the law is explicable as fundamentally due to (1) the special circumstances and special nature of the Damascus revelation and

---

141. Dunn, "A Light to the Gentiles," 93, 99. For this argument Dunn cites E. P. Sanders, *Paul, the Law, and the Jewish People*, 25-26; H. Räisänen, *Paul and the Law*, 249-50.

142. Dunn, *The Theology of Paul*, 129-61, also recognizes these negative statements, although he emphasizes Paul's intention to defend the law.

(2) the greater depth and consistency of Paul's theological thinking that was set in motion by the Damascus experience.[143]

(a) Paul was a Pharisee who sought blameless righteousness through observance of the law, and a "zealot" who fought for the integrity of the law and the purity of Israel (Phil 3:2-6; Gal 1:13-14).

(b) He persecuted the Hellenist Christians for proclaiming Jesus, crucified under the curse of the law, as the Messiah, for criticizing the temple and the law related to the temple cult in the name of Jesus Christ, and for associating with the gentiles and thereby damaging the purity and integrity of Israel.

(c) To such a Paul, Jesus appeared as the vindicated Christ and exalted Lord, the Son of God. This encounter on the Damascus road convinced Paul, first of all, of the truth of the Christian kerygma that Christ vicariously bore the curse of the law for our sins (Gal 3:13; Rom 8:3; 4:25; 3:24-26; 1 Cor 15:3; 2 Cor 5:21; etc.).[144] So he realized that now salvation depends on appropriating the divine redemption that had been wrought in Christ, or God's righteousness that had been revealed in Christ, rather than on observing the law.

(d) With God's call for him to be an apostle, Paul, an "enemy" of God, experienced God's forgiveness, justification, and reconciliation (Rom 4:5; 5:10; 2 Cor 5:11-21), and he was overwhelmed by the grace of God in Christ which was personally applied to him (Gal 2:19-21; see also Rom 1:5; 12:3; 15:15; 1 Cor 3:10; 15:9-10; Gal 1:15; 2:9; cf. also Eph 3:2, 7, 8; 1 Cor 7:25; 2 Cor 4:1; 5:14).

(e) The realization that Christ's death was the eschatological atonement implicitly assumes Paul's positive appreciation that the law had executed the divine will of salvation with its pronouncement of a curse on Christ hanging on a tree. However, 1 Cor 2:8 suggests that Paul also thought that the law's pronouncement of a curse on Christ was wrong.[145] Thus, there seems to be a

---

143. We do not know how much the Hellenists (the Hellenist Jewish Christians) articulated their doctrine of justification for their gentile mission. If some of them parted company with Paul and eventually became the opponents Paul had to deal with in 2 Cor (e.g., G. Friedrich, "Die Gegner des Paulus im 2. Korintherbrief," in *Abraham unser Vater* [O. Michel Festschrift; ed. O. Betz, M. Hengel and P. Schmidt; AGSU 5; Leiden: Brill, 1963], 181-215), they would not have been sympathetic to Paul's doctrine of justification with its radical rejection of the (works of the) law. Then this difference between them and Paul in spite of their common engagement in the gentile mission will also have to be explained in terms of the two factors of Paul. Those who explain the origin of Paul's doctrine of justification only in terms of his gentile mission owe a satisfactory explanation as to why the Hellenists did not develop the same doctrine in spite of their gentile mission.

144. In the following, I summarize my argument in ch. 4, pp. 157-63.

145. See ch. 4, p. 157 below; cf. also Beker, *Paul the Apostle*, 185-86; M. D. Hooker, "Paul and Covenantal Nomism," *Paul and Paulinism: Essays in Honour of C. K. Barrett* (ed. M. D. Hooker and S. G. Wilson; London: SPCK, 1982), 55.

dialectic in Paul's understanding of the law in connection with the crucified Christ: on the one hand, it properly represented God's will to save humankind through the vicarious death of Jesus Christ; but, on the other hand, it led sinful human beings to execute "the Lord of glory."[146] Paul felt the negative side of the dialectic acutely, as he was conscious of the fact that his own zeal for the law resulted in opposing God's salvation in the crucified Christ. This is probably what Paul means when he says, "I through the law died to the law, that I might live to God" (Gal 2:19).[147]

(f) Thus, this revelatory experience coincided with Paul's experience of the endowment of the Holy Spirit.[148] The overwhelming experience of the Spirit led him to see the promises of God in Ezek 36–37 and Jer 31 fulfilled. So out of his reflection on those Scriptures he developed his distinctive antitheses of "the flesh-the Spirit" and "the law-the Spirit."[149] Thus, the experience of the revelation of Christ and the endowment of the Spirit led Paul to do something unthinkable for the Pharisees, and even for other Jewish Christians, and associate the law with sin, the flesh, and death, beyond simply denying it as a means of obtaining righteousness.

(g) Paul learned of Jesus' teaching and ministry ("the Jesus-tradition"), especially his "disregard for the rules of the covenant" (Mark 2:15-17; Matt 11:19/Luke 7:34)[150] and his teaching critical of the food laws as Pharisaically interpreted (Mark 7:1-23/Matt 15:1-20),[151] as they were directly relevant to the gentile mission which the Hellenists were pursuing and he had been opposing. So he realized that it was no longer faithfulness to the law but faith in Jesus Christ that determined membership in the covenant and therefore that gentiles could be made righteous through faith in Christ, or brought into the community of the people of God in Christ.

(h) Thus, he formulated his gospel of salvation (or justification) by God's grace, through faith in Christ, without works of the law.

(i) His apostolic call to the gentiles stimulated the formulation of his doctrine, and his gentile mission was theologically supported by it.

(j) This gospel was constantly challenged by the Judaizers. Although he won the approval of the Jerusalem apostles for that gospel (Gal 2:1-10), the

---

146. Cf. Dunn, *The Theology of Paul*, 155-59, who also speaks of the "two sides" of the law or the law "divided."

147. Cf. Dunn, *The Epistle to the Galatians*, 143.

148. See pp. 115-23 below.

149. See pp. 158-63 below.

150. Dunn, "A Light to the Gentiles," 101.

151. Ibid., 92. Cf. J. D. G. Dunn, "Jesus and Ritual Purity: A Study of the Tradition-History of Mark 7.15," in *Jesus, Paul and the Law*, 37-60.

Judaizers' challenge continued in Antioch, Galatia, and so on. So his defense of his gospel naturally took, in part, the form of exposing the weakness of the law.[152]

I offer this as a much more coherent explanation of the rise of the Pauline doctrine of justification by God's grace, through faith in Christ and without works of the law, than the theory of Dunn and his fellow New Perspectivists that the doctrine was developed fifteen to seventeen years after Paul's conversion and then only out of a tactical necessity for his gentile mission. Not having experienced the appearance of the crucified Jesus as the vindicated Christ in the same kind of circumstances as Paul did, probably many Jewish Christians could not perceive the problem of the law as acutely and deeply as Paul, so that they continued with their traditional faithfulness to the law. Apparently their commitment to the law was so great that they did not allow it to be affected by Jesus' law-critical teaching and ministry,[153] nor even by their recognition of Christ's death as the eschatological atonement (1 Cor 15:3; Gal 3:13; cf. also Rom 3:24-26; 4:25). Out of such a firm commitment to the law, they may have thought that the institution of the new covenant in Christ and the endowment of the Spirit meant they should keep the law all the more faithfully, as the Qumran sect understood that the new covenant and the presence of the Spirit in their community meant precisely that (cf., e.g., CD 6; 1QH 7:6ff.; 14:13ff.). They may have interpreted Ezek 36:27-28 (11:19-20) and Jer 31:31-34 in this way, whereas from those Scriptures Paul developed his antitheses "the law–the Spirit" and "the flesh–the Spirit."[154] The two diverse exegeses of the Old Testament texts — the Jewish Christian and the Pauline — may have been due to the different conditions in which they experienced the appearance of the crucified Jesus as the vindicated Christ and the endowment of the Spirit. This possibility again highlights the importance of the circumstances and nature of the Damascus Christophany as a revelatory moment for Paul. At any rate, Dunn cannot use the apparent absence of any law-critical atti-

---

152. Theologians such as the authors of the Fourth Gospel and the Letter to the Hebrews also pass negative judgments on Judaism (with its central temple system) as radically as Paul does. But it is only Paul who makes specifically the law the central topic of his polemic in three letters (Rom, Gal, and Phil). The reason is twofold: (1) his persecution of the Hellenists out of his Pharisaic/zealotic concern for the law predisposed his appreciation of Christ in terms of the end of the law; and (2) the Judaizers' repeated challenges against him on the points of the law required him to discuss the law repeatedly.

153. Dunn, "A Light to the Gentiles," 92, rightly recognizes Mark 7:1-23/Matt 15:1-20 as evidence of "the tension between law and gospel" "already present in Jesus' own ministry."

154. See pp. 158-63 below.

tude of Jewish Christians as an argument against Paul's early development of his law-critical doctrine of justification from his Damascus experience. It can be evidence against Paul's interpretation of the crucified Christ as the end of the law no more than against Jesus' "disregard for the rules of the covenant"[155] and the Jewish Christian kerygma of Christ's death as the eschatological atonement for our sins.

What Gospel Did Paul Preach before the
Antiochian and Galatian Controversies?

Dunn's concentration on God's call of Paul to the gentile mission in isolation from his revelation of the christological/soteriological gospel in Paul's testimonies about the Damascus event (Gal 1:13-17; 1 Cor 9:1; 15:8-10; Phil 3:2-9) not only gives the impression that the gospel of Christ was relevant only to the gentiles but not to the Jews,[156] but also leaves the gospel unexplained. Dunn denies that Paul persecuted the Hellenist Christians because he saw in their preaching of the crucified Christ the law-Christ antithesis implicit; he further denies that some fundamental christological and soteriological insights were as immediately involved in the Damascus experience as the apostolic call to the gentiles. These denials inevitably render him unable to explain what gospel Paul preached shortly after the Damascus call. Dunn just keeps on saying that with his apostolic call to the gentiles Paul immediately began to preach the gospel to the gentiles. But what gospel? In none of his writings on Paul's conversion/call does he address this issue. Even in his essay "Paul's Conversion — A Light to Twentieth Century Disputes," whose main section takes the form of an exposition of Gal 1:13-16, he picks up only the themes of "Judaism," "zeal," and "gentiles," completely ignoring the "revelation" of the "gospel of God's Son," which is in fact the main point of the passage.[157] Likewise, in his commentary on Galatians, he again neglects to explain the con-

155. Dunn, "A Light to the Gentiles," 101.
156. See above, pp. 20-21.
157. Dunn, "Paul's Conversion," 85-91. In an obvious allusion to the Damascus revelation in 2 Cor 4:4-6, Paul speaks of "the light of the gospel of the glory of Christ" and of God's having shed light in his heart so that he might enlighten others with that gospel. But Dunn tries forcefully to shut this "light of the gospel" off and keep us in the dark about the gospel that was revealed to Paul on the Damascus road, even in his essay "Paul's Conversion — A Light to Twentieth Century Disputes." Clearly it is a mistake for Dunn to see in the Damascus event only "the light to the gentiles" but not "the light of the gospel" as well. How could Paul be or bring "the light to the gentiles" when he had no "light of the gospel"?

tent of "the gospel" that Paul received through "a revelation of Jesus Christ" (Gal 1:11-12).[158]

In the commentary, Dunn does note: "The fact that Christ was the content both of the 'revelation' to Paul and of Paul's consequent preaching is bound to be significant. . . . The implication clearly is that it was a new perception of Christ which made the transformation (from zealot within Judaism to 'apostle to the Gentiles') both possible and necessary." Yet again Dunn sees the significance of the christological revelation only in terms of the removal of the boundary between the Jews and the gentiles. Again he explains this with his pet theory that this came about with Paul's "recognition that God had acknowledged as indeed his Son the very one whom the law had consigned, like the Gentiles, to the status of an outsider." But then he immediately adds: "This is different from the oversystematized claim that Paul's conversion was itself his choice between the Either-or of the law or Christ." So Dunn once more expresses his belief that the revelation of Jesus as God's Son — whom the law had condemned as an accursed sinner — had no effect on Paul's understanding of the law. Dunn is not able to say anything, either, about the soteriological insights that Paul could have drawn from the revelation. Therefore, when Dunn ends his exposition of Gal 1:16 with the remark, "That Christ is the content of the gospel is a characteristic Pauline emphasis (Rom i.3-4, 9; xv.19; 1 Cor i.23; ii.2; 2 Cor i.19; Gal iii.1; Phil i.15, 27; 1 Thess iii.2; see also on ii.2 and iv.14),"[159] his failure to address such questions as why this is so, what connection this might have with the Damascus revelation, what it means, and so on, is all the more glaring. Thus, Dunn is not able to explain "the gospel" that Paul claims to have received through the revelation of Jesus Christ on the Damascus road.

Paul claims that the gospel he received through the revelation of Jesus Christ was the gospel that he preached to the Galatians (Gal 1:11-17), "the gospel of Christ" that the Galatians had first received from him but were now deserting (vv. 6-8). That was the gospel which, having received on the Damascus road, without consulting the Jerusalem apostles, he simply began to preach in the regions of Arabia and Damascus (vv. 16b-17). Three years thereafter, he visited Jerusalem for a fortnight "to get to know" Cephas, and there he saw James also (vv. 18-19). Unless any sort of imagination is totally barred from the historical reconstruction, we can suppose that during the fortnight the discussion between Paul and Peter would have been centered on Jesus, the gospel, their apostolic calls, and mission to the Jews and the gen-

---

158. Dunn, *The Epistle to the Galatians*, 51-68.
159. All quotations in this paragraph are from Dunn, *The Epistle to the Galatians*, 67.

tiles. But apparently that meeting did not cause any change to his gospel significant enough for mention. When Paul goes on to narrate his mission in Syria and Cilicia and the Judean churches' glorification of God for his "preaching the faith that he once tried to destroy" (vv. 21-24), the general impression conveyed is that Peter rather nodded to the gospel which Paul had been preaching since his reception of it on the Damascus road.

Paul goes on to report (Gal 2:1-10) that "fourteen years" thereafter he went to Jerusalem and laid (privately) before the "reputed" leaders there "the gospel which [he] preach[ed] among the gentiles." Here Paul clearly implies that there was a specific reason for this and that it was because his practice of not requiring circumcision of gentile believers was called into question. He took Titus, an uncircumcised gentile Christian, along to the conference apparently for a demonstration effect. In spite of the pressure of the "false brethren," he did not yield on this issue, "so that the truth of the gospel might be preserved" for the gentile Christians like the Galatians. And the Jerusalem apostles fully recognized that Paul had been "entrusted with the gospel of uncircumcision,"[160] and so they added nothing. With this language of his having been "entrusted [πεπίστευμαι] with the gospel of uncircumcision" (2:7), Paul alludes to the Damascus event and refers back to his earlier report of it in 1:11-16. This is made clear in his substantiating remark in 2:8: "For he who worked [ἐνεργήσας] for Peter to make him an apostle to the circumcised, also worked [ἐνήργησεν] for me to make me an apostle to the Gentiles."[161] This is made still clearer with the following remark in 2:9: "When they perceived the grace that was given to me." Ἡ χάρις ἡ δοθεῖσά μοι is Paul's frequent shorthand for the apostleship that he received on the Damascus road.[162]

A clear implication of this way of speaking of his gospel is that Paul sees his gospel essentially unchanged from its beginning at the revelation on the Damascus road through his private conversation with Peter after two to three

160. Paul's designation of his gospel as τὸ εὐαγγέλιον τῆς ἀκροβυστίας here is conspicuous in view of the fact that he refers to the gentiles as τὰ ἔθνη throughout in the context (Gal 1:16; 2:2, 8, 9, 12, 14, etc.). Paul's use of this phrase, especially in contrast to τὸ εὐαγγέλιον τῆς περιτομῆς for Peter's gospel, seems to be making clear that it was explicitly understood in Jerusalem that his gospel for the gentiles dispensed with the requirement of circumcision. If the two phrases were used in the minutes of the formal agreement, it may be that Paul and the Jerusalem apostles used them for that purpose.

161. Cf. the rendering of NEB: "For God whose action made Peter an apostle to the Jews, also made me an apostle to the Gentiles." See Kim, *Origin*, 26 n. 1, against the common exegesis of this verse as if Paul were arguing here for his claim to have been "entrusted with the gospel of uncircumcision" on the basis of the success of his missionary work which showed that in it God was at work.

162. See Kim, *Origin*, 25-26.

years and through his conference with the Jerusalem apostles after about six-teen years to his first preaching in Galatia or to the present time of writing the Letter to the Galatians.[163] It is, of course, difficult to reconstruct accurately the shape and content of the gospel that Paul preached before his first letter that has survived, be it 1 Thessalonians or Galatians. However, from his defense of his gospel in Gal 1–2, at least one thing is clear: from the beginning Paul's gospel dispensed with the requirement of circumcision for gentile believers. At least in this respect Paul seems to see his gospel as having remained constant. His report of the Antioch conflict in Gal 2:11-14 suggests that the gospel that he preached during his Antiochian ministry dispensed with the food/purity laws as well. Circumcision and the purity laws that prevented Jews from eating with gentiles belonged together as badges of God's covenant people.[164] Hence it is a reasonable guess that Paul's gospel dispensed with the food/purity laws as well as circumcision from the beginning. So then Paul's gospel remained constant at least in dispensing with these "works of the law" from the beginning to the time of writing Galatians. Dunn would agree with this reasoning up to this point.

On what ground then did Paul dispense with those elements of the law concerned with circumcision and food and purity? Dunn's consistent answer is that he did this because he saw Christ's death as having "broken through that boundary [between Jew and gentile] and abolished the law in its bound-ary-defining role."[165] This understanding came to Paul on the Damascus road when he saw his judgment of the crucified Jesus as cursed by God (Deut 21:23), that is, as put out of the covenant into the position of the gentile sin-ner (28:58-68), overturned by God's vindication of him. This experience led Paul to understand "that God must therefore favor the cursed one, the sinner outside the covenant, the Gentile."[166] Did Paul realize on the Damascus road only this significance of Christ's death on the cross? In view of Dunn's ada-mant refusal to see any more christological and soteriological insights present

163. Cf. Hengel and Schwemer, *Paul between Damascus and Antioch*, 303: "Paul could not have argued with such incisive sharpness in Gal. 1.10-12; 3.1-5; 4.8-19 and 5.12 and kept recall-ing the beginnings of the community if at that time he had presented quite different views, more ready for compromise, about circumcision and literal observance of the Torah. In the ap-ostolic defence there is no sign of a repudiation of the — fatal — charge that his preaching had been different earlier, and that on the decisive point, the question of the law, he had been more generous. Thus, despite all the sharpness of the controversy, Galatians is above all a precise *rec-ollection* of the gospel which the apostle preached at a much earlier time." Cf. also Donaldson, "Zealot and Convert," 664; Witherington, *Grace in Galatia*, 114.

164. See Acts 15 contra Dunn's separation of them (above, n. 98).

165. Dunn, *The Epistle to the Galatians*, 149.

166. Dunn, "A Light to the Gentiles," 100; *Partings*, 123; *The Theology of Paul*, 226-27.

in the Damascus Christophany, I have already noted the problematic implication of Dunn's minimalistic view, that it makes the gospel practically irrelevant to the Jews.[167] But here I must point out another problem of the minimalistic view: how odd Paul's "gospel" to the gentiles would have been if it only announced that through the crucifixion and resurrection of Israel's Messiah the God of Israel had shown his favor to the gentiles and welcomed them into his covenant relationship without requirements such as circumcision and the food laws, so that they could have table-fellowship with Jewish believers! Would anybody — Paul or any of his gentile hearers — have considered this announcement a "gospel"? Is there any evidence that Paul's initial gospel was only this?

On the contrary, the evidence shows that from the beginning Paul's gospel was centered on the much more fundamental significance of Christ's death, that he died vicariously for the sins of humankind, for both the Jews and the gentiles. In several instances, Paul indicates that the gospel he first preached to the recipients of his epistles was centered on Christ's death as the eschatological atonement for humankind (e.g., 1 Cor 2:2; 15:1-5; Gal 1:4; 3:1; 1 Thess 1:10; 5:9-10). His most systematic exposition of his gospel is centered on the revelation of God's righteousness in Christ's vicarious sacrifice of atonement (Rom 1:16-17; 3:21-26). Now then, is it conceivable that this central element of Paul's gospel was only a later addition? Galatians 1:4 and 3:1 clearly deny this; the two verses suggest that the gospel first preached by Paul to the Galatians was centered on Christ given up to the death on the cross for our sins, and that Paul rebukes the Galatians for deserting this gospel (1:6; 3:2) and defends this gospel as the gospel that he had received through the revelation of Jesus Christ (1:11-17).

That Christ's vicarious sacrifice for our sins was the central element of the gospel that Paul received on the Damascus road may be inferred also from his persecution of the Hellenist Christians. Even Dunn agrees that the Hellenists rejected the Jerusalem temple out of their belief that Christ's death was the eschatological atonement that ended all sacrifices.[168] After seeing the crucified Jesus as vindicated by God on the Damascus road, Paul joined them. It would be most unnatural if Paul had failed to see the appearance of the risen Christ as a confirmation of their belief. So we will have to conclude that at Damascus Paul accepted their kerygma that Christ died for the sins of humankind.[169] It is difficult to understand why Dunn consistently ignores this

---

167. See above, pp. 20-21.
168. Dunn, *Partings*, 60-71.
169. Hengel and Schwemer, *Paul between Damascus and Antioch*, 99, suggest the possibility

aspect of Paul's Damascus experience in all his writings on Paul's conversion and call. However, once Paul saw God's confirmation of Jesus' death under the curse of the law as his messianic act of vicarious atonement, he must have quickly begun to understand that on the cross Christ vicariously bore the sins of the world (Rom 8:3; 2 Cor 5:21) and the curse of the law (Gal 3:10) in order to redeem us from the curse of the law (Gal 3:13; 4:4-5; cf. 1:4) and bring us into the right relationship to God (Rom 3:24-26; 4:25; 2 Cor 5:21).[170] So then, the gospel that Paul received from the Damascus Christophany was not that God was in favor of the gentiles because he vindicated Jesus whom he had put into their cursed position, but rather that God so loved the world — both the Jews and the gentiles — that he gave Christ Jesus his Son up to the death on the cross for the eschatological atonement for their sins. This is the reason why Paul calls his message the "gospel" (εὐαγγέλιον).

In Gal 2:19-21, Paul indicates how he personally appropriated Christ's vicarious death for himself on the Damascus road. Here he speaks of his death in order to obtain a (new) life, and elaborates it in terms of "having been crucified with Christ" (συνεσταύρωμαι). This reminds us of what he says in Romans 6:1-11 of the event of becoming a believer: to believe that Christ died "for us" is to actualize Christ's vicarious death for ourselves, by recognizing that we were included in Christ crucified, our inclusive substitute, and so it is to have our "old person" "crucified together with" Christ (συνεσταυρώθη) (vv. 3-6). The purpose of this is for us to participate in the resurrection life of Christ or "to walk in the newness of life" (vv. 4-5). This dying in/with Christ and obtaining a new life in Christ by faith is dramatized by baptism. Our old person died with Christ with regard to sin, so that we are freed from the enslavement of sin (vv. 6-7). We shall participate in Christ's resurrection life fully in the future, and yet, already at present, we, freed from sin, live a new life, and this new life is "for God" (vv. 8-11).[171]

In Gal 2:19-21 Paul expresses basically the same thought, except that here he makes it his personal experience and he speaks of the law instead of sin. The event of his coming to faith was also an event of actualizing Christ's vicarious death for himself. At the Damascus Christophany he realized that Christ died "for our sins," and by believing it he actualized Christ's vicarious death for

---

that already in Damascus Paul received the substance of the pre-Pauline gospel quoted in 1 Cor 15:3-5.

170. The formulations themselves of these pregnant sentences may have taken some time, but their substance must have been clear to Paul very soon after the Damascus revelation. See pp. 131-34 below, contra Dunn's interpretation of Gal 3:10-14.

171. For an exposition of Paul's view of faith-baptism as expressed in Rom 6:1-11, see Kim, *Origin*, 301-7.

himself. This dying with/in Christ came about when he was driven by the law to commit the sin of opposing Christ and persecuting his church. So it was "through the law." His old person died in/with Christ with regard to the law as well as to sin, so that he was now freed from the enslavement of the law. All this had the purpose that he might live a new life, a life that is "for God" (cf. Rom 7:4, 6). He movingly elaborates this: "I have been crucified with Christ; I no longer live, but Christ lives in me; and the life I now live in the flesh I live by faith in the Son of God who loved me and gave himself for me" (Gal 2:20). In this description of his experience of coming to faith in Christ on the Damascus road, the reference to Christ as the "Son of God" seems to echo his earlier report of the Damascus Christophany (Gal 1:16), while the giving-up formula echoes his earlier reference to Christ "who gave himself for our sins" (1:4), which was part of his fundamental discovery at the Damascus Christophany. In conclusion he makes a summary reference to God's saving event made effective to him as "the grace of God" (2:21), and this seems to echo his reference to God's grace in his apostolic call (1:15; 2:9) as well as that to God's call of the Galatians in "the grace of Christ" manifested in Christ's self-giving for our sins (1:6). So what Paul says of the event of other Christians' coming to faith *(Gläubigwerden)* in Rom 6:1-11 (cf. also 7:4-6) and what he implies of the event of his Galatian converts' coming to faith may be seen as the generalized applications of what he himself experienced in appropriating Christ's vicarious death for himself by faith at the Damascus Christophany.

All this discussion makes it clear that Paul dispensed with the works of the law not on the strange ground that God's vindication of the cursed Christ meant his favor for the gentiles but rather on the ground that Christ's death was the eschatological atonement and that both the Jews and the gentiles were to obtain a new life of righteousness for God by appropriating that saving event through faith. This is why in Gal 2:21 he contrasts the attempt for justification through the law with Christ's death ("If righteousness were through the law, then Christ died to no purpose") and sees the former as "nullify[ing] the grace of God." This is why in Gal 1:6 he declares the Galatians' attempt for justification through the law as rejecting the grace of Christ manifested in his death of vicarious atonement (1:4).

All this means then that Paul derived his doctrine of salvation by God's grace, through faith, but without works of the law from his Damascus experience and that he formulated it quite early. It was the essence of his gospel that he preached to the gentiles and occasionally also to the Jews. To explain salvation he employed diverse metaphors: justification, reconciliation, adoption, new creation, and so on. So sometimes he formulated his gospel in the category of justification, especially when he had God's judgment in view or when the issue was about the gentile believers' standing in the proper covenantal relationship with God. As we have seen, Dunn himself recognizes that the principle of the doctrine of justification through faith alone was implicit in the Damascus revelation. But he sees it laying dormant for fifteen to seventeen years until the Antiochian and Galatian controversies woke it up. I have countered that this view ignores the factor of Paul's zeal for the law in his persecution of the Hellenist Christians.[172] Now I must add that this is also to ignore the fundamental soteriological insight Paul drew from the Damascus revelation, that Christ's death was the eschatological atonement. Seeing the nature of the factors involved in Paul's formulation of the doctrine of justification, such as Paul's former zeal for the law, his soteriological insight that Christ's death was the eschatological atonement, his own experience of God's grace of forgiveness, his experience of the Holy Spirit, his apostolic call to the gentiles, and the Jesus tradition,[173] it appears more realistic to think that Paul formulated the doctrine shortly after the Damascus revelation.

In my essay "The 'Mystery' of Romans 11:25-26 Once More," I have attempted to set as the *terminus ad quem* of Paul's formulation of the "mystery" of Rom 11:25-26 Paul's first visit to Jerusalem for a fortnight consultation with Peter (Gal 1:18), that is, two to three years after the Damascus revelation.[174] It seems realistic to suppose that Paul also formulated his doctrine of salvation (or justification) within that initial period of his apostolic ministry.[175] Many may protest that dates it too early. To them I would reply with the analogy of Dunn's formulation of his program of the "New Perspective on Paul." Within five years after E. P. Sanders's *Paul and Palestinian Judaism* (1977), Dunn was able to think through Judaism, the law, and Paul's theology, and formulate a new interpretation of Paul's soteriology, overturning the traditional Reformation interpretation.[176] If Dunn was able to formulate the New Perspective on Paul on the basis of Sanders's book within five years, why could Paul not have formulated his "new perspective" on the law and righ-

172. See above, pp. 22-45.

173. See above, p. 43.

174. See below, pp. 248-55.

175. Cf. Hengel and Schwemer, *Paul between Damascus and Antioch*, 95-98, who conclude their argument for the Damascus origin of Paul's doctrine of justification with the affirmation: "I would think that on the basis of his newly-gained missionary experience Paul was already in a position on his visit to Jerusalem after around three years to explain his gospel and the commission associated with it quite clearly to Cephas/Peter (and James), and also to sum it up conceptually," p. 98.

176. Dunn's programmatic essay, "The New Perspective on Paul," was first delivered as the Manson Memorial Lecture at the University of Manchester in November 1982 and was reprinted in his *Jesus, Paul and the Law*, 183-214.

teousness on the basis of the Damascus revelation within three years? I would argue that Paul's conditions pushed him toward the formulation of his "new perspective" much more powerfully than Dunn's conditions pushed him toward the formulation of his New Perspective.[177] For example, could the impact of the Damascus Christophany upon Paul be compared with the impact of Sanders's book on Dunn? Or Paul's personal engagement in his subject matter (salvation!) with Dunn's personal engagement in his subject matter (a largely academic discussion)? Or Paul's knowledge of Judaism with Dunn's knowledge of Judaism? Surely we are not to underestimate the creative power of Paul, as we do not underestimate that of Dunn. To portray Paul as having failed for so long as a few *years* (let alone fifteen to seventeen years) since his conversion and call to see the problems of circumcision, food and purity regulations, sabbath and festivals, posed in his gentile mission and to think through the problem of the law in the light of Christ's eschatological atonement, is to make him an extremely slow thinker. But from his letters, it is plain that slow and shallow thinking was not one of his weaknesses.

Only because right from the early period of his apostleship on he was quite clear about the principle of salvation by God's grace, through faith in Christ, but without works of the law, could Paul begin his preaching the gospel to the gentiles immediately after his apostolic call and go on preaching the same gospel in spite of constant challenges from the Judaizers.[178]

The Doctrine of Justification Developed Only for the Gentile Mission?

In agreement with the New Perspective School as a whole, Dunn repeatedly insists that Paul developed his doctrine of justification in order to defend against Jewish nationalism the gentile converts' membership in the people of God without works of the law.[179] So, for example, Dunn asserts that "wherever Paul poses the antithesis [between faith in Christ and works of the law] in his writings (explicitly or implicitly), he does so within the context of and as part of what amounts to a redefinition of the people of God." And Dunn illustrates this assertion with Phil 3 as well as Gal 3 and Rom 9–10.[180]

177. Cf. Hengel and Schwemer, *Paul between Damascus and Antioch*, 105: "We should not doubt that the process of rethinking began the moment Paul's life changed, and that for this highly gifted Jewish scribe its course was very intense."
178. For the witness of 1 Thessalonians to this, see ch. 2 below.
179. See above, p. 3.
180. Dunn, "A Light to the Gentiles," 99.

But elsewhere Dunn admits that in Phil 3 "the acceptability of Gentiles to God is not to the fore."[181] In still another place Dunn grants that Phil 3:7-9 as well as Rom 4:4-5; 10:2-4 can be read in the traditional way, as Paul's rejection of one's attempt to achieve one's own righteousness by strict observance of the law in favor of obtaining God's righteousness through faith in Christ. But Dunn immediately adds his disapproval of this way of reading the texts by saying: "The only question is whether those who read them that way have shifted the issue from one of Israel's works of the law vis-à-vis Gentile acceptability to the more fundamental one of the terms of human acceptability by God." Dunn thinks that this shift may be visible in Eph 2:8-9 but it is not in the undisputed Pauline letters.[182] In a way it is ironic that in Eph 2 where Paul's explicit concern is about reconciliation and union between the gentile believers and the Jewish believers as well as reconciliation of both groups to God through God's grace in Christ (vv. 11-22) Dunn is willing to see the principle of salvation *sola gratia/fide* in terms of the fundamental question of human acceptability by God without human achievement, whereas in places like Phil 3:7-9 and Rom 4:4-5 where there is no question of Jew-gentile relationship he refuses to do so.

Be that as it may, Dunn's view that Paul enunciates the doctrine of justification *sola gratia/fide* without works of the law only within the context of redefining the people of God or arguing for the inclusion of gentile believers in the people of God cannot be sustained. It is immediately contradicted by Rom 5–8, where Paul expounds his doctrine of justification without any reference to the inclusion of gentile believers in the people of God.[183] To be sure, Dunn tries to see even Rom 5:12-21 in terms of the Israel-gentile relationship when he says:

> Fundamental here is the recognition that God has a righteousness to fulfill as creator as well as his righteousness as Israel's covenant God. What Paul does in both Romans and Galatians is, in effect, to go behind the more restricted covenant obligation to Israel back to the more basic covenant obligation to

---

181. Dunn, "Paul and Justification by Faith," 93.
182. Dunn, *The Theology of Paul*, 370-71.
183. Cf. J. M. G. Barclay, *Obeying the Truth* (Edinburgh: T & T Clark, 1988), 246-48, who, recognizing "the generalized nature of some of Paul's remarks in Rom 4" and "the generalizing tendency" in Rom 5–7, says, "If Rom 1–4 is *purely* about Jews and Gentiles, it is difficult to relate these chapters to Rom 5–8" (p. 247, his italics). In Rom 9–11 also Paul's main concern is not about defending the gentile converts' inclusion in the people of God against Jewish restrictiveness, but rather about the Jews' unbelief and *Unheil!* So also T. R. Schreiner, *The Law and Its Fulfillment* (Grand Rapids: Baker, 1993), 106.

54

the creation and humankind as a whole. In Romans he goes behind Moses to
Adam (Rom 5:12-21).[184]

But it is not at all clear that in Rom 5:12-21 Paul "goes behind Moses to
Adam" in order to highlight God's "covenant obligation to the creation and
humankind as a whole." What is clear in that passage is rather that Paul
does *not* contrast Moses and Adam with each other nor the Jewish
particularistic perspective (or God's covenant to Israel) and the universal-
istic perspective (or God's covenant to the whole human kind) with each
other. Therefore, it is a mistake to see in Rom 5:12-21 any concern to overcome Jewish particularism.[185]

It is curious to note Dunn's shifting (self-contradicting?) opinion here:
on pages 370-71 of his *The Theology of Paul the Apostle* he insists that within
Paul's genuine letters his argument for the doctrine of justification does not
shift "the issue from one of Israel's works of the law vis-à-vis Gentile acceptability to the more fundamental one of the terms of human acceptability by
God." But on the next page of the same book, noting how Paul developed his
doctrine of justification from the Antioch incident as reflected in Gal 2:16,
elaborated the theme of justification by faith alone in Gal 3, and "carefully
and fully restated" it in Rom 3–4, Dunn states: "What is particularly interesting for us here is the fact that Paul expounded justification by faith in a way
which not only addresses the argument over the terms of Gentile acceptance,
but also presses beyond to provide a fundamental statement of human dependence on God"![186]

In Galatians, it may be granted, Paul presents his doctrine of justification
primarily in terms of Jew and gentile alike becoming children of Abraham
and people of God by faith, and in Gal 2:11-21, the "works of the law" are focused on the covenant distinctives of Israel such as circumcision and the food

---

184. Dunn, "Paul and Justification," 94.

185. For his thesis that the primary concern of Paul in Romans is "to establish the inclusion of the Gentiles in equal terms with Jews into God's salvific blessing" and that "only in the
course of arguing for [this] theme does Paul refer to the justification by faith apart from the
law" (Chae, *Paul as Apostle to the Gentiles*, 292), Chae finds it difficult to secure enough material
from Rom 5–8 for discussion. So he struggles to fill the mere nine-page space (pp. 206-14) in his
378-page book with an exposition of the four chapters in the central section of Romans in support of his thesis. There are many problems with his dissertation (which takes the New Perspective somewhat to the extreme), but this one criticism should be enough to show the failure of
his thesis. On the importance of Rom 5–8, cf. R. N. Longenecker, "The Focus of Romans: The
Central Role of 5:1–8:39 in the Argument of the Letter," in *Romans and the People of God* (G. D.
Fee Festschrift; ed. S. K. Soderlund and N. T. Wright; Grand Rapids: Eerdmans, 1999), 49-69.

186. Dunn, *The Theology of Paul*, 372.

laws. But, in Gal 3:10-14[187] onward, if not already in 2:11-21, Paul begins to broaden the issue to the more fundamental question of salvation by God's grace rather than by human achievement.[188] Also, in presenting his doctrine of justification in Romans, he does show his concern for the inclusion of the gentile believers as well as the Jewish believers in the people of God or in the sphere of salvation (1:16-17; 3:21-24, 27-30; 4:9-17; 10:12). But in Romans as a whole Paul's main concern is to declare that because of the revelation of God's righteousness in Christ justification can now be obtained through faith in Christ without works of the law.[189] The former concern is inserted here and there only as a corollary of this main concern (especially Rom 3:27-30).

The reason why in Galatians the context of Paul's discussion of the doctrine of justification is predominantly the issue of inclusion of gentile believers in the people of God is that that issue was the presenting problem there. In the face of the Judaizers' demand for the Galatian believers to be circumcised, Paul naturally expounded the doctrine of justification in such a way as to repudiate that demand the most effectively. This is bound to give the impression that the doctrine serves only the purpose of defending the membership of gentile believers in the people of God without works of the law. But as we shall observe in 1 Thessalonians,[190] Paul preaches the gospel in terms of justification by faith even in a context where there is no question of the Jew-gentile relationship. And even in Galatians (especially 2:19-21; 3:10-14, 21-22; 4:4-5; 5:4-5) he expounds the doctrine of justification to enunciate the principle of obtaining God's salvation or acquittal at the last judgment through faith without works of the law, beyond affirming that both Jewish and gentile believers become children of God through faith alone. Therefore, the more generalized way of expounding the doctrine of justification in Romans and Phil 3 is not to be viewed as signifying that the doctrine was first formulated in Galatians in connection with the Jew-gentile issue and was

187. See below, pp. 130-43.

188. Cf. S. Westerholm, *Israel's Law and the Church's Faith* (Grand Rapids: Eerdmans, 1988), 117-18; G. Stanton, "The Law of Moses and the Law of Christ: Galatians 3:1–6:2," *Paul and the Mosaic Law* (WUNT 89; ed. J. D. G. Dunn; Tübingen: Mohr-Siebeck, 1996), 103-4.

189. Cf. J. M. G. Barclay, "Paul and the Law: Observations on Some Recent Debates," *Themelios* 12 (1987): 11-12. Though sympathetic to the New Perspective, Barclay observes that there is "an important line of development in Paul's thought whereby the issue of 'works' and 'grace' becomes increasingly generalized in Paul's letters" and that in Romans "Paul begins to discuss works, law and faith in abstract terms which give some basis for later Western, and even Lutheran, theological traditions." Barclay develops this thesis more fully in his *Obeying the Truth*, 246-51. As I argue presently, however, we are to understand the difference between Galatians and Romans not in terms of a "development" but rather in terms of "contextualization."

190. See the next chapter.

then gradually generalized. The difference between Galatians and Romans in the way the doctrine is presented is determined rather by their divergent contexts and purposes.

"Works of the Law"

At any rate, it is good to find Dunn recognizing (albeit ambivalently) that in Rom 3–4 "Paul expound[s] justification by faith in a way which not only addresses the argument over the terms of Gentile acceptance, but also presses beyond to provide a fundamental statement of human dependence on God."[191] This recognition, then, surely should affect his interpretation of the phrase "works of the law." But strangely it does not. Ever since his programmatic essay "The New Perspective on Paul,"[192] Dunn's interpretation of "works of the law" has been very controversial. The intense controversy has led him to clarify it but not to change it in any substantial way.

Dunn's interpretation of the phrase "works of the law" starts from the axiom that the Judaism of New Testament times was "covenantal nomism" as defined by E. P. Sanders and not a religion of earning righteousness through one's good works.[193] Dunn defines "works of the law" as "what the law required *of Israel as God's people.*" It was Israel's response to the grace of God's

191. Dunn, *The Theology of Paul,* 372.

192. Dunn, "The New Perspective on Paul," 191-203; "Works of the Law and the Curse of the Law," 219-32; "Paul and Justification by Faith," 95-99; "Paul's Conversion," 92; *The Theology of Paul,* 354-66. His view was anticipated by J. B. Tyson, " 'Works of the Law' in Galatians," *JBL* 92 (1973): 423-31. It is supported by Wright, "Curse and Covenant: Galatians 3:10-14," in *The Climax of the Covenant,* 150; *What Saint Paul Really Said,* 132; cf. also Sanders, *Paul, the Law and the Jewish People,* 46. But it is rejected by many; for a few examples, see Westerholm, *Israel's Law,* 117-21; C. E. B. Cranfield, " 'The Works of the Law' in the Epistle to the Romans," *JSNT* 43 (1991): 89-101; M. Silva, "The Law and Christianity: Dunn's New Synthesis," *WTJ* 53 (1991): 351-53; Schreiner, *The Law and Its Fulfillment,* 51-57; J. A. Fitzmyer, *Romans* (AB; New York: Doubleday, 1993), 338-39; Stuhlmacher, *Biblische Theologie I,* 241-42; M. A. Seifrid, "Blind Alleys in the Controversy over the Paul of History," *TynBul* 45 (1994): 77-85; D. J. Moo, *The Epistle to the Romans* (NICNT; Grand Rapids: Eerdmans, 1996), 207-17. See now also J. C. de Roo, "The Concept of 'Works of the Law' in Jewish and Christian Literature," in *Christian-Jewish Relations through the Centuries* (ed. S. E. Porter and B. W. R. Pearson; JSNTSup 192; Sheffield: Academic Press, 2000), 116-47.

193. Apparently Dunn has elevated Sanders's notion of Judaism as "covenantal nomism" to the status of a dogma, so much so that even in his more recent writings (e.g., "Paul and Justification by Faith," 95; "Paul's Conversion," 84; *The Theology of Paul,* 354) he simply repeats his assumption of it, paying no attention to the criticisms of that notion or the attempts to modify it (below, pp. 143-52).

election of them as his people; it was keeping their part of the covenant with Yahweh; and therefore it was what their righteousness consisted of.[194] So it "marked out Israel's set-apartness to God and separation from the nations."[195] It refers to "all or whatever the law requires."[196] However, the Maccabean crisis reinforced the focus on certain laws such as circumcision and the purity laws as the decisive issues in defining and defending Israel's set-apartness, so that in the context where the relationship of Israel with the gentiles was at issue, attention was focused on those laws.[197] Then, in Gal 2:16; 3:2, 5, 10; Rom 3:20, 27-30; 4:2-6; 9:11, 30-32; and 11:6 Dunn finds Paul consistently using the phrase "works of the law" in this sense; with it Paul does not refer to doing good works in general but to doing the laws that sharply express the covenant distinction of Israel from the gentiles.[198]

Since the presenting problem in the Antioch incident was connected with the food laws and in the Galatian controversy was the Judaizers' attempt to impose circumcision on the gentile Christians there, in Gal 2:16; 3:2, 5 the immediate attention is naturally on those laws, which express the Jews' covenant distinctiveness. But already there Paul elevates the question of observing circumcision and the food laws to the level of trying to obtain justification through the efforts of law observance (2:19-21). This is clear in Gal 3:10-14.[199] Many have questioned Dunn's interpretation of "works of the law" in Rom 3:20 as referring only to the Jewish sense of privilege and distinctiveness.[200] For with it Paul clearly refers also to the fact that the Jews are committed to keep the moral commandments but fail to keep them (Rom 2:17-24; 3:9-18). The "works" in Rom 3:27 and "works of the law" in 3:28 must have the same general sense of law observance as in Rom 3:20.[201] Stephen Westerholm and others have found it an easy job to repudiate Dunn's interpretation of "works" in Rom 4:4-5 in terms of the Jewish covenant distinctives.[202] Dunn recognizes

---

194. Dunn, *The Theology of Paul*, 355.

195. Ibid., 356.

196. Ibid., 358.

197. Ibid., 357-58.

198. Ibid., 359-66.

199. See pp. 141-43 below.

200. Dunn, *The Theology of Paul*, 362-63. Those questioning Dunn's interpretation include S. Westerholm, *Israel's Law and the Church's Faith: Paul and His Recent Interpreters* (Grand Rapids: Eerdmans, 1988), 118-19; Schreiner, *The Law and Its Fulfillment*, 65-70; Seifrid, "Blind Alleys," 82-83; Moo, *Romans*, 207-10, 214-16.

201. So Cranfield, "The Works of the Law," 95-96.

202. Westerholm, *Israel's Law*, 113-21; Schreiner, *The Law and Its Fulfillment*, 99-100; Seifrid, "Blind Alleys," 82-84; cf. also D. G. Moo, " 'Law,' 'Works of the Law,' and Legalism in Paul," *WTJ* 45 (1983): 94-97; Barclay, *Obeying the Truth*, 246.

that the traditional interpretation of them as good works done in an attempt to gain righteousness is "wholly understandable" and that the deutero-Pauline epistles confirm this interpretation (Eph 2:8-9; 2 Tim 1:9; Tit 3:5).[203] Nevertheless, Dunn labors hard to reject this interpretation,[204] but his argument is quite hazy.[205] Commenting on Rom 4:6 ("David speaks of the blessedness of the person to whom God reckons righteousness without works"), Dunn says: "David's righteousness was to be understood in terms of his being forgiven, of his sins not being reckoned (4.7-8), rather than in terms of his being circumcised and *practising the other works of the law*."[206] It is quite revealing that to explain "works" in Rom 4:6, Dunn has to add "practising the other works of the law" here. Clearly Dunn cannot see "works" here referring only to the Jewish covenant distinctives such as circumcision and the food laws! But why is he nevertheless insisting that with "works of the law" Paul refers only to the Jewish covenant distinctives? Why does he not take into account his own insight that Paul generalizes the doctrine of justification in Rom 3–4? It is a puzzle how Dunn is able to see "works" in Rom 9:11b refer to the Jewish covenant distinctives when it clearly refers to "doing something good or bad" (πραξάντων τι ἀγαθὸν ἢ φαῦλον) in the foregoing clause (v. 11a), in contrast to God's election of grace.[207] In Rom 9:32 and 11:6, too, it is much more natural to interpret "works" (set there in contrast to God's righteousness and God's grace respectively) as referring to good works of law observance in general than to the Jewish covenant distinctives.[208]

Thus, Dunn's attempt to interpret the phrase "works (of the law)" only in terms of the Jewish covenant distinctives when it appears in the Pauline formulation of his justification doctrine is not successful. Our brief discussion of the passages in which it appears suggests rather that although in some passages in Galatians it has especially in view the Jewish covenant distinctives such as the laws of circumcision, purity, and festivals, it usually refers more generally to the deeds done in obedience to the law which are considered as

203. Dunn, *The Theology of Paul*, 354, 366-67. It is regrettable that Dunn does not accord any respect to this earliest interpretation by Paul's pupils of his doctrine of justification. Cf. Marshall, "Salvation, Grace and Works," 339-58. See n. 268 below.

204. Dunn, *The Theology of Paul*, 366-67.

205. Silva, "The Law and Christianity," 352-53 n. 26, criticizes Dunn's strange exegesis of Rom 4:4-5 in his commentary, *Romans 1–8* (WBC; Waco: Word, 1988), 203-4. Dunn's explanation in his *The Theology of Paul*, 366-67, does not appear transparent either.

206. Ibid., 364 (Dunn's rendering of Rom 4:6; my italics)

207. Cf. Cranfield, "The Works of the Law," 97.

208. Cf. ibid., 97-99. In spite of his sympathy with the New Perspective, even Barclay, *Obeying the Truth*, 249-50, recognizes the general character of "works" in Rom 9:11 and 11:5-6. Cf. also Marshall, "Salvation, Grace and Works," 356.

human achievements or as good works done to earn God's favor. The reason why Paul can bundle the Jewish covenant distinctives together with the other deeds of the law and oppose them to faith in Christ is that he perceives the former as well as the latter as human achievements. In other words, Paul is opposed to "works of the law" not because he thinks they prevent the gentiles from becoming members of the people of God, as Dunn claims, but rather because he perceives them as human, therefore inadequate attempts to earn justification.

The Antithesis between Faith in Christ and "Works of the Law"

Only this interpretation seems to be capable of explaining Paul's regular contrast of "works (of the law)" with faith and grace in his doctrine of justification (Rom 3:20-26, 27-30; 4:2-6; 9:11, 30-32; 11:6; Gal 2:16, 21; 3:2, 5, 10-14; etc.). In contrast, Dunn's interpretation cannot explain it. We can see this by observing how Paul responds to the controversies in Antioch and Galatia.

As said above, Dunn insists that Paul developed his doctrine of justification in the wake of the Antioch incident in order to defend against Jewish nationalism the gentile converts' right to be included within the people of God without works of the law such as circumcision, food laws, and sabbath.[209] But Dunn notes that Paul probably failed to persuade Peter, Barnabas, and other Jewish Christians in Antioch with his arguments for the doctrine. Dunn also thinks that Paul had to break with Antioch and become an independent missionary, making first Corinth and then Ephesus the new bases of his operations (Acts 18:11; 19:10).[210] Probably Dunn is correct on both counts. If so, Paul probably failed to win over to his side the bulk of the gentile Christians in Antioch, too. They then may have decided to observe the food laws more strictly to the satisfaction of the "men from James," or to remain with their "modest level of law-observance,"[211] just accepting their second-class citizen status and their separation from the Jewish Christians at meal times. Did they choose either of the two options gladly or only reluctantly? Even if the latter was the case, they must have thought that it was still better than following Paul. Of course, our data do not allow us to draw a certain conclusion about

---

209. Dunn, *Partings*, 130-39; "Paul and Justification," 90-100; *The Theology of Paul,* 359-60.
210. Dunn, *Partings*, 134; *Galatians,* 12-13.
211. Dunn, *Partings*, 132.

these things. But we can at least say that, according to Dunn's view of the outcome of the Antioch incident, the gentile Christians there did not or could not support their would-be champion over his Jewish opponents.

We have a clearer picture of the attitude of the Galatian Christians. From Gal 1:6-9; 3:1-5; 4:8-11, 12-20, 21; 5:1-6, 7-12; etc., it is clear that the gentile Christians in Galatia were all but won over by the Judaizers to get circumcised and place themselves under the yoke of the law. They apparently wanted to have circumcision in their flesh as a tangible sign of being God's people, in addition to their faith in Christ, and welcomed the idea that believers in Christ should keep the law in order to progress in sanctification. So much so that Paul had to write the most impassioned letter and employ all sorts of argument, at times quite desperately, to dissuade them from the Judaizers' "gospel."

In this situation, why did Paul object to their becoming members of God's people by faith in Christ *and* works of the law as the Judaizers insisted? The Judaizers were not denying that the gentiles *could* become members of God's people. They were insisting only that they could become such by getting circumcised and keeping the law in addition to believing in Christ. If, as Dunn claims, at Damascus Paul had received only the apostolic call to the gentiles and if his concern had been merely about the gentiles becoming members of God's people, why could he not happily have gone about doing his gentile mission in the way the Judaizers demanded — calling for faith in Christ *and* circumcision? It would have been much easier for the former "zealot" for the law! What was wrong with the Galatian Christians trying to get circumcised? What was wrong with the gentile Christians observing the food laws? Did Paul operate with the modern idea of "nationalism" and decide that imposing the law on the gentiles was a bad expression of "Jewish nationalism," that is, Jewish "racism" and "imperialism"?[212] Apparently the

212. In this post-Holocaust age, any attempt to exonerate even the ancient Jews of what modern people deem negative may be laudable. But in order to exonerate them of a "works-righteousness" religion, the New Perspectivists as a whole and Dunn especially tend to present them emphatically as what in our modern language can only be termed as "racists" and "(religious) imperialists" (cf. Barclay, *Obeying the Truth*, 250: "cultural imperialism"; see also p. 72 below). It is debatable whether this does greater justice to the historical data and is more desirable than the traditional view. If the excesses of the traditional view of the Judaism of New Testament times as a religion of works-righteousness can be moderated by a due consideration of the overall covenantal framework of Judaism (i.e., by taking up the positive contribution of the New Perspective), and especially if the view can be dissociated from its misuse for anti-Semitism, it may be preferable as well as being better grounded on the historical data than the view of the New Perspectivists that denies any element of works-righteousness in Judaism, because the former at least contains a respect for the great devotion of the Jews to their religion and ethics. Neither the traditional view of Judaism, which practically pays little

Galatian Christians did not mind doing the works of the law, and possibly the gentile Christians in Antioch did not mind it, either. In this situation, is it not rather odd to think that Paul objected to works of the law in order to protect them from Jewish nationalism? Just to deny the Jewish claim to their privileges which his gentile converts did not mind recognizing, would Paul have waged such life-and-death struggles against the Judaizers' attempts to combine faith in Christ and "works of the law" (cf. Gal 1:6-9; 2:11-21)?[213]

The reason for Paul's objection to works of the law must lie elsewhere. His rejection of Jewish nationalism cannot account for his regular contrasting of faith in Christ to the works of the law. Why did he say that "if justification were through the law, then Christ died in vain," and that seeking justification through works of the law is to "nullify the grace of God" (Gal 2:21)?[214]

---

attention to its overall covenant framework, nor the New Perspective, which completely denies an element of works-righteousness in Judaism, seems to do justice to Judaism. Probably it is best to understand the Judaism of New Testament times as a covenantal nomism with an element of works-righteousness. See pp. 143-52 below. Cf. R. Barry Matlock, "Sins of the Flesh and Suspicious Minds: Dunn's New Theology of Paul," *JSNT* 72 (1998): 86: "Substitute for 'legalism' in the traditional reading 'nationalism' in Dunn's, as the perverted attitude toward the law and its observance that is the real target of Paul's attack, and the old perspective fits Dunn right down to the ground, complete with Dunn's own version of traditional preoccupations with prideful 'boasting' in works and smug 'self-righteousness' in one's religion" (I owe the reference to Matlock's article to my colleague Donald A. Hagner).

213. Cf. D. A. Campbell, "The ΔΙΑΘΗΚΗ from Durham: Professor Dunn's *The Theology of Paul the Apostle*," *JSNT* 72 (1998): 101, who points out that Paul's opposition to the Jewish claim to their circumcision and other distinctive practices as their ethnic prerogatives should logically have led to a demand that such practices be made freely available to all, rather than to the *sola fide* principle.

214. Cf. the strange exegesis of this verse in Dunn, *The Epistle to the Galatians*, 148-49. Dunn takes "the grace of God" here as referring to " 'the grace of God' manifested in [Paul's] calling and in his successful missionary work (i.15; ii.9)." Then Dunn comments: "It was of the essence of that grace, in Paul's experience and understanding, that it was to be freely extended to the Gentiles as well. So any retreat back into a Judaism, or Jewish Christianity, which insisted that Jew and Gentile should eat separately was to render invalid the whole gospel — as indeed also Israel's own election (Rom xi.5-6)!" I find it difficult to grasp the logic here. Any attempt to deny the gentile believers' full participation in the fellowship of God's people may be considered as rendering invalid God's grace given to Paul, i.e., making his apostleship for the gentiles invalid (Rom 1:5; 12:3; 15:15; 1 Cor 3:10; Gal 2:9). But why is it also rendering "the whole gospel" invalid? This conclusion is possible only if we take "the grace of God" here as referring not to God's grace manifested in Paul's apostolic calling but to God's grace manifested in his giving his Son up to the vicarious death on the cross. This "grace of God" is in fact what Paul has just referred to in v. 20 ("the Son of God who loved me and gave himself for me") and is about to refer to again by pointing to Christ's atoning death in the following clause of v. 21. So Paul is saying that the Jewish Christians' insistence on the works of the law is in effect to deny the efficacy of Christ's atoning death and make God's grace in Christ's death null and void.

Dunn himself seems to recognize that Paul's opposition to works of the law involved more than Jewish nationalism. For, expounding the faith of Abraham which was "reckoned to him as righteousness" (Rom 4:3, 9, 22), Dunn says:

> Abraham's own advanced years and the barrenness of Sarah's womb made it almost impossible to envisage the promise being fulfilled in anything like the normal course of events. But Abraham believed in confident hope: that was the character of his faith — not dependent on or qualified by any legal enactment, but dependent solely on God. This was the trust in the Creator God which Adam had failed to exercise. Abraham gave the glory to God which humankind had refused to give ([Rom] 1.21). This was the character of a faith far more fundamental than Abraham's subsequent faithfulness, more fundamental than Israel's relation with its covenant God. This was the faith of the creature wholly reliant upon and confident in God's promise because it was God who promised ([Rom] 4.21). . . . This, then, is what Paul meant by justification by faith, by faith alone. It was a profound conception of the relation between God and humankind — a relation of utter dependence, of unconditional trust. Human dependence on divine grace had to be unqualified or else it was not Abraham's faith, the faith through which God could work his own work. That was why Paul was so fiercely hostile to the qualification which he saw confronting him all the time in any attempt to insist on works of the law as a necessary accompaniment of or addition to faith. God would not justify, could not sustain in relationship with him, those who did not rely wholly on him. Justification was by faith, by faith alone.[215]

It is surprising to find this traditional Reformational interpretation of Paul's doctrine of justification in Dunn. It is especially interesting to note how Dunn here contrasts faith, unqualified dependence on God's grace, to dependence on "any legal enactment," "Abraham's subsequent faithfulness," "Israel's relation with its covenant God," and "works of the law." By doing this, he is suggesting not only that "works of the law" are expressions of Israel's faithfulness to the covenant with God, or their observance of their side of the covenant requirements, but also that to insist on "works of the law" is to depend on a legal enactment. Therefore, is he not betraying unwittingly an assumption that "works of the law" are merits that Israel presents to God for rewards as in a legal transaction? He may protest about this exegesis of his statements. But his statements, so exegeted, seem to be bringing out correctly the sense of Paul's argument in Rom 4.

215. Dunn, *The Theology of Paul,* 378-79.

PAUL AND THE NEW PERSPECTIVE

In verses 4-8, in order to explain that the faith that brings about justification is to depend entirely on the grace of God's forgiveness, Paul does enunciate the principle that "works" are organically connected with "due/wage." In the rest of the chapter, Paul demonstrates that Abraham was justified by his faith, his "unconditional trust" in God, and that his justification was not a "due" or "wage" for any "work" like circumcision. This is all the more significant if, as Dunn and many others correctly believe,[216] Paul is reacting in Rom 4 against the widespread Jewish interpretation of Abraham's faith (Gen 15:6) in terms of his offering of Isaac (Gen 22).[217] Citing 1 Macc 2:52 as an exposition of Gen 15:6 ("Was not Abraham found faithful when tested, 'and it was reckoned to him as righteousness'?"), Dunn finds it significant that the example of Abraham's faith and justification is found within Mattathias's roll call of the heroes of zeal (1 Macc 2:49-68).[218] Then, noting how the zealous acts of Phinehas (Num 25:6-13) and of Simeon and Levi (Gen 34) are celebrated in Ps 106:30-31 and in *Jub* 30:17 respectively, echoing the language of Gen 15:6 ("was reckoned to him/them as righteousness"), Dunn concludes: "Evidently Gen. 15.6 was understood within Israel's tradition of 'zeal' as indicating the faithful devotion to Israel's covenant distinctiveness which God counted as righteousness."[219] So Dunn thinks that Paul, himself a former "zealot," is reacting against this tradition.[220]

But the trouble with this interpretation is that Abraham's offering of Isaac has nothing to do with Israel's covenant distinctiveness, being just a good work of perfect obedience to God's command. In his exhortation for his sons to be zealous for the law in 1 Macc 2:49-68, Mattathias lists the examples of Abraham, Joseph, Joshua, Caleb, and David along with Phinehas, Elijah, Daniel, and so on, not for their devotion particularly to Israel's covenant distinctiveness but for their faithful keeping of the law in general. Even Daniel is praised "for his innocence" rather than for his devotion to Israel's covenant distinctiveness. This seems to suggest that for Mattathias "zeal" for the law does not have the narrow focus on Israel's covenant distinctiveness, but

216. E.g., Dunn, *The Theology of Paul*, 375-76; U. Wilckens, *Der Brief an die Römer (Röm 1–5)* (EKKNT; Zürich: Benziger; Neukirchen: Neukirchener, 1978), 262; J. A. Fitzmyer, *Romans*, 372; K. Haacker, *Der Brief des Paulus an die Römer* (THKNT; Leipzig: Evangelische Verlagsanstalt, 1999), 98-99.

217. For this Dunn, *The Theology of Paul*, 375 n. 167, cites Jdt 8:26; Sir 44:19-21; *Jub.* 17:15-18; 18:16; 19:8; 'Abot 5:3; Philo, *Abr.* 192; Josephus, *Ant.* 1.223-25; Pseudo-Philo 40.2, 5; 4 Macc 14:20. See also Jas 2:21-23.

218. Dunn, *The Theology of Paul*, 375-76.

219. Ibid., 376.

220. Ibid.

64

rather has the broad sense of a fervent commitment to all the commandments of God in the law as a whole, although in the situation of defending the
purity of Israel as in the cases of Phinehas and Elijah it is best expressed in
terms of devotion particularly to Israel's covenant distinctiveness. At any rate,
Abraham's offering of Isaac was not a case of defending Israel's covenant or
purity against gentile defilement, but an extremely "zealous" act of obeying
God's command. Therefore, if, as is likely, the Jewish tradition of interpreting
Abraham's faith in terms of his offering of Isaac is the foil against which Paul
expounds his doctrine of justification by faith in Rom 4, he is not repudiating
the attempt to connect justification with devotion to Israel's covenant distinctiveness in particular but rather with the good works of keeping the law in
general.[221]

221. Cf. Fitzmyer, *Romans*, 372-74, who points out how Abraham's faith and deed were
understood as merits in the Jewish tradition. If the tradition of interpreting Gen 15:6 in
terms of zeal for Israel's covenant distinctiveness as in Ps 106:30-31 and *Jub.* 30:17 was well
established and in Rom 4 Paul reacts against this tradition, as Dunn suggests, we should expect Paul to argue in Rom 4 against that "tradition" to the effect that Gen 15:6 should not be
interpreted in the sense of Ps 106:30-31 and *Jub.* 30:17. But in Rom 4 there is no such argument. So we can only conclude that Paul was not conscious of that "tradition" in Rom 4.
Dunn, *The Theology of Paul*, 376, tries to enlist 4QMMT for his theory here. In the letter written to the "evil priest" in Jerusalem the writer lists his rulings and expresses his hope that "at
the end of time, you may rejoice in finding that some of our words/practices are true/correct.
And it shall be reckoned to you as righteousness in doing what is upright and good before
him." Seeing an allusion to Gen 15:6 here, Dunn interprets this to mean that "righteousness is
reckoned in accord with one's faithfulness in observing the rulings and the works of the law
which distinguished the Qumran community's halakah." But it must be pointed out that the
writer of 4QMMT, as he addresses his fellow Jew, does not have "Israel's covenant distinctiveness" in view. If he regards the evil priest and his followers as not doing "works of the law"
(מעשי תורה) and therefore being outside of the covenant, it is not because he believes that
they do not have "Israel's covenant distinctives" but rather because he believes that they are
not observing the law as correctly and faithfully as his Qumran community. So he is not saying that they would be justified if they observed "the rulings and the works of the law which
distinguished the Qumran community's halakah," but rather, if they observed the law as correctly (i.e., as interpreted by him) and faithfully as his Qumran community. In other words,
what is at stake is not devotion to "Qumran distinctiveness" as such (let alone "Israel's covenant distinctiveness") but the degree of correctness and faithfulness in observing the law.
Thus, 4QMMT supports neither Dunn's interpretation of the phrase "works of the law" nor
his present argument that in the Jewish tradition Gen 15:6 was interpreted in the sense of
righteousness reckoned for devotion specifically to Israel's covenant distinctiveness. On the
contrary, it bears the assumption that at the last judgment justification will be given for those
who have accurately and faithfully observed the law, i.e., that justification is for doing the
works of the law exactly. Cf. Fitzmyer, *Romans*, 338-39. See now J. C. de Roo, "The Concept of
'Works of the Law' in Jewish and Christian Literature," especially pp. 122-47, for a thorough
and convincing repudiation of Dunn's interpretation of 4QMMT.

Thus, Paul's contrast of faith in Christ to works of the law is comprehensible only when the latter is understood as referring to good works rather than to Israel's covenant distinctives. He makes this clear especially with his illustration of this point with the case of Abraham in Rom 4.

The Forensic and Ethical Dimensions of Justification

Dunn's and some of his fellow New Perspectivists' interpretation of "works of the law" as the distinctives of Israel as God's covenant people is related to their understanding of Paul's doctrine of justification predominantly in the sense of obtaining membership in the covenant people of God or in the family of Abraham. Of course, they justify their interpretation on the basis of the fact that the concept of "righteousness"/"justification" in the biblical tradition is fundamentally relational and covenantal. However, Paul's doctrine of justification also has a forensic dimension, so that it often refers to acquittal or deliverance from God's wrath at the last judgment (e.g., Rom 8:30-34; 1 Thess 1:9-10) and to its anticipation in the present (e.g., Rom 1:16–3:26; 5:1, 9; 1 Cor 6:11). The forensic dimension may be perceived as the initial and decisive step of restoration to the proper relationship to God, as it refers to forgiveness of sins that have breached the covenantal or proper relationship to God, and declaration of the forgiven sinners to be in the right.[222] Dunn does recognize the forensic dimension of justification.[223] But when he repeatedly asserts that Paul developed his doctrine of justification in order to defend against Jewish nationalism the gentile converts' right to be included within the people of God,[224] the forensic dimension of justification is practically lost. N. T. Wright also strongly emphasizes that "righteousness" means "a covenant status," and "justification" is "membership language,"[225] having to do with "the question of how you define the people of God."[226] He makes efforts even more than Dunn to integrate the forensic dimension of justification within the covenantal framework.[227] However, I am not sure whether he is entirely successful. Further, while I grant that in Galatians, because of the

---

222. It goes without saying that the forensic dimension also has the structure of "already — but not yet" typical of the Pauline eschatology.

223. Dunn, *The Theology of Paul,* 340-46.

224. Dunn, "A Light to the Gentiles," 99; *Partings,* 130-39; "Paul and Justification," 90-100; "Paul's Conversion," 92; *The Theology of Paul,* 359-79.

225. Wright, *What Saint Paul Really Said,* 124.

226. Ibid., 120.

227. Ibid., 120-33.

presenting problem of the Judaizers' demand for gentile converts' circumcision, Paul presents the doctrine of justification primarily in terms of Jew and gentile alike becoming children of Abraham and people of God by faith,[228] I am not persuaded that we should see Paul doing the same in Romans and Phil 3:2-16. Dunn himself seems to have doubts about this in the case of the latter text.[229] Although in Galatians the main emphasis falls on the gentile believers becoming members of God's covenant people, there is also the idea of their redemption from the curse of the law (3:10-14; 4:4-6). By contrast, in Romans, although the covenantal framework forms the broad background, the forensic dimension of justification, deliverance from the wrath of God, seems to receive the main emphasis (1:16–8:39). Where the forensic dimension is mainly in view, the sins (ἁμαρτία) or trespasses (παράπτωμα) from which justification or acquittal is supposed to be made cannot be limited to the transgression of the commandments that specially mark Israel off as the covenant people of God (circumcision, food laws, and sabbath). Instead, they are often specified as transgression of the religious and ethical commandments of the law (e.g., Rom 1:18–3:20; 5:15-21; 6:1-23; 7:4-25), and believers are said to be justified in spite of the fact that they have not kept those commandments (e.g., Rom 3:21-26; 5:1-11; 8:1-4). As we shall see in the next chapter, the doctrine of justification implicit in 1 Thess 1:9-10; 4:1-8; 5:9-10 has religious and moral transgressions in view, and it has no direct connection with the idea of obtaining membership in God's people.

First Corinthians 6:9-11 expresses Paul's doctrine of justification in a way quite similar to 1 Thessalonians (especially 4:1-8):

> Do you not know that the unrighteous will not inherit the kingdom of God? Do not be deceived; neither the immoral, nor idolaters, nor adulterers, nor sexual perverts, drunkards, nor revilers, nor robbers will inherit the kingdom of God. And such were some of you. But you were washed, you were sanctified, you were justified in the name of the Lord Jesus Christ and in the Spirit of our God.[230]

The evil deeds listed here are forbidden in the law of Moses. For Paul, "the unrighteous" (ἄδικοι) are those who commit such religious and moral sins.

---

228. See above, pp. 55-57.

229. Cf. Dunn, "Paul and Justification," 93.

230. Even if v. 11 is based on a pre-Pauline tradition, which I doubt, we can interpret it within the context of Paul's theology, insofar as Paul makes use of it for his argument. It is regrettable that Wright misses this important passage, noting only 1 Cor 1:30, in his discussion on the doctrine of justification in the Corinthian correspondence (*What Saint Paul Really Said*, 122-23).

Here the epithet does not refer to gentiles' lack of the covenant distinctives of Israel. "Some" of the Corinthian Christians used to be "unrighteous" people, not because they had not been circumcised and did not keep the Jewish food laws and festival days, but because they committed those religious and moral sins (cf. Rom 1:18-32). There is nothing here that would remind us, either positively or negatively, of the idea of "justification" or becoming "righteous" by keeping the commandments concerning circumcision, food, and sabbath. What is here is only the implication that they as "righteous" people should not commit those religious and moral sins.

Paul, a pious Jew, may be expected to advise the Corinthians to keep the commandments of the law that forbid those sins, in order to become "righteous" people. But he does not do that.[231] Instead, he says that they were already "justified" (ἐδικαιώθητε), and he implies that their justification took place when they were transferred into the sphere of Jesus Christ's lordship with their profession of faith in his name (cf. Rom 10:9) and received the Spirit of God at their baptism. Here the implication is not only that they were justified by God's grace and through their faith, but also that *they were justified without themselves keeping those religious and ethical commandments of the law.* It is significant that here Paul does not refer to the law, even while he lists some concrete sins forbidden in the law and speaks of his converts' "justification" and their need to remain as the "righteous" people of God. Therefore, it is a reasonable supposition that if he were asked to put his doctrine of justification implicit here into an explicit formula, he would probably state that justification is by God's grace and through faith and without "works of the law." In view of his frequent use of the phrase "works of the law" as well as the attestation of its Hebrew equivalents in the Dead Sea Scrolls (4QFlor 1:7; 4QMMT 3:29; 1QS 5:21; 6:18), we may suppose that here he would employ the phrase "without works of the law" (χωρὶς ἔργων νόμου) as a shorthand for "without keeping the religious and ethical commandments of the law," some of which are here concretely illustrated.

With their transference into the sphere under Christ's lordship, the Corinthian Christians have entered into the kingdom of God, for Christ as God's Son exercises God's kingship or lordship on his behalf in the present (1 Cor 15:24-28; Col 1:13). They have become God's people. But the kingdom of God is to be consummated in the future, so that complete "inheritance" of the kingdom of God remains an eschatological hope. Having been acquitted of their past evil deeds and made God's righteous people,[232] it is essential now

---

231. As he does not do that in 1 Thess 4:1-8; see pp. 88-90 below.

232. W. Schrage, *Der erste Brief an die Korinther (1 Kor 1,1–6,11)* (EKKNT VII/1; Zürich: Benziger/Neukirchen: Neukirchener, 1991), 433, correctly interprets ἐδικαιώθητε in v. 11 in the

that they be sustained as God's righteous people in order to obtain that eschatological hope at the last judgment on the day of the Lord Jesus Christ (1 Cor 1:7-8; 5:11-13; 2 Cor 5:10). Thus, in our passage, the concept of justification does appear connected with the concept of God's people. However, the main emphasis does not fall on that connection but rather on the acquittal of those who are made God's people, from their past (religious and ethical) sins, and on their need to remain the "righteous" people of God, free from those sins, to be able to obtain the consummation of salvation at the parousia of the Lord Jesus Christ. Thus, our passage indicates that in connection with justification we are to think not just of membership in God's people, but also of the forensic and ethical righteousness of God's people.

In our passage Paul does not elaborate on how the Corinthian Christians might remain the "justified" or "righteous" people of God, avoiding the sins here listed. But by alluding to the fact that they were justified with their transference into the sphere of Christ's lordship and with their receiving the Holy Spirit, he may be implying what he expounds in Rom 6 and 8:3-17 (Gal 5:16-26) respectively. In view of Paul's silence on the law, is it too much if we see here implied Paul's theological decision that lies behind the Spirit-law antithesis of Rom 7–8, as in 1 Thess 4:8?[233]

If it is not too much, we may conclude that in our passage Paul implies (1) that justification is on the basis of Christ's work and through the Holy Spirit, rather than through keeping the religious and ethical commandments of the law, that is, "works of the law," and (2) that the "justified" remain "righteous" unto the consummation of salvation by walking according to the Spirit, rather than by observance of the law.

As in 1 Thessalonians, so also in 1 Cor 6:9-11 we find Paul preaching his gospel in terms of justification by grace, through faith, and without works of the law, even where there is no question of the Jew-gentile relationship. In such cases, justification is presented primarily in its forensic sense, beyond the sense of becoming members of God's covenant people, and the implicit contrast is drawn between grace/faith and keeping the religious and ethical commandments rather than keeping the commandments promoting Israel's covenant distinctives. In Romans the forensic sense of justification is, to say the least, as strong as its covenantal sense of becoming the people of God. That is the reason why in the epistle the phrase "works of the law" usually re-

---

sense both of *Gerechtsprechung* and *Gerechtmachung,* and endorses C. K. Barrett's forensic interpretation coupled with an appreciation of the "ethical undertone and implication" (*Commentary on the First Epistle to the Corinthians* [BNTC; 2d ed.; London: Black, 1971], 142).

233. See pp. 154-63 below.

fers to the good works of observing the religious and ethical commandments of the law, as we have seen.

The Problem of the Law and Liberation from It

Only with the understanding that by "works of the law" Paul means the good (meritorious) works of keeping the law in general can we also account for his lengthy and at times polemical treatments of the problem of the law in Gal 3–4 and Rom 7–8. If in rejecting "works of the law" in his doctrine of justification Paul had only Israel's covenant distinctives in mind, as Dunn claims, why does he highlight the weakness of the law itself (Rom 5:20; 7:5; 8:3; Gal 3:21)? Why does he in Rom 7 illustrate with a moral commandment ("Thou shalt not covet," 7:7) the Adamic human being's and Israel's dilemma of willingness but inability to keep the law and therefore the impossibility of their being justified by the law?[234] Why does he in Rom 2:17-24; 3:9-20 charge Israel of failing to keep the moral laws (e.g., the commandments in the Decalogue), in his attempt to demonstrate that justification by "works of the law" is impossible? Why does he in Rom 8 and Gal 5 refer to various acts of moral righteousness as τὸ δικαίωμα τοῦ νόμου that the Holy Spirit is said to enable those who are justified by faith in Christ to fulfill? Why does he or how can he speak of the law as having been weakened by the flesh and so being unable to justify its adherents (Rom 8:3)? I suppose that most of the Jews could fulfill the "works of the law" (as defined by Dunn) without much difficulty. In the areas of the law that showed their covenant distinctiveness, the law was not weakened by the flesh nor were the Jews weakened by the flesh! All these arguments of Paul make sense only if by "works of the law" he means not just keeping Israel's covenant distinctives but observance of the law as a whole as good works.[235]

---

234. Accepting D. J. Moo's argument ("Israel and Paul in Romans 7.7-12," *NTS* 32 [1986]: 122-35), Dunn, *The Theology of Paul*, 99-100, now recognizes that the "I" in Rom 7:7-13 represents Israel as well as Adam. As a result, this problem should become all the more serious to him because in Rom 7 Paul must be understood as saying that the Israelites cannot be justified by the law because they cannot keep the law perfectly, rather than because their insistence on their covenant distinctives is nationalistic and contrary to God's will.

235. This has been pointed out by many: e.g., Westerholm, *Israel's Law*, 118-19; Schreiner, *The Law and Its Fulfillment*, 51-57, 65-68, 77-81; Seifrid, "Blind Alleys," 82-83; Moo, *Romans*, 214; but Dunn tends to treat their arguments in a cavalier fashion. Cf. M. Silva, "The Law and Christianity: Dunn's New Synthesis," *WTJ* 53 (1991): 352-53.

In discussing "the blessings of justification," Dunn refers to what Paul expresses "with such intensity of feeling in Galatians":

> It is that justification by faith means *liberty,* and, most important of all, liberty from the law. The antithesis of Paul's gospel of justification, as equally open to Gentiles, was a divine righteousness restricted in its scope by the law and in effect to those who practised the works of the law. Hence Paul's fear in Gal 2.4: that the Gentile Galatians' freedom might be lost if the demand for circumcision was accepted.[236]

According to Dunn's theory, Paul's gospel of justification would indeed have liberated God's righteousness from its restricted application only to the Jews. But, of course, Paul is not referring to this kind of liberation when he talks about the blessing of justification in terms of liberation. He is referring to the liberation of the justified people. Then is he referring merely to exemption from the duties of circumcision, food laws, and festival days? It is confusing because Dunn goes on to say:

> Here again it simply needs to be underlined that Paul experienced his coming to faith in Christ as one of liberation. The practice of the law, which had previously been his delight, he now regarded as a kind of slavery, the slavery of the spiritually immature ([Gal.] 4.1-3). This, of course, is the language of hindsight. But if his language resonated in any degree with his Galatian converts, they too must have experienced justification by faith as a liberation, initially at least. Paul assumes a similar resonance in his play on the metaphor of slavery and manumission in Rom. 6.16-23, and the cry of relief in Rom. 8.2 echoes that of Gal. 5.1. Not least of Paul's delights in justification by faith was that it had liberated from what he now recognized to have been a spirit of slavery, whose motivation was fundamentally one of fear (Rom. 8.15).[237]

If "works of the law" were not regarded as meritorious works for God's justification but only as affirmations that God's righteousness belonged only to the Jews, why would Paul have felt liberation when he came to faith in Christ? According to Dunn, it could not have been in the sense that the law had forced him to observe its commandments ever more exactly to earn justification. In what sense would he have regarded his former life as slavery to the law? If he had not felt that the law as a *paidagogos* was constantly forcing him to be a "good boy" with its sanction of reward and its threat of punishment,

---

236. Dunn, *The Theology of Paul,* 388 (his italics).
237. Ibid., 388-89.

why would he have seen his life under the law as slavery (Gal 3:23-25; 4:1-3)? What was the nature of the freedom from the law that he experienced when he came to faith in Christ?

Why or how could the Galatian converts have "initially" experienced justification by faith as a liberation? According to Dunn, in Gal 5:1 Paul thinks of the Galatian Christians' submission to the law as their enslavement to the Jews.[238] This is, of course, a most unlikely interpretation. Strange though it is, it is an interpretation rather consistent with Dunn's assumption of "works of the law" as the Jewish covenant distinctives or the Jewish national identity markers: accepting the law or, more exactly, "works of the law," therefore, the Galatian Christians are falling into subservience to the Jews.[239] But the liberation that they "initially" experienced with Paul's gospel of justification must have had nothing to do with the "works of the law." Surely their apostle Paul did not first require them to get circumcised and keep the food laws and the festival days and then only later tell them they did not have to do these because they were justified by faith alone! When they had not had the "works of the law" imposed on them in the first place, how could their justification be a liberation from them or from the law? Thus, the freedom that the Galatian Christians experienced with Paul's gospel of justification cannot have been one from the Jewish covenant distinctives nor even from the law of Moses as a whole. It was rather freedom from "the elemental forces of the world" (Gal 4:3, 9) to which their own religious law that was functionally analogous to the Jewish law belonged. They had been held enslaved to the "fear of infringing its taboos and boundaries"[240] lest some disaster should befall them. When they accepted Paul's gospel of justification by grace and through faith, they were liberated from this fear and this slavery. But with the acceptance of the yoke of the law of Moses under the instigation of the Judaizers they were in danger of falling back into the same kind of slavery in which they would constantly have to bear the "fear of infringing [the] taboos and boundaries" of

---

238. Dunn, *The Epistle to the Galatians*, 263.

239. Leading Dunn to such a strange exegesis of Gal 5:1, his assumption unwittingly reveals its own falsehood.

240. This phrase is from Dunn, *The Epistle to the Galatians*, 226. But Dunn strangely links it only to the law as misunderstood by the Judaizers, as if (1) the Galatians had first been liberated from the law of Moses and (2) the law of Moses in itself (i.e., as not misunderstood by the Judaizers) did not engender "fear of its taboos and boundaries." Nevertheless, it is significant that Dunn recognizes that the law as misunderstood by the Judaizers does engender "fear of its taboos and boundaries." With this recognition, then, is he not tacitly admitting that the "works of the law" demanded by the Judaizers involved the principle of works-righteousness, not just Jewish nationalism?

the Mosaic law (Gal 4:8-11). Thus, Paul's talk of the Galatian Christians as having experienced liberty from the law when they accepted his gospel (5:1, 13) implicitly affirms that he preached to them his gospel of justification *sola gratia/fide* against the sanction and punishment of any law, the Mosaic law as well as their own analogous law, rather than against the Jewish covenant distinctives.

Further, the cry of relief in Rom 8:2 (cf. Gal 5:1, 13) is not evoked by liberation from Israel's covenant distinctives but from the desperate situation into which the law forces human beings: faced with the *Sollen* of the law ("Thou shalt not covet"), fleshly human beings inevitably fall into the dilemma of being willing but unable to keep the law or to do good and consequently into sin and death (Rom 7:7-25). The liberation is from condemnation for not having kept the law (8:1). What "fear" could Paul have recognized even from hindsight that had motivated his slavery to the law? This sort of language appears possible only when Paul recognized "fear" of failing to "stay in" the covenant relationship unless he perfectly kept the law as a whole or even the Jewish covenant distinctives (e.g., the food laws). If he recognized that he was enslaved to the law for the fear of falling out of the covenant, then he at least tacitly understood his "works of the law" to be meritorious for "staying in" the covenant, that is, for justification. But isn't it the fundamental assumption of Dunn and his fellow New Perspectivists that there was in Judaism no such understanding of "works of the law" and no such fear because the law provided a system of atonement for sins? Then what fear and slavery is Paul talking about in Romans 8:15? Dunn interprets it in terms of a sectarian's "hidden fear of failing to match up at one or other of the test points by which loyalty to these distinctives is evaluated within the sect."[241] Suggesting that he understands Romans 8:15a as springing out of Paul's own experience, he immediately adds:

> Paul presumably now understood his Pharisaic attitudes in these terms, not as an inadmissible desire to please God by good works . . . , but as a concern for punctilious exactness in obeying the law . . . , which would tend to inject something of a competitive spirit (Gal 1:14; Phil 3:6) and so also of fear, fear of failing to come up to the mark of acceptability to his fellows or of the esteem in which they held him.[242]

Since his assumption that Judaism had no idea of works-righteousness does not allow him to admit any possibility of Paul having had a "fear of failing to

241. Dunn, *Romans 1–8,* 452.
242. Ibid., 452.

come up to the mark of acceptability to" God, Dunn has to interpret "fear" in Rom 8:15 as a sociological concept (something that arises within the dynamics of a sectarian group) rather than as a theological concept (a feeling that one has before God). But I find it difficult to imagine that even after his conversion Paul would have looked back at his Pharisaic days as the period in which he had worked to keep the law with punctilious exactness only to maintain his high esteem among his fellow Pharisees. Can it be imagined that Paul's zeal to keep the law perfectly was motivated only by a "fear of failing to come up to the mark of acceptability to his fellows" but not to God? Did he keep the law only for human approval but not for divine approval? Apparently the Pharisees also believed in God's judgment according to works (cf., e.g., 4 Ezra 7:70-74; 2 Bar 24:1-2). I do not believe that Paul developed his belief in God's last judgment according to works (Rom 2:1-16; 1 Cor 3:13-15; 2 Cor 5:10; etc.) only after his Damascus conversion. Nor do I believe that only after his conversion did he develop his attitude of trying to please God (e.g., 2 Cor 5:9; Rom 12:1-2) or his belief in the need to progress in sanctification in the fear of the Lord (2 Cor 5:11; 7:1; Phil 2:12; cf. 1 Cor 9:24-27). It is a pity that in order to protect his dogma about Judaism, Dunn has to go so far as to reduce Paul's and implicitly the whole Pharisaic movement's efforts to keep the law to a mere attempt to "save face" before their fellow sectarians![243]

However, even if this unrealistic interpretation about Paul's Pharisaic past should be granted, we still have the problem of figuring out how Paul thought it was relevant to the Roman Christians. When in Rom 8:15a Paul says, "For you did not receive the spirit of slavery to fall back into fear," is Paul assuming that the Roman Christians also had an experience in some sectarianism analogous to Paul's experience in his Pharisaic sectarianism? I find it difficult to imagine this, too. Further, is it conceivable that Paul is here saying that not fear of God but fear of their fellow sectarians is resolved by their reception of the Spirit and their adoption as God's children? So then, does their/our reception of "the Spirit of sonship" resolve only their/our fear arising out of their/our sectarian mentality? Again I find it hard to imagine this.

Thus, given Dunn's assumption of Judaism as covenantal nomism with no notion of works-righteousness and his understanding of "works of the law" as meaning only Israel's covenant distinctives, it appears impossible to make sense of Paul's description of life under the law as fear-driven slavery to

---

243. To my mind, Pharisees would not have accepted Dunn's suggestion, either, that their efforts to keep the law perfectly were really geared to maintaining only their sect's distinctives. Even Paul the convert would not accept it. Both the Pharisees and Paul would have claimed that their efforts were to keep the whole law as exactly, comprehensively, and deeply as possible.

the law and of his explanation of justification in terms of liberation from the law.[244] They make sense only under the assumption of a system of works-righteousness and on the understanding of "works of the law" as meritorious good works.

All this discussion makes it impossible to explain the Pauline antithesis between faith in Christ and "works of the law" merely in terms of Paul's opposition to Jewish nationalism, the Jews' devotion to their covenant distinctives and their imposition of them on the gentiles. It reveals rather that the antithesis is really about the fundamental contrast between reliance on God's grace and reliance on human achievement.[245]

If so, Paul's rejection of "works of the law" in justification could have developed without a predetermined purpose of defending his gentile mission. With their witness to Paul's preaching of his gospel of justification *sola gratia/fide* even in contexts where there is no question of the defense of his gentile mission, 1 Thessalonians and 1 Cor 6:9-11 implicitly confirm this, as we shall see in the next chapter. Then while a big question mark is placed on the theories that Paul's rejection of "works of the law" originated in the Antioch incident or in the Galatian controversy, the possibility of its origin in the Damascus revelation of the gospel is greatly enhanced. It is much more plausible to believe that it originated from the former zealot Paul's own experience of God's grace of justification as well as his realization about Christ's death of vicarious atonement at Damascus, than to think that it originated fifteen to seventeen years later from his desire to protect the gentile converts' right to be included in the people of God.

"My/Their Own Righteousness"

Our discussion thus far brings us finally to Dunn's interpretation of Paul's testimony of his conversion in Phil 3:2-10. Those who have attempted to see the origin of Paul's doctrine of justification in Paul's conversion experience on the Damascus road have found their most explicit evidence in that testi-

---

244. It is curious that in this connection Dunn, *The Theology of Paul*, 389 n. 224, approvingly cites "one of Bultmann's keener insights," that "the hidden side of 'boasting' and 'putting confidence in the flesh' is *fear*" (R. Bultmann, *Theology of the New Testament I* [London: SCM/New York: Scribner, 1952], 243; cf. also his *Romans 1–8*, 452). Can Dunn do this without accepting Bultmann's assumptions about Judaism and works of the law which are the basis of the statement?

245. Cf. R. H. Gundry, "Grace, Works, and Staying Saved," *Bib* 60 (1985): 12-13; Marshall, "Salvation, Grace and Works," 355-56.

mony. For there Paul speaks about surrendering his own "blameless" righteousness which he had acquired from the law, in order to obtain God's righteousness through faith in Christ. To oppose this interpretation, Dunn dutifully starts with a citation of his dogma: "the need to attain one's own righteousness was no part of traditional Jewish teaching."[246] This dogma does not allow him to take "my own righteousness" in verse 9 in its natural grammatical sense of Paul's personal righteousness, the righteousness that he attained through his faithful observance of the law. So he interprets it to mean only his sense of participation in the righteousness that belongs to Israel by virtue of the covenant, what Wright calls the "national righteousness" of Israel:[247] "It was his standing before God as a devout member of God's chosen people that Paul had previously treasured so highly (Phil 3:7-8). As such, he had rejoiced in a righteousness that non-Jews knew nothing of. It was 'his,' as one who had been 'circumcised on the eighth day,' of the people of Israel.' "[248]

As the ground of his own righteousness, had Paul listed only those items which showed his belonging to the covenant people of God ("circumcised on the eighth day, of the people of Israel, of the tribe of Benjamin, and Hebrew born of Hebrews," v. 5a-d), Dunn's interpretation could have made sense. But unfortunately for Dunn, Paul goes on to list some more items: "as to the law a Pharisee, as to zeal a persecutor of the church, as to righteousness under the law blameless" (vv. 5e-6). The latter three items clearly belong personally to Paul and not to the covenant people of Israel as a whole. So Dunn is forced to acknowledge that they are "self-chosen." But he argues: "But they cannot be considered 'self-achieved' even if self-chosen."[249] However, defying the most elementary rule of logic, this argument of Dunn seems to be born of desperation: if Paul's self-chosen Pharisaic life of observing the law with the most punctilious exactness[250] and his persecution of the church out of his zeal for the covenant and the law were not what he personally achieved, what were they? If they were not what he could claim as his personal achievement, what was the basis on which he could have *greater* "confidence in the flesh" than his Jewish opponents (v. 4b)? With Paul's testimonies about his pre-conversion

246. Dunn, *The Theology of Paul*, 369.

247. N. T. Wright, "The Paul of History and the Apostle of Faith," *TynBul* 29 (1978): 83. It is common among the other New Perspectivists also to take "my own righteousness" in Phil 3:9 and "their own [righteousness]" in Rom 10:3 in the sense of the Jewish "national righteousness," "that righteousness that the Jews alone are privileged to obtain" (E. P. Sanders, *Paul, the Law and the Jewish People*, 38; Räisänen, *Paul and the Law*, 175).

248. Dunn, "Paul and Justification by Faith," 93.

249. Dunn, *The Theology of Paul*, 370.

250. Cf. Josephus, *Bell.* 1.110; 2.162; *Vita* 191; *Ant.* 17.41; Acts 22:3; 26:5.

devotion to the law and Judaism in Gal 1:13-14 and Phil 3:4-6 in view, Dunn speaks of the "competitive covenant faithfulness," in the spirit of which Paul expressed his "satisfaction that he had outstripped his less faithful contemporaries."[251] So Paul "sought to outdo other Jews in the degree and quality of . . . Torah-keeping," and "that extra degree of faithfulness would have ensured that in terms of covenant obligation ('righteousness') he was 'without reproach.' "[252] Even while saying these quite correctly, Dunn still maintains that in Philippians 3:4-6 Paul was not conscious of his personal achievement. What a strange argument! Am I failing to understand Dunn or am I unfair to him if I again perceive a self-contradiction in his argument? If Paul was not conscious of his personally achieved righteousness but only the "national righteousness" of Israel in Phil 3:2-10, should he not have referred to it as "*our own* righteousness," including his Jewish opponents in his claim, insofar as they, by virtue of their being zealous Jews, evidently also participated in the "national righteousness"? Why did he instead implicitly compare *"my own"* superior "righteousness" with their inferior righteousness? The simple truth is that in Phil 3:2-10 Paul claims to have achieved during his pre-conversion days with his "extra degree of faithfulness" to the law a "righteousness" that was "without reproach," a "righteousness" that gave him a greater degree of confidence "in the flesh" than his opponents could claim. This conclusion is strongly supported by our lengthy argument above for interpreting "works of the law" as obedience rendered to the law as a whole in order to attain personal righteousness.

Otto Betz appreciates the significance of the fact that Paul's sentence in Phil 3:5, "according to the law, a Pharisee," is the only definition we have of Pharisaism that was made by a Pharisee himself.[253] I would say that if we approach Paul's testimony of his Jewish past in Phil 3:2-10 without the dogma of the New Perspective School, it reveals itself as an extremely important piece of primary evidence that the Pharisaic Judaism of the first century A.D. was a covenantal nomism which contained in itself an element of works-righteousness. For a former practitioner of that Judaism himself presented it![254] And he claimed to have attained a righteousness superior to that of some of his fellow Jews, and indeed he spoke of "his own" "blameless" righ-

251. Dunn, "Paul's Conversion," 87.

252. Dunn, *The Theology of Paul,* 350.

253. O. Betz, "Paulus als Pharisäer nach dem Gesetz: Phil. 3, 5-6 als Beitrag zur Frage des frühen Pharisäismus," in *Treue zur Thora* (G. Harder Festschrift; Berlin, 1977), now reprinted in O. Betz, *Jesus: der Herr der Kirche* (WUNT 52; Tübingen: Mohr-Siebeck, 1990), 103-13.

254. See below, n. 275.

teousness that he achieved through his zealous adherence to the law, as well as of the "confidence" that he could have in it.

Since Dunn interprets "my own righteousness" in Phil 3:9 in terms of the "national righteousness" of Israel and understands its problem only in terms of Jewish nationalism but not human (i.e., fleshly) achievement, he inevitably interprets Paul's Damascus experience as follows: "what Paul experienced was not so much his acceptance as one who had previously been without acceptance by God, but primarily the shattering of his assumption that righteousness before God was Israel's peculiar privilege."[255] But if it had been so, Paul could hardly have said things like: "While we were still weak Christ died for the ungodly at the right time. . . . while we were enemies, we were reconciled to God through the death of his Son" (Rom 5:6-9), and "[God] who justifies the ungodly" (Rom 4:5).

So we have already rejected this interpretation as tantamount to the unwarranted "two covenant theory."[256] But here it must also be pointed out that this interpretation contradicts Paul's contrast of "my own righteousness that is from the law" with "the righteousness that is from God, based on faith" (v. 9). If "their own righteousness" in Rom 10:3 or "my own righteousness" in Phil 3:9 means the "righteousness that belongs to them or me" which Israel or an individual Jew affirms as "from the law," being "forgetful of its essentially gracious character ('from God'),"[257] why does Paul contrast it with "God's righteousness" (Rom 10:3) or "the righteousness from God" (Phil 3:9)? If we are to follow Dunn's interpretation, the righteousness that Israel or individual Jews have from the law is also "from God," because the law is God's gift to them as part of his covenant of grace, although they "forget" this "essentially gracious character" of it.[258] Then why does Paul not say just that they ought not to forget that their "national righteousness" *is* essentially *God's* righteousness? Why does he instead contrast "*their/my own* righteousness" with "*God's* righteousness" that is obtained through faith in God's saving act in Christ?

This contrast is all the more incomprehensible if we are to see Paul in Phil 3:7-9 and Rom 10:2-4 as "fiercely resisting his own earlier pre-Christian assumption that God's righteousness was only for Israel."[259] According to this interpretation, "my/their own righteousness" that Paul fiercely resists in the two passages is *God's* righteousness as understood as being only for Israel. If so, the Jews and the pre-conversion Paul were *not* ignorant of *God's* righ-

255. Dunn, "Paul and Justification by Faith," 93.
256. See above, p. 21.
257. Dunn, *The Theology of Paul,* 368, 370.
258. Ibid., 370.
259. Ibid., 371.

teousness; their fault was only that they thought that it was only for Israel. How can Paul say, then, that they were "ignorant" of God's righteousness (Rom 10:3)? And how can he contrast it with "my/their own righteousness"? Why does he not simply say that the Jews and he himself were ignorant that God's righteousness was not just for Israel but for all humankind? Thus, on Dunn's interpretation of "my/their own righteousness" in Phil 3:9 and Rom 10:3, it is quite incomprehensible why Paul contrasts it with God's righteousness.[260]

The contrast is understandable only if the former is not God's righteousness, but a human righteousness, a righteousness achieved by human beings. Paul regarded his former Pharisaic righteousness as his "own" (i.e., human) righteousness, even if it was achieved by obeying God's law or by keeping the terms of the God-given covenant. So, after coming to know God's righteousness in Christ, Paul could not help but bring it under the rubric of the "flesh" (vv. 3-4) and regard it as "dung" (v. 8). Thus, Paul clearly finds this human (i.e., fleshly) quality, and not a nationalistic quality, to be the problem of the righteousness that is from the law.

Hence it is plausible to think that Paul discovered this truth when on the Damascus road he personally experienced the revelation of God's righteousness in Christ's vicarious death and resurrection. In the light of the revelation, his own attempts to attain "blameless" righteousness even by persecuting the church turned out to be a sin, an act of enmity to God (Rom 5:10). But God forgave him, reconciled him to himself, and even called him to be an apostle of Christ (2 Cor 5:14-21).[261] Thus, Paul personally experienced God's righteousness or God's grace and his justification thereby. Therefore he gave up his own law-righteousness as a mere fleshly righteousness. Out of this experience he developed his doctrine of justification by God's grace and through faith in Christ. Paul's testimony in Phil 3:2-11 makes this reasonably clear, while providing us with little ground for thinking that Paul developed the doctrine to counter Jewish nationalism and secure the right of his gentile mission.[262]

This discussion about Phil 3:2-11 brings us to Rom 9:30–10:4, a passage in which I think Paul applies his personal experience described in Phil 3:2-11 to Israel as a whole.[263] Just as in Phil 3:9 he interprets "my own righteousness"

260. Cf. Cranfield, "The Works of the Law," 98.

261. See ch. 6 below.

262. Dunn himself recognizes that in Phil 3 "the acceptability of Gentiles to God is not to the fore" ("Paul and Justification by Faith," 93).

263. Cf. Kim, *Origin,* 3-4, 298. Dunn, "Paul and Justification," 92, also recognizes that there is a close similarity in the language of Phil 3:7-9 and Rom 10:3. Therefore, in discussing the im-

in terms of the Jewish "national righteousness," so here in Rom 10:3 Dunn interprets "their own" righteousness as righteousness that belongs to them (Israel) and not others, that is, in terms of "righteousness as Israel's covenant prerogative, the privilege of Jews only and not of Gentiles."[264] But as "my own righteousness" in Phil 3:9 cannot be taken in the sense of the Jewish "national righteousness," as we have seen above, "their own" righteousness in Rom 10:3 cannot be taken in that sense, either. Since I argued above at length that "works of the law" cannot be confined to Israel's covenant distinctives, we may assume that "works" in Rom 9:32 should be taken in the sense of observance of the law in general.

Paul charges the Jews that "being ignorant of the righteousness from God" they are "seeking to establish their own" righteousness. In Rom 9:31-32 he indicates that they are seeking to establish their own righteousness by works of the law. He grants that they are doing it with a great zeal, but he thinks that this zeal is "not in accordance with knowledge" (10:2). He immediately elaborates that the ignorance is an ignorance of "the righteousness that comes from God" (10:3), but he suggests in 9:32 that it is also an ignorance of the fact that righteousness is to be attained through faith and not by works of the law. Thus, the problem that Paul sees with the Jews is that being ignorant of God's righteousness and of the fact that it is attained through faith they insist on establishing their own righteousness through works of the law. But why is their insistence on establishing their own righteousness through works of the law a problem? In 9:31 Paul suggests that it is because by works of the law they cannot "reach the law" or "live up to the law."[265] So in 9:30–10:4 Paul seems to recapitulate the point he established in Rom 2:12–3:26: not only the gentiles but also the Jews fail to attain righteousness because they do not or cannot keep the law perfectly (cf. Gal 3:10-14).[266] Now God's righteousness has been revealed in Christ's atoning

---

pact of Paul's conversion/call on his theology, it is more proper to start with the Philippians passage and seek to interpret the Romans passage in the light of the former, since the former is directly concerned with Paul's conversion, while the latter reflects it only indirectly. As Dunn himself concedes (*The Theology of Paul*, 369-70), in the former, " 'my own' can be more readily understood as 'what I have gained.'" Is this a reason why in discussing the impact of Paul's Damascus experience on his theology ("Paul and Justification by Faith," 91-93) Dunn strangely starts with the phrase "their own [righteousness]" in the Romans passage and moves to the phrase "my own righteousness" in the Philippians passage, rather than the other way around? Cf. also Dunn, *The Theology of Paul*, 368-71.

264. Dunn, "Paul and Justification," 92; also *The Theology of Paul*, 368.

265. Dunn, *Romans 9–16*, 582, interprets εἰς νόμον οὐκ ἔφθασεν as "has not lived up to the law."

266. See pp. 141-43.

death, so that it is obtained through faith in Christ. Therefore Christ means the end to every attempt to attain righteousness through the (works of the) law (10:4).

Thus, together with Gal 3:10-14,[267] Phil 3:2-11, and several other passages, Rom 9:30–10:4, when exegeted without the presupposition of the New Perspective School, provides an extremely valuable piece of primary evidence that the pious Jews of the first century A.D. sought to attain their own — personal, and not "national" — righteousness through zealous observance of the law.[268]

Conclusion

This study has shown that James D. G. Dunn's thesis that at the Damascus Christophany Paul received only God's call to the gentile mission and that Paul developed his doctrine of justification only in the wake of the Antioch incident in order to defend the gentile believers' right to be included in God's people is untenable. The interpretations of many Pauline statements concerning justification and the law that Dunn advances in support of the thesis or as consequences of the thesis have proved to be highly questionable.

This critical interaction with Dunn's interpretation of the Damascus event has led me to confirm my original thesis that the two elements of the event belong inseparably together: the revelation of the gospel of Jesus, the Christ, Lord, Son of God, and Image of God, and the apostolic call to the gentiles. There were two more elements in the Damascus event: the endowment of the Holy Spirit upon Paul and the revelation of the "mystery" of Rom 11:25-26, the divine plan of salvation concerning the salvation of the gentiles prior to the salvation of the Jews. I came to discover the former only recently from my study on Paul's interpretation of his apostolic call in the light of Isa 42, while the latter was part of my original thesis.[269] These two elements are

---

267. See pp. 141-43.

268. On Rom 9:30–10:4 C. K. Barrett, *Paul: An Introduction to His Thought* (Louisville: Westminster/Knox, 1994), 83, comments: "Thus — in Paul's view — his contemporaries were seeking to establish a righteousness of their own (as Paul himself had done, Phil 3:6, 9) by doing works required by the law." Barrett also appreciates the importance of Paul's evidence for our understanding of first-century Judaism when he says, "He is a rash man, whether Christian scholar or even Jew, who supposes that he understands first-century Judaism and first-century Jewish Christianity better than Paul did" (p. 9; similarly again on p. 78). Cf. also Gundry, "Grace, Works, and Staying Saved," 19; Marshall, "Salvation, Grace and Works," 356-58.

269. Kim, *Origin*, 83-98.

discussed in chapters 3 and 7 respectively of this book. Against Dunn's exclusive stress on Paul's call to the gentile mission, I would conclude that not that element alone but the four elements combined together made a passionate apostle of Christ to the gentiles out of a Pharisee and "zealot" for the law and Judaism.

Paul developed his doctrine of justification by God's grace through faith in Christ without works of the law from his experience of seeing Jesus crucified under the curse of the law as vindicated by God on the Damascus road, that is, from his experience of the revelation of God's righteousness in Christ crucified. The doctrine was born out of his reflection on that revelation in critical interaction with his own Pharisaic devotion to the law for "his own righteousness" and his zeal for the law which had led him to persecute the church. Paul found the doctrine confirmed not only by his experience of the Holy Spirit but also by the teaching and ministry of Jesus.[270] This doctrine, aided by the insights of the Adam-christology/soteriology which is also rooted in the Damascus revelation, provided Paul with the theological justification for his gentile mission. Therefore, the doctrine belongs to the center of Paul's gospel, and it is not a mere tactical maneuver which he developed fifteen to seventeen years after his conversion and call in order to fight the Judaizers in defense of his gentile mission.

Paul presents his doctrine of justification in various ways: in Galatians, faced with the demand of the Judaizers for the gentile Christians' circumcision, he presents it more in terms of obtaining the covenantal status or membership in God's people, although he does not totally neglect the forensic and ethical dimension of it there; in 1 Thessalonians and 1 Cor 6:9-11, where there is no question of the Jew-gentile relationship, he presents the doctrine more in the forensic and ethical sense, with the covenantal sense only in the background;[271] and in Romans he combines both the covenantal sense and the forensic/ethical sense, although the latter seems to come to the fore more than the former. In Galatians, because of the presenting problem there, with the phrase "works of the law" Paul focuses on the Jewish covenant distinctives of circumcision, food laws, and festival days, although even there he broadens its sense to cover observance of all the religious and ethical commandments of the law (see especially Gal 3:10-14). Where he presents the doctrine of justification primarily in the forensic sense, the phrase "works of the law" cannot mean observance only of the

---

270. For a more detailed summary about the development of the doctrine, see above, pp. 42-44.

271. See the next chapter.

Jewish covenant distinctives but of all the religious and ethical commandments of the law. To that extent, the traditional interpretation of the doctrine of justification by grace and through faith without works of the law in
terms of acquittal of sinners by God's grace apart from their own good
works of observing all the religious and ethical commandments of the law
is legitimate. The traditional interpretation may need to be augmented by
the consideration of the fundamental, covenantal dimension of the doctrine of justification which the New Perspectivists stress. It appears that
further work is needed to clarify the relationship between the covenantal
and forensic dimensions of justification.

Using the phrase "works of the law" in the sense of observance of all the
religious and ethical commandments of the law, Paul sets out his doctrine of
justification by grace and through faith without works of the law both in critical reaction to his past Pharisaic attempt to attain "his own" righteousness by
works of the law and in polemical reaction to the Judaizers' attempt to impose the law on the gentile Christians. My examination of Paul's arguments
against the (works of the) law in unfolding his doctrine of justification has
led to the conclusion that Paul, the former Pharisee and "zealot" for the law,
provides an extremely valuable piece of evidence that the Judaism of the first
century A.D. contained an element of works-righteousness within its framework of covenantal nomism.

This is, of course, contrary to the fundamental assumption of the New
Perspective School. With many new inquiries into the Judaism of New Testament times, it is increasingly clear that Sanders's definition of Judaism as
covenantal nomism is in need of correction,[272] and therefore that we cannot
simply elevate it to the status of a dogma, as Dunn and some of his fellow
New Perspectivists have done.[273] The pendulum which had swung too far toward the side of denying any element of works-righteousness in Second Temple Judaism has begun to swing back. When it eventually finds its equilib-
rium, we may see that neither the traditional view of Judaism as a religion of
pure works-righteousness nor the New Perspective that totally denies any element of works-righteousness in Judaism is right, but that Judaism was a cove-

---

272. Cf. the works cited on pp. 143-52 below. See further the important work of M. A.
Elliott, *The Survivors of Israel: A Reconsideration of the Theology of Pre-Christian Judaism* (Grand
Rapids: Eerdmans, 2000); also T. Eskola, *Theodicy and Predestination in Pauline Soteriology*
(WUNT 2/100; Tübingen: Mohr-Siebeck, 1998), esp. 28-60; idem, "Paul, Predestination and
'Covenantal Nomism' — Re-Assessing Paul and Palestinian Judaism," *JSJ* 28 (1997): 390-412.

273. Cf. J. C. Beker, "Echoes and Intertextuality: On the Role of Scripture in Paul's Theology," *Paul and the Scriptures of Israel* (JSNTSup 83; ed. C. A. Evans and J. A. Sanders; Sheffield:
Academic Press, 1993), 68.

nantal nomism with an element of works-righteousness.[274] Paul's data, when studied properly, will make a real contribution to this better understanding of first-century Judaism, as they provide primary and direct evidence.[275]

274. "Synergistic nomism" may be a more accurate definition of the Judaism of Paul's day than "covenantal nomism"; cf. Eskola's two works cited in n. 272 above; also Gundry, "Grace, Works, and Staying Saved," 36; T. Laato, *Paul and Judaism: An Anthropological Approach* (Atlanta: Scholars Press, 1995), 167; D. A. Hagner, "Paul and Judaism. The Jewish Matrix of Early Christianity: Issues in the Current Debate," *BBR* 3 (1993): 122.

275. Although he starts with the presupposition of Sanders's notion of Judaism as a covenantal nomism, H. Räisänen, *Paul and the Law* (WUNT 29; Tübingen: Mohr-Siebeck, 1983; 2nd ed. 1987) recognizes that Paul depicts Judaism as a legalistic religion of works-righteousness. So it may be a credit to him that he does not allow his presupposition of Judaism as a covenantal nomism to lead him to a distortion of Paul's picture of Judaism. The only problem is that he allows the presupposition to lead him to declare that Paul's picture itself is a distortion of Judaism. While he does not unduly force Paul to bear witness to Judaism in accordance with the script of a twentieth-century person — namely Sanders — Räisänen is in effect charging Paul for bearing false witness. With the charge, Räisänen betrays that he has more faith in the twentieth-century scholar's description of first-century Judaism than Paul's witness to it. But C. K. Barrett represents many of us with his counsel that it is not a wise thing to do (above, n. 268). Cf. Kim, *Origin*, 345-58. Alan F. Segal, *Paul the Convert: The Apostolate and Apostasy of Saul the Pharisee* (New Haven: Yale Univ. Press, 1990), 34-71, recognizes Paul as "an important witness" to the experiences of apocalyptic visions of the *kabod Yahweh* on the heavenly throne in the first-century Judaism that later developed into *merkabah* mysticism (quotation from p. 40). We should, likewise, recognize him as an important witness to the element of works-righteousness in first-century Judaism.

CHAPTER 2

Justification by Grace and through Faith in 1 Thessalonians

No Doctrine of Justification in 1 Thessalonians?

While James Dunn dates the formulation of Paul's doctrine of justification to the Antioch incident,[1] some scholars see the doctrine as arising out of the Galatian controversy. But agreeing that the doctrine originated in Paul's struggles with the Judaizers, whether in Antioch or in Galatia, they both tend to see the doctrine only within the context of Paul's defense of his gentile mission. Those who think that the doctrine originated out of the Galatian controversy tend to date Galatians late, shortly before Romans, during the so-called third missionary journey of Paul. One of their pet arguments for this view has been to point to 1 Thessalonians and claim that in that epistle, which they consider to be the first surviving epistle of Paul, the doctrine is absent.[2] Although he sees the doctrine as having originated from the Antioch incident, Dunn also employs this argument.[3] Therefore, an examination of 1 Thessalonians will help us understand better the status and nature of the doctrine as well as its age.

Certainly in 1 Thessalonians there is no discussion about "justification" nor a polemic against the works of the law. However, recently Martin Hengel and Rainer Riesner have shown that the doctrine of justification by grace and

---

1. See p. 3 above.

2. E.g., U. Schnelle, "Der erste Thessalonicherbrief und die Entstehung der paulinischen Anthropologie," *NTS* 32 (1986): 218; J. Becker, *Paulus: Der Apostel der Völker* (Tübingen: Mohr-Siebeck, 1989), 294-50.

3. James D. G. Dunn, *The Epistle to the Galatians* (BNTC; London: Black; Peabody: Hendrickson, 1993), 18-19.

through faith is clearly present in 1 Thessalonians.[4] With them, we must be clear, first of all, about what to expect from 1 Thessalonians. It is only a short letter that Paul hastily composed to ward off the (possible) charge of his having abandoned the church too quickly, to encourage the besieged church, and to deal with some of its specific questions and needs. Paul sent the letter to his converts, who were on good terms with him (1 Thess 3:5; cf. 2 Cor 8:1-4), only a few months after his departure from them, during which time there was no agitation of the Judaizers in their midst. So Paul had no reason in that letter to develop his argument for the doctrine of justification without works of the law, as he did in Galatians and Romans.[5] Nevertheless, there are many signs that the principle of salvation by grace and through faith alone was central to the teaching Paul had imparted to them.

Salvation as Deliverance from the Wrath of God through Christ's Atoning Death

Paul conceives of salvation in terms of deliverance from the wrath of God at the last judgment in the parousia of the Lord Jesus Christ (1:10; 5:9, 23; cf. also 4:6). So it is evident that Paul preached[6] to the Thessalonians the gospel in terms of justification, that is, acquittal at the last judgment. This salvation is based on Christ's death of vicarious atonement, and Paul makes this clear with the death-formula of the traditional kerygma: "For God has not destined us for wrath, but to obtain salvation through *our Lord Jesus Christ, who*

4. M. Hengel and A. M. Schwemer, *Paul between Damascus and Antioch* (Louisville: Westminster/Knox, 1997), 301-10; R. Riesner, *Paul's Early Period: Chronology, Mission Strategy, Theology* (Grand Rapids: Eerdmans, 1998), 394-403.

5. Writing to the Roman Christians at the conclusion of his mission in the eastern hemisphere of the Roman Empire in order to woo their support for his mission into Spain (Rom 15:14-33), Paul felt it necessary to introduce his gospel to them fully in order to dispel any misunderstanding of or mistrust in him that some of them might have because of his controversies with the Judaizers in the east. His impending journey to Jerusalem and the prospect of a conference with the leaders of the Jerusalem church also led him to use the occasion of writing Romans as a rehearsal of his presentation for the conference. These circumstances required him to expound in Romans his gospel in terms of justification *sola gratia/fide* and without works of the law. This view does not necessarily deny that part of the purpose of Romans may also have been to help the Christians in Rome with their practical problems arising, e.g., from the Jew-gentile relationship. Cf. K. P. Donfried, ed., *The Romans Debate* (rev. ed.; Peabody: Hendrickson, 1991).

6. In 1 Thess 4:6 Paul says that he "already told and forewarned" (προείπαμεν . . . καὶ διεμαρτυράμεθα) the Thessalonians about the Lord being ἔκδικος, one who metes out just punishment, at the last judgment.

86

died for us" (5:9-10; cf. also 4:14).[7] In 1 Cor 15:1-5, where Paul cites the full version of the traditional kerygma as the "gospel," he indicates that faith is the means whereby we avail ourselves of the salvation in Christ's death and resurrection. Paul suggests this also in 1 Thess 4:14: εἰ γὰρ πιστεύομεν ὅτι Ἰησοῦς ἀπέθανεν καὶ ἀνέστη, οὕτως καὶ ὁ θεὸς τοὺς κοιμηθέντας διὰ τοῦ Ἰησοῦ ἄξει σὺν αὐτῷ.

Here is a grammatical anomaly, in that the protasis is a conditional clause, but the apodosis starts with a comparative and inferential conjunction. This anomaly seems to result from many thoughts being compressed. The protasis with εἰ clearly states a reality rather than a hypothetical condition;[8] yet it is formulated as a conditional clause in order to invite the readers to identify themselves with the confession once more.[9] The protasis is a *pistis*-formula (to believe + the clause stating Christ's death and resurrection as the saving event — cf. 1 Cor 15:3-5).[10] But the use of the name "Jesus" instead of "Christ" and the verb ἀνέστη instead of ἐγήγερται both seem to suggest that here Paul is citing a credal formula older than 1 Cor 15:3-5. Even so, the older formula also must have contained a phrase expressing the atoning effect of Jesus' death, because as a form of the *pistis*-formula it must have made clear why Jesus' death and resurrection was the eschatological saving event. First Thessalonians 5:9-10 suggests that at least Paul so understood it. Then he must be abbreviating the old confession to the bare facts of Jesus' death and resurrection in order to make it directly relevant to the subject under discussion: the death and resurrection of believers.[11] ὅτι Ἰησοῦς ἀπέθανεν καὶ ἀνέστη or its fuller version in 1 Cor 15:3b-5 is the essence of the "gospel" (1 Cor 15:1-3a). Acceptance of this gospel preached is "faith." Hence πιστεύειν is used in connection with the gospel. "Faith" as acceptance of this "gospel" preached actualizes the objective saving event proclaimed in the "gospel," and so it is the means of availing ourselves of Christ's atoning death. Note also how by having "God" as the subject in the inferential and comparative apodosis Paul gives away his unexpressed assumption in the protasis that behind Jesus' death and resurrection God was at work. Thus, 1 Thess 4:14 implies the usual Pauline thoughts that God sent Christ to be the atonement for our sins

7. Paul's own testimony in 1 Cor 1:17-25; 2:1-5 suggests that during his Thessalonian mission he concentrated on preaching "Christ crucified." Cf. Riesner, *Paul's Early Period,* 402.

8. Cf. Blass-Debrunner-Rehkopf, 372. 1.

9. So T. Holtz, *Der erste Brief an die Thessalonicher* (EKKNT; Zürich: Benziger/ Neukirchen: Neukirchener, 1990), 190.

10. Cf. W. Kramer, *Christ, Lord, Son of God* (London: SCM, 1966), 19-64.

11. Cf. C. Wanamaker, *The Epistles to the Thessalonians* (NIGTC; Grand Rapids: Eerdmans, 1990), 168.

(Rom 3:25-26; 4:25; 2 Cor 5:21; etc.), that "God who raised the Lord (Jesus) will also raise us up" (1 Cor 6:14; similarly also 2 Cor 4:14), and that by believing these we obtain God's salvation in Christ.[12]

Therefore, 1 Thess 1:10; 4:14; 5:9-10, 23 contain basically the same thought as the classical expression in Rom 3:24-26 of Paul's gospel of justification by faith in Christ's atoning death.

God's Sovereign Initiative and Grace

Further, Paul emphasizes that salvation is God's work from start to finish. "God has destined us . . . to obtain salvation through our Lord Jesus Christ who died for us" (5:9-10). God not only has provided the means of salvation, namely the atoning death and resurrection of Christ, but he has also predestined us to appropriate that salvation in Christ. God has chosen us (1:4) and called us "into his kingdom and glory" (2:12; cf. also 4:7). The divine election and call are out of his love (1:4). Thus, Paul stresses God's sovereign initiative and grace for our salvation. Paul speaks of the life of God's elect people in terms of sanctification. It requires their efforts for moral rectitude (4:3-4), but it is grounded on God's call and dependent on his continual provision of "his Holy Spirit" (4:7-8). Paul concludes his letter with a reassuring affirmation of the perseverance of the saints: "He who calls you is faithful, and he will do it," that is, God who is faithful will go on sanctifying his elect and preserve them blameless to the last judgment at the parousia of the Lord Jesus Christ (5:23-24; cf. also 3:12-13).[13]

Not by Works of the Law but by the Holy Spirit

In 4:1-8 Paul reminds the Thessalonians of the "commands" he imparted to them for a life of pleasing God, the "commands" which he imparted διὰ τοῦ κυρίου Ἰησοῦ, that is, with the authority of the Lord Jesus, as they were in fact the Lord's commands which he as his apostle represented (vv. 1-2). Then, setting forth "the will of God" in terms of their "sanctification," he strongly urges the Thessalonian Christians to abstain from sexual immorality, in which their idolatrous heathen neighbors are engaged (vv. 3-6a). He re-

---

12. Cf. Hengel and Schwemer, *Paul between Damascus and Antioch*, 305.

13. Cf. E. Best, *The First and Second Epistles to the Thessalonians* (BNC; London: Black, 1972), 149-50, for an appropriate comment on 1 Thess 3:12-13.

inforces this exhortation by reminding them of God's call for sanctification and of his judgment and still further by warning that anyone who disregards his commands really disregards God (vv. 6b-8).

This passage clearly implies that Paul no longer considers "the will of God" in terms of the Torah but in terms of the commands of the Lord Jesus which he represents as his apostle. Romans 2:18 shows that Paul is aware of the fundamental Jewish understanding that the will of God is defined in terms of the Torah. Further, what Paul presents here as "the will of God" revealed in the Lord Jesus is in fact what the Torah teaches as "the will of God." Yet Paul does not refer to the Torah but emphatically appeals to "the Lord Jesus." This clearly suggests the assumption that Christ has superseded the Torah as the means of the revelation of "the will of God" (cf. Rom 10:4). Therefore, it is implied that Christians no longer live a life of pleasing God by Torah observance. Even if the Christian way of life that pleases God involves in reality observance of the injunctions that the Torah also issues, it is not perceived as doing works of the law but a "new obedience"[14] enabled by the Holy Spirit (4:8). Thus, 4:1-8 implicitly contains the Pauline theses expounded in length in Galatians and Romans: Christ has superseded the Torah, and the Christian life of pleasing God is not Torah observance (which is doing the "works of the law") but obeying "the law of Christ" (Gal 6:2; cf. 1 Cor 9:21) through the power of the Holy Spirit (Rom 8:1-17).

This is made clearer by the echo of Ezek 36:26-27; 37:6, 14 in 4:8,[15] as those Ezekiel texts form, together with Jer 31:31-34, the scriptural basis for Paul's Spirit-law and Spirit-flesh antitheses in Rom 8; 2 Cor 3; and Gal 5.[16] In Ezek 36:27 the Spirit is promised for the age of the new covenant in order to enable perfect obedience to the law. But in our Thessalonians passage the Spirit is suggested as the agent of sanctification against fornication, lustful passion, defrauding, and impurity, yet without any reference to the law. Indeed, there is no reference to the law in the whole epistle of 1 Thessalonians. From this fact, Volker Rabens infers an indirect intimation of Paul's Spirit-law and Spirit-flesh antitheses here.[17] If so, 1 Thess 4:1-8 indirectly intimates

14. A term taken from E. Käsemann, "Gottesgerechtigkeit bei Paulus," in *Exegetische Versuche und Besinnungen.* vol. 2 (2d ed.; Göttingen: Vandenhoeck, 1965), 184; cf. J. M. G. Barclay, *Obeying the Truth: Paul's Ethics in Galatians* (Studies of the New Testament and Its World; Edinburgh: T & T Clark, 1988; Minneapolis: Fortress, 1991), 214-15.

15. E.g., Holtz, *Thessalonicher,* 167; I. H. Marshall, *First and Second Thessalonians* (NCBC; Grand Rapids: Eerdmans, 1983), 114; M. M. B. Turner, *The Holy Spirit and Spiritual Gifts* (rev. ed.; Peabody: Hendrickson, 1998), 109.

16. See pp. 158-63 below.

17. V. Rabens, "The Development of Pauline Pneumatology," *BZ* 43 (1999): 178-79. See below, pp. 155-63.

also Paul's doctrine of justification. For the Spirit-law and Spirit-flesh antitheses are essential building blocks of Paul's doctrine of justification.

Paul's Initial Preaching (1:9b-10)

In 1:9b-10 Paul summarizes the report of the conversion of the Thessalonian Christians that circulates in Macedonia and Achaia: καὶ πῶς ἐπεστρέψατε πρὸς τὸν θεὸν ἀπὸ τῶν εἰδώλων δουλεύειν θεῷ ζῶντι καὶ ἀληθινῷ καὶ ἀναμένειν τὸν υἱὸν αὐτοῦ ἐκ τῶν οὐρανῶν, ὃν ἤγειρεν ἐκ [τῶν] νεκρῶν. Ἰησοῦν τὸν ῥυόμενον ἡμᾶς ἐκ τῆς ὀργῆς τῆς ἐρχομένης.

Some critics think that Paul is here quoting a pre-Pauline baptismal hymn[18] or missionary preaching.[19] For this view, they point to the fact that the language is very strongly colored by the Old Testament/Judaism, especially Hellenistic Judaism; that many words are unusual in Paul: ἐπιστρέφειν, θεὸς ζῶν καὶ ἀληθινός, ἀναμένειν, ῥύεσθαι, also δουλεύειν; that Paul usually speaks of serving the Lord rather than God; that there are close affinities with Paul's sermons in Acts 14:15-17 (ἀπὸ τούτων τῶν ματαίων ἐπιστρέφειν ἐπὶ θεὸν ζῶντα) and 17:22-31 (cf. also Heb 6:1-2); and that there is no characteristic Pauline emphasis on *theologia crucis*.[20]

But Holtz argues that great differences among Acts 14:15-17; 17:22-31; 1 Thess 1:9-10; and Heb 6:1-2 make it difficult to speak of a common schema underlying them all, let alone a fixed formula.[21] Then how un-Pauline are those words cited above? Second Corinthians 3:16 and Gal 4:9 show that Paul himself could have used ἐπιστρέφειν after the Hellenistic Jewish usage for conversion to God (cf. *Jos. Asen.* 54:10; *T. Zeb.* 9:8; *T. Jud.* 23:5; *T. Iss.* 6:3).[22] Θεὸς ζῶν καὶ ἀληθινός, the biblically well-established expression effectively used especially in the context of rejecting pagan idolatry,[23] could most naturally have suggested itself to Paul in his call for the gentiles to turn away from the "so-called gods and lords" (1 Cor 8:5) and "dumb idols" (1 Cor 12:2) toward the God who has so convincingly revealed himself in Jesus Christ as the living and real God. How else could Paul have compared God and idols? The

18. G. Friedrich, "Ein Tauflied hellenistischer Judenchristen," *TZ* 21 (1965): 502-16.

19. U. Wilckens, *Die Missionsreden der Apostelgeschichte* (WMANT 5; Neukirchen: Neukirchener, 1974), 81-91.

20. See Best, *Thessalonians*, 85-87.

21. Holtz, *Thessalonicher*, 55; also Wanamaker, *Thessalonians*, 85.

22. See Holtz, *Thessalonicher*, 58; also Wanamaker, *Thessalonians*, 85.

23. For the biblical and Jewish references, see Best, *Thessalonians*, 82; Holtz, *Thessalonicher*, 58-59.

connection of δουλεύειν with θεὸς ζῶν καὶ ἀληθινός as its object here was clearly dictated by the preceding phrase of the Thessalonians "turning to God," which was the most natural way of speaking about gentiles' conversion to God. Had "the Lord Jesus Christ" stood here instead of "God" as the object of the δουλεύειν, it would have been very awkward. In fact, Paul's language and ideas in Gal 4:8-9 are quite similar to those in our formulation. Ἀνα-μένειν is a *hapax legomenon* in the New Testament, and while the Hellenistic Jewish literature (e.g., *Jos. Asen.; T. 12 Patr.*) prefers ῥύεσθαι to σῴζειν, not just Paul but the New Testament as a whole prefers σῴζειν and seldom uses ῥύεσθαι.[24] So the appearance of the two words here does not necessarily speak for the origin of our formulation from a certain quarter in the New Testament Christianity outside the Pauline. In fact, Paul would not be happy if we exegete ῥύεσθαι in Rom 7:24 only in a non-eschatological sense and insist that its meaning is essentially different from what the word means in our formulation. By quoting Isa 59:20 in Rom 11:26 Paul speaks of Christ as coming as the eschatological deliverer (ὁ ῥυόμενος) in a way rather similar to what he says here in 1 Thess 1:10 (cf. also Col 1:13). In fact, the idea of deliverance from "the wrath of God" at the last judgment must be considered as typically Pauline. The other words and ideas in our formulation are also well attested in Paul. Galatians 4:8-9 shows that Paul was quite capable of speaking of the conversion (ἐπιστρέφειν) of gentiles from serving (δουλεύειν) false gods (τοῖς φύσει μὴ οὖσιν θεοῖς) to serving the real God without any reference to the cross of Christ (cf. also Rom 1:18–2:16).

Thus, there is no basis for emphasizing the un-Pauline character of the language and ideas of our formulation. This examination confirms only two things: (1) the statement about gentiles' conversion strongly reflects the language of Hellenistic Judaism (cf. *Jos. Asen.* 54:5-10 [= 11:10-11]). (2) Gal 4:8-9 and to some extent also 1 Cor 8:5-6 + 12:2 and Rom 1:18–2:16 corroborate the idea in our passage that Paul himself did have a call for conversion from idols to the real God at the center of his missionary preaching among gentiles. Thus, in Acts 14:15-17; 17:22-31 Luke may have faithfully recounted the gist of Paul's actual sermons. Even if he has composed the sermons himself, he has composed them in a way everybody, Paul included, would have preached in the given situations. Hence the affinities between the passages in Acts, on the one hand, and our passage and the other Pauline passages, on the other hand.

So we conclude that 1 Thess 1:9b-10 echoes a central aspect of Paul's preaching among the gentiles in Thessalonica and elsewhere, and that to-

24. Cf. Holtz, *Thessalonicher,* 59 n. 193.

gether with Gal 4:8-9; 1 Cor 8:5-6 + 12:2; Rom 1:18–2:16 it shows that this aspect of Paul's preaching retained some important elements of the Hellenistic Jewish language and ideas. Of course, 1 Thess 1:9b-10 represents the whole picture of Paul's preaching no more than Gal 4:8-9; 1 Cor 8:5-6; 12:2; or Rom 1:18–2:16 does. As 1 Thess 4:14 and 5:9-10 show, salvation through the death and resurrection of Jesus Christ stood at the center of his preaching in Thessalonica, just as the rest of Galatians, 1 Corinthians, and Romans indicate that he preached *theologia crucis* in Galatia, Corinth, and elsewhere. However, in 1 Thess 1:9b-10 he presents a summary of only that aspect of his preaching, namely a call for conversion from idolatry to the real God to be assured of the eschatological redemption through his Son, because apparently that aspect had excited the Thessalonian believers the most so as to become the talking-point among the people of Macedonia, Achaia, and elsewhere (1 Thess 1:8-9a).

The first result of their conversion was that they came to "serve the living and true God." The second result was that they came to have a strong hope for the eschatological redemption through God's Son. Here the "Son" of God is identified (1) with "Jesus," (2) as the one "whom [God] raised from the dead," (3) as the one who will come again "from heaven," and (4) as the one "who will deliver us from the coming wrath." This description presupposes an understanding of Jesus provided by, for example, Rom 1:3-4; 1 Cor 15:24-28; Phil 2:9-11; 3:20-21. By raising him from the dead God has exalted Jesus to sit at his right hand in heaven and thus installed him as his Son ("heir") (cf. Heb 1:2-3; Rev 3:21).[25]

How does Paul think Jesus will deliver us from God's wrath? It is a merit of I. Howard Marshall to ask this question and try to answer it in reference to 1 Thess 5:9-10 and Rom 5:9.[26] First Thessalonians 5:9-10 shows Paul linking Jesus' deliverance of us from God's wrath to his vicarious death for us. How can Jesus' death bring about our redemption from God's wrath? In Rom 5:9 Paul answers: his atoning death brings about our justification in the present, which will be confirmed at the last judgment so that "we shall be saved through him from the wrath." We may safely assume that in proclaiming his gospel (1 Thess 1:5), which is partly echoed in 1:9b-10, he included in it at least the thought of 1 Thess 5:9-10. Did he also elaborate the thought as in Rom 5:9? Pointing to the absence of the righteousness/justification language

25. Cf. Best, *Thessalonians*, 83; Marshall, *Thessalonians*, 59; also M. Hengel, " 'Sit at My Right Hand!' The Enthronement of Christ at the Right Hand of God and Psalm 110:1," in *Studies in Early Christology* (Edinburgh: T & T Clark, 1995), 119-225.
26. Marshall, *Thessalonians*, 59.

in 1 Thessalonians, many critics would deny this. But then how else would he have explained the link between Jesus' death of vicarious atonement and our deliverance from God's wrath at the last judgment, which is after all an act of "justification"?

It is interesting that in 1:9b-10 Paul uses the christological title "Son" of God in connection with deliverance from God's wrath at the last judgment. Paul usually connects the title "Lord" to the themes of the exaltation and parousia of Christ,[27] and in this letter also he is shortly to explain the parousia of the "Lord" (4:13–5:11; cf. also 3:13; 5:23). If 1:9b-10 presupposes the exalted Christ's sitting at the right hand of God in heaven, as suggested above, the title "Lord" would have been more natural here because that title stands in Ps 110:1, the scriptural basis on which all the references to Christ's sitting at the right hand of God are made in the New Testament. But why is the "Son" of God used here?[28] This question calls for a comparison with Gal 4:4-5; Rom 7:24–8:4; 8:31-39; and 1:2-4, 9 + 16-17.[29]

In Gal 4:4-5 Paul speaks of God having "sent forth his Son . . . in order to redeem [ἐξαγοράσῃ] those who are under the law." This redemption refers to the "redemption from the curse of the law" (ἐξηγόρασεν ἐκ τῆς κατάρας τοῦ νόμου) which Christ has wrought by bearing the curse of the law vicariously for us on the cross (Gal 3:13). Since "the curse of the law" is none other than the expression of or the basis for the wrath of God, redemption from the curse of the law is deliverance (ῥύεσθαι) from the wrath of God. In Rom 7:24–8:4 Paul has the natural human being enslaved to the law of sin cry out in desperation, "Who will deliver [ῥύσεται] me from this body of death?" Then Paul answers that God has wrought the deliverance through Jesus Christ. God did this by sending his Son to bear in his body the condemnation (κατάκριμα) for our sins on our behalf. The result of this saving act of God in his Son is liberation from condemnation, that is, deliverance from the wrath of God. Thus, as in Gal 4:4-5 so also in Rom 7:24–8:4 Paul presents the Son of God as the agent of God's work of deliverance from his wrath.

Having expressed at the climax of his exposition of the gospel of justification his certainty of the consummation of salvation ("glorification") of those whom God has predestined, called, and justified (Rom 8:28-30), Paul shouts defiantly in Rom 8:31-39, "If God is for us, who is against us?" "Who shall bring any charge against God's elect?" and "Who is to condemn?" To negate

---

27. Kramer, *Christ, Lord, Son of God*, 65ff., 173ff.

28. See below, p. 195.

29. The comparison will show that the title "Son of God" is an essential component of the statement in 1 Thess 1:10, not a secondary one (contra Kramer, *Christ, Lord, Son of God*, 126).

these absolutely, Paul first refers to God's love: "He who has not spared his Son but gave him up for us all, will he not also give us all things with him?" Second, Paul refers to the fact that the God who has elected us is the judge who declares us righteous. Third, Paul refers to the work of Christ (v. 34): Χριστὸς ['Ιησοῦς] ὁ ἀποθανών, μᾶλλον δὲ ἐγερθείς, ὃς καί ἐστιν ἐν δεξιᾷ τοῦ θεοῦ, ὃς καὶ ἐντυγχάνει ὑπὲρ ἡμῶν. Christ died for our sins and so made atonement for them, so that no one can condemn us. Furthermore, he was raised victorious over all the evil forces, and he is sitting at the right hand of God as God's pleni-potentiary (= God's Son). It is he who intercedes for us, so that even if anybody brings any charge against us, there will be no condemnation for us. Then, fi-nally, Paul powerfully affirms that no person or thing can separate us from the love of Christ or the love of God in Christ (vv. 35-39).

For the reference to Christ's resurrection and sitting at the right hand of God (μᾶλλον δὲ ἐγερθείς, ὃς καί ἐστιν ἐν δεξιᾷ τοῦ θεοῦ) in verse 34, the title "Lord" or "Son of God" would have been more fitting. The analogies of Gal 4:4-5 and Rom 7:24–8:4 suggest that in this context of speaking about deliv-erance from condemnation, the title "Son of God" could have been used. But instead the title "Christ" is used here because that title is firmly fixed in the death formula (Χριστὸς ['Ιησοῦς] ὁ ἀποθανών).[30] However, since verse 34 is a continuation of the thought in verse 32 (ὃς γε τοῦ ἰδίου υἱοῦ οὐκ ἐφείσατο ἀλλὰ ὑπὲρ ἡμῶν πάντων παρέδωκεν αὐτόν), we may assume that in verse 34 Paul thinks of Christ as having wrought atonement or redemption for us as the Son of God (as in Gal 4:4-5 and Rom 7:24–8:4) and as having been ex-alted as the Son of God to sit "at the right hand of God" (cf. Rom 1:3-4; 1 Cor 15:24-28). Here, therefore, Paul is affirming that Christ as the Son of God de-livers us from condemnation through the intercession he offers for us at the right hand of God (vv. 34c-e; cf. Heb 4:14-16), as well as through the atone-ment he wrought on the cross (vv. 32a, 34b; cf. Rom 3:24-26; 4:25). While the latter is the same thought as in Gal 4:4-5 and Rom 7:24–8:4, the former is an additional thought. With it Paul seems to be making our justification at the last judgment doubly secure.

The two elements (atonement and intercession) of the Son's work of de-livering us from God's wrath or condemnation which are suggested in Rom 8:34 seem to be implicitly assumed also in 1 Thess 1:10.[31] If the reference to the death of the Son of God in the context of speaking about deliverance from God's wrath here leads us to interpret 1 Thess 1:10 in connection with Rom 8:32a + 34b as well as Gal 4:4-5, Rom 7:24–8:4 and 1 Thess 5:9-10, the picture

30. Cf. Kramer, *Christ, Lord, Son of God,* 26ff.
31. Cf. Hengel, "Sit at My Right Hand!" 159.

94

of the Son of God sitting at the right hand of God, which is implied here, leads us to interpret our verse in connection with Rom 8:34c-e. At the last judgment in his parousia, the Son of God will deliver us from God's wrath not only on the basis of the atonement he wrought on the cross, but also through his active intercession for us. Since in our verse the reference to the death of the Son of God is only oblique and not emphasized, the element of his intercession comprises the main focus while the element of his atonement remains in the background.

Since Christ as the Son of God delivers us from condemnation or the wrath of God through his self-sacrifice on the cross for our atonement and through his intercession at the right hand of God at the last judgment, Paul likes to define or summarize his gospel in terms of the Son of God.[32] So his gospel concerns the Son of David who has been installed as the Son of God at God's right hand through his resurrection (Rom 1:3-4, 9), and this gospel is the good news of God's justification of sinners or God's deliverance of sinners from his wrath (Rom 1:16-18; 3:21-26; 5:1-11; etc.).[33] There is a sort of *inclusio* between introducing the gospel in this way in Rom 1:3-4, 9 + 16-18 and concluding his exposition of the gospel in terms of the Son of God who delivers us from condemnation in Rom 8:31-39. Having found that the gospel Paul preached to the Thessalonians (1 Thess 1:5), namely, the gospel of the Son of God who will deliver us from God's wrath (1 Thess 1:10), is essentially the same as the gospel preached in Rom 7:24–8:4; 8:31-39; 1:3-4 + 16-18; Gal 1:16; 4:4-5, we may now claim that Paul preached to the Thessalonians the same gospel as to the Romans and the Galatians, namely the gospel of justification by grace.

Observing the close similarity between Paul's gospel echoed in 1 Thess 1:9b-10 and the Hellenistic Jewish conversion preaching, Peter Stuhlmacher notes the three essential differences between them, one of which is: whereas in the latter monotheism is tied to the Torah, especially to the first commandment as the summary of the whole Torah, in the former there is no reference to the Torah.[34] It is indeed remarkable that Paul, the former Pharisee and "zealot" for the law (Gal 1:13; Phil 3:6), speaks about the gentiles' conversion to and service of God without any reference to the Torah and circumcision. It is astonishing that such a Paul should speak about the deliver-

---

32. Cf. Seyoon Kim, *The Origin of Paul's Gospel* (WUNT 2/4; Tübingen: Mohr-Siebeck, 1981, 1984; Grand Rapids: Eerdmans, 1982), 132-36.

33. See ibid., 132-33, for the unity of the two definitions of the gospel in Rom 1 (vv. 3-4, 9 and vv. 16-17).

34. P. Stuhlmacher, *Das paulinische Evangelium: I. Vorgeschichte* (FRLANT 95; Göttingen: Vandenhoeck, 1968), 261-62.

ance from God's wrath at the last judgment without any reference to the Torah but with the emphatic reference to Jesus the Son of God. This is in line with what we observed above in connection with 1 Thess 4:1-8. This fact suggests that the principle of *solus Christus* for justification had already been well established in Paul's formulation of the gospel. It in turn implies that Paul had renounced his former Pharisaic view of the Torah as the means for human beings' proper relationship to God and that he had come to a negative judgment on the Jewish conception of proper relationship to God as governed by the Torah.

By Faith Alone

With this Paul's emphasis on "faith" in 1 Thessalonians fits perfectly. We have already noted from 1 Thess 4:14 and 5:9-10 that to the Thessalonians as to others (Rom 3:24-26; 1 Cor 15:1-5; Gal 2:16-21; etc.) Paul taught that faith was the means whereby they were to appropriate Christ's atoning death proclaimed in the gospel. Faith is clearly regarded as acceptance of the gospel or the preached word of God (1:5-8; 2:13). Appreciating this as "a good 'Lutheran Reformation' stamp," Martin Hengel notes the significant fact that the term πίστις appears eight times in 1 Thessalonians (1:3, 8; 3:2, 5, 6, 7, 10; 5:8), while it appears only seven times each in 1 and 2 Corinthians and five times in Philippians.[35] In most of these cases the reference is made to "your faith" (ἡ πίστις ὑμῶν) (1:8; 3:2, 5, 6, 7, 10). The Thessalonians are defined simply as "you, the believers" (ὑμῖν τοῖς πιστεύουσιν) (2:10, 13), and they are said to have become an example "to all the believers" (πᾶσιν τοῖς πιστεύουσιν) in Macedonia and Achaia (1:7). All these facts indicate that faith is regarded as the determinative factor for the Thessalonians' Christian existence. This surely reflects the fact that Paul "wrote into the heart of the

---

35. Hengel and Schwemer, *Paul between Damascus and Antioch*, 304-5. From this prevalence of "faith" in the Thessalonian correspondence (cf. also 2 Thess 1:3-4, 10, 11; 2:13), Dunn, *The Theology of Paul*, 371-72, also concludes that teaching faith as the means of appropriating salvation offered in the gospel "was already a fundamental feature of [Paul's] message, quite apart from the dispute over 'works of the law.'" However, he immediately adds, "But then the issue of 'works of the law' emerged in the internal Christian dispute over the terms on which the gospel could be offered to Gentiles. And in that dispute the classic antithesis was formed: 'no human being is justified by works of the law but only through faith in Jesus Christ' (Gal 2.16)." So Dunn again tries to persuade us to believe that Paul, the former Pharisee and "zealot" for the law, emphatically taught faith as the means of appropriating salvation in Christ without having considered its relationship to the Sinai system of the covenant and the law. I find it difficult to believe this.

community what faith is and what it is based on during the brief stay when he brought it into being."[36]

Thus, 1 Thessalonians contains all the elements of Paul's doctrine of justification: predestinarian election of grace, Christ's atonement and intercession, deliverance from God's wrath at the last judgment, the appropriation of the gospel through faith, a life of sanctification according to the Holy Spirit, and the perseverance of the saints,[37] except the actual terminology of δικαιοῦν/δικαιοσύνη (but cf. 2 Thess 1:5-10). But there is no reference to the Torah, and its absence is especially striking in those contexts (1 Thess 1:9-10; 4:1-8) where the subject matters treated would have naturally led a person with a background of "zealotic" Pharisaism to refer to the Torah.

The Absence of the Terminology "Righteousness/Justification"

The absence of the terminology "righteousness/justification" has led many to the view that Paul developed his doctrine of justification subsequent to his writing 1 Thessalonians and in the situation of struggle with the Judaizers in Antioch and Galatia. But did the struggle with the Judaizers in Antioch and Galatia lead Paul to *coin* the terminology of "righteousness/ justification" *for the first time* to express restoration to a proper relationship to God through his acquittal? Or did it only help him sharpen the issue of whether for that restoration only faith in Christ was necessary or the works of the law were also necessary? In Paul's and Luke's accounts of the Antiochian conflict and in Galatians there is nothing to indicate the former. It would be a strange thesis that Paul began to use the central Old Testament-Jewish term "righteousness/justification" for the first time in his struggle with the Judaizers. Given the Old Testament-Jewish background, it would be equally strange if in speaking of Christians' deliverance from God's wrath at the last judgment (1 Thess 1:10; 5:9-10) and also of the Lord as ἔκδικος (1 Thess 4:6, one who metes out ἐκδίκησις, 2 Thess 1:8) Paul did not use the very appropriate Old Testament-Jewish term. So it seems that the absence of the terminology "righteousness/justification" in 1 Thessalonians is due to the fact that in the epistle Paul did not feel a particular need to use the term itself explicitly. "Justification" is not the only Pauline soteriological category which is not terminologically referred to in the epistle; some other

36. Hengel and Schwemer, *Paul between Damascus and Antioch*, 305.
37. Cf. ibid., 307.

soteriological terms such as "adoption," "reconciliation," and "new creation" are not mentioned either. Paul did not refer to them because he had no need to do so in the short letter which he wrote with specific purposes other than that of expounding his gospel.

Conclusion and Corollaries

At any rate, from our discussion so far we can safely conclude that the doctrine of justification by grace and through faith is materially present in 1 Thessalonians as a whole and implicitly contained in the echo of Paul's gospel preaching in 1:9b-10. From the teaching on the doctrine of justification contained in the epistle we can draw some significant corollaries concerning that doctrine.

(1) First Thessalonians is not to be used as evidence for the view that the doctrine was a late development or that it was not central for Paul's theology.

(2) The gospel was preached in terms of that doctrine even where there was no question of controversy with the Judaizers or defense of Paul's gentile mission.

(3) Justification is understood first and foremost as God's forensic act of acquittal at the last judgment (deliverance from God's wrath).[38] Certainly the Thessalonian Christians who have been saved or justified are God's elect people (1 Thess 1:4), the people whom God "calls into his own kingdom and glory" (2:12), "the ἐκκλησία . . . in God the Father and the Lord Jesus Christ" (1:1). But no direct connection is made between justification and obtaining membership in God's people. Thus, the pet theory of the New Perspectivists that emphasizes the meaning of justification as obtaining membership in God's people at the expense of its forensic meaning is not supported.

(4) In 1 Thess 4:1-8 we have observed how the Torah is implicitly replaced with the Lord Jesus Christ in connection with "the will of God" and again how obedience to the Torah is implicitly replaced with obedience to the Holy Spirit in connection with moral requirements for sanctification. This suggests that when Paul sets "works of the law" in contrast to faith in Christ in his explicit formulation of the justification doctrine he refers by the former not just to the identity markers of the Jews as God's covenant people but to all the requirements of the law, including the moral requirements.

(5) While everywhere Paul presented his gospel in the category of justifi-

38. Cf. Hengel and Schwemer, *Paul between Damascus and Antioch*, 307.

cation by grace and through faith as well as in other categories, he did not feel the need to expound the doctrine of justification apologetically unless his gospel was challenged by the Judaizers. In the controversies with the Judaizers, however, he not only had to expound the doctrine and substantiate it scripturally, but especially had to defend it against the requirement of works of the law. This was what happened in Galatians and Romans (cf. also Phil 3). But in Thessalonica he did not face the challenge of the Judaizers, and so he went about preaching the gospel to the gentiles there in his usual way or in the way adapted to their needs. So Paul's gospel reflected in 1 Thessalonians must be appreciated not only as a specimen of the early version of his gospel, but also as a specimen of the version of the gospel that he preached to the gentiles when there was no controversy with the Judaizers. It is particularly significant to find out that this specimen is clearly centered on the doctrine of justification by grace and through faith.

Appendix: Justification in the Corinthian Correspondence

We can say similar things about 1 and 2 Corinthians. Although there is neither exposition nor defense of the doctrine of justification in those epistles, there are many signs that Paul preached the gospel in terms of justification by grace and through faith (e.g., 1 Cor 1:30; 6:9-11; 10:16-17; 11:23-26; 15:3-5; 2 Cor 3:1–4:6; 5:10, 14-21),[39] applying its principle also to the critique of the Corinthians' typically Hellenistic view of wisdom/knowledge as the means of salvation (see especially 1 Cor 1–4).[40] The doctrine is not *unfolded* in the Corinthian correspondence because in Corinth it was not challenged by the Judaizers. The frequent argument for the late development of the doctrine on the basis that it is not expounded in the Corinthians correspondence and in 1 Thessalonians ignores not only those many signs of the doctrine in the Corinthian correspondence, but also the fact that Paul wrote Romans in Corinth at the conclusion of the Corinthian controversies, which are reflected in the Corinthian correspondence. It is scarcely imaginable that, having had no well-thought-out doctrine of justification during the period of the Corinthian correspondence, Paul suddenly and miraculously developed it instantly when writing Romans in Corinth at the conclusion of

39. See pp. 67-70 above for an exposition of the doctrine of justification present in 1 Cor 6:9-11 as well as for the similarities between 1 Thess 4:1-8 and 1 Cor 6:9-11.

40. Cf. P. Stuhlmacher, *Biblische Theologie des Neuen Testaments*, vol. 1 (Göttingen: Vandenhoeck, 1992), 333-34.

the Corinthian conflicts. The nature of the issues in the Corinthian conflicts explains quite well why Paul did not feel the need to expound the doctrine of justification in the Corinthian correspondence in the way he did in Galatians and Romans.[41]

41. Cf. the wise observations of Hengel and Schwemer, *Paul between Damascus and Antioch:* "The differences [of Romans] from I and II Corinthians generally are striking, although he is writing to the Romans from Corinth, and he had difficulty enough in resolving the problems there. Here in particular the fronts in the community which he had founded had been quite different, and in his letters Paul was always deliberately concerned to address quite specific problems in the community. They are far removed from the abstract theological treatises" (p. 302); similarly again: "it is important to reflect that in all the letters Paul always goes into the special questions and needs of those whom he is addressing. He is anything but a rigid 'dogmatic' theologian, and therefore he can present the same message, the gospel entrusted to him, with rich and varied metaphors and from different aspects, depending on the situation" (p. 308). See also pp. 66-70 above.

CHAPTER 3

Isaiah 42 and Paul's Call

It is widely recognized that in Gal 1:15-16 Paul alludes primarily to Isa 49:1, 6, and secondarily also to Jer 1:5, and so the scholarly consensus is that here Paul interprets his Damascus call in the light of the calls of the Servant of the Lord, Ebed Yahweh, and the prophet Jeremiah.[1] This is no doubt true in view of the close verbal agreements between Gal 1:15-16 and the Old Testament texts: καλεῖν (= Isa 49:1, 6; cf. τίθημι in Jer 1:5; 1 Cor 12:28); ἐκ κοιλίας μητρός μου (= Isa 49:1; cf. Jer 1:5); ἐν τοῖς ἔθνεσιν (= Isa 49:6; Jer 1:5). Since Gal 1:24 seems to allude to Isa 49:3 and Gal 2:2 to Isa 49:4,[2] the call of the Ebed of Isa 49 appears to be in the forefront of Paul's mind while he recalls his own call to apostleship on the road to Damascus.

Concerning the call of the Ebed, however, Isa 49 does not seem to be the only Ebed passage in Paul's mind. Isaiah 42, the first of the so-called Servant Songs, which is in many ways closely related to Isa 49, the second Servant Song, seems to be equally prominent in Paul's mind. It has occasionally been observed that in 2 Cor 4:4-6 Paul does allude to Isa 42:6-7 as well as Isa 49:6 and Gen 1:3 (cf. also Isa 9:1),[3] since the passage appears to reflect both the εἰς φῶς ἐθνῶν of

---

1. Most recently, e.g., R. E. Ciampa, *The Presence and Function of Scripture in Galatians 1 and 2* (WUNT 2/102; Tübingen: Mohr-Siebeck, 1998), 111-18; K. O. Sandness, *Paul — One of the Prophets?* (WUNT 2/43; Tübingen: Mohr-Siebeck, 1991), 61-65.

2. Sandness, *Paul,* 61-62, and lit. cited there.

3. C. M. Martini, "Alcuni Temi Letterari di 2 Cor 4,6 e i racconti della conversione di San Paolo negli Atti," in *Studiorum Paulinorum Congressus Internationalis Catholicus 1961* (AnBib 17-18, vol. 1; Rome: Editrice Pontificio Istituto Biblico, 1963), 469-73; Seyoon Kim, *The Origin of Paul's Gospel* (WUNT 2/4; Tübingen: Mohr-Siebeck, 1981, 1984; Grand Rapids: Eerdmans, 1982), 10; C. K. Stockhausen, *Moses' Veil and the Glory of the New Covenant* (AnBib 116; Rome: Editrice Pontificio Istituto Biblico, 1989), 165-66. Cf. also J.-F. Collange, *Énigmes de la deuxième Épître de Paul aux Corinthiens* (SNTSMS 18; Cambridge: Cambridge University Press, 1972),

Isa 42:6; 49:6 and the ἀνοῖξαι ὀφθαλμοὺς τυφλῶν of Isa 42:7. It seems to echo further ἐν σκότει and ποιήσω αὐτοῖς τὸ σκότος εἰς φῶς of Isa 42:7 and 16 respectively. This interpretation is well supported by the tradition of Paul's call in Acts 26:16-18, which clearly alludes to Isa 42:7, 16 (+ Isa 61:1), while showing several parallels in vocabulary and idea to 2 Cor 4:4-6.[4] So, from 2 Cor 4:4-6, in which most commentators see an allusion to Paul's experience of the Damascus Christophany, we can surmise that he interpreted his Damascus call in the light of Isa 42 in terms of opening the eyes of the blind with the light of the gospel of God's glory in the face of Christ. However, many more features in Paul's letters further confirm that he did indeed interpret his Damascus experience in the light of Isa 42.

God "Was Pleased (εὐδόκησεν) . . ."

First of all, the εὐδόκησεν in Gal 1:15, which has not so far been accounted for in spite of its being a typically biblical term, seems to come from Isa 42:1. רָצְתָה נַפְשִׁי of Isa 42:1 is rendered προσεδέξατο αὐτὸν ἡ ψυχή μου in the Codex Sinaiticus (S) of LXX, but in Codex Marchalianus (Q) and Syro-Hexapla, as well as in the text of Eusebius's Isaiah-Commentary, it is rendered (ὁ ἐκλεκτός μου) ὃν εὐδόκησεν ἡ ψυχή μου. The latter is also the text of Isa 42:1-4 cited in Matt 12:18-21 and alluded to in Matt 3:17 pars. In the LXX רצה (qal) of MT is rendered more often εὐδοκεῖν (21 times) than προσδέχεσθαι (12 times).[5] According to J. Ziegler, Codex Q is "the best witness to the old Isaiah-text."[6] Thus, it is very likely that Paul knew the LXX Isa 42:1b as ὁ

139, cited from R. P. Martin, *2 Corinthians* (WBC; Waco: Word, 1986), 80; P. Jones, *La deuxième Épître de Paul aux Corinthiens* (CEB; Vaux-sur-Seine, 1992), 91.

4. E.g.,

Acts 26:16-18	2 Cor 4:4-6
(1) Paul's commission	Paul's commission
(2) vision of God	vision of God
(3) existence under Satan	under "the god of this age"
(4) [blinded — presupposed]	blinded
(5) turning to God (ἐπιστρέφειν)	[implied: turning to God; cf. 3:16-18 (ἐπιστρέφειν)]
(6) from darkness to light	from darkness to light

Cf. C. Burchard, *Der dreizehnte Zeuge* (FRLANT 103; Göttingen: Vandenhoeck, 1970), 128-29, who supposes on some other grounds that the third account of Paul's conversion/call in Acts (26:12-18) is based on the Pauline tradition.

5. See Hatch-Redpath, *A Concordance to the Septuagint*, vols. 1 and 2 (Graz: Akademische Druck- u. Verlagsanstalt, 1975), *s.v.*

6. J. Ziegler, *Septuaginta: Isaias* (*Vetus Testamentum Graecum;* Göttingen: Vandenhoeck,

ἐκλεκτός μου ὃν εὐδόκησεν ἡ ψυχή μου, and it seems equally likely that with the εὐδόκησεν in Gal 1:15 he alludes to that text.

God's "Call" to Be "a Light to the Gentiles"

In Isa 42:6-7 God calls (ἐκάλεσα) the Ebed in righteousness and gives (ἔδωκα) him to be "a covenant to the people and a light to the gentiles (εἰς φῶς ἐθνῶν), to open eyes that are blind, to free captives from prison, and to release those who sit in darkness." Of course, this is very similar to Isa 49:1, 6, where the Lord calls (ἐκάλεσε) and gives (ἔδωκα) the Ebed to be "a light to the gentiles [εἰς φῶς ἐθνῶν], so that [he] may bring my salvation to the ends of the earth." (Note that the universal outreach of the Ebed's mission is emphasized also in Isa 42:1, 4, 10ff.). It is widely recognized that in Gal 1:15-16 Paul thinks of Isa 49:1, 6, but it is quite probable that he is also thinking of Isa 42:6-7. The καλέσας and ἐν τοῖς ἔθνεσιν in Gal 1:15-16 could echo Isa 42:6-7 as much as Isa 49:1, 6. It is likely that Paul combines the two almost identical texts that concern the call of the same Servant of the Lord in the same context of the same book Isaiah. He is again combining these two texts in 2 Cor 4:4-6, as shown above.

"I Immediately Went Away to Arabia"

With their characteristic sensitivity to details, M. Hengel and A. M. Schwemer ask why, after the apostolic commission at Damascus, Paul went immediately (εὐθέως, Gal 1:16) to Arabia (Gal 1:17), of all places. They suggest several theological and practical reasons.[7] Such practical and theological considerations must have been decisively supported by Isa 42:11, where the Ebed called to be a bearer of light and salvation to the gentiles leads the inhabitants of Kedar and Sela to sing praises to the Lord. קֵדָר refers to a North-Arabic tribe,[8] and in Isa 60:7 it is identified with Nebaioth, the oldest son of Ishmael, from whom, according to Josephus (*Ant.* 1.220-221), the Nabataeans took their name.[9] סֶלַע ("Rock") was the old name of Petra of the Hellenistic-Roman period.[10] In fact,

---

1967), 29; cf. also D.-A. Koch, *Die Schrift als Zeuge des Evangeliums* (BHT 69; Tübingen: Mohr-Siebeck, 1986), 48-49.

7. M. Hengel and A. M. Schwemer, *Paulus zwischen Damaskus und Antiochien* (WUNT 108; Tübingen: Mohr-Siebeck, 1998), 178-84.

8. K. Elliger, *Deuterojesaja*, vol. 1, *Jesaja 40,1–45,7* (Biblischer Kommentar, Altes Testament 11/1; Neukirchen-Vluyn: Neukirchener, 1978, 1989), 247.

9. Cited from Hengel and Schwemer, *Paulus*, 190.

LXX renders סֶלַע Πέτρα in Isa 42:11. So, for Paul both קֵדָר and סֶלַע would have referred to Arabia, the Nabataean kingdom, whose leading city was Petra during his time. This conjecture is supported by the Targum, which has simply "the wilderness of Arabia" for both.[11] Thus, Paul's first missionary attempt in "Arabia" immediately after his apostolic commission (Gal 1:15-17) seems to indicate that he indeed interpreted his call to an apostleship to the gentiles on the Damascus road in the light of Isa 42.

If Paul went to Arabia "immediately," his interpretation of his call in the light of Isa 42 must have been equally immediate! This immediacy militates against the view that he began to interpret his Damascus experience years later or that Gal 1:15-17 represents only a later interpretation of it for an apologetic, rhetorical, or paradigmatic purpose at the time of writing Galatians.[12] While confirming the view that Paul went to Arabia indeed to preach the gospel, which is the most natural interpretation of Paul's statement in Gal 1:15-17, this new discovery of Isa 42:11 as the basis for Paul's choice of Arabia as his first mission field also makes us bid farewell to both the psychologically comfortable theories that Paul went to Arabia for meditation and that he turned to gentile mission years later only upon failing with his Jewish mission.[13]

"Chosen" and "Set Apart"

If so much of Gal 1:15-17 can be seen as echoing Isa 42, can the concept of God's setting Paul apart (ἀφορίσας) in Gal 1:15 also be an echo of Isa 42?

10. Elliger, *Deuterojesaja* 1, 247.

11. Actually it was Professor O. Betz who first spotted Πέτρα in LXX Isa 42:11 when I presented to him my ideas about Isa 42, comparing the MT and LXX texts of the chapter. Subsequently Professor Hengel also commented that the view here presented was quite plausible.

12. Contra B. R. Gaventa, "Galatians 1 and 2: Autobiography as Paradigm," *NovT* 28 (1986): 310-26; G. Lyons, *Pauline Autobiography* (SBLDS 73; Atlanta: Scholars Press, 1986), 123-76; P. Fredricksen, "Paul and Augustine: Conversion Narratives, Orthodox Traditions, and the Retrospective Self," *JTS* 37 (1986): 3-34. For a more detailed critique of their positions, see pp. 11-12.

13. Seeing that Paul followed the guidance of Isa 42:11 in choosing his first mission field, we may presume that he continued to look for guidance in the Scriptures such as Isa 66:18-21 and Gen 10 in planning his missionary itinerary, as recently Rainer Riesner, *Paul's Early Period: Chronology, Mission Strategy, Theology* (trans. Doug Stott; Grand Rapids: Eerdmans, 1998), 245-53, and James M. Scott, *Paul and the Nations: The Old Testament and Jewish Background of Paul's Mission to the Nations with Special Reference to the Destination of Galatians* (WUNT 84; Tübingen: Mohr-Siebeck, 1995), have plausibly suggested.

Traugott Holtz, a pioneer in the investigation into the Old Testament allusions in Gal 1:15-16, has suggested that Paul probably derived the concept from Isa 41:9: ἐκάλεσά σε, καὶ εἶπά σοι, παῖς μου εἶ, ἐξελεξάμην σε.[14] His supporting argument that ἐκλέγειν is a material, though not a linguistic, parallel to ἀφορίζειν seems to be well grounded in view of H. Seebass's explanation of the Old Testament background of the former:

> Überall, wo בחר in bezug auf Personen vorkommt, bezeichnet es die Auswahl aus einem Ganzen — im allgemein aus dem Ganzen des Volkes — , dergestalt dass der Gewählte in bezug auf das Ganze eine Funktion wahrnimmt. בחר hat dabei durchaus die Komponente des Abgrenzenden, aber gerade so, dass das durch בחר Abgegrenzte um so klarer der Gesamtheit zu Diensten stand.[15]

Our only regret is that Holtz failed to take Ἰακὼβ ὁ παῖς μου . . . Ἰσραὴλ ὁ ἐκλεκτός μου of Isa 42:1 together with Ἰσραὴλ παῖς μου Ἰακὼβ ὃν ἐξελεξάμην . . . ἐκάλεσά σε, καὶ εἶπά σοι, παῖς μου εἶ, ἐξελεξάμην σε of Isa 41:8-9. Having seen how much of Gal 1:15-17 can be explained in terms of Isa 42, it is easier to think that with the ἀφορίσας με in Gal 1:15 Paul thinks of the ὁ ἐκλεκτός μου of Isa 42:1 rather than the equivalent phrase of Isa 41:8-9. However, Paul could easily have combined the two passages, which appear close to each other and speak about the same selection and call of the servant of Yahweh. Karl O. Sandness criticizes Holtz's attempt to see the ἀφορίσας of Gal 1:15 as echoing the idea of divine selection in Isa 41:9 for neglecting the cultic background of ἀφορίζειν or its denotation of consecration.[16] But in alluding to the Servant's selection (ἐκλέγειν/ἐκλεκτός) of Isa 41:8-9 and 42:1 with the verb ἀφορίζειν in Gal 1:15, Paul may have also alluded to the ἡγίακά σε of Jer 1:5, the text which is widely recognized as having been in Paul's mind in Gal 1:15-16. Paul's ἀφορίζειν in Gal 1:15 seems to be a suitable word for the combination of the ideas of selection and consecration.[17] If, as many commentators think, the ἀφορίζειν in Gal 1:15 was also intended to allude to Paul's present true set-apart-ness in contrast to his Pharisee (פרוש) days, we can understand even better why he chose the word instead of using the ἐκλέγειν/ἐκλεκτός from Isa 41:8-9 and 42:1. So we conclude that the ἀφορίσας of Gal

---

14. T. Holtz, "Zum Selbstverständnis des Apostels Paulus," *ThLZ* 91 (1966): 321-30, now reprinted in his *Geschichte und Theologie des Urchristentums* (WUNT 57; Tübingen: Mohr-Siebeck, 1991), 132-33.

15. H. Seebass, בחר, *ThWbAT* 1, 603.

16. Sandness, *Paul*, 63 n. 57.

17. In the important text of Lev 20:26 ἀφορίζειν also seems to combine the two ideas of selection and consecration. I owe this reference to Professor Stuhlmacher.

1:15 reflects the combination of the ἐκλέγειν/ἐκλεκτός from Isa 41:8-9 and 42:1, and the ἡγίακά σε of Jer 1:5.

"The Old Things" and "The New Things"

In connection with Paul's declaration that with the new creation in Christ, τὰ ἀρχαῖα παρῆλθεν, ἰδοὺ γέγονεν καινά (2 Cor 5:17), commentators have tended to pay attention only to Isa 43:18-19. No doubt that text is alluded to there.[18] But along with that text, he also seems to allude to Isa 42:9 because the two passages and Isa 48:6 belong together as an expression of Deutero-Isaianic expectation for God's new saving act.[19] Actually הָרִאשֹׁנוֹת הִנֵּה־בָאוּ/ τὰ ἀπ᾽ ἀρχῆς ἰδοὺ ἥκασι of Isa 42:9 may stand closer to τὰ ἀρχαῖα παρῆλθεν of 2 Cor 5:17 than the similar phrase in Isa 43:18. Nevertheless, again Paul may well be combining the similar statements (Isa 42:9; 43:18-19) from the same context of the same book.

To Preach the Gospel of God's Saving Judgment or His Righteousness

In Isa 42:1, 3 the Ebed is commissioned to deliver מִשְׁפָּט to the gentiles. Its exact meaning within the original context of Deutero-Isaiah is disputed.[20] However, if Paul interpreted his apostolic commission in the light of Isa 42, what could the מִשְׁפָּט have meant for him?

As LXX renders the word κρίσις (cf. Tg: דִּינָא), Paul could have understood it as God's judgment. Indeed the summary of his preaching in one of his earliest, if not the earliest, letter indicates that God's eschatological judgment belonged to the center of his preaching (1 Thess 1:10; cf. also 2 Thess 1:5ff.). Romans 1:18 indicates that "the wrath of God" remained at the center of his gospel to the end of his effective preaching ministry. So he warned his audience and his converts of "the day" of God's last judgment (Rom 2:1-16;

18. See, besides commentaries, e.g., O. Betz, " 'Fleischliche' und 'geistliche' Christus-erkenntnis nach 2 Korinther 5,16," *ThBeitr* 14 (1983); now in his *Jesus: Der Herr der Kirche* (WUNT 52; Tübingen: Mohr-Siebeck, 1990), 124; G. K. Beale, "The Old Testament Background of 2 Corinthians 6:14–7:1," *NTS* 35 (1989): 553-54.

19. Cf. P. Stuhlmacher, "Erwägungen zum ontologischen Charakter der καινὴ κτίσις bei Paulus," *EvTh* 27 (1967): 11-12; Kim, *Origin*, 18.

20. Cf. Elliger, *Deuterojesaja* 1, 205ff.; K. Baltzer, *Deutero-Jesaja* (KAT 10/2; Gütersloh: Gütersloher Verlagshaus, 1999), 174-75.

1 Cor 1:8; 3:13; 2 Cor 1:14; Phil 1:10-11; 2:16; 1 Thess 5:2; etc.): "For we must all appear before the judgment seat of Christ, so that each one must receive good or evil, according to what he has done in the body" (2 Cor 5:10).

However, the message that Paul was commissioned to deliver to the gentiles was a *good* news of salvation, namely the message of God's redemption through the atoning death of Christ Jesus his Son, through which God will justify believers at the last judgment and in fact makes that justification proleptically effective to them already in the present (Rom 3:21-26; 4:25; 5:1-11; 8:3-4, 28-39; 2 Cor 5:21; etc.). Paul referred to this redemptive act of God as God's δικαιοσύνη (Rom 1:17; 3:21-26; etc.). So Paul's "gospel" included the fearful judgment of God, but it was in the end a good news about God's saving "righteousness" in Christ and about believers' justification on the basis of it (Rom 1:16-18). Hence Paul's Thessalonian converts can confidently "wait for [God's] Son . . . Jesus who delivers us from the wrath to come" (1 Thess 1:10), and the Roman Christians can rely on the intercession of the exalted Son of God, Jesus Christ, at the last judgment (Rom 8:32-34) because he "was given up (to death) for our trespasses and raised up for our justification" (4:25).[21] In fact, "there is no condemnation for those who are in Christ Jesus," for God has already wrought atonement through his Son for our justification (8:1-4). "Therefore, since we have been justified by faith, we have peace with God through our Lord Jesus Christ, through whom we have obtained access to this grace in which we stand, and we rejoice in our hope of sharing the glory of God" (5:1-2).

This brief reflection on the character of Paul's message, the gospel of God's justifying righteousness in the face of the coming judgment of God, leads us to wonder whether Paul may not have understood the מִשְׁפָּט of Isa 42:1, 3 in the dual sense of God's judgment and his justifying righteousness, or better, in the sense of God's justifying righteousness at his judgment.[22]

Apart from Paul's own actual preaching, the text of Isa 42 itself also strongly supports this hypothesis: not only can מִשְׁפָּט be rendered δικαιοσύνη as well as κρίσις,[23] but within Isa 42 itself the message of מִשְׁפָּט to be delivered by the Ebed has to be understood as a "good news" of salvation, for it is "to

---

21. I learned to take Rom 4:25 and 8:33-34 together in this manner from a paper read by Stuhlmacher at the Fifth Tübingen-Durham Colloquium, September 20-24, 1999.

22. Here Stuhlmacher reminds me of 1QS 11:3 + 12-15, where מִשְׁפָּט is the praying person's justification provided by God's righteousness, and Betz points out Isa 56:1, where מִשְׁפָּט, יְשׁוּעָ, and צְדָקָה appear in close association with one another, the latter two being synonymous.

23. Although the usual LXX rendering for מִשְׁפָּט is κρίσις, it is rendered δικαιοσύνη six times in LXX (Prov 16:11; 17:23; Mal 2:17; Isa 61:8; Ezek 18:19, 21). See Hatch-Redpath, *Septuagint Concordance*, s.v.

open the eyes that are blind, to free captives from prison and to release from the dungeon those who sit in darkness" (v. 7). And so the message is to turn the nations to God so that they may rejoice in his salvation and glorify him for his salvation (vv. 10-17).[24] It is precisely such preaching of this message of salvation that Deutero-Isaiah refers to as בָּשַׂר and its messenger as מְבַשֵּׂר (Isa 40:9; 41:27; 52:7; 60:6; 61:1-2), from which Paul's and the New Testament's term "gospel" (εὐαγγέλιον: בְּשׂורה; cf. Tg. Isa. 53:1) is rightly understood to have originated.[25] (See further below.)

Thus the saving מִשְׁפָּט that the Ebed is commissioned to deliver to the gentiles in Isa 42 agrees well with the gospel of God's saving judgment, i.e., justification, that Paul delivers to the gentiles.[26] This seems to support further the view here propounded that Paul interpreted his apostolic commission in the light of Isa 42 as well as other Old Testament texts. Moreover, we may even presume that in the formation of Paul's gospel of justification, Isa 42, together with several other Deutero-Isaianic passages (e.g., 52:13–53:12), played an important role.

At any rate, keeping in mind both the fact that, for Paul, Jesus the Son of God embodies the gospel of God's δικαιοσύνη (Rom 1:2-4, 9, 16-17; 8:3-4; Gal 4:4-6; 1 Thess 1:10) and the fact that Paul's term εὐαγγελίζεσθαι/ εὐαγγέλιον originated from Deutero-Isaiah, we suspect that the clause ἵνα εὐαγγελίζωμαι αὐτόν (= God's Son) in Gal 1:16 may actually allude to the Ebed's task of preaching the good news of God's saving מִשְׁפָּט/δικαιοσύνη and thus bringing divine revelation and salvation to the gentiles in Isa 42:1-7 (cf. Isa 40:9; 52:7; 60:6; 61:1-2). This possibility cannot be excluded in view of the fact that so much of Gal 1:15-17 (εὐδόκησεν, ἀφορίσας, καλέσας, ἐν τοῖς ἔθνεσιν, and Ἀραβίαν) seems to be echoing Isa 42.

24. Cf. Jörg Jeremias, "מִשְׁפָּט im ersten Gottesknechtslied," VT 22 (1972): 31-42.
25. Cf. P. Stuhlmacher, Das paulinische Evangelium 1 (FRLANT 95; Göttingen: Vandenhoeck, 1968), 63-108; Biblische Theologie des Neuen Testaments, vol. 1 (Göttingen: Vandenhoeck, 1992), 315; O. Betz, "Jesu Evangelium vom Gottesreich," in Jesus: der Messias Israels (WUNT 42; Tübingen: Mohr-Siebeck, 1987), 232-54.
26. So O. Hofius, "Das Gesetz des Mose und das Gesetz Christi," in Paulusstudien (WUNT 51; Tübingen: Mohr, 1989), 74: "Das 'Recht,' das der Gottesknecht ihnen . . . bringt, ist Gottes 'Recht der Begnadigung' [quotation from W. Zimmerli], der Freispruch für die zu Recht Verurteilten; es ist — paulinisch gesprochen — die Rechtfertigung der Gottlosen."

The Hope of the Gentiles

According to Isa 42:4, the Ebed is to go about unfaltering and undaunted until he establishes מִשְׁפָּט on earth and "in his instruction the islands set their
hope." The Greek codices and versions of LXX render verse 4c וּלְתוֹרָתוֹ אִיִּים
יְיַחֵלוּ as καὶ ἐπὶ τῷ ὀνόματι αὐτοῦ τὰ ἔθνη ἐλπιοῦσιν.[27] This is also the version cited in Matt 12:21. If Paul understood the מִשְׁפָּט here as God's saving
judgment, he could have interpreted the Ebed's "instruction" (תורה) in verse
4c in terms of his instruction about God's saving judgment or God's
δικαιοσύνη. As the Ebed, Paul preaches or "instructs" the gentiles about God's
saving judgment or justification, and so the gentiles can set their hope in this
"instruction" or message of the Ebed/Paul for their justification at the last
judgment.[28] This line of thinking may underlie Paul's talk of the believers'
"rejoicing in [their] hope of sharing the glory of God" (Rom 5:2; cf. 8:18-25).
If Paul had read in verse 4c the תורה in its technical sense of the Mosaic Law,
he would have replaced it with the gospel of God's Son, Jesus Christ, which
was revealed to him at his Damascus call (Gal 1:11-17). And he would have
been inclined to understand 4c in a way similar to Matt 12:21 and LXX to
mean that the gentiles set their hope in the name of Jesus Christ, God's Son,
whom he proclaims as the gospel. When in Rom 15:12-13 he cites Isa 11:10
according to LXX (ἐπ' αὐτῷ τὰ ἔθνη ἐλπιοῦσιν), which is quite different from
MT (אֵלָיו גּוֹיִם יִדְרֹשׁוּ), to express the same thought, Paul may have Isa 42:4
also in mind.

Unfaltering and Undaunted, to the Ends of the Earth

According to Isa 42:4, the Ebed is to go about with his mission unfaltering
(לֹא יִכְהֶה/ἀναλάμψει in LXX) and undaunted (לֹא יָרוּץ/οὐ θραυσθήσεται)
even in the face of opposition and persecution, "until [God's] saving judgment is established on earth." Now, is this not exactly the spirit of Paul, who
tirelessly pursues his apostolic mission to the ends of the earth, quite unfal-

27. So all the LXX MSS: see the Rahlfs edition; but Ziegler's Göttingen edition corrects it
with νόμῳ according to MT.
28. Stuhlmacher pointed out to me the importance of 1 Cor 4:17 (cf. also 2 Cor 3:6; 5:19)
in this context. There Paul speaks of "my ways [ὁδούς] in Christ [which] I teach everywhere in
every church." This verse not only reminds us of the fact that Paul understood his ministry also
as a teaching ministry but also suggests that he understood his teaching as a new הלכה/דרך/
תורה (cf. also Phil 4:9; Acts 19:8-10). By his "ways" Paul must mean not just "doctrines" or "ethics," but both together.

tering and undaunted in the face of so much opposition and persecution (see only 2 Cor 11:23-29!)? Perhaps Paul does this partly because in Isa 42:4 he saw prefigured his mission to the ends of the earth to preach God's saving judgment (δικαιοσύνη) and bring all the gentiles to the obedience of faith in the name of the Lord Jesus Christ (Rom 1:5). So he presses on with his mission unfailingly, from Jerusalem as far round in a circle as Illyricum, and indeed to Spain on from Rome, so that all the gentiles might hear of the saving name of the Lord Jesus Christ (Rom 15:15-21).

"A Covenant to the People"

According to Isa 42:6, the Ebed is called not only to be "a light to the gentiles" but also to be "a covenant [בְּרִית/διαθήκη] to the people." Karl Elliger helpfully explains the difficult idea of the latter thus:

> Yahweh has made the person he called a "commitment for the עם" just as a "light for the nations." . . . As the called person is made to be one who brings light to the nations, so he is also made to be one who is obligated by Yahweh to the advantage of the עם. The meaning and purpose of ברית is, of course, the usual thing: life, well-being, peace, which the Hebrew calls שׁלום. The called person is guarantee, personal guarantee for the salvation of the עם; for that Yahweh has determined him. The agreement in content between ברית and אור is not to be overlooked.[29]

Then Elliger goes on to argue that the עם here does not refer to Israel but is the same as the גּוֹיִם.[30] In Gal 1:16 where, as generally recognized, Isa 49:6 and, as argued here, Isa 42:6 are alluded to, Paul clearly interprets the ἐθνῶν of the εἰς φῶς ἐθνῶν of Isa 42:6 and 49:6 as the gentiles. Then would he have seen the עם/ γένος also as a reference to the gentiles? In spite of the strange switch that LXX makes from rendering the עם/γένους in Isa 42:6 to ἐθνῶν in Isa 49:8,[31] it is quite probable that Paul interpreted the עם of both Isa 42:6 (as in LXX S* C' Bo Syp Cypr) and 49:8 as referring to Israel, the people of God, in contradistinction to the גּוֹיִם of Isa 42:6 and 49:6 which he saw as referring to the gentiles.

Furthermore, if Paul indeed consulted Isa 42 and 49 in order to interpret his apostolic commission, how would he have understood the part of the Ebed's commission to be a "covenant to the people" (וְאֶתֶּנְךָ לִבְרִית עָם/καὶ

29. Elliger, *Deuterojesaja* 1, 234-35 (my translation).
30. Ibid.; cf. Baltzer, *Deutero-Jesaja*, 179-80.
31. See the next note.

110

ἔδωκά σε εἰς διαθήκην γένους),[32] which appears in both Isa 42:6 and 49:8, 6 in parallelism to the other part of Ebed's commission, to be a "light to the gentiles" (וְאֶתֶּנְךָ] לְאוֹר גּוֹיִם]/[ἔδωκά σε] εἰς φῶς ἐθνῶν)? Surely it is more natural to suppose that he saw his apostolic commission in the light of both parts of the commission of the Ebed in Isa 42:6//49:8, 6 rather than just one part of it. Therefore, Paul most likely saw his commission in terms of being a "covenant" for Israel as well as a "light" to the gentiles.

Unlike the latter, an allusion to the former idea of being a covenant to Israel has not so far been detected in Paul's letters. However, if we look afresh at his intense concerns for the salvation of Israel in the light of Elliger's explanation cited above, we can see such a self-understanding of Paul reflected in them.[33] In Rom 11:1 Paul says, "I ask, then, has God rejected his people?" and answers vehemently, "By no means!" Then he points to himself as proof for this answer: "For I also am an Israelite, of the seed of Abraham, of the tribe of Benjamin." To this James Dunn comments, "The answer at first seems rather ludicrous, as though Paul was saying, 'The fact that *I* have understood and believed the word of faith is sufficient proof that God has not rejected Israel,' as though Paul was setting himself up as a representative of his whole people, or even as progenitor of a reconstructed people!" Having denied this meaning, Dunn goes on to say: "Certainly what comes to expression is Paul's consciousness of being one of the covenant people."[34]

Dunn is quite right in sensing the gravity of Paul's way of answering with the emphatic "I" (ἐγώ) in Rom 11:1. His emphasis on Paul's consciousness of being a member of Israel, the covenant people of God, is also quite proper. However, it is not easy to understand why Dunn plays down the equally important element of Paul's consciousness of being a Christian here. It is surely one-sided to conclude, as Dunn does, "It is not because he is a Christian that Paul can dismiss the suggestion that God has repudiated his people . . . but because he is an Israelite, because he is so conscious that he belongs to God's people. It is precisely as a Jew that Paul reaffirms God's faithfulness to the Jews."[35] No, it is rather *as a Jew and Christian* or *as a Christian Jew* — one who by faith in the Messiah Jesus has come to have God's purpose of electing Israel realized in his person — that Paul reaffirms God's faithfulness to his election of the Jewish people.[36] Since Paul is about to talk about the present existence

32. Note the change from γένους in 42:6 to ἐθνῶν in Isa 49:8.

33. Cf. K.-W. Niebuhr, *Heidenapostel aus Israel* (WUNT 62; Tübingen: Mohr-Siebeck, 1992), 158-75.

34. All quotes in J. D. G. Dunn, *Romans 9–16* (WBC 38B; Waco: Word, 1988), 644.

35. Ibid.

36. Cf. Niebuhr, *Heidenapostel,* 171.

of a "remnant," a group of Christian Jews, in whom God's purpose of election has been realized (Rom 11:5), in Rom 11:1 he certainly does not intend to exclude other Jewish Christians. However, when in Rom 11:2-4 he illustrates the present situation with the story of Elijah from 1 Kings 19, he draws a parallel between Elijah and himself, who both charge Israel with unfaithfulness, as well as a parallel between the remnant at the time of Elijah and the remnant at the present time.[37] It means, therefore, that Paul is presenting himself here as a representative of the redeemed Israel, if not actually the leader of the group.[38]

In Rom 10:1-4 Paul describes the failure of the Jews in terms of an unenlightened zeal for God and a mistaken attempt to establish their own righteousness on the basis of the works of the law (Rom 9:31-32) in ignorance of God's righteousness. It is significant that he describes the failure of the Jews in the same way as he usually describes his own pre-conversion past (Gal 1:13-14; Phil 3:5-6; cf. also 2 Cor 4:4, 6; 5:16). So in his affirmation of the Jews' regrettable failure to submit to God's righteousness we can hear an undertone of a contrast with his own submission to God's righteousness (Phil 3:7-11; Gal 1:15-16; cf. also 2 Cor 4:6; 5:16-21). In this context, he says that he has an intense desire in his heart for the salvation of his fellow Israelites and earnestly prays for it. Clearly he is praying that the Jews would "convert" as he did. Thus, in this passage also, Paul seems to present himself implicitly as a representative of the redeemed Israel. Then, as a representative of the redeemed Israel, he is earnestly praying for the salvation of the whole Israel.

In Rom 9:1-3 Paul solemnly testifies to the "great sorrow and unceasing anguish" in his heart about the failure of the Jews and says, "For I could pray that I myself were accursed and cut off from the Messiah for the sake of my brethren, my kinsmen according to the flesh." Commentators rightly think that here Paul has in mind the model of Moses interceding for his people after they had fallen into the sin of worshiping the Golden Calf and praying that

---

37. So E. Käsemann, *An die Römer* (HNT; Tübingen: Mohr-Siebeck, 1980), 291; Dunn, *Romans*, 645-46; D. J. Moo, *The Epistle to the Romans* (NICNT; Grand Rapids: Eerdmans, 1996), 677.

38. Cf. Käsemann, *Römer*, 289, 291; C. E. B. Cranfield, *The Epistle to the Romans* 2 (ICC; Edinburgh: T & T Clark, 1986), 544; Moo, *Romans*, 677; Niebuhr, *Heidenapostel*, 167-71. In Rom 2:19 (ὁδηγὸν εἶναι τυφλῶν, φῶς τῶν ἐν σκότει) Paul appears to describe the Jewish sense of mission towards the gentile world in terms of the Ebed's role in Isa 42:6-7; 49:6. Then, when in Gal 1:15-16; 2 Cor 4:4-6 he interprets his own commission in terms of the same role of the Ebed and when through his gentile mission he seeks to fulfill that commission, he is clearly regarding himself as a representative of Israel who fulfills in a representative way the purpose of God's election and commission of Israel.

God blot him out of his book if he would not forgive them (Exod 32:30-32). Seeing that Moses wished to obtain God's forgiveness of Israel by a willingness to sacrifice himself for atonement for their sins, Paul is similarly willing to sacrifice himself for the salvation of Israel. Then it is probable that Paul is here implicitly reflecting his "consciousness of playing a role of decisive salvation-historical significance, like Moses."[39]

Thus Paul's intense concerns for salvation of the Jews in the three passages of Romans (9:1-3; 10:1-4; 11:1-5), together seem to implicitly reflect his consciousness of being a representative destined to fulfill an important salvation-historical role for the Jews. This impression is strengthened if we consider the fact that apparently he sees his gentile mission as decisive for the salvation of the Jews as well as the gentiles. In expressing his understanding of God's *Heilsplan* in Rom 11:25-26, "A hardening has come upon part of Israel, until the full number of the gentiles come in, and so all Israel will be saved," Paul implies that the eventual salvation of "all Israel" is in a way dependent on his gentile mission. For as a "special" apostle to the gentiles (ἐθνῶν ἀπόστολος,[40] Rom 11:13; cf. also Gal 2:7-9),[41] he is specially responsible for bringing in the full number of the gentiles, which would lead to the lifting of the hardening of Israel and to Israel's eventual salvation. So he works feverishly and tirelessly to bring in the full number of the gentiles, and seeks to go to the ends of the world for this purpose. But even before his gentile mission is complete, he is eager to use his gentile mission as an instrument of Israel's salvation: apparently encouraged by Deut 32:21 (Rom 10:19), Paul deliberately demonstrates the success of his gentile mission in order to provoke the Jews to jealousy and thus save "some" of them even now (Rom 11:11-15). Thus, in both Rom 11:25-26 and 11:13-14 Paul indirectly suggests that his apostolic ministry is an instrument for the salvation of the Jews as well as the gentiles and therefore that his apostleship has a decisive salvation-historical role for the Jews as well as the gentiles.[42]

---

39. Dunn, *Romans*, 525, referring to J. Munck, *Christ and Israel* (Philadelphia: Fortress, 1967), 29. This conclusion can be further supported by a consideration of 2 Cor 2:14–3:18 in which Paul alludes to the call of Moses (2:16; 3:4-5) in defense of his own apostolic sufficiency and compares/contrasts his ministry of the new covenant with Moses' ministry of the old covenant. See S. J. Hafemann, *Paul, Moses, and the History of Israel* (WUNT 81; Tübingen: Mohr-Siebeck, 1995), esp. 107-10.

40. Cf. Moo, *Romans*, 691 n. 40: "ἐθνῶν ἀπόστολος may be something of a title."

41. Cf. Dunn, *Romans*, 656.

42. So ibid., 655-58; Käsemann, *Römer*, 302-3; J. Munck, *Paul and the Salvation of Mankind* (Richmond: John Knox Press, 1959), 275-79; Niebuhr, *Heidenapostel*, 171-75; R. H. Bell, *Provoked to Jealousy* (WUNT 2/63; Tübingen: Mohr-Siebeck, 1994), 156-66, 336-50. Moo, *Romans*, 692, objects to this interpretation by pointing to the "modest" number ("some of them") that Paul hopes to win here. But with "some," although Paul may be expressing some

Now would it be wrong to connect this self-understanding of Paul to the dual role of the Ebed in Isa 42:6//49:8, 6? Paul's intense concerns for the salvation of the Jews as their representative and his work for it, indirect and circuitous as it is — do they not correspond to Elliger's explanation of the meaning of the Ebed's being given as a "covenant" to Israel? Paul's self-understanding reflected in Rom 9–11 — or in his entire apostolic ministry — seems to correspond exactly to the dual role of the Ebed: to be a "covenant" to Israel and to be a "light" to the gentiles. Regarding the dual role of the Ebed, Paul seems to be convinced that the latter is his primary task and the means of fulfilling the former as well. If my theory of the "mystery" of Rom 11:25-26 as having originated together with Paul's call to apostleship[43] is correct, we can understand why in his mind Paul arranged the dual role of the Ebed the way he did. Since, according to the divine *Heilsplan* embodied in the "mystery," the gentile mission was the most urgent task, he naturally emphasized his commission to be a bearer of divine light and salvation to the gentiles. However, since he would ultimately fulfill the role of being a covenant to Israel only by means of fulfilling his gentile mission, he could not emphasize the former. His deference to Peter and the other apostles before him (Gal 2:7-8), the division of the mission field with them (v. 9), and his bitter struggle with some sections of the Jewish church all made him also wary of referring explicitly to his commission to be a covenant to Israel.[44] Nevertheless, these considerations make it quite probable

---

modesty, he does not mean a "modest number," i.e., a small number (cf. Bell, *Provoked*, 161-62). This is clear from Paul's use of the same expression (τινες) in 1 Cor 9:22 as well as in Rom 11:17. Just as in Rom 11:17 he does not mean that only a small number of the Jews have become reprobate, so also in 1 Cor 9:22 Paul surely does not mean that he makes all the efforts to save only a small number of gentiles and Jews! He is the one who, having fully preached the gospel in the eastern hemisphere of the Roman empire, savors his ambition to preach the gospel in the western hemisphere as well, even to Spain, in order to bring "*all* the gentiles" to the obedience of faith in the Lord Jesus Christ (Rom 1:5; 15:18-20). So he is rather the one who seeks to bring "the full number of the gentiles" into the kingdom (Rom 11:25). This he can achieve only when he completes his mission. While on the way to that goal, the fruit he can show at each juncture of his mission will always be only "some." So the "some" in Rom 11:14 should also be understood in the same sense: the full number of the gentiles in the kingdom will lead to the salvation of "*all* Israel," but until that goal is reached, Paul can go on saving only "some" Jews by demonstrating the success of his gentile mission whenever the opportunity presents itself. In other words, the "some" in both Rom 11:14 and 1 Cor 9:22 should be interpreted as a tentative number in contrast to the eschatological "*all* Israel" and "the *full* number of the gentiles" in Rom 11:25.

43. Kim, *Origin*, 74-99; Kim, "The 'Mystery' of Rom 11.25-26 Once More," *NTS* 43 (1997): 412-29, reprinted in this volume, ch. 7. See below, pp. 123-25.

44. Nevertheless, in his reference to himself as "a minister of the new covenant" in comparison with and contrast to Moses, the servant of the old covenant, in 2 Cor 3 this self-understanding may be reflected. See n. 39 above.

that Paul interpreted his apostolic commission in the light of the dual commission of the Ebed in Isa 42:6//49:8, 6.

"I Will Put My Spirit on Him"

In Isa 42:1 the Lord puts his Spirit upon the Ebed, thus empowering him to carry out his important mission of delivering God's saving judgment to the gentiles and thus being a bearer of light and salvation to them as well as being a covenant to Israel. If Paul interpreted his apostolic commission in the light of Isa 42, surely he would not have missed this decisive idea.

(1) Gordon D. Fee's Observation

Though so far no direct evidence has been found for linking Paul's apostolic commission to endowment of the Holy Spirit, recently Gordon D. Fee, the author of an imposing work on the Holy Spirit in Paul,[45] has attempted to show that Paul's understanding of the Spirit is determined by "his own experience of the eschatological Spirit in his Damascus road conversion."[46] Recognizing that the agendas of Paul's letters were set by their recipients and that they provide only indirect evidence for his conclusion, Fee proceeds in three steps. First, under nine headings, he "set[s] forth in summary fashion the central features in Paul's understanding of the Spirit — a topic that is so pervasive in his theology and of such a nature as to demand an experienced reality as its origin."[47] Second, Fee notes that whenever Paul reminds his converts of their conversion he invariably refers to the role played in it by the Spirit. The passages in which Paul does this are of two kinds: one, the "passages where the Spirit is mentioned in a presuppositional manner" (1 Cor 2:4-5; 6:11; 1 Thess 1:5-6, 9-10; 2 Thess 2:13-14),[48] and the other, the "passages where the Spirit is highlighted as being crucial to the argument" (2 Cor 3:3; Gal 3:1-5).[49] Fee especially highlights how crucial the Galatian Christians' experience of the Spirit at

---

45. Gordon D. Fee, *God's Empowering Presence: The Holy Spirit in the Letters of Paul* (Peabody: Hendrickson, 1994).

46. Gordon D. Fee, "Paul's Conversion as Key to His Understanding of the Spirit," in *The Road from Damascus* (ed. R. N. Longenecker; Grand Rapids: Eerdmans, 1997), 167-83; quotation from 167.

47. Ibid., 167.

48. Ibid., 173-74.

49. Ibid., 175-76.

their conversion is to Paul's entire argument in Gal 3–6. Fee's third step is to examine the numerous "confessional" texts in which, while affirming the saving event, Paul indicates himself together with his readers as recipients of the Holy Spirit, including Gal 3:13-14; 4:4-7; Rom 8:15-16; 2 Cor 1:21-22; and Rom 5:1-5.[50] All these "confessional" texts allude to the moment of the conversion of "us." But Fee particularly highlights Rom 5:5 ("the love of God has been poured out in *our* hearts through the Holy Spirit who has been given to us") as "almost certainly reflecting . . . [Paul's] experience of the Spirit at the time of his own conversion."[51]

(2) Romans 5:1-11 and 1 Corinthians 2:4-10

Fee's three-step argument as a whole is a quite convincing demonstration that Paul received the Holy Spirit at his Damascus conversion/call, as Luke also testifies (Acts 9:17-18).[52] We would further support it by observing how, in Rom 5:1-11, such an important role is played by the words that remind us of Paul's Damascus conversion: "enemies," "reconciliation," "peace," and probably also "the ungodly." Clearly, in describing generally the justification and reconciliation of the believers, Paul is reflecting on the experience of justification and reconciliation he himself received while on his way to Damascus as an "enemy" of Christ/God (cf. 2 Cor 5:11-21).[53] So his affirmation of the endowment of the Holy Spirit in this context (Rom 5:5) can be looked upon as clear evidence of his receiving the Spirit at his Damascus conversion. Similarly, we would strengthen Fee's argument on 1 Cor 2:4-5 by observing how in 1 Cor 2:8-10 Paul reflects his Damascus Christophany experience: when he encountered the crucified Jesus as "the Lord of glory" on the Damascus road, he received the revelation of God's secret wisdom, the divine counsel of saving the world through the crucified Christ.[54] The most significant point here for our

50. Ibid., 177-81.

51. Ibid., 180.

52. When we argue here for the endowment of the Spirit at Paul's apostolic commission at Damascus, we are not presuming to know how the endowment took place nor excluding the possibility that it may have taken place a few days after his initial encounter with the risen Lord, as Luke suggests. We are interested only in ascertaining that in the course of the event(s) in which Paul received the Lord's call to his apostleship he came to experience the endowment of the Holy Spirit and that he saw this experience in the light of Isa 42:1 and 61:1 (see below).

53. Cf. Seyoon Kim, "2 Cor 5:11-21 and the Origin of Paul's Concept of 'Reconciliation,'" *NovT* 39 (1997): 360-84, reprinted in this volume, ch. 6.

54. See Kim, *Origin,* 74-82; confirmed by Sandness, *Paul,* 86-88, 116; and C. C. Newman, *Paul's Glory-Christology* (NovTSup 69; Leiden: Brill, 1992), 237-38.

present purpose is that for this experience Paul states: "God revealed to us [his secret wisdom] through the Spirit" (v. 10). While still somewhat indirect, this offers clear evidence for linking the Spirit to Paul's Damascus experience.

(3) 2 Corinthians 1:21-22

However, 2 Cor 1:21-22 presents the most interesting evidence: "Now the one who makes us firm [or secure] [βεβαιῶν] together with you unto Christ, and anointed [χρίσας] us is God, who indeed sealed [σφραγισάμενος] us and gave [δούς] us the down-payment [ἀρραβῶνα] of the Spirit in our hearts." We cannot attempt a detailed exegesis of this difficult passage here. Most recent commentators take the thrice repeated "us" here (the object of the three aorist participles) as including the Corinthians as well as Paul and his colleagues. They do so because they see verse 22 to be a sort of baptismal or confessional language which naturally applies to all believers (cf. 2 Cor 5:5; Rom 8:21; Eph 1:14). But then they show themselves greatly perplexed in explaining the remarkable aorist participle χρίσας here and also how suddenly Paul turns to make a general affirmation about the baptismal experience of himself and the Corinthian church.

Erich Dinkler, who has provided the most detailed baptismal interpretation of our passage, thinks that the participle χρίσας describes the baptismal pouring of water and refers to God's acceptance of the baptized into the eschatological community of the saints. However, Dinkler apparently cannot quite ignore the technical sense the verb has accrued from its Old Testament background. So he says that what is in view here is "the anointment for the *office* of the believer in Christ to which the χάρισμα-granting χρίειν is directed," and elaborates that what is meant here is similar to 1 John 2:20, 27, although in the latter χρῖσμα refers more to the Spirit himself received at baptism.[55] In line with this, Ralph P. Martin considers whether the verb refers to the bestowal of the gifts of the Spirit upon believers for ministry.[56] Since in the New Testament only Jesus is said to have been anointed to be the Messiah (Luke 4:18; Acts 4:27; 10:38; Heb 1:9), and since, as most recent commentators think, the verb is suggested in our passage by the titular sense of the preceding Χριστόν, Margaret Thrall specu-

---

55. E. Dinkler, "Die Taufterminologie in 2. Kor 1,21f.," in *Signum Crucis: Aufsätze zum Neuen Testament und zur christlichen Archäeologie* (Tübingen: Mohr-Siebeck, 1967), 107 (his emphasis).

56. Martin, *2 Corinthians*, 28.

lates that Paul may mean that all believers are consecrated at baptism to kingship, to share in Christ's reign.[57]

But does this line of interpretation suit the context? Why suddenly in the middle of his apostolic defense would Paul make such a general confessional or baptismal statement for himself *and* the Corinthian church? In fact, of all the commentators, Dinkler has the merit of explicitly raising the question of whether his line of interpretation of our passage as a general statement of baptism suits the context.[58] He argues that it does: by reminding the Corinthian church of the fact that they have already been bound to a unity with Paul himself in Christ through baptism, Paul is saying that "the church should have known how impossible for [him] a yes-and-no at the same time is."[59] However, I must confess I simply fail to make sense of this argument.

As 2 Cor 1:17, 23 indicates, in the context Paul's concern is to defend his behavior of not having come to Corinth as he had promised. The general run of Paul's argument in 2 Cor 1:12–2:4 appears to be as follows: the cancellation of my planned visit to Corinth was not an insincere decision born of "fleshly wisdom" (1:12) or "fleshly planning" (1:17). It was made, rather, according to the grace of God (1:12), and it was to spare you, the Corinthians (1:23-2:4). God, whose word I and my colleagues are commissioned to preach, is a faithful God, who has faithfully fulfilled all his promises in and through his Son Jesus Christ. It is this God who is making it sure at present (βεβαιῶν)[60] for us to go on belonging to Christ so as to participate in his eventual salvation, as he does the same for you (1:7; cf. also 1:14).[61] As those

57. M. Thrall, *The Second Epistle to the Corinthians*, vol. 1 (ICC; Edinburgh: T & T Clark, 1994), 155. Fee, *Empowering*, 291-92, waffles: emphasizing the uniqueness of χρίσας here, he wants to take it seriously in view of not only its Old Testament background but also the Lucan report of the Jesus tradition, but then he immediately reduces its meaning to "made us Christ's people." Somehow Fee is able to exegete the sense as "By joining them [Paul and the Corinthians] to the Anointed One, God has thereby anointed them as well." But then he immediately corrects it with a reference to "the OT traditions of the anointing of kings and priests and, especially in Isaiah, the anointing of the Messiah with the Spirit," and says that "[this] usage is what Paul picks up on here." However, Fee immediately weakens his comment: "But Paul does not further press the metaphor, nor should we." This sort of vacillation seems to betray only the weakness of the line of interpretation that takes "us" in our passage as inclusive of the Corinthians.

58. Dinkler, "Taufterminologie," 115.

59. Ibid., 116. Note how Dinkler quietly drops any reference to "the anointment for the *office* of the believer in Christ" (part of his own interpretation of χρίσας) in his summary statement about the meaning of our passage.

60. Cf. Bauer-Aland, *Wörterbuch*, on ὁ βεβαιῶν in 2 Cor 1:21: "der uns festmacht in Christus = zur treuen Jüngern macht."

61. βεβαιῶν in 1:21 must be related to βεβαία in 1:7 (cf. P. Barnett, *The Second Epistle to the Corinthians* [NICNT; Grand Rapids: Eerdmans, 1997], 80), and σὺν ὑμῖν in 1:21 is probably to

who are constantly confirmed by such a faithful God to go on belonging to Christ so as to participate in his eventual salvation, we have conducted ourselves in holiness and sincerity. For this our conscience bears witness and we (or rather "I") can call God also to bear witness (note the *inclusio* in 1:12 and 1:23).[62]

In the context of such an argument,[63] Paul speaks of God having "anointed us" and "sealed us and given us the down-payment of the Spirit in our hearts." It appears that this set of statements is to be seen in contrast to the "fleshly wisdom" and "fleshly planning" which Paul denies in 1:12, 17 respectively. In other words, Paul is here setting up his usual antithesis between σάρξ and πνεῦμα. He does so in order to affirm that in canceling his visit to Corinth he did not act according to the flesh but according to the Spirit, which is the same as "according to the grace of God" (1:12). In the light of this general run of Paul's argument, then, the older commentators appear to be correct in taking "us" in 1:21b-22 as referring to Paul and his colleagues, and especially to Paul.[64] It would be strange if having specifically separated "you" from ἡμᾶς in verse 21a, Paul would include "you" in the immediately following ἡμᾶς in verse 21b. Since the ἡμᾶς in verse 21a clearly refers to Paul and his colleagues, so the ἡμᾶς in verse 21b must also refer

be understood in the light of Paul's hope expressed in 1:7. Paul's hope is "firm" for the Corinthians not only in the sense that his *act* of hoping for their eventual salvation is not wavering but more in the sense that the *object* of his hope (their eschatological salvation) is an assured thing (because God is confirming them). So Paul is saying in v. 21a: "as God is confirming you (implied in 1:7), so he is confirming us, i.e., he is confirming us together with you").

62. Victor P. Furnish, *II Corinthians* (AB; Garden City: Doubleday, 1984), 150, speaks of Paul returning in 1:23 to the subject of the cancelled visit of 1:15-17, and thereby implicitly takes 1:18-22 as a digression; similarly also Fee, *Empowering*, 294. Holding a similar view, Thrall, *The Second Epistle to the Corinthians*, 159, thinks that in 1:23 "there is some slight contrast with what [Paul] has just been saying about the activity of God." But such views seem to underline only that their interpretation of 2 Cor 1:21-22 as a general statement applying to Paul *and* the Corinthians is not correct.

63. Having given a somewhat confusing explanation, Martin, *2 Corinthians*, 29, comes in the end to a summary of Paul's argument similar to ours.

64. H. A. W. Meyer, *Kritisch-exegetisches Handbuch über den zweiten Brief an die Korinther* (Göttingen: Vandenhoeck, 1870), 159; A. Klöpper, *Kommentar über das zweite Sendschreiben des Apostels Paulus an die Gemeinde zu Korinth* (Berlin: Reimer, 1874), 144-46; J. A. Beet, *Two Corinthians* (London: Hodder, 1882), 328; J. Denney, *The Second Epistle to the Corinthians* (London: Hodder, 1894), 50-51; A. Plummer, *The Second Epistle of Paul to the Corinthians* (ICC; Edinburgh: T & T Clark, 1925), 39; P. Bachmann, *Der zweite Brief des Paulus an die Korinther* (Leipzig: Deichertsche, 1922), 77-81; R. H. Strachan, *The Second Epistle of Paul to the Corinthians* (London: Hodder, 1935), 59, following Moffatt's translation of the NT. See also P. L. Hammer, "Canon and Theological Variety," *ZNW* 67 (1976): 87. Does this contrast between the old commentators' "individual" interpretation and the recent commentators' "collective" interpretation reflect the difference of their *Zeitgeister*?

to them only. Likewise, the "us" and "our" in verse 22 must do the same. The emphatic ἐγώ in 1:23 makes it clear that throughout the apologetic section of 1:12–2:4 Paul is thinking mainly of himself, since the cancellation of the planned visit was the decision he made as the leader of his team (Silvanus, Timothy, and perhaps other assistants). This is made clear in 2:1-4. Then, in 1:21-22, in order to affirm that his cancellation of the planned visit was born of holiness and sincerity from God, Paul appeals not only to the faithful God's present upholding (βεβαιῶν) of him in the sphere of Christ's redemption, but also to the faithful God's anointment of him with the Spirit for his apostolic ministry. Thus, here Paul seems to be referring to his apostolic commission on the Damascus road.[65] Most significantly, he uses the word χρίσας for it, and understands his apostolic commission as God's anointment with the Spirit.[66]

For the sake of clarity, Paul's thought in the passage may be paraphrased thus: Having sealed me as his own and anointed me as his apostle through the Spirit, the faithful God is continually confirming me to go on belonging to the sphere of Christ's redemption through that Spirit, who is God's guarantee for my eventual participation in the consummated salvation in Christ. Being

65. Certainly Paul would not deny that blessings the same as or analogous to those described with the three aorist participles here have been given also to his Corinthian readers. The only question here is whether in our passage he is explicitly drawing them into his statements, disrupting the run of his argument. Contra Fee, *Empowering*, 292 n. 27.

66. The three aorist participles are to be taken together. The relative clause for God's sealing and endowing with the Spirit is probably an elaboration of ὁ . . . χρίσας, particularly aiming at emphasizing the endowment of the Holy Spirit (cf. Fee, *Empowering*, 291). The appearance of the present participle βεβαιῶν before the aorist participles seems to be dictated by the need to connect the thought of the truthful God immediately to his act of confirming Paul that goes on in the present, since that need is paramount in the context. What is described subsequently with the three aorist participles has only a supportive role for the affirmation in v. 21a. There may also be a chiasmus intended here:

A: ὁ δὲ βεβαιῶν ἡμᾶς σὺν ὑμῖν εἰς Χριστὸν
  B: καὶ χρίσας ἡμᾶς θεός,
  B': ὁ καὶ σφραγισάμενος ἡμᾶς
A': καὶ δοὺς τὸν ἀρραβῶνα τοῦ πνεύματος ἐν ταῖς καρδίαις ἡμῶν.

Note the correspondence between the "technical" terms βεβαιῶν and ἀρραβῶν as well as between χρίσας and σφραγισάμενος. God sealed him as his own (B') and anointed him as his apostle (B). And having endowed him with the Spirit as the guarantee (ἀρραβῶν, "deposit") for his continuous act of confirming Paul to the consummation of salvation in Christ (A'), God indeed continues confirming (βεβαιῶν) Paul in the present through that Spirit to remain as a faithful believer/servant in the sphere of Christ's redemption (A). This chiastic structure seems to help explain both the emphatic position of the statement about the endowment of the Spirit and its connection with the main concern in the passage (A).

such a person, I did not make my decision on the travel plan according to the flesh but rather according to the Spirit.

If this interpretation is correct, 2 Cor 1:21-22 provides direct evidence for Paul's understanding of his apostolic commission in terms of God's "anoint-ment" with the Holy Spirit, and as such the passage makes it highly likely that Paul interpreted his Damascus call in the light of Isa 42, where God commis-sions the Ebed by endowing his Spirit upon him (v. 1).

Now, we may ask whether 2 Cor 1:21-22 itself might not at least echo Isa 42. Apart from (1) the idea of the endowment of the Spirit, we could consider the following four additional possibilities: (2) behind the idea of God's hold-ing Paul fast (βεβαιῶν) there may lie the idea of God's "upholding" the Ebed in Isa 42:1 (אֶתְמָךְ־בּוֹ/αὐτοῦ ἀντιλήψομαι), which is properly elaborated on in terms of God's keeping and strengthening him in 42:6 (וְאַחְזֵק בְּיָדְךָ וְאֶצָּרְךָ/ καὶ κρατήσω τῆς χειρός σου καὶ ἐνισχύσω σε); (3) the idea of God's sealing Paul as his own may reflect God's election of the Ebed in Isa 42:1 (בְּחִירִי/ὁ ἐκλεκτός μου); (4) the remarkable participle χρίσας could be a reference to God's endowment of his Spirit upon the Ebed in Isa 42:1 read in the light of its early interpretation in Isa 61:1 (πνεῦμα κυρίου ἐπ᾽ ἐμέ οὗ εἵνεκεν ἔχρισέ με εὐαγγελίσασθαι/רוּחַ אֲדֹנָי יְהֹוִה עָלָי יַעַן מָשַׁח יְהֹוָה אֹתִי לְבַשֵּׂר);[67] and (5) Paul's idea of God's faithfulness and his own truthfulness may echo the Ebed's commission to establish God's saving judgment in truthfulness (לֶאֱמֶת יוֹצִיא מִשְׁפָּט/εἰς ἀλήθειαν ἐξοίσει κρίσιν). These five points establish a close parallelism on the level of ideas between 2 Cor 1:21-22 and Isa 42:1-3, 6. When considered in the light of the other arguments in this essay for the like-lihood of Paul's using Isa 42 for interpretation of his Damascus call, the five correspondences cannot be judged arbitrary or accidental.

(4) 2 Corinthians 3:16-18

Second Corinthians 3:16-18 may provide another piece of evidence for Paul's experience of the Spirit at his Damascus conversion/call. I have already ar-gued that in 2 Cor 3:6–4:6 Paul reflects his Damascus experience of seeing the exalted Lord Jesus Christ appearing in divine glory/image and his being com-missioned to be a minister of the new covenant, and that in 2 Cor 3:16-18 he applies his experience of conversion to the Lord as, in a way, typical for all

---

67. For Isa 61:1-4 as an intertextual interpretation of the Servant Songs in Isa 42 and 49, cf. C. Westermann, *Das Buch Jesaja: Kapitel 40–66* (ATD; Göttingen: Vandenhoeck, 1966), 290-92; F. F. Bruce, *This Is That* (Exeter: Paternoster, 1968), 84. See p. 123 below.

Christians.[68] If this thesis is correct, is it not significant for our present concern that in this context he emphasizes the Spirit, indicating that the Lord to whom believers convert is the Spirit (vv. 16-18) and that his ministry of the new covenant is a ministry of the Spirit (vv. 6, 8)?

(5) The Signs of an Apostle

Further, Paul's reference to "the signs of an apostle" (τὰ σημεῖα τοῦ ἀποστόλου) verifies that Paul understood himself as commissioned with the power of the Holy Spirit. He claims that during his Corinthian mission he performed "the signs of an apostle," which he explains as "signs and wonders and mighty works" (2 Cor 12:12). When he comes to summarize his gentile mission up to the time of his writing Romans, he speaks of "what Christ has wrought through me to win the obedience of the gentiles, by word and deed, by the power of signs and wonders, by the power of the Holy Spirit, so that from Jerusalem and as far round as Illyricum I have fully preached the gospel of Christ" (Rom 15:18-19). First Corinthians 2:4; Gal 3:5; and 1 Thess 1:5 confirm that throughout his missionary work Paul indeed performed those signs and wonders and mighty works by the power of the Holy Spirit. In all these passages he makes it clear that his preaching of the gospel was not in "word" alone but it was accompanied by the "deed" of those wonders performed through the Holy Spirit.[69] It is most interesting to note that in Rom 15:18 Paul looks at what he wrought as, in reality, what Christ wrought through him. So the miracles he performed were in fact the works of Christ, and Christ performed them by the power of the Holy Spirit. Just as Jesus, while on earth, had preached the gospel of the kingdom of God and authenticated it through his healing miracles, so the risen and exalted Christ Jesus, now operating through his apostle Paul, preached the gospel and authenticated it through the mighty works of the Holy Spirit. Thus in his gospel

---

68. Kim, *Origin*, 5-13, 229-33; now confirmed by Hafemann, *Paul,* esp. 411-12, 415-16, who has recently provided the most exhaustive study on 2 Cor 3, as well as by Sandness, *Paul,* 131-45, and Newman, *Glory-Christology,* 229-40, 245-47. Cf. also A. Segal, "Paul's Thinking about Resurrection in Its Jewish Context," *NTS* 44 (1998): 406-9; *Paul the Convert: The Apostolate and Apostasy of Saul the Pharisee* (New Haven: Yale University Press, 1990), 59-61. See ch. 5, especially pp. 178-84.

69. Cf. J. Jervell, "Die Zeichen des Apostels: Die Wunder beim lukanischen und paulinischen Paulus," in *Studien zum Neuen Testament und seiner Umwelt* 4 (1979), esp. 68-74, who argues for an understanding of "the signs of an apostle" by observing how closely Paul binds his preaching with miracles and how he attributes his miracles to the Holy Spirit.

preaching Paul truly represented Christ, so that in it Christ was revealed. In this way was Paul an *apostle* of Christ. Therefore, the signs and wonders that Paul wrought by the power of the Spirit, revealing as they did that Christ was operating in and through him, were "signs" of Paul being Christ's *apostle* or empowered agent (cf. *Ber.* 5:5). Such an understanding of his apostleship would not have been possible without his consciousness of having been commissioned by Christ as his apostle with the power of the Holy Spirit.[70] Thus, Paul's term "the signs of an apostle" and his testimony about his apostolic mission as constantly accompanied by the mighty works of the Holy Spirit strongly suggest that he understood himself to have been anointed with the Holy Spirit to his apostleship.

Therefore, we conclude that Paul could well have seen the Ebed's commission with the endowment of the Spirit in Isa 42:1 as prefiguring his own apostolic commission.

Then the question arises whether in this context Paul may not also have appreciated Isa 61:1-3, where the Lord's "sending" of the servant (ἀπέσταλκέ με/שְׁלָחַנִי) is described in close parallelism to the commission of the servant in Isa 42. If Paul did, he may have taken the word χρίσας in 2 Cor 1:21 from Isa 61:1 and the idea of anointment with the Spirit from Isa 61:1 as well as Isa 42:1. No doubt, he would also have appreciated the whole notion of God's "sending" his servant εὐαγγελίσασθαι (לְבַשֵּׂר) and κηρύξαι in Isa 61:1 (cf. Gal 1:16 and compare esp. 1 Cor 1:17 [ἀπέστειλέν με Χριστὸς . . . εὐαγγελίζεσθαι] with Isa 61:1 [ἔχρισέν με εὐαγγελίσασθαι . . . ἀπέσταλκέ με . . .]). Note how Acts 26:16-18, which is close to 2 Cor 4:4-6, explains Paul's call through a combined allusion to Isa 42:7, 16 and 61:1.

The Hardening of Israel

There is an increasing recognition that in Rom 11:7-10 Paul alludes also to Isa 6:9-10 in his combined citation of Deut 29:3, Isa 29:10, and Ps 69:23-24.[71]

---

70. The Jesus tradition such as Mark 6:7/Matt 10:1/Luke 9:1-2 and the tradition of the risen Lord's commissioning apostles with the power of the Holy Spirit, such as John 20:21-22; Acts 1:8; cf. also Matt 28:18-20; Mark 16:17-18, may also have contributed to the understanding of the miracles performed by the apostles through the power of the Spirit as "signs of an apostle." If so, such tradition(s) would have made Paul all the more conscious of the endowment of the Spirit at his apostolic commission.

71. Dunn, *Romans 9-16*, 640-41, referring to C. H. Dodd, *According to the Scriptures* (London: Nisbet, 1952), 38; Hafemann, *Paul*, 375; Stockhausen, *Moses' Veil*, 141-42; see also Nestle-Aland, 27th ed.

Further, Scott J. Hafemann clearly shows that the "juxtaposition between Israel's hardened condition . . . and the one who 'returns to the Lord' . . . in 2 Cor. 3:14 and 3:16" reflects Isa 6:9-10a and Isa 6:10b respectively.[72] This allusion to Isa 6:9-10 in 2 Cor 3:14-16 is rather similar to that in Matt 13:13-15/ Mark 4:12/Luke 8:10 and to that in John 12:40[73] (cf. also Acts 28:26-27). So, in common with other representatives of the primitive church, Paul seems to have found in Isa 6 one of the important prophecies about Israel's hardening (cf. Acts 28:26-27).

Now it appears that Isa 42:18-20 could also have contributed to Paul's understanding of Israel's hardening. For Isa 42:18-20 (LXX) builds a close parallel to Isa 6:9-10: the people of Israel, having been made deaf and blind, are unable to hear or to see. In the difficult MT Isa 42:18-20, first, "you deaf ones" and "you blind ones" are called to hear and see (v. 18); and then they are identified as the Ebed Yahweh (v. 19); and finally "he" is said to "see many things but does not pay attention" and has the open ears but does not hear. But LXX Isa 42:18-20 identifies the blind ones with the servants (pl. παῖδες/ δοῦλοι) of God and the deaf ones with their rulers. Elliger thinks that in MT Isa 42:19 the identification of the deaf and blind ones with the Ebed Yahweh indicates that, unlike the Ebed in Isa 42:1, the Ebed in Isa 42:19 is not an individual but a collective, that is, the people of Israel (cf. Isa 41:8).[74] Some such interpretation seems to be reflected in the LXX text. So, guided by the LXX, Paul could have seen Israel's obduracy or God's hardening of them also in Isa 42:18-20 (see further vv. 21-25). Thus, just as Isa 42:1, 4, 7, as we argued above, helped Paul to understand his commission to be a bearer of light and salvation to the gentiles, and just as Isa 42:6, again as we argued above, likewise helped him to be conscious of his commission to be a covenant to Israel, so Isa 42:18-20 could also have contributed to his understanding of Israel's hardening.

In *The Origin of Paul's Gospel*, I submitted that the "mystery" of Rom 11:25-26 originated from Paul's interpretation of the revelation and call he had received at the Damascus Christophany chiefly in the light of Isa 6 and 49, and in a recent essay I sought to strengthen this thesis.[75] From Isa 6:9-10 (LXX), I argued, Paul learned of God's hardening of Israel and its limited du-

72. *Paul*, 391-93; quotation from 391; Stockhausen, *Moses' Veil*, 163-64, sees both πωρόω in 2 Cor 3:14 and τυφλόω in 2 Cor 4:4 reflecting Isa 6:10; cf. also Dodd, *Scriptures*, 38.

73. The similarity between 2 Cor 3:14; 4:4-6; and John 12:40 in their common reflection of Isa 6:10 has been strongly argued by Stockhausen, *Moses' Veil*, 163-67.

74. Elliger, *Deuterojesaja*, 283.

75. Kim, *Origin*, 74-99; Kim, "The 'Mystery' of Rom 11.25-26 Once More," 412-29, reprinted in this volume as ch. 7.

ration (ἄχρι οὗ in Rom 11:25 = ἕως πότε; . . . ἕως ἄν . . . in Isa 6:11). Then from Isa 49:6 he learned of his commission first to be a bearer of light and salvation to the gentiles to the ends of the earth, and from Isa 6:13 and 49:5-6 he learned that all Israel was eventually to be saved and that he was to be responsible also for it. This was the reason why in the "mystery" of Rom 11:25-26 he saw the period of Israel's hardening limited until the full number of the gentiles came into the kingdom of God and why he connected his gentile mission of bringing the full number of gentiles into the kingdom (Rom 15:15-24) with Israel's salvation in Rom 11:11-14.

My argument that Paul obtained the idea of Israel's hardening in Rom 11:25 from Isa 6:9-10 is now strengthened by the increasing recognition that in Rom 11:7-10 and 2 Cor 3:14-16 he actually speaks of Israel's πώρωσις in allusion to Isa 6:9-10.[76] Isaiah 6:10 (LXX) has παχύνομαι. However, in citing Isa 6:10, John 12:40 uses instead its "near synonym" πωρόω.[77] With πωρόω, Rom 11:7 and 2 Cor 3:14 clearly indicate that Paul understood Isa 6:10 in the same way.[78] This makes it highly likely that the πώρωσις in the "mystery" of Rom 11:25-26 also reflects Isa 6:9-10.

Now, if, as argued above, Paul saw Isa 42:18-20 together with Isa 6:9-10 for Israel's hardening, then within Isa 42 he would have found most of the building materials for the "mystery" of Rom 11:25-26: Israel's present hardening, the gentiles' readiness to praise God and set their hope in God (vv. 4, 10-12; see sect. 7 above), his commission to be a bearer of light and salvation to the gentiles, and also to be a covenant to Israel.

On the form- and tradition-historical grounds, it is to be presumed that Paul saw his Damascus Christophany in the light of Isa 6,[79] and Paul's allusion to Isa 6:9-10 in Rom 11:7-10 and 2 Cor 3:14-16 and his use of the key word πωρόω in those passages make this understanding fairly certain. Paul's use of Isa 49 in interpreting his call is well recognized. Now that we have seen that Paul probably used Isa 42 also and that Isa 42 contains some of the important building materials for the "mystery" of Rom 11:25-26, I would like to supplement my thesis on the "mystery": Paul interpreted his experience of revelation and call at the Damascus Christophany in the light of Isa 42 as well as Isa 6 and 49, that is, in the combined light of the three Isaianic chapters, and that interpretation gave rise to his understanding of divine *Heilsplan* as embodied in the "mystery."[80]

---

76. See nn. 71-72 above.
77. Observed by Dunn, *Romans 9-16*, 640.
78. So Stockhausen, *Moses' Veil*, 163-64; Hafemann, *Paul*, 375, 390-93.
79. See pp. 247-49 below and lit. cited there.
80. Some other texts like Deut 32:21 could also have contributed to this. See J. Jeremias,

Conclusion

The above eleven observations and arguments may not all be equally convincing, yet they support one another, and their cumulative effect appears to be strong. So I conclude that Isa 42 was one of the chief Old Testament texts in the light of which Paul interpreted God's revelation and call that he had received at the Damascus Christophany. I am particularly impressed how most of the elements in Gal 1:15-17, a key text for Paul's conversion/call, can be seen as allusions to Isa 42. Seen in the light of Isa 42, some of the features in Paul's theology and ministry that have been noted (at least by some) as related to his Damascus experience receive a sharper profile: his gospel of God's saving judgment or God's righteousness, his gentile apostleship, his understanding of God's *Heilsplan,* his initial mission to Arabia, and so on. However, the most significant result of following Paul in his interpretation of his Damascus experience in the light of Isa 42 is the discovery that he was conscious of having been commissioned as an apostle *with the endowment of the Holy Spirit.* This experience of the endowment of the Spirit at his conversion/call explains best both his constant practice of connecting the *Gläubigwerden* of his converts with the endowment of the Spirit and the overwhelming importance that the Holy Spirit had in his life, thought, and work.

Isaiah 42 plays an important role in the Jesus tradition. Isaiah 42:1 is alluded to in the divine declaration of Jesus as Son and endowment with the Spirit at Jesus' baptism (Matt 3:17 pars). According to Matt 11:5/Luke 7:22, Jesus alluded to Isa 42:7, 18 along with other Isaianic texts (29:18; 35:5-6; 26:19; 61:1) to reply to John the Baptist that the prophecy was being fulfilled through him. Matthew 12:17-21 cites Isa 42:1-4 as being fulfilled in Jesus' ministry. Did Paul know at least the tradition of Jesus' messianic anointment at his baptism? Regardless of whether Jesus himself did or not,[81] his followers certainly interpreted his death and exaltation in terms of the Ebed song of Isa 52:13–53:12, and Paul consciously took this tradition over and even elaborated on it (e.g., 2 Cor 5:11-21).[82] However, in several places he applies the passages from the same Ebed song to himself: for example, Rom 10:15/Isa 52:7; Rom 10:16/Isa 53:1; Rom 15:21/Isa 52:15. How was this possible? This

"Einige vorwiegend sprachliche Beobachtungen zu Röm 11, 25-36," in *Die Israelfrage nach Römer 9–11* (ed. L. De Lorenzi; Rome: Abtei von St Paul von den Mauern, 1977), 201; now Bell, *Provoked,* esp. 269-85.

81. Cf. O. Betz, "Jesus und Jesaja 53," in *Geschichte — Tradition — Reflexion,* M. Hengel Festschrift, vol. 3: *Frühes Christentum* (ed. H. Lichtenberger; Tübingen: Mohr-Siebeck, 1996), 3-19.

82. Cf., e.g., O. Betz, "Fleischliche," 119-28; O. Hofius, "Erwägungen zur Gestalt und Herkunft des paulinischen Versöhnungsgedankens," in *Paulusstudien,* 11-14.

may be revealing once more Paul's understanding of apostleship, especially his own apostleship: as an apostle of Jesus Christ, he was really representing Jesus Christ, his sender, and he was carrying on the work of Christ; or, in his own words, "Christ worked through me . . . by the power of the Holy Spirit" (Rom 15:18-19; cf. Gal 2:20). So Paul carried on fulfilling the Ebed role of Jesus Christ, or rather the risen Christ Jesus carried on fulfilling the Ebed's role through Paul.[83] That is why Paul did not even shy away from applying the call text of Jesus, Isa 42:1, to his own apostolic call, and from using the hallowed term χρίειν for his apostolic commission (cf. Isa 61:1-3) immediately after naming "the anointed" *par excellence,* Χριστός (2 Cor 1:21).

---

83. Of course, this perspective is limited to mission, and Paul would be the first to emphasize the uniqueness and once-for-all-ness of Christ's fulfillment of the atoning role of the Ebed. Cf. J. Blank, *Paulus und Jesus* (Munich: Kosel, 1968), 227 (cited from F. Mussner, *Der Galaterbrief* [Freiburg: Herder, 1974], 83 n. 19); J. R. Wagner, "The Heralds of Isaiah and the Mission of Paul," in *Jesus and the Suffering Servant* (ed. W. H. Bellinger and W. R. Farmer; Harrisburg: Trinity, 1998), 193-222.

CHAPTER 4

Paul, the Spirit, and the Law

Galatians 3:10-14 as a Test Case

"Since no one is justified before God by the law, it is evident that 'the one who is righteous by faith shall live.' " This statement in Gal 3:11 quoting Hab 2:4 is the clearest enunciation of Paul's doctrine of justification through faith apart from (works of) the law in the whole Pauline corpus. Therefore, Gal 3:10-14 with the statement at the center is a test case for various interpretations of that doctrine.[1]

The statement is an answer to the rhetorical question that Paul twice posed the Galatians: "Did you receive the Spirit by works of the law or by hearing with faith?" (3:2, 5). Paul has answered this question first with the example of Abraham in 3:6-9: "Abraham 'believed God, and it was reckoned to him as righteousness' " (Gen 15:6). This example of Abraham, the patriarch of God's people, clearly shows what the principle is whereby human beings can establish a proper relationship to God and become his people. It is faith. Hence "it is those of faith who are" members of God's people, namely "the children of Abraham" (v. 7). This means that even gentiles, if they have faith, can be "justified," that is, properly related to God as his people. This is confirmed by Gen 12:3, which declares God's will to make Abraham the source of blessing for all the nations (v. 8). The conclusion of all this lesson from the example of Abraham is that "those of faith [ἐκ πίστεως] are blessed with Abraham who had faith" (v. 9).

Thus, the Galatian Christians received the Spirit, "were justified," and were made God's people (children of Abraham) by faith and not by works of

---

1. Cf. James D. G. Dunn, "Works of the Law and the Curse of the Law (Gal 3:10-14)," in *Jesus, Paul and the Law* (Louisville: Westminster/Knox, 1990), 225.

the law.[2] This is the case "for [γάρ] all those who are of works of the law are under a curse" (v. 10a), that is, for "all those who are of works of the law [ἐξ ἔργων νόμου]" are not blessed but rather cursed, unlike "those of faith [ἐκ πίστεως]."[3] Paul substantiates this assertion by quoting Deut 27:26 (+ 28:58-59) in verse 10b. Having thus proved from Scripture the assertion that those who rely on works of the law receive only a curse, he states the summary conclusion in verse 11: "No one is justified before God by the law," and since this is the case, "it is evident that 'the one who is righteous by faith shall live.' "[4]

Thus, the assertion of verse 11a depends on verse 10. Hence on verse 10 depends the answer to the question, Why is it that "no one is justified before God by the law"? But in verse 10 how can Paul submit Deut 27:26 as the ground for his judgment that "all those who are of works of the law are under a curse"? Traditionally it is thought that Paul does this because he has an implicit premise that no one does or can keep the law perfectly:

- Deut 27:26 declares a curse on "every one" who does not keep "all the things written in the book of the law."
- [But no one does/can keep "all the things written in the book of the law"]
- Therefore "whosoever are of works of the law are under a curse."

Representing the exaggerated Reformation perspective, however, some scholars thought that the implicit premise here was Paul's condemnation of the legalistic attitude of earning justification through works of the law. Understanding that the law demands the "doing" of it (Lev 18:5 cited in v. 12), and indeed perfect "doing" of all the commandments (Deut 27:26 cited in v. 10), those of works of the law seek to keep the law perfectly so as to earn justification before God. But this legalistic attitude, opposed as it is to faith in God's grace, is sin. Therefore, all those who rely on works of the law are under

2. Reception of the Spirit, justification, and children of Abraham are equivalent to, if not synonymous with, one another here. Cf. S. K. Williams, "Justification and the Spirit in Galatians," *JSNT* 29 (1987): 91-100.

3. The γάρ here indicates that what follows is a substantiation for the preceding 3:2-9; the ἐξ ἔργων νόμου of v. 10 builds an immediate contrast with the ἐκ πίστεως of v. 9 and then of vv. 11-12, thus showing that the section 3:10-14 is still governed by the initial question of 3:2, 5. Note also the *inclusio*: 3:2–3:14: reception of the Spirit by faith.

4. For this punctuation, cf. F. Thielman, *Paul and the Law* (Downers Grove: InterVarsity, 1994), 127-28; B. Witherington, *Grace in Galatia* (Edinburgh: T & T Clark, 1998), 348; also N. T. Wright, *Climax of the Covenant* (Edinburgh: T & T Clark, 1991), 149 n. 42. ἐν νόμῳ οὐδεὶς δικαιοῦται παρὰ τῷ θεῷ is a summary conclusion of v. 10. The opening ὅτι starts the subordinate clause, giving the reason for the main sentence δῆλον ὅτι Ὁ δίκαιος ἐκ πίστεως ζήσεται. δέ is used to contrast δικαιοῦται in v. 11 with ὑπὸ κατάραν εἰσίν/ἐπικατάρατος (ἐστιν) in v. 10.

a curse.[5] Hans Dieter Betz has gone to the extreme of suggesting that here Paul associates curse with the law itself.[6] But this is a most unnatural interpretation of the immediate connection between Paul's assertion in verse 10a and its scriptural ground in verse 10b. Deuteronomy 27:26 condemns not those who try to keep the law faithfully, but on the contrary, those who do not do that!

The Challenges of the New Perspective

More serious challenges to the traditional interpretation have come from those who have been strongly influenced by Ed P. Sanders's description of Second Temple Judaism as covenantal nomism.[7] According to Sanders, the Judaism of Paul's day did not require perfect observance of the law, but it rather understood the law to include provisions for repentance and sacrifices of atonement for transgressions committed. So those who had a basic commitment to the law could remain in the covenantal relationship to God by repenting of their sins and offering sacrifices for their atonement. Given this picture of Judaism, the implicit premise attributed to Paul in verse 10 by the traditional interpretation is judged impossible. Moreover, it is pointed out that Paul himself looks back to his Pharisaic days in terms of "blameless" righteousness according to the law (Phil 3:6). With this testimony Paul did not mean that he kept the whole law perfectly, but rather that he had "blameless" righteousness within the terms of the covenant which included provisions for repentance and atonement. Thus being in good agreement with the covenantal nomism of contemporary Judaism as described by Sanders, his testimony is taken as evidence against the traditional interpretation: Paul clearly thought that it was possible to keep the law so as to have "blameless" righteousness; and therefore it is quite improbable that Paul would argue in verse 10 that no one can keep the law perfectly so that "all those of works of the law are under a curse."[8]

Such a consideration has led many to attempt to interpret verse 10 without this premise. According to Sanders, Paul's christological decision that sal-

5. E.g., H. Schlier, *Der Brief an die Galater* (Göttingen: Vandenhoeck & Ruprecht, 1971), 132-35; D. F. Fuller, "Paul and 'the Works of the Law,' " *WTJ* 38 (1975): 28-42.

6. Betz, *Galatians* (Philadelphia: Fortress, 1979), 145-46.

7. Sanders, *Paul and Palestinian Judaism* (Philadelphia: Fortress, 1977).

8. E.g., E. P. Sanders, *Paul, the Law, and the Jewish People* (Philadelphia: Fortress, 1983), 24-25; J. D. G. Dunn, *The Epistle to the Galatians* (Peabody: Hendrickson, 1993), 171; N. T. Wright, "Curse and Covenant: Galatians 3.10-14," in *Climax of the Covenant*, 145.

vation is only in Jesus Christ led him to see Judaism as problematic: salvation is only in Christ and therefore cannot be related to the law in which Judaism is centered.[9] This is one of the fundamental insights that Sanders has presented in his epoch-making book as a corollary of his theory of Judaism as covenantal nomism. Another insight that he has emphasized is that Paul's argument for justification by faith and his critique of the (works of the) law are in defense of his gentile mission against Jewish particularism.[10] Guided by these insights, Sanders thinks that Paul cites Deut 27:26 here not because it provides a logical substantiation for his assertion that those of works of the law are cursed, but simply because as the only Old Testament passage that combines the terms "law" and "curse," it serves his purpose of condemning Jewish particularism for the sake of the inclusion of the gentiles into God's people in 3:8-14.[11] But this interpretation has drawn strong criticism because it not only fails to pay adequate attention to the actual content of Deut 27:26 but also makes Paul incomprehensibly arbitrary.[12]

As usual, standing on Sanders's theory of covenantal nomism but trying to improve on his interpretation of Paul, James D. G. Dunn has repeatedly attempted to interpret our passage from the New Perspective.[13] He has recognized that this key passage is in fact a "test case" for his sociological interpretation of the phrase "works of the law" and for the whole New Perspective.[14] According to Dunn, the phrase "works of the law" is "Paul's code for those requirements of the law in particular which brought to the sharpest focus Israel's claim to be distinctive from others as God's covenant people." So by the phrase "those of works of the law," according to Dunn, Paul refers to the Jews who, emphasizing their distinctives from gentiles and restricting covenant grace to themselves, "[rest] their confidence in Israel's 'favoured nation' sta-

---

9. Sanders, *Paul and Palestinian Judaism,* 549ff.

10. Sanders, *Paul, the Law, and the Jewish People,* 45-48, 154-60.

11. Ibid., 21-23.

12. E.g., J. M. Scott, " 'For as Many as Are of Works of the Law Are under a Curse' (Galatians 3.10)," in *Paul and the Scriptures of Israel* (ed. C. A. Evans and J. A. Sanders; Sheffield: JSOT Press, 1993), 191; B. W. Longenecker, *The Triumph of Abraham's God* (Nashville: Abingdon, 1998), 139.

13. J. D. G. Dunn, "Works of the Law and the Curse of the Law (Gal 3.10-14)," in *Jesus, Paul, and the Law* (Louisville: Westminster/Knox, 1990), 215-41; *The Epistle to the Galatians,* 168-80; *The Theology of Paul the Apostle* (Grand Rapids: Eerdmans, 1998), 361-62.

14. Dunn, "Works of the Law," 225-32. In his essay, "Paul's Conversion — A Light to Twentieth Century Disputes," in *Evangelium, Schriftauslegung, Kirche,* Stuhlmacher Festschrift, (Göttingen: Vandenhoeck & Ruprecht, 1997), 77, Dunn also designates "Paul's conversion" as a test case for the New Perspective. In ch. 1 above, we have examined that test case. So with this chapter we complete examination of Dunn's two self-chosen test cases for his New Perspective.

tus."[15] Since the law properly understood contains the promise of blessings to the nations, this nationalistic attitude of the Jews is a failure to "abide by all that has been written in the book of the law to do it." So Paul declares the Jewish "law-devotees" to be under the curse pronounced by Deut 27:26.[16] Then, on Paul's train of thought in verse 13, Dunn speculates as follows:

> Christ in his death had put himself under the curse and outside the covenant blessing (cf. Deut. 11.26; 30.19-20) — that is, put himself in the place of the Gentiles! Yet God vindicated him! Therefore, God is *for* the Gentiles; and consequently the law could no longer serve as a boundary dividing Jew from Gentile.[17]

But even N. T. Wright, who agrees with Dunn on the meaning of "works of the law" and on the emphasis of Paul's concern for the inclusion of the gentiles in our passage, finds this interpretation of Gal 3:13 "tortuous and improbable."[18] Dunn says, quite correctly, that "Paul intends 'the curse of the law' " in verse 13 "to be understood in the light of v. 10,"[19] and interprets the idea of interchange here in terms of "the law printing its curse on Jesus, as it were, so that in his death the force of the curse was exhausted, and those held under its power were liberated."[20] If we follow Dunn's interpretation, then we should understand Paul to mean that by vicariously taking up the curse of the law for the Jewish nationalistic attitude and exhausting its force, Jesus redeemed "us," both Jew and gentile, according to Dunn, from that curse.[21] The Jews are then liberated from the curse they received from the law for their nationalism. But then how are the gentiles liberated from the curse? Did they have any "curse of the law" in the sense of Dunn's interpretation, in the first place? Or did they also have the Jewish nationalism so as to incur "the curse of the law" in the sense of verse 10 as interpreted by Dunn? Of course, Dunn is far from meaning such nonsense. According to him,

> The curse which was removed by Christ's death . . . was the curse which had previously prevented [the] blessing [of Abraham] from reaching the Gentiles, the curse of a wrong understanding of the law.[22]

15. Dunn, *The Epistle to the Galatians*, 172.
16. Dunn, *The Theology of Paul*, 362; "Works of the Law," 227.
17. Dunn, "Works of the Law," 230; similarly also *The Epistle to the Galatians*, 178.
18. Wright, "Curse and Covenant," 153; similarly also C. E. B. Cranfield, "'The Works of the Law' in the Epistle to the Romans," *JSNT* 43 (1991): 92: "unconscionably tortuous."
19. Dunn, "Works of the Law," 228.
20. Dunn, *The Epistle to the Galatians*, 177.
21. Ibid., 176.
22. Dunn, "Works of the Law," 229.

Dunn goes on to say:

> As soon as we recall that "those under the law" are under the curse of the law (v. 10), the purpose of Christ's redemptive work can be specified quite properly as the removal of *that* curse, as the deliverance of the heirs of the covenant promise from <u>the ill effects</u> of the too narrow understanding of the covenant and law held by most of Paul's Jewish contemporaries, so that both Jew and Gentile can enter into the fuller scope of the covenant promise.[23]

In these two quotations, note how Dunn shifts the meaning of "the curse of the law." He is no longer using the phrase in the sense of the curse that the law pronounced on the Jews *for* their nationalistic understanding of the covenant and the law, as he did in his interpretation of verse 10. He now lets the phrase mean "the ill effects" *of* the Jewish nationalistic understanding of the law! It is no longer the curse *for* a wrong understanding of the law, but the curse *of* a wrong understanding (the appositional genitive). The curse that the law pronounced on the Jews for their nationalistic attitude could not possibly have "prevented [the] blessing [of Abraham] from reaching the Gentiles"; only the curse in the sense of "the ill effects" that their nationalistic attitude engendered could have. But then the latter is no longer the sense of the curse of the law in verse 10.

This muddle on Dunn's part about the key concept, the curse of the law in verses 10 and 13, which is a serious problem in itself, has a more serious consequence in Dunn's interpretation of the effect of Christ's redemption. In verse 10 he interprets correctly that "those who are of works of the law" refers primarily to the Jewish "law-devotees" and therefore that these Jewish "law-devotees" are said to be under the curse of the law (Deut 27:26). But Dunn's interpretation of verse 13 makes only the gentiles the real beneficiaries of Christ's redemption. Whereas Christ's redemption affects the Jews only to *correct* their "wrong understanding of the law" so that it may no longer prevent the blessing of Abraham from reaching the Gentiles, it truly delivers the gentiles from "the ill effects" of the Jewish misunderstanding of the law so that they may now receive the blessing of Abraham. A mere *correction* of the Jews' "wrong understanding of the law" can hardly be said to be redemption from the curse that the law pronounces upon their not "abiding by all that has been written in the book of the law to do it" (v. 10b; Deut 27:26).[24] In that case, the Jewish "law-devotees" declared to be under the curse of the law in

---

23. Ibid., 229-30 (Dunn's italics, and my underline).

24. Cranfield, "The Works of the Law," 92, points out that Dunn's interpretation also "sorts extremely ill with" what Paul says in Gal 2:20.

verse 10 for their failure to "abide by all that has been written in the book of the law" remain under that curse, for Christ's redemption removes only the "ill effects" of their "wrong understanding of the law" (on the gentiles)! Thus, Dunn's interpretation makes Christ's redemptive work on the cross practically irrelevant to the Jews.[25]

Dunn's confusion regarding the curse of the law in verses 10 and 13 and his "tortuous" interpretation of Christ's death as redemption from that curse, not to mention the other details such as his controversial interpretation of the phrase "works of the law," make his whole interpretation of our passage highly questionable. This means that his interpretation from the New Perspective fails at our passage, his chosen "test case"![26]

"With a rhetorical/reader response approach" C. D. Stanley seeks to interpret Gal 3:10 without the assumption of an implied premise. According to him, verse 10 functions as a threat, intended to induce the Galatians to reconsider their contemplated acceptance of Torah-observance by pointing out "its potential dangers,"[27] and Deut. 27:26 is cited in order "to define the circumstances under which its 'curse' comes to be actualized."[28] Stanley paraphrases verse 10: "Anyone who chooses to abide by the Jewish Torah in order to secure participation in Abraham's 'blessing' is placed in a situation where he or she is threatened instead with a 'curse,' since the law itself pronounces a curse on anyone who fails to live up to every single one of its requirements."[29] To be consistent with his interpretation of verse 10, Stanley has to interpret verse 13 as describing "how God in the death of Jesus Christ has opened up a way of escape for *Gentiles* from the 'negative potentiality' associated with Torah-observance."[30] But James M. Scott has no problem finding fault with this whole interpretation, as it contradicts the clear meaning of 3:13: it is not from "negative potentiality" but from "the curse of the law" that Christ redeemed us. This in turn makes it clear that the "curse" in verse 10 is not just future "negative potentiality" but the *Unheil* which "all those of works of the law"

---

25. Dunn's interpretation of the Damascus event as a whole also makes the gospel of Christ practically irrelevant to the Jews. See pp. 20-22 above.

26. At least this seems to be the verdict of the jury of scholars. Longenecker, *Triumph*, 136 n. 29, finds that Dunn's interpretation is followed only by M. Cranford, "The Possibility of Perfect Obedience: Paul and an Implied Premise in Galatians 3:10 and 5:3," *NovT* 36 (1994): 249, 254; and J. P. Braswell, " 'The Blessing of Abraham' versus 'The Curse of the Law': Another Look at Gal 3:10-13," *WTJ* 53 (1991): 73-91. Cf. also N. H. Young, "Who's Cursed — and Why? (Galatians 3:10-14)," *JBL* 117 (1998): 86 n. 36.

27. Stanley, " 'Under a Curse': A Fresh Reading of Galatians 3.10-14," *NTS* 36 (1990): 501.

28. Ibid., 499.

29. Ibid., 500.

30. Ibid., 506 (his italics).

are presently under.[31] We should not forget that for Paul both the Jews and the gentiles "*have* sinned and fall short of the glory of God" (Rom 3:23) and "the wrath of God is revealed from heaven against all ungodliness and wickedness of human beings" (Rom 1:18). Furthermore, it should be pointed out that Stanley's interpretation also requires an implied premise in verse 10: either "because he or she cannot keep the law perfectly," or "if he or she does not keep the law perfectly." Does it then have any advantage over against the traditional interpretation? It would suffer exactly the same objection from the New Perspectivists as the traditional interpretation. Besides, if it presupposes the latter form of the premise, it would make Paul appear as if he granted a possibility of receiving "blessing" or justification by perfect observance of the law, which would create an immediate conflict with the following verses, verses 11-12.

Recently Norman H. Young has presented an interpretation of 3:10 similar to that of Stanley, explicitly proposing to see the implied premise as a condition, "*if* those ἐξ ἔργων νόμου do not do all the requirements of the law."[32] According to Young, this new proposal is called for because the implied premise in the traditional interpretation cannot be maintained in the face of the challenge of the New Perspectivists.[33] But he seems to be unaware that his new proposal would face exactly the same objection as the implied premise in the traditional interpretation: Judaism did not require perfect obedience, and it had provisions for atonement, and therefore Paul would not have said that "those of the works of the law are under a curse, if they do not do all the requirements of the law"! Furthermore, apparently sensing difficulties in connecting his interpretation of verse 10 with verse 11, Young proposes to insert the same unexpressed condition into verse 11 and to read verse 11 as "it is clear that no one can be a member of the people of God by works of the law, *while at the same time abandoning any of the Sinai covenant's stipulations,* therefore those who are righteous by faith will live out their life in the covenant by faith, and not by works of the law."[34] But this is a massive eisegesis! Unlike verse 10, verse 11 does not require any premise or condition. Young has no real ground for importing "while at the same time abandoning any of the Sinai covenant's stipulations" into verse 11a and "live out their life in the covenant by faith, and not by works of the law" into verse 11b. In this interpretation, 11a and 11b are not logically connected, and so "therefore" is quite

31. Scott, "Galatians 3.10," 193.
32. Young, "Who's Cursed?" 86 (his emphasis).
33. Ibid., 83.
34. Ibid., 88-89 (his emphasis).

inappropriate. Besides, Young has to face the same question that we have put to Stanley: Is Paul here then implicitly granting the possibility of justification by perfect observance of the law? Such a view would be the exact opposite of Paul's intent in 3:10-14 and the whole Epistle to the Galatians!

The Theory of the Continuing Exile

Recently N. T. Wright and James M. Scott have, apparently independently from each other, proposed to interpret our passage in the light of the theory of a continuing exile of the Jewish nation.[35] According to them, there was a widespread perception in Second Temple Judaism that despite their return from Babylon the Jewish people were still in exile. So long as they remained under the foreign domination while the national independence and prosperity predicted by the prophets did not materialize, they thought that the exile continued and so they longed for the eschatological redemption through the Messiah. With its threat of curse and exile for Israel's disobedience to the law and its promise of blessing and restoration for her repentance and obedience, Deut 27–30 was a foundational text for this understanding and gave rise to a strong tradition-history in the various strands of the Old Testament and Judaism.

Paul's combined citation of Deut 27:26 and 29:19b (+ 28:58) in Gal 3:10 clearly suggests that he has in view the Deuteronomic passage. So, according to Wright and Scott, Paul is in Gal 3:10 reflecting the common belief in the continuing exile of Israel and declaring that the Jewish nation is under the curse of Deut 27–30 for her disobedience to the law. Scott[36] sees Gal 3:13 in the light of the divine promise of restoration of Israel after the exile (Deut 30:1-8; Dan 9:15) and the expectation of a redemption through the Messiah (e.g., *Frg. Tg.* Exod 12:42). Wright also takes 3:13 as a perfect expression of the exile-restoration scheme:

> Because the Messiah represents Israel, he is able to take on himself Israel's curse and exhaust it. Jesus dies as the King of the Jews, at the hands of the Romans whose oppression of Israel is the present, and climactic, form of the curse of exile itself. The crucifixion of the Messiah is . . . the *quintessence* of the curse of exile, and its climactic act.[37]

---

35. Wright, "Curse and Covenant," 137-56; Scott, "Galatians 3.10," 187-221.
36. Scott, "Galatians 3.10," 215-16.
37. Wright, "Curse and Covenant," 151 (his italics).

Scott[38] further believes that the reception of the Spirit referred to in 3:14 as a consequence of Christ's redemption reflects the Old Testament-Jewish expectation of the endowment of the Messiah and Israel with the Spirit at the eschatological restoration (cf. *T. Jud.* 24:3; *Jub.* 1:23-24). So, for Scott, the concepts like "curse" (3:10), "redemption" from the "curse" through "Christ" (3:13), and the reception of the "Spirit" (3:14), unmistakably suggest that Paul uses the Old Testament-Jewish exile-restoration tradition in 3:10-14.[39] Scott goes on to draw the same conclusion from the concepts like "the fullness of time," God's sending his Son for "redemption," and the reception of "adoption" and the "Spirit" in Gal 4:4-6.[40] For Scott, the fact that in Gal 3–4 the messianic restoration is emphasized in the argument for the inclusion of the gentiles in the people of God also agrees well with the tradition, which expected the gentiles' participation in the restored Israel.[41]

This is an attractive interpretation of 3:10, 13-14, and 4:4-6. However, it is not without serious difficulties. First of all, it is striking that Scott completely neglects the two verses intervening between 3:10 and 3:13-14.[42] Wright does deal with the two verses,[43] but Bruce W. Longenecker is only fair when he judges that Wright "fails to show how the extended exile theology animates these verses."[44] Wright is also unable to explain satisfactorily how the two verses are connected with both the foregoing verse 10 and the following verses 13-14 as interpreted in terms of Israel's exile and restoration. Verses 11-12 constitute vital steps in Paul's argument in the passage from verse 10 to verse 14. Therefore, unless Wright and Scott convincingly explain the connection of verses 11-12 with 10 and 13-14, their interpretations of verses 10, 13-14 in terms of Israel's exile will remain questionable.

Both Longenecker and Mark A. Seifrid question the assumption of Wright and Scott that in Second Temple Judaism there was a widespread and well-established belief in the continuing exile.[45] Seifrid further denies any substantial influence of the belief on Paul either before or after his conversion.[46] However, even if it may be questioned whether the majority of the

---

38. Scott, "Galatians 3.10," 212, 216; similarly also Wright, "Curse and Covenant," 154.

39. Scott, "Galatians 3.10," 215.

40. Ibid., 217-19.

41. Ibid., 219-20.

42. Cf. Longenecker, *Triumph*, 138.

43. Wright, "Curse and Covenant," 148-50.

44. Longenecker, *Triumph*, 138 n. 35.

45. Ibid., 137-38; Seifrid, "Blind Alleys in the Controversy over the Paul of History," *TynBul* 45 (1994): 86-89.

46. Seifrid, "Blind Alleys," 89-91.

Jews during the New Testament period held to a well-articulated and coherent theory of the Babylonian exile still continuing, there is no question that they generally felt the great prophecies of restoration (Deutero-Isaiah, Ezekiel, etc.) had not yet been fulfilled, and so they longed for the final and full restoration of Israel at the end time.[47] The latter feeling may have led some Jews to regard their present situation in terms of an "intermediate" state (between the first stage fulfilled and the final restoration to come at the end).[48] But it may have led some Jews who were particularly struck by the present malaise of the Jewish existence to think in terms of a continuation of the exile and see a hopeful sign of its end in the fortune-turning events that they had recently experienced or were intensely anticipating. The Jews generally thought in the pattern of covenantal threats (exile) and promises (restoration).[49] For example, 2 Maccabees apparently perceives in the Maccabean victory a sign of the end of the exile (cf. 2 Macc 15:37).[50] The Qumran covenanters appear to have thought that the continuing exile ended with the foundation of its community (cf. 1QH 3:19-20).[51] During his pre-conversion days Paul may have joined Pharisaism in order to fulfill the condition of Israel's restoration with a whole-hearted obedience to the law (Deut 30:1-8).[52] Then he may have thought of Israel as a whole to be either in the "intermediate" state or still under the condition of exile.

However, even if it is granted that the majority of the Jews during the New Testament period held to a well-articulated and coherent theory of the Babylonian exile still continuing, the view of Wright and Scott that in Gal 3:10, 13-14 Paul represents that theory is questionable. If the theory had been so powerfully at work during the New Testament period as they claim, Paul's Judaizing opponents in Galatia would also have shared it.[53] If so, how would they have looked at the Christ crucified, the one who died under the "curse of the law" (Deut 21:23; 27:26)? They must have become Christians because, on the assumption of the theory of a continuing exile, they believed Jesus the

47. Thus, it may be necessary to distinguish between a well-articulated and coherent theory of the continuing exile and the widespread expectation of the eschatological restoration. Cf. Longenecker, *Triumph*, 138; E. P. Sanders, *Jesus and Judaism* (Philadelphia: Fortress, 1985), 87.

48. Seifrid, "Blind Alleys," 88, thinks that Tobit and *Pss. Sol.* display this belief.

49. Seifrid, "Blind Alleys," 87; cf. also Thielman, *Paul*, 49-55.

50. Cf. Seifrid, "Blind Alleys," 88.

51. Cf. ibid., 89.

52. Cf. Roland Deines, *Die Pharisäer: ihr Verständnis im Spiegel der christlichen und jüdischen Forschung seit Wellhausen und Graetz* (WUNT 101; Tübingen: Mohr-Siebeck, 1997), 544-45.

53. So Wright, "Curse and Covenant," 141; Scott, "Galatians 3.10," 214. Scott thinks Paul's Galatian addressees also knew it.

Messiah had brought the exile to an end. Then they must have understood the "curse of the law" as something that the Messiah bore vicariously. That is to say, they must have shared Paul's view read out of 3:13 by Wright and Scott: Christ had redeemed them (the Jews) from the curse of the law, that is, from the exile, that had befallen the Jews because of their failure to keep the law (Deut 27–30). Now, then, when they had been redeemed from the curse of the law, why were they still insisting on keeping the law? Were they saying, "Now that Christ has redeemed us from the curse of the law that had befallen us for our *past* disobedience, let us keep the law all the more conscientiously and let us make the gentile Christians also keep the law"?[54] Had this been the argument of the Judaizers — on the assumption of the theory of a continuing exile, which seems to be the only option — would Paul have argued back as he did in 3:10-14?

First of all, why would he have stated in verses 10 and 13 what his opponents (and his readers) were already taking for granted — even with scriptural substantiation at that? Given the well-established theology of the extended exile and its termination through the Messiah, it has to be assumed that the Judaizers, if not Paul himself, had taught the Galatian Christians of the redemption through Christ in terms of redemption from "the curse of the law" or the extended exile of Israel. Would not verse 13 then have been gratuitous, and the scriptural substantiation from Deut 21:23 even more so?

According to Scott, by stating in verse 10 that the curse of Deut 27:26 had fallen on Israel and still remained on them, Paul sought to answer his own question, "Did you receive the Spirit by works of the law, or by the hearing of faith?" (Gal 3:2, 5): "Paul was answering in effect that the former possibility was completely ruled out on the basis of OT/Jewish tradition: the law did not bring the Spirit, but rather a long-term curse on Israel."[55] But then why did he not write, "*Israel* [or *the Jews*] is under a curse," but instead, "*All those who* [ὅσοι] are of works of the law are under a curse"? In writing thus, he clearly sought to state something else than what his opponents and readers might have taken for granted. He wrote ὅσοι ἐξ ἔργων νόμου here rather than simply "the Jews" because he wanted to draw a generalized conclusion from the proof-text of Deuteronomy and apply it to others as well as the Jews. These others he had in view must have included both the Jewish *Christian* agitators (cf. 2:16) and the Galatian (i.e., *gentile*) Christians attracted to the agitators

---

54. Cf. C. K. Barrett, *Freedom and Obligation* (Philadelphia: Westminster, 1985), 23-26, for the view that Deut 27:26 was originally used by the Judaizers against Paul's disregard of the commandments of the law.

55. Scott, "Galatians," 241-42.

(cf. 3:2, 5).[56] If so, here he had already left behind the thought of *Israel's* exile or at least driven it into the background!

Wright would not agree with this judgment. Apparently being conscious of Paul's individualizing and generalizing ὅσοι, while sticking to his theory of the extended exile, he tries to show the run of Paul's argument in 3:10 as follows:

On the assumption (I) that

a. Israel as a whole is under the curse if it fails to keep Torah;
b. Israel as a whole failed to keep Torah;
c. therefore Israel is under the curse,

Paul is arguing (II) that

a. all who embrace Torah are thereby embracing Israel's national way of life;
b. Israel as a nation has suffered, historically, the curse that the Torah held out for them if they did not keep it;
c. therefore all who embrace Torah now are under this curse.[57]

But this would be an extremely clumsy argument, which Wright normally would not like to attribute to Paul! From a. and b. in the above argument (II), the conclusion c. does not necessarily follow. A quite different conclusion can be drawn: "Therefore all who embrace Torah now must keep the law perfectly, to avoid Israel's mistake." The Judaizers would be the first to argue in this way. Thus, even Wright cannot solve the problem of the individualizing and generalizing ὅσοι in 3:10.

We may ask further: why is it that "all those who are of the works of the law are under a curse"? For anybody who operates on the basis of the covenantal curses and blessings of Deut 27–30, the exactly opposite inference from Deut 27:26 would be in order: "all those who are *not* of the works of the law (i.e., all those who do not keep the law) are under a curse."[58] Therefore, on the assumption of a well-established theory of a continuing exile, Paul's Judaizing opponents in Galatia would have the better of the argument here: just as Israel was cursed and sent into exile for her disobedience to the law, so all those who do not keep the law will be cursed. Hence the need for obser-

---

56. So H. J. Eckstein, *Verheissung und Gesetz: Eine exegetische Untersuchung zu Galater 2,15–4,7* (WUNT 86; Tübingen: Mohr-Siebeck, 1996), 123.

57. Wright, "Curse and Covenant," 147.

58. Cf. Longenecker, *Triumph*, 135.

vance of the law! This consideration also suggests that when Paul writes "all those who are of the works of the law are under a curse" and backs it up with a quotation from Deut 27:26, he cannot be thinking in terms of the notion of Israel's extended exile.

No Alternative to the Traditional Interpretation

Thus, both 3:13 and 3:10, the two verses which Wright and Scott regard as the clearest evidence of the extended exile theology, actually present difficulties to their interpretation in terms of that theology. This leads us to bid farewell to the attractive theory of Israel's continuing exile as an aid for interpretation of Gal 3:10-14. So, then, quite independent of the theory, we have to seek to answer the question, Why is it that "all those who are of the works of the law are under a curse"? On what premise would the quotation from Deut 27:26 be a logical support for the statement? Deuteronomy 27:26 (cited in 3:10) is a statement in a negative form of the principle of Lev 18:5 (cited in 3:12): He who keeps the law will have life in it (Lev 18:5), but he who does not keep it will be cursed (Deut 27:26). According to this scheme, when it is said that "all those who are of the works of the law are under a curse," it must be because they are thought of as not keeping the law although they are "of the works of the law." But are not "those of the works of the law" by definition law-keepers? But then in what sense are they thought of as not keeping the law so as to incur a curse? This line of reasoning seems to lead us inexorably to the word πᾶσιν in Deut 27:26 cited in 3:10: "those of the works of the law" are thought of as not keeping the law because they do not keep "*all things* written in the book of the law."[59] The phrase "those of the works of the law" implies their commitment to keep the law. But then why, in spite of that commitment, do they not keep "*all things* written in the book of the law"? The only answer available appears to be: because they *cannot* keep "*all things* written in the book of the law." Thus, the premise implicit in the declaration of 3:10a seems to be that no one can keep the law perfectly (cf. Gal 5:3). Then 3:10 has a coherent logic in itself and runs smoothly into verse 11:

• It is written, "Cursed is every one who does not abide by all things written in the book of the law to do them."

59. The word πᾶσιν appears only in the LXX version, and its Hebrew equivalent does not appear in the MT. By citing Deut 27:26 according to the LXX, Paul clearly intends to emphasize both the requirement to keep all the commandments and the impossibility thereof.

- [But no one can keep *all things* in the book of the law.]
- Therefore, all those who are of the works of the law are under a curse.
- [Thus] by the law no one is justified before God.
- Therefore it is evident that "he who is righteous by faith shall live" (Hab 2:4).

This line of logic further develops smoothly into verses 12-14: The law has to do with something else than the "by faith [ἐκ πίστεως]" attitude,[60] for it enunciates the fundamental principle "The one who does them will live by them" (Lev 18:5), quite contrary to the principle of Hab 2:4. But it is impossible to obtain righteousness and life through works of the law, so that all those who rely on works of the law are in fact under a curse. However, the good news is that Christ has redeemed us[61] from the curse that the law had pronounced on us for our failure to keep the law of God (cf. Rom 1:18–3:20; 7:4-25), by bearing the curse vicariously for us on the cross (Deut 21:23). The purpose of this redemption was not to save the Jews[62] only but to have the blessing promised to Abraham, the salvation of the gentiles (Gal 3:8; Gen 12:3; 18:18), also come true. The purpose was for us to receive by faith the life-giving Spirit promised for the age of the new covenant (cf. Ezek 36–37).

60. Cf. Dunn, *The Epistle to the Galatians*, 175.

61. The first person plural in vv. 13-14 is to be interpreted as referring to both the Jews and the gentiles. The Jerusalem church which formulated "Christ was delivered [to death] for our trespasses" (Rom 4:25a) and the Hellenistic Jewish church which formulated "Christ died for our sins" (1 Cor 15:3) (cf. M. Hengel, *The Atonement* [London: SCM, 1981], 35-39) may naturally have referred the 1st p. pl. primarily to the Jewish people. But as soon as Paul delivered to the gentiles the formulae as the kernel of the gospel, it was expanded to refer to all humankind. This corresponds to Paul's belief that through their idolatry, immorality, and so on not only the Jews but also the gentiles transgressed the will or law of God revealed in creation and written in their conscience (Rom 1:18-32; 2:12-16; 7:7-25). The integration of the Adamic and Israel perspectives in Rom 7:7-25 (cf. Wright, *Climax*, 197-98; Dunn, *The Theology of Paul*, 99-100) seems to suggest that Paul perceived Israel as the heir of Adam's destiny to represent all humankind. Even D. J. Moo, *The Epistle to the Romans* (NICNT; Grand Rapids: Eerdmans, 1996), 428, 449, who tries to minimize the presence of the Adam perspective in favor of the Israel perspective in Rom 7, admits that through "paradigmatic significance of Israel's experience with the Mosaic law" Paul speaks to the situation of all people "because what is true of Israel under God's law through Moses is true *ipso facto* of all people under 'law' " (cf. 2:14-15; 7:4). Then he could have understood that Christ's death for Israel was also for all humankind.

62. It would be absurd to think that Christ's redemption on the cross was only for the salvation of the gentiles. Here Paul mentions only it, omitting mention of the salvation of the Jews, because in the context he is concerned to address the gentile Christians in Galatia and explain how they can benefit from Christ's redemption by faith alone and why they therefore should not join in the Jewish efforts to keep the law.

Since all the attempts so far proposed to interpret our passage without the implied premise have failed, while the traditional interpretation with the implied premise makes perfect sense, we have to accept it as the right exegesis of our passage. The objections to it have not arisen from within the passage or its context or even Pauline theology in general. In fact, Rom 1:18–3:26 and 7:4–8:17 have basically the same structure of argument and make the same points as Gal 3:10-14, namely: (a) the inability of the Jews (as well as the gentiles) to keep the law perfectly; (b) their plight of falling short of God's glory or of standing under the power of sin and death and therefore under the wrath of God; and (c) their redemption through Christ's death of vicarious atonement. Thus, it is clearly wrong to think that Paul could not have said that "all those who are of the works of the law are under a curse" because they cannot keep the law perfectly. *In Rom 2:1–3:20, 23 and 7:4-25 he says precisely that!*[63]

The Judaism of Paul's Day

The objections to the traditional interpretation with the implied premise have arisen only from the general consideration of the character of the Judaism of Paul's day, or, to be more specific, from Sanders's definition of its character. Therefore we are bound to examine the latter.

There are some, however, who assume the Second Temple Judaism to have been covenantal nomism as Sanders described but still find no alternative to the traditional interpretation of our passage.[64] For them, the implied premise has to be explained as a product of Paul's new Christian convictions. Thus Bruce Longenecker suggests that having experienced God's saving grace in Christ, which made him think of it as restricted to those "in Christ," Paul came to see Jewish ethnocentric covenantalism as "nothing but works to ef-

---

63. Cf. H. Räisänen, *Paul and the Law* (WUNT 29; Tübingen: Mohr-Siebeck, 1983), 95-101, 109-13. Right up to his recent writing on Rom 2–3, Dunn continues his one-sided emphasis on Paul's charge of the overconfidence of the Jews in their covenantal status, without adequately acknowledging his equally serious charge of their transgressions of the law in that Romans passage (*The Theology of Paul,* 116-19, 145). Against this, see, e.g., S. Westerholm, *Israel's Law and the Church's Faith* (Grand Rapids: Eerdmans, 1988), 118-19; T. R. Schreiner, *The Law and Its Fulfillment* (Grand Rapids: Baker, 1993), 56-57. However, Dunn now recognizes that in Rom 7:7-13 Paul integrates the story of Israel within the story of Adam and that thus Paul is indicating "that Israel was bound up in the solidarity of human frailty and failure and was firmly caught in the nexus of sin and death as any Gentile" (*The Theology of Paul,* 99-100). Then would Dunn still object to the conclusion here presented?

64. E.g., Räisänen, *Paul,* 94-96; Longenecker, *Triumph,* 139.

fect their salvation, despite their own convictions that their works are in response to grace."[65] So Paul separates Jewish "works" from divine "grace" in Rom 9:32 and 11:5-6, and understands the former in terms of "wages" in Rom 4:4-5. His reevaluation of Judaism in the light of his new Christian convictions climaxes in Rom 7, where he depicts "the Jew" as "completely incapable of doing the law, despite the best of intentions." Precisely this view is presupposed in Gal 3:10. According to Longenecker, the Judaism so reevaluated by the Christian Paul "has little semblance to the traditional Jewish view that he held in his pre-Christian days (cf. Phil 3:6)."[66]

This is basically a restatement of Sanders's famous dictum that Paul's exclusive soteriology (salvation only in Christ) obtained at his conversion led him to fault Judaism and reject it.[67] And it comes close to the thesis of Heikki Räisänen, that Paul distorted Judaism as a legalistic religion,[68] although, unlike Räisänen, Longenecker tries to suggest that given Paul's new Christian view of grace in Christ, such a reevaluation of Judaism is understandable. But even Dunn, who stands on the basic premise of Sanders's theory of Judaism as covenantal nomism, finds it difficult to accept Sanders's picture of an "idiosyncratic," "arbitrary and irrational" Paul.[69] The same criticism applies to Räisänen's thesis. No doubt Paul's new Christian perspective obtained at his conversion must have yielded a picture of Judaism somewhat different from what he used to cherish in his Pharisaic days. But if the former had "little semblance" to the latter, Longenecker, like Räisänen, has the task of showing how Paul could have imagined he could argue effectively against his Jewish opponents with "such profoundly novel depictions of traditional forms of Judaism and Jewish experience."[70] There must be some continuity between the Judaism that Paul practiced as a Pharisee and the Judaism that he now criticizes as a Christian.

So we are bound to inquire whether it was at all possible within the Judaism of Paul's day to think that since no one can keep the law perfectly all those who are of the works of the law are under the curse of the law. If Second Temple Judaism was indeed covenantal nomism that emphasized God's gracious election and atonement as Sanders has described it, of course, it would have been impossible. Although Sanders's notion of Judaism as covenantal

65. Longenecker, *Triumph*, 140-41.
66. Ibid., 141.
67. Sanders, *Paul and Palestinian Judaism*, 549-50.
68. Räisänen, *Paul*, 188.
69. Dunn, "The New Perspective on Paul," in *Jesus, Paul, and the Law*, 187.
70. Longenecker, *Triumph*, 141. Cf. Seyoon Kim, *The Origin of Paul's Gospel* (WUNT 2/4; Tübingen: Mohr-Siebeck, 1981, 1984; Grand Rapids: Eerdmans, 1982), 351.

nomism has received broad consent in New Testament scholarship, there have also been attempts to modify or correct it. So Martin Hengel makes a fundamental criticism of Sanders's covenantal nomism that it ignores the "positive will" of the Jewish religion or its representatives, as it operates only with the concepts of "getting into" the covenant through divine election and "staying in" it through law observance. Merely "staying in" the covenant is "the absolutely minimum goal," and it is impossible to think that all the various groups within Judaism wanted simply the same minimum goal. In fact, "no religion, let alone its active, self-conscious and especially successful representatives [e.g., the Pharisees], could be content with such a minimum goal."[71] So, for Hengel, a more adequate description of the structure of a religion must involve such questions as "*what* it wants, *why* it wants it, and *with which means* it seeks to arrive at it."[72]

Mark A. Seifrid has observed in 1QS and *Pss. Sol.* how the Qumran covenanters and those (Pharisees?) who are represented as the "righteous" or "pious" in *Pss. Sol.* are distinguished from the rest of the Jews and how the saving blessings of the covenant are restricted to the former. While in both documents the covenant structure is maintained and salvation is attributed to God's mercy, that covenant promise of mercy is made available only to those who are faithful to the covenant. Thus, a measure of individualism is developed and salvation is conceived of as contingent upon personal righteousness, faithful observance of the law.[73] So, to put it in the language of Hengel, the Qumran

---

71. Hengel, "E. P. Sanders' 'Common Judaism,' Jesus und die Pharisäer," in *Judaica et Hellenistica: Kleine Schriften I* (WUNT 90; Tübingen: Mohr-Siebeck, 1996), 394.

72. Ibid., 394 (his emphasis).

73. M. A. Seifrid, *Justification by Faith: The Origin and Development of a Central Pauline Theme* (NovTSup 68; Leiden: Brill, 1992), 78-135; summary in his "Blind Alleys," 76. T. Laato, *Paul and Judaism: An Anthropological Approach* (Atlanta: Scholars Press, 1995), esp. 147-68, arrives at a similar conclusion through his analysis of the Jewish optimistic anthropology in contrast to Paul's pessimistic anthropology. Pointing out the fact that in the Jewish literature which is concerned with eschatological salvation "obedience [to the law] is the criterion and condition for eschatological salvation" (p. 55), T. Eskola, *Theodicy and Predestination in Pauline Soteriology* (WUNT 2/100; Tübingen: Mohr-Siebeck, 1998), 54-60, observes that with regard to such literature Sanders's "covenantal nomism" is really a "synergistic nomism," insofar as it requires obedience to the law for "staying in" the covenant and eventually obtaining eschatological salvation. Eskola appeals to C. F. D. Moule's observation: "in observing that a Jew was in the Covenant-area by no merit but by the grace of God, it must not be overlooked that Sanders does, nevertheless, agree that obedience to the Torah was necessary for staying within the Mosaic Covenant, within which one is initially placed by the sheer grace of God. If the Jew was 'in' (i.e. within the Covenant) unless he deliberately put himself 'out' by flagrant transgression, this does not alter the fact that 'staying in' does therefore depend on observance: a code of laws does play an essential part, though not in the initiation of 'salvation,' which is by pure grace, yet in its

covenanters and "the righteous" in *Pss. Sol.* wanted better righteousness than that of their less pious compatriots; they wanted it for God's mercy or salvation; and they sought to arrive at it by ever more faithful observance of the law. They were not content with the minimum goal of merely "staying in" the covenant, like the rest of the Jews. Or, to be more precise, thinking that those Jews who were not as faithful to the law as they, were not "staying in" the covenant, they made extra efforts to keep the law in order to stay in the situation where they could obtain the covenant promise of God's mercy and salvation.

Confirming an insight that E. Sjöberg developed long ago,[74] recently Friedrich Avemarie has showed that rabbinic soteriology is based on two contrary principles: election and recompense.[75] The former affirmed that those who belong to Israel, the elect people of God, would have a share in the world to come, while the latter held that those who fulfill the law would be rewarded with life in the world to come. Both principles are well evidenced in the rabbinic literature, and they stand next to each other without any connection between them. So the rabbinic tradition does not arrange them in a hierarchy, giving one priority over against the other. Rather, it "brings election and recompense to a balance in constantly changing proportions, sometimes even to the extent of an apparent absolutization of one and ignoring of the other."[76] If this is so, not only those who have emphasized only the principle of recompense (e.g., F. Weber and P. Billerbeck), but also those who have made the principle of election dominant (e.g., G. F. Moore and E. P. Sanders) are wrong.

Criticizing Sanders for dismissing several Mishnaic statements that are detrimental to his thesis,[77] C. L. Quarles[78] has specifically repudiated his as-

---

maintenance. . . . I am asking whether 'covenantal nomism' itself is so far from implicit 'legalism'" ("Jesus, Judaism, and Paul," in *Tradition and Interpretation in the New Testament: Essays in Honor of E. Earle Ellis* [ed. G. F. Hawthorne and O. Betz; Grand Rapids: Eerdmans; Tübingen: Mohr-Siebeck, 1987], 48). Cf. also D. A. Hagner, "Paul and Judaism. The Jewish Matrix of Early Christianity: Issues in the Current Debate," *BBR* 3 (1993): 122.

74. E. Sjöberg, *Gott und die Sünder im palästinischen Judentum* (Stuttgart: Kohlhammer, 1939).

75. F. Avemarie, "Erwählung und Vergeltung: Zur Optionalen Struktur Rabbinischer Soteriologie," *NTS* 45 (1999): 108-26; cf. also K. R. Snodgrass, "Justification by Grace — To the Doers: An Analysis of the Place of Romans 2 in the Theology of Paul," *NTS* 32 (1986): 78.

76. Ibid., 108.

77. Cf. also Kim, *Origin*, 347; R. Gundry, "Grace, Works, and Staying Saved in Paul," *Bib* 60 (1985): 19; Snodgrass, "Justification by Grace," 78; Seifrid, *Justification*, 59-61; G. N. Stanton, "The Law of Moses and the Law of Christ," in *Paul and the Mosaic Law* (WUNT 89; ed. J. D. G. Dunn; Tübingen: Mohr-Siebeck, 1996), 105.

78. C. L. Quarles, "The Soteriology of R. Akiba and E. P. Sanders' *Paul and Palestinian Judaism*," *NTS* 42 (1996): 185-95.

sertion, "There is no hint in Rabbinic literature of a view such as that of Paul in Gal 3:10 or of 4 Ezra, that one must achieve legal perfection."[79] Quarles has persuasively argued that *m. 'Abot* 3:16-17 and *b. Sanh.* 81a show older rabbis like R. Gamaliel II holding the rigorous views similar to those of Paul in Gal 3:10 (i.e., the requirement to keep all the commandments of the law and pessimism about human ability to do it) and R. Akiba countering such views with his more humane view of God's judgment according to the majority of works.[80] Further, G. N. Stanton has pointed to Justin Martyr's *Dialogue with Trypho the Jew* 8:4 as an important piece of evidence against Sanders's notion of covenantal nomism. For there Justin, who does not know Galatians, represents Trypho the Jew as pleading with Justin to "do all the things that are written in the law" (τὰ ἐν τῷ νόμῳ γεγραμμένα πάντα ποίει) in order to find mercy from God.[81]

So it seems that "covenantal nomism" as Sanders has defined it needs to be modified to accommodate the strands of thought in Second Temple Judaism that accorded saving value to deeds of the law beyond Sanders's sense of merely "staying in" the covenant.[82] And it appears that the more conscientious and zealous for law observance one was, the more one emphasized the saving value of law observance. Now, according to his own testimonies (Phil 3:5-6; Gal 1:13-14), Paul was a Pharisee who pursued "blameless" righteousness with a great zeal for the law and the traditions. His zeal for the law with which he sought to advance beyond his peers in Judaism may have been motivated by a premise like that of the pious/righteous of *Pss. Sol.* or the Qumran covenanters that God's mercy would be given only to those who observed the law faithfully.[83] Then it is conceivable that he understood passages like Lev 18:5 and Deut 27:26 as requiring him to observe

79. Sanders, *Paul and Palestinian Judaism*, 137.

80. Quarles, "Soteriology," 185-95; cf. also H. J. Schoeps, *Paul: The Theology of the Apostle in the Light of Jewish Religious History* (Philadelphia: Westminster, 1959), 177; Avemarie, "Erwählung," 111.

81. Stanton, "The Law of Moses," 104-6.

82. See now the important study of M. A. Elliott, *The Survivors of Israel: A Reconsideration of the Theology of Pre-Christian Judaism* (Grand Rapids: Eerdmans, 2000). This fresh and thorough study of pre-Christian Jewish literature effectively repudiates the notion of "nationalistic election theology" in Judaism, i.e., "covenantal nomism" in Sanders's terms, and convincingly demonstrates "a highly individualistic and conditional view of covenant" (p. 639). Thus the work deprives the New Perspective School of its basis in Judaism and so makes its proposed revolution in Pauline studies abortive. See also de Roo, "The Concept of 'Works of the Law' in Jewish and Christian Literature," in *Christian-Jewish Relations Through the Centuries* (ed. S. E. Porter and B. W. R. Pearson; JSNTSup 192; Sheffield: Academic Press, 2000).

83. Cf. Seifrid, *Justification*, 174.

all the commandments of the law to obtain righteousness and life in the world to come, as, according to *b. Sanh.* 81a, R. Gamaliel II understood Ezek 18:5-9.[84]

However, the New Perspectivists like to point out that the law contained provisions for atonement such as repentance and temple sacrifices and that therefore keeping the law included doing those things. So, according to them, when Paul says that in his Pharisaic days he had "blameless" righteousness under the law (Phil 3:6), he does not mean that he never transgressed a commandment. Rather, his statement presupposes atonement for his occasional transgressions through repentance and sacrifices. Interpreting Phil 3:6 in this way, the New Perspectivists like to use his testimony to support their notion of Judaism as covenantal nomism and to reject the traditional interpretation of Gal 3:10: claiming himself to have had "blameless" righteousness through his law observance and atoning works during his Pharisaic days, Paul could hardly say that "all those who are of works of the law are under a curse" because they cannot keep the law perfectly.[85]

This consideration leads N. T. Wright to see Paul in Gal 3:10 referring not to individuals but to the nation Israel as a whole and assuming that Israel as a nation failed to keep the law so that she is under the curse of the exile.[86] We have already observed that the individualizing and generalizing ὅσοι (instead of "Israel") and πᾶς in 3:10 militate against this interpretation. Further, we have to remember that the Jewish theology of atonement was meant not only for individuals but for the nation as a whole. The rituals especially on the Day of Atonement were thought to atone for the sins of the nation as a whole, not just individuals (cf. Lev 16; *m. Yoma* 4:2; 6:2; 8:9).[87] So under the assumption of Sanders's covenantal nomism, Paul would also not be able to say that Israel is under a curse because she has failed to keep the law. But in fact, as Wright himself is eager to point out, during Second Temple Judaism many Jews did perceive of their national malaise in terms of the curse of Deut 27–30 for their failure to keep the law (Dan 9; etc.).[88] If, in spite of the atonement theology, the Jewish nation could be thought of as falling under the curse of the law for

84. Cf. Quarles, "Soteriology," 193-94.

85. See note 8 above.

86. Wright, "Curse and Covenant," 145-47.

87. Cf. G. F. Moore, *Judaism in the First Centuries of the Christian Era* (Cambridge, Mass.: Harvard University Press, 1927), 1:499-502; J. C. Rylaarsdam, "Atonement, Day of," *IDB*, 1:313-16.

88. Thus, Wright's two emphases, the theory of Judaism as covenantal nomism with readily available atonement and the theory of the Jewish belief in the continuing exile for their national sins, seem to be in serious tension, if not outright contradiction, with each other, unless it is to be resolved in the way suggested here below.

their failure to keep the law,[89] could individual Jews not also be so regarded? If the Jews around New Testament times thought that atonement for their sins was as readily available as the New Perspectivists insist, why did R. Gamaliel II "weep" for not being able to keep the law perfectly?[90] This clearly suggests that some Jews could think of the requirement of perfect observance of the law quite apart from atonement practices.

This consideration raises the question of how much Paul is, in fact, thinking of the Torah's provisions of atonement for sins in Phil 3:6. The phrase of Phil 3:6b stands at the climax of the enumeration of his merits, both of his impeccable pedigree and of his extraordinary achievements (3:5-6), on the ground of which he thinks he can claim a greater confidence in the Jewish existence ("the flesh") than his Jewish opponents (3:4). If he is conscious of the Jewish practices of atonement here as much as the New Perspectivists suggest, what is the meaning of ἐγὼ μᾶλλον in verse 4b? It is obvious that Paul's Jewish opponents in Philippi are also very zealous for the law and righteousness. They must also have had their occasional sins atoned for through repentance and sacrifices. Then they must also have "blameless" righteousness. In fact, according to the theory of the New Perspectivists, every sincere Jew in Second Temple Judaism could claim the same, insofar as he or she maintained a sincere commitment to the law. Then what is the point of Paul's claiming that he could have a greater confidence in the law-righteousness than his Jewish opponents? Clearly here Paul is suggesting that not only his pedigree but also his achievement as a zealous Pharisaic law-keeper exceeded that of his opponents.[91] Is Paul then suggesting that he observed better than his opponents the Torah's provisions for atonement as well as the other commandments? Perhaps that he repented of his sins more promptly and sincerely than they? But would Paul have recognized as "blameless" those who often failed to keep the commandments and had to repent their sins frequently (cf. Luke 18:9-14)? Doesn't Phil 3:2-6 rather carry the connotation that he tried to keep the commandments of the law as perfectly as possible so as to need to repent as little as possible?[92]

89. Cf. I. G. Hong, *The Law in Galatians* (JSNTSupp 81; Sheffield: JSOT, 1993), 141; Thielman, *Paul,* 154, 285 n. 37.

90. Cf. Scott, "Galatians 3.10," 201-3 against the theory of readily available atonement in Judaism.

91. See pp. 76-78 above.

92. Probably the more zealous one was for law-observance, the less one tried to rely on atonement. This spirit may be reflected in *Pss. Sol.* There is no reference to the cultic atonement. There is a reference to the righteous one's atonement "for (sins of) ignorance by fasting and humbling his soul" (3:8) (R. B. Wright, "Psalms of Solomon," in *The Old Testament Pseudepigra-*

If so, in Phil 3:2-6 Paul is not very much conscious of the atonement provisions. Therefore, his claim to have had "blameless" righteousness should be understood as a claim to have kept all the commandments of the law as interpreted by the Pharisees[93] (cf. Luke 18:21). As the Qumran Essenes criticized the Pharisees as "seekers after smooth things" for their tendency to interpret the commandments in such a way as to make them fulfillable (4QNah 1:2, 7; 2:2-3; 3:3, 8), they might not have assessed Paul's Pharisaic righteousness as he did. After getting to know the righteousness that is from God and through faith in Christ, Paul himself came to evaluate his Pharisaic righteousness differently (Phil 3:9). However, judging according to the Pharisaic standard that he adopted, during his Pharisaic days he saw himself as "blameless."

The Qumran *Rule of the Community* shows how such a language of perfection was possible with law observance at the time of Paul: 1QS speaks of the organization of the council of the community with "twelve men and three priests, *perfect in all that is revealed of all the Law*" (8:1–9:26).[94] However, as Otto Betz observes,[95] the Qumran covenanters who could, "before human beings," speak of themselves as perfect and holy, as "children of light" in contrast to the "children of darkness" (cf. 1QS 2:1-10; 5:18-26), also confess in prayer "before God" their inadequacies and failures, acknowledging that all the works of righteousness are enabled only by God (1QS 11:9-11; 1QH 1:21-27; 3:23ff.; 4:29ff.). Probably we should understand Paul the Pharisee in analogy to the Qumran covenanters: he made extreme efforts to keep all the commandments and thought he had achieved "blameless" righteousness according to the Pharisaic standard that was respected among his fellows. Yet he was also conscious of his inadequacies and failures.[96] He may sometimes have "wept" like Gamaliel II in *b. Sanh.* 81a at the insurmountable task of keeping all the commandments (cf. Rom 7).[97] Then he would not have taken easy so-

---

pha [ed. J. H. Charlesworth; Garden City: Doubleday, 1985], 2:655). But that is the only reference to atonement in the whole book. Cf. J. Schröter, "Gerechtigkeit und Barmherzigkeit: Das Gottesbild der Psalmen Salomos in seinem Verhältnis zu Qumran und Paulus," *NTS* 44 (1998): 572 n. 53.

93. Verse 6c is to be understood in the light of the phrase in v. 5: "according to the law, Pharisee."

94. Quotation from 1QS 8:1-2. Cf. O. Betz, "Paulus als Pharisäer," in *Jesus: der Messias Israels* (WUNT 42; Tübingen: Mohr-Siebeck, 1987), 107.

95. Betz, "Pharisäer," 107; cf. Kim, *Origin*, 53.

96. Cf. Sanders, *Paul, the Law, and the Jewish People*, 24, who also shows how in Judaism one could claim to be blameless and yet admit occasional sins.

97. In my book *Origin*, 52-54, I argue that in describing the plight of the Adamic human being under the law from his Christian perspective in Rom 7, Paul uses his own experience with the law as raw material. This view is endorsed by S. Westerholm, *Israel's Law and the Church's*

lace in the thought that repentance and perhaps also sacrifices in the temple would take care of his failures. Nor would he have in despair given up his efforts to keep the law. Rather, he would have resolved himself all the more, like the Qumran covenanters (cf. 1QS 5:1-10, 20-26; 8:20–9:6), to keep the law with greater perfection.[98]

Thus, it seems to be important to recognize that in the Judaism of Paul's day, just as there was the idea of salvation through works of the law alongside and in spite of the doctrine of election, so there was also the emphasis on perfect observance of the law alongside and in spite of the doctrine of atonement. Of course, before his conversion Paul was fully conscious of God's election of and covenant with Israel (Rom 9–11!) and probably also of the doctrine of atonement. Yet his autobiographical data (Gal 1:13-15; Phil 3:2-9) seem to suggest that he was one who put more emphasis on achieving his own righteousness through law observance than relying on the doctrines of election and atonement. Presumably this is one of the reasons why in charging the Jews of their failure to keep the law (Rom 2:1–3:20; 7:4-25), he does not refer to repentance and the other means of atonement in Judaism at all, something that has surprised so many students of Judaism and Paul. In arguing for justification not by works of the law but by faith, he is satisfied just with showing the Jews' failure to keep the law (Rom 2:1–3:20) and their inability to keep the law perfectly (Rom 7:4-25), but does not feel the need to go on with another round of argument that the temple sacrifices are defective and have been superseded by Christ's sacrifice,[99] as the author of Hebrews does. This fact seems to suggest that the Judaism he practiced during his Pharisaic days did not put much emphasis on the means of atonement. Apparently his Judaism was one that sought righteousness by observing the law as perfectly as possible so as to need repentance and sacrifices as little as possible.

The Judaism presupposed in Gal 3:10 as traditionally interpreted appears to be this kind of Judaism. Now that it is made plausible by the work of Hengel, Seifrid, Avemarie, Quarles, Stanton, Elliott, and others, who have corrected Sanders's covenantal nomism, and it is shown here to accord well with Paul's own testimonies about his Pharisaic past, it should not be regarded as a new creation of Paul in the light of his new Christian convictions. There is no

---

Faith (Grand Rapids: Eerdmans, 1988), 152; cf. Moo, *Romans*, 424-31, who argues for a combination of the view that ἐγώ denotes Paul himself with the view that ἐγώ denotes Israel. "*Ego* is not Israel, but *ego* is Paul in solidarity with Israel" (431).

98. Cf. E. Käsemann, *An die Römer* (2d ed.; Tübingen: Mohr-Siebeck, 1974), 193.

99. Of course, Paul presupposes this at many places (e.g., Rom 3:24-26; 8:3; 2 Cor 5:21) but explicitly argues for it nowhere.

question of Paul distorting Judaism or arguing against a figment of his own imagination. He was addressing the actual Judaism in which many pious Jews sought righteousness and life through perfect observance of the law in spite of their repeated failure at this, as he saw that Judaism represented by the Judaizing opponents in Galatia.

However, Paul the Pharisee would not have said that since no human being can keep the law perfectly "all those who are of the works of the law are under a curse." As we said above, even when he found himself unable to keep the law perfectly, he would not have abandoned the efforts to do it but rather would have resolved all the more to attempt it. The statements in Gal 3:10 (as traditionally interpreted) cannot be made by one who remains within the system of the law as his only viable world. They can be made only by one who, having found an alternative to it, has stepped outside of it. So only from his Christian standpoint could Paul have made those statements. Therefore, it is a reasonable hypothesis that once he had experienced God's righteousness in Christ, he began to view his and his people's failure to keep the law perfectly no longer as a spur for even greater efforts for perfect law observance but rather as a sign that no one could actually keep the law perfectly.

Revelation of God's Righteousness in the Crucified Christ

It has often been observed how often Paul contrasts law observance with faith in the crucified Christ (Rom 3:21-26; 7:1-6; 8:2-4; 10:2-4, 5-8; Gal 2:16-21; 3:1-4, 13-14; 5:11; 6:12-14). It belongs to Paul's fundamental Christian conviction that Christ's death was the eschatological atonement for all humankind (Rom 3:25-26; 4:25; 1 Cor 15:3; 2 Cor 5:21; Gal 1:4). It was God's act of redemption, so that it was the revelation of God's righteousness (Rom 1:16-17; 3:21-26; 8:3-4; 10:3-4; 1 Cor 1:30). Therefore, anyone, Jew or Gentile, can now avail him or herself of this redemption: he or she can make the atonement effective for his or her sins and thus be restored to the right relationship to God, the creator, that is, be justified or obtain righteousness. The means to this is simply faith, acceptance of the Christ-event and trust in it (Rom 1:16-17; 3:21-26; Gal 2:16; Phil 3:9; etc.).

Now, seen from the standpoint of this conviction, how would his own and his fellow Jews' efforts to obtain righteousness and life through law observance have appeared to Paul? On the Jewish Christian agitators' attempt to keep the law for righteousness, he says that it is to deny the atoning effect of Christ's death and nullify God's grace (Gal 2:21). On the unbelieving Jews who keep on trying to obtain their own righteousness with zeal for God and

152

the law,[100] he says that they are ignorant of God's righteousness in Christ and so are failing to submit to it (Rom 10:2-4). Why should they submit to God's righteousness in Christ, giving up their attempt to obtain their own righteousness through law observance? The main reason is that, while they have not attained their goal of righteousness by law observance (Rom 9:31), God has provided Christ as the "end [τέλος] of the law for righteousness to every one who believes" (10:4). However, in verses 5-13 Paul seems to imply another, related reason. He cites Lev 18:5 in Rom 10:5 as in Gal 3:12: "He who does them [the commandments] will live in them." Then he contrasts the way of obtaining life through law observance with the way of obtaining salvation through faith in God's redemption already accomplished in Christ. Since by citing Deut 30:11-14 Paul emphasizes how easy rather than impossible a task the latter is, the point of the contrast with the former seems to lie in the former being difficult or impossible.[101] Unfortunately Israel pursued righteousness not by the easy way of faith but by the difficult way of works of the law, and so they failed to reach the goal in spite of their exceedingly zealous pursuit (Rom 9:31-32). This judgment bears the implication that they failed to obtain righteousness and life through law observance because that way is impossibly difficult. Thus Rom 9:30–10:13 implies that in the light of the recognition of Christ as the end of the law for righteousness, Paul judges that the Jews' attempt to obtain righteousness by law observance has been a failure and that this way of obtaining it is in fact impossible.

This means that in the light of God's righteousness in Christ, his and his fellow Jews' imperfect law observance appeared to Paul no longer as a spur for ever greater efforts for perfect law observance but only as a sign that no one could actually keep the law perfectly. Thus, for Paul the Christian, the promise of Lev 18:5 began to appear as unattainable and so the threat of Deut 27:26 for those under the law as real. Therefore, he drew the conclusion from Deut 27:26 that all those who tried to obtain righteousness and life through law observance were in fact under the curse of the law (Gal 3:10). And so he could understand God's redemption in Christ specifically in terms of redemption from the curse of the law (Gal 3:13; cf. also 4:4-5; Rom 8:2).

---

100. For this, see above ch. 1, sec. 13, contra the New Perspectivists' view that in Rom 10:2-4 Paul refers to the "national righteousness" of Israel rather than individual Jews' righteousness (N. T. Wright, "The Paul of History and the Apostle of Faith," *TynBul* 29 [1978]: 83; Sanders, *Paul, the Law, and the Jewish People*, 38, 42-45; Dunn, *The Theology of Paul*, 368-71). Cf. Gundry, "Grace," 13-14, 16-19; Westerholm, *Israel's Law*, 114-16; Schreiner, *The Law and Its Fulfillment*, 106-14.

101. So Joseph A. Fitzmyer, *Romans: A New Translation with Introduction and Commentary* (AB 33; New York: Doubleday, 1993), 587; cf. also Moo, *Romans*, 644-60.

The Flesh/Law–Spirit Antithesis

However, it is to be recognized that Rom 9:30–10:13 only implies that Paul derived from God's righteousness in Christ's atoning death the conclusion that no one can actually keep the law perfectly and therefore "no one is justified by works of the law" (Rom 3:20; Gal 2:16) but instead "all those who are of works of the law are under a curse."

The explicit ground that Paul provides for his argument for the inability to keep the law perfectly and the impossibility of obtaining righteousness through law observance is usually set in terms of the flesh-Spirit or the law-Spirit antithesis. This is nowhere clearer than in Romans 7. There Paul speaks of the inability of the Adamic humanity as a whole and Israel in particular to keep the law perfectly and of their resulting predicament of condemnation and death, from which only Christ redeems them (Rom 7:24-25; 8:1-4).[102] The fundamental problem is that we human beings are fleshly beings. Because we are of the fleshly nature (7:14) or exist in the flesh (7:5), we are dominated by sin (7:14), so that we are unable to do the good we want, but we are forced to do the evil we do not want (7:19). The law cannot help us because, holy, just, good, even spiritual and life-promising though it is (7:10, 12, 14), the law is weakened by the flesh (8:3) and is exploited by sin to arouse our sinful passions (7:5, 8-10, 13) and to bring us only condemnation and death (7:9-11, 13). From this "law of sin and death" God has redeemed us by letting his Son Jesus Christ vicariously bear his condemnation of sin (8:2-3). The purpose of God's redemption through his Son was for "the just requirement of the law [to] be fulfilled in us, who walk not according to the flesh but according to the Spirit" (8:4). In verses 5-8 Paul then contrasts those who live according to the Spirit with those who live according to the flesh. The minds of the latter are hostile to God and do not, indeed cannot, submit to God's law, so that they cannot please God and they receive only death. By contrast, those who walk according to the Spirit receive life and peace because, it is implied, they submit to God's law (cf. Gal 5:13-26; Rom 13:8-10; 1 Cor 9:21; Gal 6:2) and please God. Our divine deliverance from existence according to the

---

102. The view that in Rom 7:7-25 Paul describes from his Christian standpoint the experience of Adam and the humanity represented by him with the law has been popular (e.g., Käsemann, *An die Römer*, 183-90; P. Stuhlmacher, *Paul's Letter to the Romans* [Louisville: Westminster, 1994], 106-7; J. D. G. Dunn, *Romans 1–8* [Waco: Word, 1988], 378-86). But Moo, *Romans*, 428-67, argues that here Paul describes Israel's experience with the law, reflecting also his own experience insofar as he was in solidarity with Israel. However, even Moo is not denying an allusion to Adam completely (ibid., 429). We are to see both perspectives integrated in Rom 7. See n. 61 above.

flesh to existence according to the Spirit has taken place in Christ Jesus, through his vicarious suffering. This is basically what Paul means with the complicated sentence in 8:2: "the law of the Spirit of life in Christ Jesus has set [you/me] free from the law of sin and death."

The argument in Rom 7:7-25 for the inability to fulfill the law perfectly and the impossibility of obtaining life through law observance is an explicit unfolding of the argument of Gal 3:10-11a. The statement in Rom 8:3-4 about God's redemption in Christ is basically the same as that in Gal 3:13. The explanation of the purpose of God's redemption in Christ in terms of our new existence according to the Spirit in Rom 7:6 and 8:4 is equivalent to that in Gal 3:14b. Thus Rom 7:4–8:17 may be regarded as an unfolding of the summary statements in Gal 3:10-14. Further, the claim that those who walk according to the Spirit fulfill the just requirement of the law (Rom 8:4) is paralleled by Gal 5:13-25. In view of the close parallelism between Rom 7:7–8:17 and Gal 3:10-14 + 5:13-25, we may also take the statement about the law in Gal 3:21 together with some of the statements about the law in Rom 7:7–8:17. We may see the sentence of an unfulfilled condition in Gal 3:21b ("If a law had been given which could give life, then righteousness would indeed be by the law") as unfolded in Rom 7:4–8:17: although the law is holy, just, good and spiritual (7:12-14) and even promises life (7:10; cf. Lev 18:5), it has no power to give life. Instead it is weakened by the flesh (8:3) and is exploited by sin to arouse our sinful passions (7:5, 8-10, 13) and to bring us only condemnation and death (7:9-11, 13). No doubt, this is what is meant when Paul speaks of "the letter that brings death" in contrast to "the Spirit that gives life" (2 Cor 3:6; cf. Rom 7:6; also 2:27).

Thus it is clear that Paul's view on human inability to fulfill the law perfectly and the impossibility of obtaining righteousness through law observance is immediately connected with the new Christian experience of the Spirit, although it is ultimately grounded in the appreciation of the revelation of God's righteousness in the redemptive death of the crucified Christ.

The Origin of the Flesh/Law–Spirit Antithesis

Both the antithesis the flesh–the Spirit and the antithesis the law–the Spirit are distinctive features of Paul's theology.[103] Recently Jörg Frey has propounded the thesis that Paul formulated the flesh-Spirit antithesis by developing the dualism of the Palestinian Jewish wisdom tradition in the light of

---

103. Cf. M. Turner, *The Holy Spirit and Spiritual Gifts* (Carlisle: Paternoster, 1996; Peabody: Hendrickson, 1998), 118.

the experience of the Spirit in the gospel.[104] Chiefly from the various Qumran documents that have recently been published, Frey shows how the concepts of the sinful "flesh" and the spirits opposing each other developed as the traditional ethical dualism was cosmically and eschatologically expanded.[105] He thinks that Paul's concepts of the sinful "flesh," the cosmic powers fighting with each other, and the flesh-Spirit antithesis reflect this background. Yet with Paul the Spirit became clearly dominant and the flesh-Spirit antithesis became a much clearer concept. These Pauline developments took place out of the experience of the saving power of the Spirit.[106]

Further, there is an essential difference between the Pauline and the Jewish language of "flesh" and "Spirit," and it is in relation to the law. In the Jewish wisdom tradition human beings are designated as "flesh" for their disobedience to God and his law, and the insight mediated by the "Spirit" is thought to motivate the pious to better obedience to the law. But for Paul, law observance is associated with the "flesh" (Gal 3:3; Phil 3:3-4), and those who are led by the Spirit are no longer "under the law" (Gal 5:18) because they have crucified their flesh (Gal 5:24) and died to the law (Rom 7:6).[107] According to Frey, this fundamental devaluation of the law resulted from Paul's call experience: Paul was called when he was a "zealot for the traditions of the fathers" (Gal 1:14), and from this he realized that "this zeal [was] πεποιθέναι ἐν σαρκί, that is, opposed to God's saving act in Christ."[108]

Frey's explanation of the religion-historical background of Paul's distinctive flesh/law-Spirit antithesis is quite convincing, and his proposal to see the antithesis in the light of Paul's conversion/call experience is headed in the right direction. There has been much reflection as to what Paul could have realized about the law once he discovered on the Damascus road, on the one hand, that the Jesus crucified under the curse of the law (Deut 21:23; Gal 3:13) was the Messiah and Lord exalted by God, and, on the other hand, that his zeal for the law had led him into the sin of opposing God's saving act in Christ. From the former discovery he clearly could have derived his insight that Christ vicariously bore the curse of the law for our sins (Gal 3:13; Rom 8:3; 4:25; 2 Cor 5:21). Then he must have appreciated that the law had executed the divine will of salvation with its pronouncement of the curse on Christ hanging on a tree. But at the same time he must have realized that now

---

104. J. Frey, "Die paulinische Antithese von 'Fleisch' und 'Geist' und die palästinisch-jüdische Weisheitstradition," *ZNW* 90 (1999): 53-73.

105. Ibid., 53-67.

106. Ibid., 72-73.

107. Ibid., 74.

108. Ibid., 74.

salvation depended no longer on keeping the law but on appropriating the divine redemption that had taken place in Christ. Hence the attempt to obtain righteousness by law observance is to declare that Christ died in vain (Gal 2:21). However, the former discovery seems to have also led Paul to thinking that the law's pronouncement of a curse on Jesus was wrong.[109] There is at least a hint of this in 1 Cor 2:8. There, by saying, "If [the rulers of this age] had known [God's wisdom], they would not have crucified the Lord of glory," Paul implies that they crucified Jesus wrongly, out of ignorance of God's wisdom. The "rulers of this age" represented the wisdom of this age according to which both the Greeks and the Jews rejected Christ (1 Cor 1:18-25). The wisdom by which the Jewish rulers turned Jesus over to the Roman rulers for crucifixion came from the law. It was the law by which they judged Jesus as a false messiah. So, if the law was not wrong in itself, it at least lent itself to be misused by sinful human beings, "the flesh," for the crucifixion of "the Lord of glory."

Accordingly, there seems to be a dialectic in Paul's understanding of the law in connection with the crucified Christ: on the one hand, it properly represented the divine will to save humankind through the vicarious death of Jesus Christ; but on the other hand, it led sinful human beings to execute "the Lord of glory." The negative side of the dialectic must have been felt acutely when Paul discovered how his own zeal for the law resulted in opposing God's salvation in the crucified Christ. This seems to be expressed in Gal 2:19: "I through the law died to the law, that I might live to God."[110] Thus it appears that the combination of the two elements of the Damascus revelation — (1) Jesus crucified under the curse of the law as the risen Lord exalted by God and (2) his zeal for the law turning out to be sin — led Paul to something unthinkable for a Pharisee, that is, associating the law with sin and the flesh, beyond simply denying it as a means of obtaining righteousness.

Paul's Experience of the Holy Spirit at His Conversion/Call and Its Impact on His Theology

In chapter 3 we saw how Isa 42, in the light of which Paul interprets his apostolic call, suggests his endowment with the Holy Spirit at his apostolic call and

109. Cf. J. C. Beker, *Paul the Apostle* (Philadelphia: Fortress, 1980), 185-86; M. D. Hooker, "Paul and Covenantal Nomism," in *Paul and Paulinism*, C. K. Barrett Festschrift (London: SPCK, 1982), 55; contra J. D. G. Dunn, " 'A Light to the Gentiles,' or 'The End of the Law'? The Significance of the Damascus Road Christophany for Paul," in *Jesus, Paul, and the Law*, 93.
110. Cf. Dunn, *The Epistle to the Galatians*, 143.

how various passages in his letters confirm it, just as Acts 9:17-18 does. There we have also seen how such an overwhelming experience marking the beginning of his Christian life leads him to define the beginning of his converts' Christian life also in terms of the reception of the Spirit (see above all Gal 3:2-5, but also 1 Cor 2:4-5; 6:11; 1 Thess 1:5-6, 9-10; 2 Thess 2:13-14; 2 Cor 3:3).

Apparently the overwhelming experience of the Spirit at his conversion and call led Paul to see the promises of God in Ezek 36–37 and Jer 31 as fulfilled,[111] for the prophetic passages are alluded to in 2 Cor 3, where he reflects on his call to be a minister of the new covenant at the Damascus Christophany in comparison and contrast with Moses' call to be the minister of the old covenant at the Sinai theophany (Exod 32–34). Paul's designation of himself as a minister of "the new covenant" (3:6a) is a clear allusion to the promise of the new covenant in Jer 31:31-34. His characterization of the new covenant in terms of the Spirit (3:6b) and his talk of the Corinthians being "the letter of Christ . . . written with the Spirit of the living God, not on tablets of stone but on tablets of the hearts of flesh" (3:3), allude to God's promise in Ezek 36:26-27 (also 11:19) to give to his people his Spirit and a new heart, namely a "heart of flesh," in place of the "heart of stone" (cf. also Jer 31:33). When, by contrast, Paul implicitly characterizes the Mosaic ministry of "the old covenant" (3:14) as the "letter" (v. 6) or as something "carved in letters on stone" (v. 7; also v. 3), it is clear that he devalues the Mosaic covenant in the light of his conviction that the new covenant promises of Jer 31 and Ezek 36–37 have been fulfilled. It is significant that in this context he designates the Mosaic covenant as the "letter" that "kills" in contrast to the Spirit that "gives life." According to Scott Hafemann, by "letter" here Paul refers to the Torah which is not accompanied by the Spirit or which is given to the Israelites who have not received the Spirit.[112] This means that having received the Spirit, Paul began to see in the light of the promises of Ezek 36–37 and Jer 31 the problem of the law. Whereas the Spirit brings about righteousness (2 Cor 3:9; Ezek 11:20; 36:27; Jer 31:33-34), freedom[113] (2 Cor 3:17; cf. Jer 30:8-10; Ezek 34:27-

---

111. The Jesus tradition, especially the eucharistic tradition (1 Cor 11:23-26), could have helped him in this. Cf. Seyoon Kim, "Jesus, Sayings of," in *Dictionary of Paul and His Letters* (ed. G. F. Hawthorne, R. P. Martin, and D. Reid; Downers Grove: InterVarsity Press, 1993), 474-92, reprinted as ch. 8 in this volume.

112. S. J. Hafemann, *Paul, Moses, and the History of Israel* (Tübingen: Mohr-Siebeck, 1995), 438-51. But Hafemann's anthropocentric interpretation or his repeated contention that in 2 Cor 3 Paul does not perceive any problem with the old covenant/the law *per se* but only the problem of Israel's hearts to which the law was given, is probably one-sided. Was not the absence of the Spirit in the law or the inability of the law to change the hearts of Israel an inherent weakness of the law itself (cf. Gal 3:21)?

113. It seems the best to understand "freedom" here in terms of the allegory of Gal 4:21-31

28), and indeed life (2 Cor 3:6; Ezek 37:4-14), the law brings about only condemnation (2 Cor. 3:9) and death (3:6, 7). So here we can see that Paul's experience of the Spirit at his conversion and call led him to build the law-Spirit antithesis.

In Ezek 36:26-27 God promises to redeem the people of Israel and give them a new heart, a "heart of flesh," and his Spirit, so that they may "walk in my statutes . . . and keep my judgments and do them" (ἵνα ἐν τοῖς δικαιώμασίν μου πορεύησθε καὶ τὰ κρίματά μου φυλάξησθε καὶ ποιήσητε/אֶת אֲשֶׁר־בְּחֻקַּי תֵּלֵכוּ וּמִשְׁפָּטַי תִּשְׁמְרוּ וַעֲשִׂיתֶם). This statement strongly reminds us of what Paul says in Rom 8:3-4: God's redemptive act in his Son had the purpose "that the righteous requirement of the law might be fulfilled in us, who walk not according to the flesh but according to the Spirit" (ἵνα τὸ δικαίωμα τοῦ νόμου πληρωθῇ ἐν ἡμῖν τοῖς μὴ κατὰ σάρκα περιπατοῦσιν ἀλλὰ κατὰ πνεῦμα). In the two passages, note

- the common theme of redemption,
- the common reference to the Spirit,
- the common key word δικαίωμα,
- the common concept of "walking" (πορεύομαι/הלך and περιπατεῖν), and also
- the parallelism between φυλάσσειν καὶ ποιεῖν and πληροῦν.

In Ezek 36:27 LXX חֹק is rendered δικαίωμα and מִשְׁפָּט as κρίμα, but in the parallel passage Ezek 11:20 LXX the former is rendered πρόσταγμα and the latter δικαίωμα (cf. Exod 21:1, 9; Num 36:13; 1 Sam 2:12; 8:9). So חֻקַּי וּמִשְׁפָּטַי/τὰ

---

as M. Thrall, *The Second Epistle to the Corinthians* (ICC; Edinburgh: T & T Clark, 1994), 1:275-76, suggests (following Emerling, 37). There Hagar, the slave woman, represents the Sinai covenant and produces slave children according to the flesh, who live by law observance. But Sarah, the free woman, represents the new covenant and produces free children according to the Spirit, who live by faith in the promise of God. If this interpretation is correct, then we must see Paul implying in 2 Cor 3 as well as in Gal 4:21-31 that the Jews under the law are in slavery. Since in 2 Cor 3 Paul speaks of righteousness and life as the effects of the ministry of the new covenant in the power of the Spirit at least in part from the perspective of Ezek 36–37 and Jer 31, he may be doing the same with regard to "freedom" here. With the word he may be summarizing the liberation (esp. Jer 30:8-10; Ezek 34:27-28) and restoration of Israel from the captivity which the contexts of Jer 31 and Ezek 36–37 are talking about as coming together with the giving of the new covenant, the new heart, and the Spirit. If so, the Jews who insist on the Mosaic covenant are seen as being in the place of the Israel of the captivity, and the Christians in the place of the liberated Israel. Then the law is seen as an enslaving power. Just as in 2 Cor 3:6 the "life" in Ezek 37:4-14 is taken to mean the comprehensive eschatological salvation rather than just the politico-economical well-being of Israel restored from the captivity, so in 2 Cor 3:17 the liberation in Jer 30:8-10 and Ezek 34:27-28 seems to be taken to refer to the eschatological "freedom" from all the evil forces, including the law and its adverse effects.

δικαιώματά μου καὶ τὰ κρίματά μου of Ezek 36:27 or חֻקֹּתַי יֵלֵכוּ וְאֶת־מִשְׁפָּטַי/ προστάγματά μου καὶ τὰ δικαιώματά μου of Ezek 11:20 may be taken as equivalent to τὸ δικαίωμα τοῦ νόμου of Rom 8:4. Thus it seems likely that Rom 8:4 is a rephrasing of Ezek 36:26-27.

This view is further supported by the fact that Ezek 36:27-28 (and 11:19-20) appears to be echoed in Rom 8:9, 14. In Rom 8:9, 14 Paul identifies the Spirit of God as the Spirit of Christ. In v. 9 Paul says that Christians are those in whom the Spirit of God dwells and therefore that "if any one does not have the Spirit of Christ, he is not of his [i.e., Christ's]." In verse 14 Paul expresses the same thought in the affirmative: "all those who are led by the Spirit of God, they are sons of God." This idea that those who have the Spirit of God/ Christ indwelling them are the children or people of God/Christ seems to be an echo of Ezek 36:27-28 (and 11:19-20), where God promises the redeemed Israel that he will put his Spirit within them and make them his people: "And I will put my Spirit within you . . . and you shall be my people and I will be your God." Further, Rom 8:11 ("If the Spirit of him who raised Jesus from the dead dwells in you, he who raised Christ from the dead will give life to your mortal bodies also through his Spirit which dwells in you") could well be an allusion to Ezek 37:4-14, where God promises to breathe his Spirit into Israel dead like "dry bones," and resurrect them and give them life. Thus, Rom 8:9, 11, 14 with the additional evidence that Ezek 36–37 forms a basis for Paul's statements in Rom 8:1-17 makes it highly probable that Rom 8:3-4 is partly a rephrasing of Ezek 36:26-27.[114]

Ezekiel 36:26-27 promises that God's Spirit would enable the redeemed Israel with the "heart of flesh" to fulfill the righteous requirement of the law, what the exiled Israel with "the heart of stone" could not do. In Rom 8:3-4, Paul says that this promise has been fulfilled in God's redemption through his Son. Accordingly, the redeemed Israel given the Spirit and the new "heart of flesh" in Ezek 36:26-27 are the redeemed who "walk according to the Spirit" in Rom 8:4, and the unredeemed Israel with the "heart of stone" in Ezek 36:26 are the unredeemed who "walk according to

114. After observing the parallels between Rom 8:1-17 and Ezek 36–37 (+ 11:19-20), I found H. Hübner, *Biblische Theologie des NT*, vol. 2, *Die Theologie des Paulus* (Göttingen: Vandenhoeck, 1993), 301-5, who perceives Ezek 36–37 to be an important background for Rom 8:1-17. He also thinks that Ezek 36:27 could stand behind Rom 8:4. But he does not observe the parallels between Rom 8:9, 14 and Ezek 36:27-28 and between Rom 8:11 and Ezek 37:4-14. Of his observations, only the correspondence between the πνεῦμα τῆς ζωῆς of Rom 8:2 and the πνεῦμα ζωῆς of Ezek 37:5 is interesting for our present purpose. Noting the importance of Ezek 36–37 for Paul's pnematology, Turner, *Holy Spirit*, 123, also thinks that the phrase "the Spirit of God" in Rom 8:9a mirrors the "my Spirit" of Ezek 36–37.

the flesh" in Rom 8:4, that is, the unredeemed Israel (and the Adamic humanity represented by them) of Rom 7. So Paul is suggesting in Rom 8:3-4 that in fulfillment of the promise of Ezek 36:26-27 (and the other related prophetic texts) God has redeemed his people in Christ and given them the Spirit and a new responsive heart so that they might fulfill the just requirement of the law and obtain righteousness and life. Thus, in Rom 8:1-17, one of the two passages where Paul develops the Spirit-flesh antithesis (cf. Gal 5:13-26), he makes the fundamental statement (vv. 3-4) by rephrasing Ezek 36:26-27. This strongly suggests that Paul's Spirit-flesh antithesis is at least partly grounded on Ezek 36:26-27 and the related texts (Ezek 11:19-20; Jer 31:31-34).[115]

The flesh-Spirit antithesis thus developing out of Paul's reflection on Ezek 36–37 in the light of his Spirit experience at his conversion/call is quite understandable. But why did this reflection lead him also to the law-Spirit antithesis rather than to an emphasis on more conscientious law observance with the power of the Spirit, which seems to be the more obvious demand of those passages?[116] By saying that the redeemed do fulfill the δικαίωμα of the law by walking according to the Spirit in Rom 8:4, he is in fact faithful to the intention of Ezek 36:27-28, as we have seen. So Paul does exhort the redeemed to fulfill the righteous requirement of the law by walking according to the Spirit (Gal 5:13-26; Rom 13:8-10). However, he is opposed to Christians keeping the law of Moses in the way the Jews do. In this dual attitude there is reflected the dialectic of Paul's view of the law. The law is the true representation of God's will, and so it is holy, just, good, and spiritual. Therefore, the redeemed should fulfill its just requirement through the power of the Spirit. Yet the law is weak and is manipulated by the evil forces of sin and the flesh, so that it cannot give life.

Above we surmised that this dialectic developed from Paul's threefold realization at his conversion/call: (1) that the law had properly represented the divine will to save humankind through the vicarious death of Jesus Christ on

---

115. D. Wenham, *Paul: Follower of Jesus or Founder of Christianity?* (Grand Rapids: Eerdmans, 1995), 275-80, shows it to be quite possible that Paul knows the tradition of Jesus' Gethsemane prayer and reflects it in Rom 8. If so, Jesus' saying, "Be awake and pray that you may not enter into temptation; the spirit is indeed willing, but the flesh is weak" (Matt 26:41/Mark 14:38), may also have played a part in this development. If this can securely be established, Paul's flesh-Spirit antithesis may provide a good illustration of Paul's method of theologizing through reflection on the Jesus tradition as well as on the Old Testament in the light of his Damascus revelatory experience.

116. Cf. the Qumran understanding of the new covenant and of the Spirit as meaning more perfect law observance; e.g., CD 6; 1QH 7:6ff.; 14:13ff.; Frey, "Antithese," 74.

the cross; (2) yet it had led sinful human beings to execute "the Lord of glory"; and (3) that his own zeal for the law turned out to be a sin of opposing God's salvation in the crucified Christ. Now we can see how Paul's experience of the Spirit at his conversion/call must have reinforced the negative side of the dialectic of the law. In the light of his Spirit experience, he could now see that his Pharisaic zeal for the law was really a blind zeal (2 Cor 3:16-18; 4:6), the zeal of a man with a "heart of stone" (Ezek 11:19; 36:26), a man of the flesh. Therefore, with such a Pharisaic zeal he could not truly fulfill the just requirement of the law. He then began to see the problem of his fellow Jews in the light of his own experience: they had zeal for God and his law, but it was a blind zeal (Rom 9:31; 10:2), a zeal of the people with "stony hearts" and "veiled" and "hardened" minds (2 Cor 3:14-15).

The real problem was that the law could not lift the "veil" and replace the "heart of stone" with a soft and responsive "heart of flesh," which was possible only in Christ (2 Cor 3:14-15). Having experienced on the Damascus road how his turning to the Lord, the Spirit, resulted in the removal of the "veil" and the "heart of stone" (2 Cor 3:16-18; 4:6), he could now see this fundamental problem of the law. So he realized that there was an inherent correspondence between the fact that the Mosaic law was written on the stone tablets and the fact that those who are under the law have the "stony hearts" or "hardened minds" (2 Cor 3:3, 7, 14). He probably realized also that because of the structural weakness of the law, the people of Israel had been "stiffnecked," blinded and hardened ever since they received the law at Sinai (Exod 32:9; 33:3, 5; 34:9; Isa 6:9-10; 29:10-12; Jer 5:21-24; Ezek 12:2). When the law is responded to by those who have the "stony hearts" or "hardened minds," the consequences are only condemnation and death (2 Cor 3:6, 7, 9). Just as there is a correspondence between the law written on the stone tablets and the "stony hearts" of the Jews, so there is also a correspondence between the Spirit and the "flesh hearts" of the Christians (2 Cor 3:3). The Spirit touches the "hearts of flesh" (2 Cor 3:3) and so brings about righteousness and life (2 Cor 3:6, 9). Thus, Paul's reflection on Ezek 36–37 in the light of his Spirit experience at his conversion/call led him to the law-Spirit antithesis as well as the flesh-Spirit antithesis.

Against Friedrich W. Horn's view that Paul came to develop his Spirit-law and Spirit-flesh antitheses only in his struggle against his Jewish Christian opponents, Volker Rabens argues that the Spirit-law antithesis is implicitly intimated also in 1 Thess 4:8.[117] Rabens builds his case on Max Turner's argument that Paul's allusion to Ezek 37:6, 14 (cf. 36:26-27) (LXX) in 1 Thess 4:8 suggests that

---

117. Rabens, "The Development of Pauline Pneumatology," *BZ* 43 (1999): 178-79.

"Paul had already understood the Spirit of prophecy in the congregation as the 'life-giving' recreative Spirit of Ezekiel's promised New Covenant . . . some time before he came to use that theologoumenon as a powerful weapon in his argument against the Judaizers in 2 Corinthians 3 and beyond."[118] Rabens notes that in Ezek 36:27 the Spirit is promised in order to enable obedience to the law and that in 1 Thess 4:8 the Spirit is suggested as the agent of sanctification and yet without any reference to the law both in the immediate context and in the whole epistle of 1 Thessalonians. This suggests that "the Spirit has in some sense superseded the law."[119] Further, noting how Paul sets the gift of the Spirit in opposition to fornication, lustful passion, defrauding, and impurity (4:3-7), Rabens concludes that "this contrast clearly foreshadows what Paul would later (if Gal was indeed written so much later . . .) formulate *expressis verbis* as the πνεῦμα κατὰ σαρκός – opposition (e.g., Gal 5:17 . . .)."[120]

A similar observation can be made from 1 Cor 6:10-11[121] and also 3:1. This means that the Spirit-law/flesh antithesis was developed independent of his struggle against the Judaizers and could also be used in other contexts. This enhances the likelihood that it is a fundamental insight originating from the Damascus experience/the Jesus tradition.

Conclusion

Thus, out of his experience of the revelation of the crucified Jesus as the exalted Lord and of the endowment of the Spirit while zealously pursuing righteousness through works of the law, Paul developed the Spirit-law antithesis as well as the Spirit-flesh antithesis. Moreover, he did so by reflecting chiefly on Ezek 36–37 (+ 11:19-20) and Jer 31:31-34 as one who had seen the promises of the new covenant, the Spirit, a new heart, righteousness, and life in those texts fulfilled. The revelation of the crucified Jesus as the embodiment of God's righteousness and the endowment of the Spirit at his conversion/call led him to see the structural weakness of the law, its association with the flesh and sin. So he concluded that it was impossible to keep the law perfectly and it was impossible to obtain righteousness and life through law observance.[122]

118. Turner, *Holy Spirit*, 109.

119. Rabens, op. cit., 178.

120. Ibid., 179.

121. See pp. 67-70 and 99-100 above and cf. Rabens, op. cit., 179; also Turner, *Holy Spirit*, 110-11.

122. Therefore, to the extent that only from his Christian perspective did Paul begin to see the impossibility of keeping the law and of obtaining righteousness through law observance,

So he had to break with the law and his Pharisaic Judaism and trust only in God's redemption in Christ (Gal 2:18-21). Lamenting over his fellow Jews' zealous but futile pursuit of righteousness through works of the law, he now longed that they might also obtain the "freedom" from the law of sin and death (Rom 8:2; 2 Cor 3:17; Gal 5:13), that is, righteousness and life, by faith in Christ, the eschatological embodiment of God's righteousness (Rom 9:1-5; 10:1-4). He gave himself totally to his apostolic task of bringing all the gentiles to the obedience of faith in Christ for their salvation. And he fought the Judaizers fiercely against their mistaken attempts to bring his gentile converts under the yoke of the law.

So, at Gal 3:10-14, the test case, the traditional interpretation turns out to be right and the New Perspective wrong. An implication of this conclusion is that the passage can be taken as an important piece of evidence that at least some Jews of Paul's day sought to obtain righteousness through perfect law observance.

Sanders is right to say that Paul's thought moved from solution to plight. However, he is not right if he means thereby that the pre-Christian Paul had no awareness of the plight of law observance at all, as we have seen above. Cf. F. Thielman, *From Plight to Solution* (NovTSup 61; Leiden: Brill, 1989). For Paul, his Christian perspective led him to a clearer understanding of the plight of law observance than he and his fellow Jews had hitherto perceived, rather than to creating the plight *ex nihilo*. Only so could his arguments against the Judaizing Christians and the Jews in Galatians and Romans make sense. Cf. S. Westerholm, "Sinai as Viewed from Damascus: Paul's Reevaluation of the Mosaic Law," in *The Road from Damascus* (ed. R. N. Longenecker; Grand Rapids: Eerdmans, 1997), 157.

CHAPTER 5

Christ, the Image of God
and the Last Adam

Summary of My Thesis

In my book *The Origin of Paul's Gospel*, the chapter on Paul's christology that deals with "Christ the εἰκὼν τοῦ θεοῦ" occupies the central place.[1] In it I submit that Paul's distinctive conception of Christ as "the image of God" originated from the Damascus Christophany and that the εἰκών-christology developed further into Paul's Adam-christology and Wisdom-christology. Along with this main thesis, I also submit two minor theses: that Paul's designation of Christ as the Son of God based on the Damascus Christophany corresponds to Jesus' intention in his self-designation as the Son of Man, and that the Damascus Christophany contributed to Paul's conception of the church as the body of Christ and the true Israel. In the next chapter I follow up the main thesis by proposing that Paul's distinctive transformation-soteriology was the soteriological application of his εἰκών-christology and therefore was also ultimately rooted in the Damascus Christophany.[2]

To outline briefly the course of my argument for these theses, I first of all ascertain that in the New Testament only Paul uses the terms εἰκών and μορφή, and he uses them abundantly to designate Christ as the εἰκών or μορφή of God (2 Cor 4:4; Col 1:15; Phil 2:6), to refer to the εἰκών of Christ (Rom 8:29; 1 Cor 15:49; 2 Cor 3:18), and to speak of our being "conformed" (συμμορφοῦσθαι) to or "transformed" (μεταμορφοῦσθαι) into the εἰκών of

---

1. Seyoon Kim, *The Origin of Paul's Gospel* (WUNT 2/4; Tübingen: Mohr-Siebeck, 1981, 1984; Grand Rapids: Eerdmans, 1982), ch. 6, 136-268.
2. Ibid., 319-26.

Christ (Rom 8:29; 1 Cor 15:49; 2 Cor 3:18; Phil 3:21; cf. also 1 Cor 15:52; Gal 4:19; Phil 3:10; Col 3:9-10; Eph 4:24; Rom 12:2). This fact, little appreciated in scholarship even to this day, immediately raises the question of how Paul came to develop these unique conceptions.

In the second stage of my argument, I examine various theories about the origin of the εἰκών-christology, especially the theory that it is derived from the Adam-christology. But an extended discussion on the diverse religion-historical approaches only confirms the conclusion of E. Käsemann that the origin of Paul's Adam-christology itself has not been clarified.[3] This state of affairs leads me to reverse the priority of Paul's Adam-christology and his εἰκών-christology and consider the possibility that Paul derived his conception of Christ as the Last Adam from his prior conception of Christ as the εἰκών of God.

So the third stage of my argument naturally begins with the linguistic data. Here I examine the terms εἰκών and μορφή and their cognates and synonyms, including their Semitic equivalents: ὁμοίωμα, ὁμοίωσις, ἰδέα, σχῆμα, צלם, דמות, מראה, תמונה, תבנית, and so on. Then I examine various descriptions of epiphany visions in the Old Testament and the Jewish literature. In the survey, the most prominent place is given to the visions of God or his כבוד on the throne of the chariot (מרכבה) "appearing like a human being" (דמות כמראה אדם/ὁμοίωμα ὡς εἶδος ἀνθρώπου) in Ezek 1 and in the subsequent chapters of Ezekiel. The discussion of the theophany vision in Ezek 1 is followed by a survey of the well-known visions in Dan 7, *1 En.* 46, *4 Ezra* 13 and Rev 1, which, standing both form-critically and tradition-historically under the influence of Ezek 1, describe a heavenly figure appearing "like a son of man." Then the *Testament of Abraham* is examined, which again unmistakably reflects the influence of the tradition of Ezek 1. There Abraham in his ascension sees Adam sitting on a golden throne and appearing ὁμοία τοῦ δεσπότου (sc. God) (Rec. A. 11), Abel sitting on a fiery throne and appearing "like a son of God" (ὅμοιος υἱῷ θεοῦ) (Rec. A. 12), and the personified Death appearing "like the sun" (ἡλιομόρφους) and "wearing the form of an archangel" (ἀρχαγγέλου μορφὴν περικείμενος) (Rec. A. 16). Then I examine three passages: Josephus's rendering of the story of the divination by the medium of Endor (*Ant.* 6.332-33), *4 Ezra* 5:37, and *T. Benj.* 10:1. Although they do not betray any direct influence of the tradition of Ezek 1, they are interesting nevertheless since they support the conclusion that can be drawn from Ezek 1, Dan 7, *1 En.* 46, *4 Ezra* 13, Rev 1 and *T. Ab.* that words such as מראה, דמות, תבנית, ὁμοίωμα, εἰκών, μορφή, ἰδέα, and σχῆμα are commonly employed to

---

3. E. Käsemann, *An die Römer* (2nd ed.; HNT 8a; Tübingen: Mohr-Siebeck, 1974), 136.

describe with their earthly analogies God, heavenly beings, or other invisible beings seen in epiphanic visions or dreams. This conclusion is supported also by many accounts of theophanies and angelophanies in the Old Testament, besides Ezek 1, which describe God or an angel appearing in the *form* of a human being (e.g., Gen 18; 19; 32:22-32; Exod 33; Isa 6; Dan 8:15; etc.). Therefore James Barr and Gerhard von Rad are justified in their view that the affirmation of human beings as having been made in the "image" of God in Gen 1:26-27 was based on the theophanic experiences of seeing God appearing in the form of human beings.

I further back up the conclusion by ascertaining how in Wisdom of Solomon and in Philo the personified Wisdom and Logos as *Theophanieträger* are spoken of as the εἰκών of God (e.g., Wis 7:26; Philo, *Leg.* i.43; *Conf.* 62; 146-47). I appreciate especially Philo's interpretation of the theophany to Jacob in Gen 31:13: in this theophany God appears "assuming the εἰκών of angel," which is also the εἰκών of a human being. So at Bethel Jacob did not directly see God himself but his εἰκών, which is the Logos, the angel of God (*Somn.* 1.227-41). With this interpretation as well as his designation of the Logos as the (arch-)angel, the Son of God (*Conf.* 62) and the δεύτερος θεός (*QG* 2.62), Philo clearly reflects the theophany vision tradition of Ezek 1 which develops into the rabbinic *merkabah* mysticism.

From the conclusion of the linguistic and form- and tradition-historical studies that εἰκών and μορφή are the words regularly used for the being seen in epiphany visions in the Old Testament and Judaism, a hypothesis develops quite naturally: Paul's designation of Christ as the εἰκών of God is based on his experience of an epiphany of Christ as the εἰκών of God, that is, on his experience of the Christophany on the road to Damascus. So the fourth stage of my argument is to prove this hypothesis by exegeting the Pauline passages containing εἰκών and the related terms and by demonstrating that his experience of the Damascus Christophany is reflected in those passages: Gal 1:16; 1 Thess 1:10; Col 1:15; 2:9; Phil 3:20-21; 1 Cor 2:8; 1 Cor 15:44-49; and 2 Cor 3:1–4:6. Of all these, I find the last-mentioned to be conclusive evidence that Paul derived his conception of Christ as the εἰκών of God from the Damascus Christophany. For not only is the whole passage concerned with demonstrating Paul's commission as an apostle and servant of the new covenant at the Damascus Christophany, in comparison with and contrast to Moses' commission as the servant of the old covenant at the Sinai theophany (Ex 33–34), but it also uses the expressions in 4:4-6 (cf. also 3:16-18), which, as the majority of commentators acknowledge, clearly allude to the Damascus Christophany. At the Damascus Christophany in which he received his apostolic commission as well as his gospel, Paul saw "the δόξα of God in the face of Christ" and so perceived Christ as the εἰκών of God (2 Cor 4:4-6). Both the synonymous use of δόξα (כבוד) and εἰκών (דמות/צלם) and the idea of "beholding the δόξαν κυρίου [כבוד יהוה] as in a mirror" (κατοπτριζόμενοι) (3:18) are strongly reminiscent of Ezek 1 and the theophanic tradition that originated from Ezek 1. This suggests that Paul is describing his call vision in the form of the call vision of Ezek 1.[4]

Thus, in four stages, I submit my main thesis that Paul's εἰκών-christology is rooted in the Damascus Christophany. Alongside this main thesis, I submit two minor theses, one concerning Jesus' self-designation, "the Son of Man," and Paul's designation of Jesus as the Son of God, and the other concerning Paul's conception of the church as the body of Christ and the true Israel. While the main thesis derives from a mainly form-critical examination of Ezek 1 and the various epiphany visions in the Old Testament and the Jewish literature, the minor theses derive from a tradition-historical consideration of the similar material, especially the tradition of the *merkabah*-vision of Ezek 1.

For the latter, I survey the research done by O. Procksch, A. Feuillet, M. Black, H. R. Balz, and above all C. C. Rowland on the tradition of the vision of God appearing in the form of a human being on the *merkabah*-throne in Ezek 1 as it is reflected in Dan 7; *1 En.* 14; 37-71; *4 Ezra* 13; 4Q405; Rev 1; 4–5; *Apoc. Ab.* 17-18; *T. Ab.; Tg. Gen.* 28:12; *b. Ḥag.* 14b; *2 En.; 3 En.;* etc. The survey leads me to endorse their conclusion that the heavenly figure appearing "like a son of man" in Dan 7; *1 En.* 37-71; *4 Ezra* 13 is a product of hypostatization of the כבוד יהוה appearing דמות כמראה אדם in Ezek 1:26-28.[5] Arguing that

---

4. In 2 Cor 4:4 Paul speaks about Christ as being "the εἰκών of God," but in 3:18 he speaks about the εἰκών of Christ. With regard to δόξα, he makes a similar switch: in 3:18 and 4:4 he refers to the δόξα of Christ, but then in 4:6 he speaks about "the δόξα of God in the face of Christ." This apparently incongruous way of speaking is not sufficiently appreciated by commentators. With the analogy of Philo's speaking of Jacob as having seen the image of God, the Logos, and the image of the Logos at the theophany at Bethel (*Somn.* 1.227-41), such language is best explained as the result of Paul's experience of the Damascus Christophany. In the Damascus Christophany Paul saw "the light phenomenon of the 'glory of God' clearly display[ing] human contours" (to borrow the interpretation of Ezek 1:26 by G. von Rad, *Old Testament Theology* [London: SCM, 1975], 1:146), and the human contours turned out to be those of the exalted Christ. So he speaks of "the glory of God in the face of Christ." But since the glory of God shone in the face of Christ, i.e., Christ appeared so glorified, he at the same time speaks about that glory as the glory of Christ. Since the human contours which were displayed by the glory of God were those of Christ, Paul saw the "image" (i.e., the human contours) of Christ. But since those human contours (i.e., "image") were so exalted and divine as they were displayed by "the glory of God," Paul perceived them as the "image of God."

5. Although I note Rowland's insistence on the contribution in this development which

parallel to the binitarianism so developed (God as "the Ancient of Days" and a second divine figure כבר אנש, "like a son of man," on the heavenly throne[s]) in the apocalyptic literature, the conception of Wisdom and Logos as the bearer of theophany in the Wisdom literature and Philo also developed from the same *merkabah*-vision tradition of Ezek 1,[6] I present the conjecture that the two streams — the apocalyptic and the Wisdom — of the development of binitarianism converge in the conception of Metatron in *3 Enoch*.

This means that the one "like a son of man" in Dan 7:9-14 is a divine figure who is enthroned on the throne next to that of God, the Ancient of Days (note the plural כרסון/θρόνοι in v. 9), so as to be invested and delegated with God's "dominion, glory and kingdom." Since that figure is interpreted as the symbol and corporate head of the people of God ("the saints of the Most High") in Dan 7:18, 22, 27, M. Black seems to be right in his interpretation that Dan 7 has in view the *apotheosis* of Israel, the elevation of God's people to God's throne or their participation in God's "dominion, glory and kingdom," in fulfillment of their destiny as the covenant people of God. Appreciating C. F. D. Moule's view that when Jesus designated himself with the unique, arthrous phrase, "*the* Son of Man," he was doing so in reference to the "son of man" of Dan 7:13, I suggest that with this self-designation Jesus claimed to be the Son of God whom Daniel saw appearing "like a son of man." Jesus could have interpreted the one "like a son of man" of Dan 7 as the Son of God from the fact that he comes with the clouds of heaven, the vehicle of theophany, to be enthroned at God's side and invested with God's "dominion, glory and kingdom" and also from the fact that he is the symbol and corporate head of God's people, God's children. I argue that Jesus' consciousness of his unique filial relationship to God, his *Vollmachtsanspruch* as the executor of God's kingly reign, his ingathering of his followers into the kingdom of God, and his invitation for them to participate in his filial relationship to God bear witness to the fact that he understood both his identity and his mission in terms of the Son of Man of Dan 7.[7]

Then I examine Gal 1:16 and 1 Thess 1:10 in which some scholars hear an

---

was made by the Old Testament concept of מלאך יהוה as the bearer of theophany or mediator of God's presence in theophany (Kim, *Origin*, 242), I fail to integrate it with the hypostatization of the כבוד יהוה of Ezek 1.

6. So now also Andrew Chester, "Jewish Messianic Expectations and Mediatorial Figures and Pauline Christology," in *Paulus und das antike Judentum* (ed. M. Hengel and U. Heckel; WUNT 58; Tübingen: Mohr-Siebeck, 1991), 52.

7. I have sought to substantiate this thesis further in my monograph, *"The 'Son of Man'" as the Son of God* (WUNT 30; Tübingen: Mohr-Siebeck, 1983; Grand Rapids: Eerdmans, 1985).

echo of "the Son of Man" in "the Son of God."[8] With a form- and tradition-historical consideration I support their view. When the exalted Jesus Christ appeared in glory to Paul on the Damascus road, he perceived him in the form and tradition of theophanic visions in the Old Testament and Judaism with which he was familiar, and so he thought he was seeing a heavenly, divine being כבר אנש or דמות כמראה אדם, or an exalted human being in the εἰκὼν τοῦ θεοῦ and "like a son of God," as the כבוד יהוה was blazing in the face of the figure (2 Cor 4:6). In view of the pattern in the descriptions of epiphanic visions in the Old Testament and Judaism, it is not difficult to imagine that some such process took place in Paul's mind at the Damascus Christophany.[9] So, in recounting his experience of the revelation (ἀποκάλυψις) of Christ on the Damascus road in Gal 1:16, he could have referred to "the revelation of the Son of Man." In view of Dan 7 and Jesus' apocalyptic sayings about the coming of the Son of Man for judgment and deliverance, the title "the Son of Man" would fit in well in 1 Thess 1:10. Further, seeing that at the Damascus Christophany Paul could have seen the exalted Christ appearing "like a son of man," we can well imagine that he could have called Jesus "the 'Son of Man'" of Dan 7 and spoken in 1 Thess 1:10 about our "waiting for the Son of Man" to deliver us from God's wrath. But since the figure seen at the Damascus Christophany turned out to be the man Jesus of Nazareth, he came to understand the vision in terms of seeing the exalted Jesus Christ as the Son of God and the Image of God. So in Gal 1:16 he refers to the revelation of "the Son (of God)" rather than "the Son of Man." The ἀποκάλυψις of the Son of God from heaven on the Damascus road was a prolepsis of his eschatological ἀπο-

---

8. E.g., E. Schweizer, "ὁ υἱὸς τοῦ θεοῦ," *TDNT* 8:370, 383; U. Wilckens, "Der Ursprung der Überlieferung der Erscheinung des Auferstandenen," in *Dogma und Denkstrukturen* (E. Schlink FS; ed. W. Joest and W. Pannenberg; Göttingen: Vandenhoeck, 1963), 83-84 n. 67; G. Friedrich, "Ein Tauflied hellenistischer Judenchristen," *TZ* 21 (1965): 502-16. See further J. Dupont, "Filius meus est tu," *RSR* 35 (1948): 525; L. Cerfaux, *Christ in the Theology of St. Paul* (New York: Herder and Herder, 1959), 440-41.

9. See Kim, *Origin*, 214-16 for the pattern in the descriptions of epiphanic visions in the Old Testament and Judaism: a heavenly, divine figure appearing in a vision is regularly described as being "like" a human being (e.g., Ezek 1:26; 8:2; Dan 7:13; 8:15; 10:16, 18; *1 En.* 46:1; *4 Ezra* 13:3), while a human being exalted to heaven or translated into the supernatural realm is said to appear "like" God or a son of God (e.g., *T. Ab.* Rec. A. 12; 16; Dan 3:25; 1 Sam 18:13-14; Rev 2:18). From the data, I infer that "the glorious, supernatural figure appearing in a vision can in himself be described either as being 'like a son of man' (= 'like a man') or 'like a son of God' (= 'like God'), and what determines the seer's choice of one expression or the other depends on whether the figure is already known (or later turns out) to be a divine being or an exalted man" (pp. 215-16). In other words, the choice of the expression is dictated by the necessity to avoid tautology.

κάλυψις, and as such it provided Paul with the ground of hope for the latter. Therefore, in 1 Thess 1:10 Paul speaks about our "waiting for the Son [of God] from heaven . . . Jesus, who will deliver us from the wrath to come." It is quite likely that Paul knew Jesus' self-designation "the 'Son of Man.'" But he did not use it as a title for Jesus. One of the reasons may have been that it would be incomprehensible and misleading to his audience. But I suggest that the more important reason was probably that he understood that Jesus had referred to himself as "the 'Son of Man'" in the sense of the Son of God whom Daniel saw as one "like a son of man" (Dan 7), and he saw him at the Damascus Christophany exactly as the Son of God appearing "like a son of man." So, by designating him as the Son of God, Paul sought to correspond to Jesus' intention in his self-designation as "the 'Son of Man.'"

The second minor thesis that I present by examining Paul's Damascus Christophany in connection with the tradition of the throne-theophany of Ezek 1 is that that Christophany contributed to the formation of Paul's conception of the church as the body of Christ and as the true Israel. If G. Scholem is right with his suggestion that 2 Cor 12:2-4 evidences Paul's acquaintance with the *merkabah* mysticism that originated from the throne-theophany vision of Ezek 1 and that Paul's reference to "the body of glory" in Phil 3:21 likewise points to the influence of the שׁעור קומה speculation, measurement of God's body and its limbs seen in a *merkabah*-vision,[10] I argue that Paul's vision of Christ's "body of glory" (Phil 3:21) or "spiritual body" (1 Cor 15:44) at the Damascus Christophany, which must be seen within the context of the *merkabah*-vision tradition, could have been one of the various factors that led him to conceive of the church as the body of Christ and of Christians as members or limbs of that body (1 Cor 12:12-27). Further, from a comparison of the Damascus Christophany with the Targumic and Rabbinic tradition on Gen 28:12 as well as Dan 7, in which Jacob or the one "like a son of man" appears enthroned in heaven as the inclusive representative of the people of God, I suggest that it is possible that the Damascus Christophany led Paul to conceive of Christ as the inclusive representative of the people of God and therefore of the church as the true Israel (Gal 6:16; Phil 3:3; cf. John 1:51).

Having submitted these minor theses, on whose plausibility, however, my main thesis does not depend,[11] I return to my main thesis and pursue how the

---

10. Cf. G. Scholem, *Jewish Gnosticism, Merkabah Mysticism and Talmudic Tradition* (New York: The Jewish Theological Seminary of America, 1965), 17-18; *On the Mystical Shape of the Godhead* (New York: Schocken, 1991), 278.

11. Kim, *Origin*, 239.

insight of Christ as the εἰκών of God obtained from the Damascus Christophany developed in Paul's theological thinking. I suggest that it developed along two lines, one Wisdom-christology and the other Adam-christology. Since in Philo and the Wisdom literature of Judaism the Wisdom/Logos of God is conceived of as the *Theophanieträger* or mediator of divine presence in theophany visions and even designated as the εἰκών of God's goodness (Wis 7:26), we can see how Paul could have started thinking of Christ, the εἰκών of God, in terms of the Wisdom of God. I suggest that another insight obtained from the Damascus experience, Christ as the end of the Torah, also contributed to the development of a Wisdom-christology, and that Paul apparently secured its basis on Jesus' self-disclosure as the final representative of the Wisdom of God (Matt 11:16-19/Luke 7:31-35; Matt 11:25-27/Luke 10:21-22; Matt 11:28-30; Matt 23:34-36/Luke 11:49-51). I submit 2 Cor 4:4-6 and Col 1:15-20 as evidence for the element of Wisdom-christology in the conception of Christ as the εἰκών of God, and appreciate the former especially, as it clearly reflects the Damascus Christophany. Paul expressed his Wisdom-christology, so originated, mainly through the vehicle of the title "Son of God" as well as the title εἰκών of God and in affirming Christ as the preexistent mediator of creation, revelation, and redemption. Thus the element of Wisdom-christology in the εἰκών-christology basically affirms the divinity of Christ.

The insight of Christ as εἰκών of God led Paul also to think of Christ in terms of Adam, because he is said to have been created in the image of God (Gen 1:26-27). Since Jesus Christ, who had been raised by God from the dead, appeared to him as the image of God on the Damascus road, and his resurrection signaled the dawn of the eschaton, Paul began to perceive of Christ as the Adam of the eschaton, ὁ ἔσχατος Ἀδάμ (1 Cor 15:45), and to develop his distinctive (first) Adam–Last Adam typology (Rom 5:12-21; 1 Cor 15:21-22, 42-49; probably also Phil 2:6-11). Thus I submit my solution to the hitherto unresolved problem of the origin of his Adam-christology. Christ as the Last Adam is conceived of as having restored the image and glory of God that the first Adam all but lost through his fall. So through his Adam-christology Paul basically affirms Christ as the perfect human being and therefore also affirms Christ's humanity.

What I have analyzed as two lines of development of the εἰκών-christology, though corresponding to the two lines of development of the theophany-vision tradition in the Old Testament and Judaism, may not really have been so conceived of by Paul. He may rather have seen them as a unity. That is suggested by 2 Cor 3:18–4:6, where the elements of both Wisdom-christology and Adam-christology appear fused together: "Christ as the εἰκών τοῦ θεοῦ is the revelation of God (2 Cor 4:4-6), i.e., the embodiment of Wisdom, but as such he is also the Last Adam who has recovered the divine image so that we may be transformed into his image (2 Cor 3:18) and become a new creature (2 Cor 4:6)" (cf. also Col 1:15-20; Rom 8:29-30).[12] Both by containing Adam-christology and Wisdom-christology combined in the εἰκών-christology and by having them all in a context that clearly alludes to the Damascus Christophany, 2 Cor 3:18–4:6 effectively confirms my fundamental thesis: Paul's εἰκών-christology originated from the Damascus Christophany, and it gave rise to both his Adam-christology and Wisdom-christology.

The conception of Christ as the εἰκών of God and as the Last Adam who has restored the image and glory of God that the first Adam lost quite naturally led Paul to conceive of salvation in terms of being "conformed" (συμμορφοῦσθαι) to or "transformed" (μεταμορφοῦσθαι) into the εἰκών of Christ (Rom 8:29; 1 Cor 15:49; 2 Cor 3:18). When Paul expresses his distinctive "transformation"-soteriology by speaking of the hope that the Lord Jesus Christ will come "from heaven" and "transform [μετασχηματίσει] our lowly body [τὸ σῶμα τῆς ταπεινώσεως] to conform [σύμμορφον] to his body of glory [τῷ σώματι τῆς δόξης]" (Phil 3:20-21), he gives a strong impression that he is visualizing the exalted Christ's body of glory which he saw appearing from heaven on the Damascus road. He does the same also in 1 Cor 15:42-54, where he calls this "body of glory" the "spiritual body" (σῶμα πνευματικόν) and the "lowly body" the "physical body" (σῶμα ψυχικόν), and explains the eschatological salvation in terms of our parting with the "image" and "physical body" of the first Adam, "the man of earth" (ὁ χοϊκός), and obtaining ("bearing" or "putting on") the "image" and "spiritual body" of the Last Adam, "the man of heaven" (ὁ ἐπουράνιος). From this it is not difficult to see how the Adam-soteriology or "transformation"-soteriology develops into the idea of "putting off τὸν παλαιὸν ἄνθρωπον . . . and putting on τὸν νέον in the knowledge after the image [κατ᾽ εἰκόνα] of its creator" (Col 3:9-10; cf. Eph 4:22-24). While holding that the transformation is to be consummated at the parousia of the Lord Jesus Christ (1 Cor 15:42-54; Phil 3:20-21; Rom 8:29-30), Paul sees that the process has already begun with our faith-baptism, when we were conformed to Christ's death, so that we might be conformed to his resurrection (εἰ γὰρ σύμφυτοι γεγόναμεν τῷ ὁμοιώματι τοῦ θανάτου αὐτοῦ, ἀλλὰ καὶ τῆς ἀναστάσεως ἐσόμεθα) (Rom 6:5), "our παλαιὸς ἄνθρωπος was crucified with Christ," so that we might live with him (Rom 6:6-8), or we "put off" τὸν παλαιὸν ἄνθρωπον and "put on" Christ or τὸν νέον (ἄνθρωπον) (Gal 3:27; Col 3:9-10).

12. Kim, *Origin*, 267.

What happened at our baptism, that is, our becoming conformed to Christ's death or the crucifixion of our old person with Christ, is actualized in the life of discipleship. Therefore, the life of discipleship, especially suffering in it, is the process by which we are being transformed into the image of Christ from one degree of glory to another (2 Cor 3:18) and in which the resurrection life of Jesus is being manifested in our mortal bodies (2 Cor 4:10-18; Phil 3:10). Therefore, it is essential that we be "not conformed [συσχηματίζεσθε] to this world but be transformed [μεταμορφοῦσθε] by the renewal of the mind" or by obeying the perfect will of God (Rom 12:2).

The Adam-Christ typology is a fundamental element in Paul's christology, anthropology (cf. Rom 1:18-32; 7:7-25!), soteriology, ethics, eschatology, and ecclesiology, in fact, in Paul's theology as a whole.[13] Seeing that it originated from the revelation of Christ as the εἰκών of God to Paul on the Damascus road, just as his doctrine of justification and reconciliation originated from the experience of the same Christophany,[14] I find Paul fully justified in his claim that he received his gospel through the revelation of Jesus Christ on the Damascus road (Gal 1:12-17).

Recent Research on the Tradition-History of the Theophany Vision of Ezekiel 1

So far went the theses that I worked out in my dissertation submitted in 1977 and published in early 1981. Since then I have been encouraged not only by the judgment of the old master Otto Michel that further research along the lines charted out by my thesis and its precursors are the most incumbent in Pauline studies today,[15] but also by the works of the increasing number of scholars who have come to stress the importance of the apocalyptic-mystical dimension in

13. Cf. Matthew Black, "Pauline Doctrine of the Second Adam," *SJT* 7 (1954): 173: "the Second Adam doctrine provided Paul with the scaffolding, if not the basic structure, for his redemption and resurrection Christology."

14. See Kim, *Origin*, 269-329.

15. Otto Michel, "Christologische Überlegungen," *TBei* 21 (1990): 32-34: "Neuerdings wird mit Recht versucht, dieses Damaskusgeschehen in die geschichtliche Umgebung der apokalyptischen Mystik einzuordnen. Nach den Forschungen von G. Scholem, C. C. Rowland und H. Odeberg stellt S. Kim das linguistische Material und die Formgeschichte der apokalyptischen Vision dar. *Die Auseinandersetzung mit dieser Forschungsgeschichte ist im Augenblick für uns das Notwendigste*" (p. 32, his italics); again: "Ohne auf den Gesamtentwurf von S. Kim einzugehen . . . , möchte ich ausdrücklich darauf hinweisen, dass S. Kim und die Lehrer, auf die er sich bezieht, einen Weg freigeben, paulinisches Denken in ein neues religionsgeschichtliches Licht zu rücken" (p. 34).

Paul's thought. To name only some of them, C. C. Rowland,[16] J. E. Fossum,[17] L. Hurtado, A. F. Segal,[18] A. Chester,[19] C. C. Newman,[20] C. R. A. Morray-Jones,[21] B. Heininger,[22] S. Meissner,[23] J. M. Scott,[24] and C. A. Gieschen[25] all emphasize the understanding that the throne-theophany tradition of Ezek 1 in Jewish apocalyptic and Wisdom literature which later developed into the *merkabah* mysticism of rabbinic Judaism provides important background for Paul's thought and that Paul's terms such as δόξα, εἰκών, and μορφή must be understood against this background.[26] Undoubtedly their works have the general effect of strength-

16. C. C. Rowland, *The Open Heaven: A Study of Apocalyptic in Judaism and Early Christianity* (New York: Crossroad, 1982), which expands substantially his dissertation, "The Influence of the First Chapter of Ezekiel on Judaism and Early Christianity" (Cambridge University, 1974), from which I drew a great deal.

17. J. E. Fossum, *The Name of God and the Angel of the Lord* (WUNT 36; Tübingen: Mohr-Siebeck, 1985), 257-338; *The Image of the Invisible God: Essays on the Influence of Jewish Mysticism on Early Christianity* (NTOA 30; Freiburg, Switz.: Universitätsverlag Freiburg; Göttingen: Vandenhoeck, 1995), 7-39.

18. A. F. Segal, *Paul the Convert: The Apostolate and Apostasy of Saul the Pharisee* (New Haven: Yale University Press, 1990), 34-71; "Paul and the Beginning of Jewish Mysticism," in *Death, Ecstasy, and Other Worldly Journeys* (ed. J. J. Collins and M. Fishbane; Albany: SUNY Press, 1995), 95-121; "Paul's Thinking about Resurrection in Its Jewish Context," *NTS* 44 (1998): 400-19.

19. Chester, "Jewish Messianic Expectations," 47-78.

20. C. C. Newman, *Paul's Glory-Christology: Tradition and Rhetoric* (NovTSup 69; Leiden: Brill, 1992).

21. C. R. A. Morray-Jones, "Paradise Revisited (2 Cor 12:1-12): The Jewish Mystical Background of Paul's Apostolate. Part 1," *HTR* 86 (1993): 177-217; "Part 2: Paul's Heavenly Ascent and Its Significance," *HTR* 86 (1993): 265-92; also "Transformational Mysticism in the Apocalyptic-Merkabah Tradition," *JJS* 43 (1992): 1-31.

22. B. Heininger, *Paulus als Visionär* (HBS 9; Freiburg: Herder, 1996), esp. 182-211.

23. S. Meissner, *Die Heimholung des Ketzers: Studien zur jüdischen Auseinandersetzung mit Paulus* (WUNT 2/87; Tübingen: Mohr-Siebeck, 1996), 140-213.

24. J. M. Scott, "The Triumph of God in 2 Cor 2:14: Additional Evidence of Merkabah Mysticism in Paul," *NTS* 42 (1996): 260-81; "Throne-Chariot Mysticism in Qumran and in Paul," in *Eschatology, Messianism, and the Dead Sea Scrolls* (ed. C. A. Evans and P. W. Flint; Grand Rapids: Eerdmans, 1997), 101-19.

25. C. A. Gieschen, *Angelomorphic Christology: Antecedents and Early Evidence* (AGAJU 62; Leiden: Brill, 1998).

26. Cf. also A. F. Segal, *Two Powers in Heaven: Early Rabbinic Reports about Christianity and Gnosticism* (SJLA 25; Leiden: Brill, 1977); I. Gruenwald, *Apocalyptic and Merkavah Mysticism* (AGAJU 14; Leiden: Brill, 1980). Segal, *Paul the Convert*, 34, 40, 48, 51, 59, insists that we should take Paul seriously as the unique first-hand witness to the existence of the precursor of merkabah mysticism in the first century A.D. But still Meissner, *Heimholung*, 157, complains that Paul's relationship to the early Jewish mysticism postulated by Jewish researchers has not been taken seriously enough in Christian scholarship.

ening my theses.[27] But, beyond that, many of these scholars specifically endorse my main thesis that Paul obtained his insight into Christ as the εἰκών of God from the Damascus Christophany.[28]

Contra James D. G. Dunn Again

In view of this recent stress on the tradition-history of the throne-theophany of Ezek 1, J. D. G. Dunn's criticism of my theses appears to be ill-informed. He attributes to me an "attempt to merge different elements of different visions into a composite form of theophanic vision (in a manner disturbingly similar to the *religionsgeschichtliche* constructs of the 'pre-Christian Gnostic redeemer myth' or the 'divine man') — particularly Ezekiel 1.26, Daniel 7.13, and the identification of the figure seen as Messiah and Son of God."[29] But this is a strange criticism, because I did not "merge different elements of different visions into a composite form of theophanic vision." I, first, observed only the language and form used in the descriptions of various epiphanic visions in order to ascertain that terms such as δόξα, εἰκών, μορφή, and their

27. Cf. also W. Stenger, "Biographisches und Idealbiographisches in Gal 1,11–2,14," in *Kontinuität und Einheit* (F. Mussner FS; ed. P.-G. Müller and W. Stenger; Freiburg: Herder, 1981), 136, who sees Gal 1:15 as "apokalytische Kurzformel für die 'Thronsaalvision.' "

28. E.g., Larry W. Hurtado, *One God, One Lord: Early Christian Devotion and Ancient Jewish Monotheism* (Philadelphia: Fortress, 1988), 118-19; Segal, *Paul the Convert*, 54, 59-71; "Paul and the Beginning of Jewish Mysticism," 111-12; "Paul's Thinking about Resurrection," 409; Chester, "Jewish Messianic Expectations," 74-77; K. O. Sandness, *Paul — One of the Prophets? A Contribution to the Apostle's Self-Understanding* (WUNT 2/43; Tübingen: Mohr-Siebeck, 1991), 141-44; C. Strecker, *Die liminale Theologie des Paulus: Zugänge zur paulinischen Theologie aus kultuanthropologischer Perspektive* (FRLANT 185; Göttingen: Vandenhoeck, 1999), 140-41; M. Bockmuehl, " 'The Form of God' (Phil. 2:6): Variations on a Theme of Jewish Mysticism," *JTS* 48 (1997): 20; see also C. Dietzfelbinger, *Die Berufung des Paulus als Ursprung seiner Theologie* (Neukirchen: Neukirchener, 1985), 73-74; Newman, *Glory-Christology*, 178, 202; S. J. Hafemann, *Paul, Moses, and the History of Israel* (WUNT 81; Tübingen: Mohr-Siebeck, 1995; Peabody: Hendrickson, 1996), 411-18; Meissner, *Heimholung*, 162, 199, 212. Gieschen, *Angelomorphic Christology*, 333-35, correctly affirms that Paul's references to the glory and εἰκών of God/Christ in 2 Cor 3:18; 4:4-6 must be understood against the background of the tradition of Ezek 1, and refers to my book, *Origin*, 193-268, but strangely adds: "but [Kim] founds his understanding of antecedents in Wisdom and Adam traditions, rather than the Glory of Ezekiel 1.26-28 and related texts" (p. 335).

29. Dunn, "A Light to the Gentiles," in *Jesus, Paul and the Law* (Louisville: Westminster/Knox, 1990), 96; he repeats this criticism in his "Foreword to Second Edition," in *Christology in the Making: A New Testament Inquiry into the Origins of the Doctrine of the Incarnation* (London: SCM, 1980; 2d ed. London: SCM, 1989; Grand Rapids: Eerdmans, 1996), xxiv.

Semitic equivalents are regularly used for God, angelic beings, or exalted human beings.[30] Then, following Procksch, Feuillet, Black, Balz, and above all Rowland, I did affirm the tradition-historical development of the throne-theophany vision of Ezek 1 in Dan 7; *1 En.* 14:37-71; 4Q405; Rev 1; 4–5; *Apoc. Ab.* 17-18; *T. Ab.; Tg. Gen.* 28:12; *b. Ḥag.* 14b; *2 En.; 3 En.;* the conceptions of Wisdom and Logos as *Theophanieträger* in Philo and Wisdom of Solomon, and others.[31] It is strange for Dunn to compare this attempt to trace the tradition-history of the throne-theophany vision of Ezek 1 with the *Religionsgeschichtliche Schule's* construction of the "pre-Christian Gnostic redeemer" or "divine man" myth. Dunn himself grants the tradition-historical links among Ezek 1, Dan 7, *1 En.* 46, *4 Ezra* 13 and Rev 1:13-14.[32] So what is he objecting to? Dunn fails to show where C. C. Rowland's attempt to trace the tradition-historical links among the theophany visions cited above went wrong.[33] Instead he not only at least partially agrees with it but now regrets that in writing his *Christology in the Making* he was not "alive to [Rowland's] Cambridge thesis (1974) ['The Influence of the First Chapter of Ezekiel on Judaism and Early Christianity'], as Kim was," and "failed to give enough attention to an important strand in Jewish apocalyptic and merkabah mysticism in which visions of a glorious archangel are prominent."[34] It is incomprehensible how he can express such a regret in the same breath as repeating his criticism of the attempt to trace the tradition-history of the throne-theophany vision of Ezek 1.[35] Now that many more scholars such as those

30. Kim, *Origin*, 205-23.

31. Ibid., 239-46.

32. Dunn, "A Light to the Gentiles," 96.

33. Accepting Rowland's demonstration of the tradition-history running through the various texts cited above, I did not in fact attempt my own demonstration of it, except to add my notes on the conception of Wisdom/Logos as *Theophanieträger* which was elucidated by H. Hegermann, *Die Vorstellung vom Schöpfungsmittler im hellenistischen Judentum und Christentum* (TU 82; Berlin: Akademie-Verlag, 1961); see my *Origin*, 241-46.

34. Dunn, *Christology in the Making*, xxiv.

35. It is even more incomprehensible how Newman, *Glory-Christology*, 179-80, can copy Dunn's criticism of me when he himself traces a similar tradition-history (in a more complex way than I have done!), speaking, e.g., of "the long-established throne vision trajectory stemming from Ezekiel 1:28" (p. 204), and adopting many of my own conclusions. In fact, Newman presents a thesis very similar to mine, though substituting "Glory" for "Image" in my thesis, or speaking of Paul's "Glory-christology" where I speak of his "εἰκών-christology." Paul nowhere directly designates Christ as the "Glory of God," and this is recognized even by Segal whose work is one of the few books from which Newman apparently has drawn much inspiration (see Segal, *Paul the Convert*, 47; "Paul and the Beginning of Jewish Mysticism," 104, 109). Newman himself admits this, but when he says: "Though Paul never made the surface argument that

cited above have joined Rowland in affirming that tradition-history, one wonders what Dunn's judgment would now be.

Concerning my main thesis that Paul derived his εἰκών-christology from seeing the exalted Christ appearing in the εἰκών of God on the Damascus road, Dunn objects to my taking 2 Cor 3:18; 4:4-6 as evidence of what Paul *saw*. For him Paul's language in those verses expresses only "the impact of the event on Paul rather than a description of the event itself."[36] However, if we read those verses in the light of the form- and tradition-history of the epiphany visions of Ezek 1, etc. as well as Paul's insistence that he saw the Lord (1 Cor 9:1; 15:8), such a dichotomy appears unnecessary and pedantic.[37] Dunn argues further:

> And the fact that Paul makes it a generalized description of Christian conversion confirms that he cannot be thinking particularly of the features which *distinguished* his conversion from those which followed (compare 1 Cor 15.8 — "last of all"). In fact the whole passage is still influenced by the Midrash on Exodus 34 (2 Cor 3.7-18), with Moses' entrance unveiled into the presence of God seen as the type of *all* Jewish conversion from old covenant to new; and the theme of divine glory (δόξα) is drawn more from there than anywhere else (2 Cor 3.7-11, 18; 4.4, 6).[38]

Christ = δόξα, one can still deduce that such an identification occurred at the convictional level for Paul" (*Glory-Christology*, 211), one wishes that he had demonstrated that occurrence at Paul's "convictional level," instead of repeating the mere assertion that Paul identified Christ as Glory (ibid., 13 et passim). I do not think that his assertion that the Pauline phrase τὸν κύριον τῆς δόξης (1 Cor 2:8) "bears out the convictional identification of Jesus as δόξα" (ibid. 204) is a sufficient demonstration. In fact, that phrase, as well as some others such as "the glory of the Lord," "the gospel of the glory of Christ," and "the knowledge of the glory of God in the face of Christ" (2 Cor 3:18; 4:4, 6), shows that Paul does not identify Christ as Glory but rather sees glory as the attendant circumstance of the exalted Christ appearing or as his attribute. This is not to deny that in Judaism כבוד/δόξα is used as a circumlocution for God and even as a technical term for God appearing on the *merkabah*-throne (e.g., Segal, *Paul the Convert*, 41) or that it is closely associated with or, at times, almost synonymous with εἰκών. But the fact remains that Paul identifies the exalted Christ whom he saw on the Damascus road as appearing with *the glory of God* shining *in his face*, as the "image" of God, not as the "glory" of God.

36. Dunn, "A Light to the Gentiles," 95.

37. Even without considering such epiphanic visions in detail, H. D. Betz, "The Concept of the 'Inner Human Being' in Paul's Anthropology," *NTS* 46 (2000): 332, is able to affirm of 2 Cor 3:18; 4:4-6: "the πρόσωπον of Jesus Christ is the mirror image (εἰκών) reflecting the heavenly δόξα/כבוד of God (3:18). . . . Considering ancient ideas about visions, it is reasonable to conclude that Paul saw Christ's πρόσωπον. If so, he interpreted Christ's πρόσωπον as the εἰκών of God."

38. Dunn, "A Light to the Gentiles," 95 (his italics).

But when he makes Moses' experience of the Sinai theophany as the type of all Jewish conversion from old covenant to new, does Paul think that the form of all Jews' conversion would be exactly the same as the former, or that there were no features in Moses' experience of the Sinai theophany that would distinguish that experience in form from the conversion experience of all Jews? There is no question that in 2 Cor 3:7-18 Paul refers to the distinctive features in Moses' experience of the Sinai theophany as reported in Exod 34. Nevertheless, when he uses Moses' experience as the type of Jews' conversion, it is not because he expects that all Jews would have the same experience as Moses in its *form*, but because he sees Moses' experience as typical in terms of the principle or theological meaning. Likewise, in terms of the principle or theological meaning rather than the *form* Paul is making his conversion experience typical of Christians' conversion experience in 2 Cor 4:4-6.[39] But in recalling his conversion experience for that purpose he cannot help but allude to the actual form of his Damascus experience. Dunn is correct in saying that the whole passage of 2 Cor 3:7–4:6 is under the influence of Exod 34. But it is a pity that he does not ask what could have led Paul to Exod 34 in his defense of his apostolic commission. For me, it is eminently sensible that discovering that what he experienced at the Damascus Christophany was quite similar to what was said of Moses' experience at the Sinai theophany in many respects, Paul went to Exod 34 to interpret his Damascus experience. For the new revelation had to be substantiated and interpreted by the revelation in the Scriptures.[40]

With the last sentence of the above quotation, Dunn seems to suggest that the theme of divine δόξα is drawn from Exod 34 "more than" the Damascus Christophany itself. But what is the point of the comparison here? Is he thereby trying to weaken my contention that Paul saw Christ appearing in divine glory? If he is, he immediately contradicts himself. For he goes on to add: "What did Paul see on the Damascus road? Christ 'clothed in glory' could be deduced from 2 Corinthians 4.4, 6 (cf. 1 Cor 15.43; Phil 3.21)."[41] So Dunn does recognize that on the Damascus road Paul *saw* Christ appearing in glory. But then immediately again Dunn expresses his disapproval of my view that Paul saw Christ exalted by God and enthroned at his right hand, saw him as the εἰκὼν τοῦ θεοῦ, as "one like a son of man," or "one like a son of God." He charges that this is "reading a tremendous amount into the few

---

39. See below, pp. 189-90.

40. In his teaching, Prof. Otto Betz used to emphasize this as a principle in Jewish thinking.

41. Dunn, "A Light to the Gentiles," 95. Newman, *Glory-Christology*, 179-80, also points out this discrepancy in Dunn (n. 37) and yet repeats Dunn's view against me that we cannot recover from Paul's interpretation of the Damascus Christophany the event itself (what he actually saw), only to contradict himself in his conclusion (pp. 246-47).

very allusive references Paul makes to the Damascus road experience it-self."[42] I have always thought that Dunn is one of the New Testament exe-getes who draws illustration materials from the Old Testament, Jewish litera-ture, and other religion-historical sources in order to exegete often "very al-lusive" statements of Paul and others in the New Testament. If he is, I cannot see why he is objecting to my exegeting passages such as 1 Cor 15:44-49; 2 Cor 3:18; 4:4-6; Gal 1:16; Phil 3:20-21 with illustrations drawn from the epiphanic visions of the Old Testament and Jewish literature since many terms used in those passages clearly point to them.[43] In the light of the lan-guage and form used in descriptions of those epiphanic visions, at least some of which Paul, the former rabbinic student, must have known because they were in his Bible and in his Jewish tradition, I can well imagine that Paul saw the exalted Christ appearing in the brilliant light of divine glory as being "like God" or in the "form" and "likeness" of God (i.e., εἰκὼν τοῦ θεοῦ), or as being "like a son of God" or "like a son of man," or as sitting on God's throne or at his right hand. The epiphanic visions which I examined in *The Origin of Paul's Gospel* and some more that other scholars (noted above) have examined bear abundant witness to seeing the appearance of di-vine figures, angelic figures, and exalted human figures in such forms. I said that I could not discuss the psychological mechanism involved in such a see-ing.[44] I have not attempted to figure out (if it is possible to figure out at all)[45] whether Paul's familiarity with such epiphanic visions guided him already in the perception of Christ while the Damascus Christophany was actually tak-ing place or whether only some time thereafter he visualized again and con-

42. Dunn, "A Light to the Gentiles," 96. Sometimes Dunn tries to give the impression that I base my thesis on the Damascus origin of Paul's εἰκών-christology only on 2 Cor 4:4-6 (ibid.; "Paul's Conversion," in *Evangelium, Schriftauslegung, Kirche* [Stuhlmacher Festschrift; Göttingen: Vandenhoeck & Ruprecht, 1997], 81). Of course, this is not true. Although I think that 2 Cor 4:4-6 provides the clearest evidence for that thesis, I also interpreted other texts such as 1 Cor 15:44-49; 2 Cor 3:18; Gal 1:16; Phil 3:20-21; Col 1:15; 2:9 as pointing to it (see Kim, *Origin*, 223-33).

43. Cf. Segal, *Paul the Convert*, 39: "With only the most general hints about Paul's conver-sion in his own writing, we must fill in the Jewish cultural context informing his experience. Ezekiel 1 was one of the central scriptures that Luke, and Paul, used to understand Paul's con-version. The vision of the throne-chariot of God in Ezekiel 1, with its attendant description of Glory *(Kavod)*, God's Glory of form, for the human figure, is a central image of Jewish mysti-cism, which is closely related to the apocalyptic tradition."

44. Kim, *Origin*, 246.

45. Cf. J. W. Bowker, " 'Merkabah' Visions and the Visions of Paul," *JSS* 16 (1971): 157-73, who suggests that being acquainted with merkabah mysticism Paul must have been meditating upon Ezek 1 and 2 on the Damascus road when the Christophany took place. But I have not found this suggestion convincing; see my *Origin*, 224 n. 3.

ceptualized what he saw in the language and form of those visions as some similarities (at least the light of glory!) in his vision led him to them. But even if the latter should be the case, Paul would be convinced of having seen Christ as the image and Son of God exalted at the right hand of God. I think that this is the reason why in the context of referring or alluding to his experience at the Damascus Christophany he designates Christ as the εἰκὼν τοῦ θεοῦ and as the Son of God (2 Cor 4:4-6; Gal 1:16; cf. Acts 9:20).[46]

Dunn asks: "May these titles not simply be referents rather than descriptions?" But in view of the illustrations from the epiphanic visions, I ask why they could not be both.[47] Why could not "the Lord of glory" (1 Cor 2:8; 9:1) and "the Son [of God]" (Gal 1:16) be Paul's designations (i.e., the referents) that resulted from his experience of seeing Christ appearing in divine glory, "like a son of God"?[48] The early Christian kerygma of Jesus as Lord and Son of God exalted at the right hand of God (Ps 110:1) would have confirmed to Paul that the person whom he saw appearing in divine glory and "like a son of God" *was* indeed the Son of God, the Lord. Dunn suggests that ὅς ἐστιν εἰκὼν τοῦ θεοῦ is a confessional formula rather than a description of what Paul saw.[49] It is indeed a confessional formula in 2 Cor 4:4, but immediately after citing it, Paul gives a hint as to how he obtained that distinctive confession, namely, from seeing "the glory of God in the face of Christ" on the Damascus road (2 Cor 4:6). After all this hard and sustained campaign against my view that Paul saw the exalted Christ as the "image of God" on the Damascus road, Dunn himself concludes: "Paul's own assertions [about his conversion] make most sense when we see the primary Christological significance of the Christophany for Paul in terms of Adam Christology. . . . In other words, *he saw Christ as the 'image of God'"!*[50] Although it is not clear how he has arrived at it, this conclusion undermines his own criticism of my view completely.

Dunn's next charge is that I claim that Paul instantaneously obtained his christology of Christ as the Wisdom, the Son of God, and so on at the Damascus Christophany. He alleges that I argue that seeing Christ as a glorious figure

---

46. Cf. Chester, "Jewish Messianic Expectations," 76-77. Surely it is significant that the only occurrence of the title "Son of God" in Acts appears in 9:20 as the summary of the gospel Paul preached immediately after the Damascus revelation and call, a parallel to Gal 1:16.

47. See Kim, *Origin*, 225, 256-57.

48. Dunn, "A Light to the Gentiles," 96, wonders how Jesus "would be expressed visually" as "Son." Clearly this sort of query arises because he completely ignores the illustration materials of epiphanic visions in Old Testament-Judaism which often report seeing an exalted figure appearing "like a son of God."

49. Ibid.

50. Ibid., 100 (my italics).

"Paul must at once have jumped to the conclusion that this was a divine figure, the figure of hypostatized Wisdom." He further alleges that having produced "a composite form of theophanic vision" by merging different elements of different visions, I "assume that the whole composite was already in play in Paul's mind at the time of his conversion, simply on the basis of the 'image' language used in 2 Corinthians 4.4."[51] Above I have already rejected his charge that I produced "a composite form of theophanic vision." But his allegation about my assumption or claim here is a gross exaggeration.[52] Explaining how Paul's experience of seeing the glorious Christ appearing "like a son of God" or "in the image of God" could have led him to affirm Christ as the Son of God and the Image of God and how he may have been aided in this by the Christian kerygma of Jesus as the Messiah, the Son of God, by the conception of the king as the "son of God" and "image of God," and by the conception of Wisdom/Logos as the daughter/son and image of God, I do say: "That this understanding of Jesus Christ really took place at the Damascus Christophany (or shortly thereafter, but, in any case, in the light of it), can be gathered from a number of Pauline passages."[53] Such language could have given the impression to some readers that I am claiming what Dunn alleges that I am. To avoid such a wrong impression, now I would put the matter more guardedly. However, to any careful reader it must be clear that this statement is made in the context of explaining how Paul could have concluded that the glorious Christ whom he saw appearing "like a son of God" and "in the image of God" *was* indeed the Son of God and the Image of God. To him it must be clear that my main concern in the context (pp. 223-33 of my book) is to establish the origin of the conception of Christ as the εἰκὼν τοῦ θεοῦ and that I do not discuss the origin of Paul's Wisdom-christology until page 258. In pages 257-67 of my book I explicitly say that the εἰκών-christology which Paul obtained from the Damascus Christophany *developed* along the two lines, Wisdom-christology and Adam-christology.[54] A clear implication in that part of my argument is that the devel-

51. The quotations are taken from ibid., 96.

52. Dunn has not been the only critic to exaggerate my alleged claim about the "instantaneous" origin of Paul's gospel right at the moment of the Damascus revelation. Other critics have also resorted to such a generalized exaggeration in order to dismiss my thesis, rather than producing a substantial argument against my explanation as to how Paul develops the various aspects of his theology as logical corollaries of the Damascus revelation.

53. Kim, *Origin*, 225-26.

54. So I find Dunn's following advice quite gratuitous: "Where the whole point of the argument is to demonstrate that a Christology, which is certainly evident later, actually emerged in Paul's thought following (or even at) the Damascus road encounter, a more carefully delineated exposition is necessary" ("A Light to the Gentiles," 96).

opment took some time. However, because both Wisdom-christology and Adam-christology originated from the εἰκών-christology, I say that both can be said to be "grounded in the Damascus Christophany."[55] This is the reason why in Paul's allusion to his Damascus experience of seeing Christ as the εἰκών of God in 2 Cor 3:18; 4:4-6, we see both Wisdom-christology and Adam-christology implied.[56] Today, I would say that the εἰκών-christology developed in Paul's mind very soon after his experience of seeing Christ as the εἰκών of God on the Damascus road, and that both Wisdom-christology and Adam-christology began to develop a little later — but not too much later. I submit this presumption on the basis of my appreciation, on the one hand, of the εἰκών terminology in epiphanic visions, and, on the other hand, of Paul's knowledge of the Old Testament-Jewish tradition and his theological acumen, which must by no means have been inferior to those of the best of our contemporary scholars who manage to learn much of biblical theology within a few years even though they are not Jews or have not had a soul-shaking experience such as Paul's Damascus Christophany.

Dunn objected also to my seeing Wisdom-christology as well as Adam-christology implicit in Paul's reference to Christ as the εἰκών of God in 2 Cor 4:4-6, preferring to interpret it only in terms of Adam-christology.[57] However, now he has apparently changed his mind on this, as in view of the passage he says: "[Paul's] recognition of the glorious heavenly figure as Christ could then be said to have been the basis of his subsequent Wisdom christology."[58] Nevertheless, he still operates with an "either-or" scheme here and struggles to argue that "the structure of thought seems to be more that of Adam than of Wisdom."[59] Yet he is able to speak about "the fundamental structure of Paul's christology in its overlap and tension between Adam and Wisdom christology" and to appreciate it as pointing the way forward to the subsequent theological conception of Christ as both God and human being.[60]

---

55. Kim, *Origin*, 267. If Dunn finds this view of mine as liable to an interpretation that at the Damascus Christophany Paul "at once jumped to the conclusion that [Christ] . . . was the figure of hypostatized Wisdom" ("A Light to the Gentiles," 96), I suppose that he should find his own statement concerning Adam-christology (ibid., 100) as liable to a similar interpretation, that at the Damascus Christophany Paul "at once jumped to the conclusion" that Christ was the Last Adam, "as the risen embodiment and therefore eschatological fulfilment of God's plan from the beginning to share his glory with the human kind he had created."

56. Kim, *Origin*, 267.

57. Dunn, "A Light to the Gentiles," 97-98. Cf. my rebuttal in my "The 'Mystery' of Rom 11.25-26 Once More," *NTS* 43 (1997): 424 n. 39; pp. 251-52 n. 39 in this volume.

58. Dunn, *The Theology of Paul*, 290.

59. Ibid.

60. Ibid., 293.

I am happy to agree with this formulation, but I would go one step further: *Paul's εἰκών-christology, containing both Wisdom and Adam motifs, encapsulates what subsequent theologians have tried to elucidate with the conception of Christ as both God and human being.*[61]

Alan F. Segal

Among the scholars who recently have stressed the importance of the tradition of the chariot-throne theophany of Ezek 1 for interpreting Paul, Alan F. Segal may be singled out as the representative. Segal has gathered up the insights of G. Scholem, C. C. Rowland, G. Quispel, J. E. Fossum, J. D. Tabor, and others,[62] as well as his own research,[63] to present Paul as an "apocalyptic-mystagogue of the first century"[64] in the most comprehensive way so far, and he is then followed by C. C. Newman, C. R. A. Morray-Jones, B. Heininger, S. Meissner, J. M. Scott, C. A. Gieschen, and others.[65] Segal repeats basically the same thesis in three different writings.[66] Here we will follow his argument as it is laid out in his much-hailed book, *Paul the Convert*, supplementing, where necessary, from the other two essays.

I find Segal presenting a thesis more or less identical with mine in its main points, with differences only in a few details. From Paul's use of the term *apokalypsis* in connection with his conversion in Gal 1, from the phrase *optasias kai apokalypseis* as well as his recounting one of his visionary experiences in 2 Cor 12:1-10 (pp. 34-37), and from Paul's use of the apocalyptic-mystical vocabulary such as *doxa, eikon, morphe* and the idea of transformation which originate from the tradition of the theophany visions (pp. 52-54,

---

61. Cf. Kim, *Origin*, 266-68; also A. Schlatter, *Theologie des Apostels* (Stuttgart: Calwer, 1922), 338 n. 1: "Der Gedanke 'Bild Gottes' liesse sich leicht als Grundgedanke benützen, der alle christologische Sätze des Paulus umfasst."

62. Cf. G. Scholem, *Major Trends in Jewish Mysticism* (New York: Schocken, 1941); *Jewish Gnosticism, Merkabah Mysticism and Talmudic Tradition* (2nd ed.; New York: Jewish Theological Seminary, 1965); G. Quispel, "Ezekiel 1:26 in Jewish Mysticism and Gnosis," *VC* 34 (1980): 1-10; "Hermetism and the New Testament, Especially Paul," *ANRW* 2:22 (forthcoming; cited from Segal, *Paul the Convert*, 323); *Things Unutterable: Paul's Ascent to Paradise in Its Greco-Roman, Judaic and Early Christian Contexts* (Lanham: University Press of America, 1986). For the works of Rowland and Fossum, see nn. 16 and 17 above.

63. Cf. Segal, *Two Powers in Heaven*.

64. Segal, *Paul the Convert*, 36.

65. For the works of these scholars, see nn. 20-25.

66. See n. 18.

59-61), Segal appreciates the fact that Paul "describes his own spiritual experiences in terms appropriate to a Jewish apocalyptic-mystagogue of the first century" (p. 35). This means that Paul's conversion is to be interpreted in the light of the tradition of the vision of God's *merkabah*-throne in Ezek 1, which is "a central image of Jewish mysticism, which is closely related to the apocalyptic tradition" (p. 39). The one "like a son of man" in Dan 7:13 is related to "the appearance of the likeness of the Glory of the Lord" in Ezek 1:26-28 (p. 41), and the notion of a mediator figure sitting on the divine throne developed from interpretations of Ezek 1:26 (e.g., *Apoc. Ab.;* 11QMelch; *2 En.* 33:10; *3 En.*) (pp. 42-43). Alongside this, there also developed the idea that certain heroes could be transformed into the angelic figure on the throne (e.g., *T. Ab.* Recension A 12-13; *2 En.* 30:8-10; *Pr. Jos.; T. Mos.;* the Exagoge of Ezekiel; *Jub.; 1 En.* 70-71) (p. 43-47). Such *merkabah* themes were developed also by Philo, especially in his descriptions of the Logos (pp. 44-45).

In the tradition of the theophany visions, "both terms, *appearance* and *image,* later become technical terms for the Glory of God" (p. 53), and "this vocabulary . . . was known to Paul and became a central aspect of Paul's explanation of the Christian message" (p. 54). Paul designates Christ as the *eikon* of God (2 Cor 4:4; Col 1:15) and the *morphe* of God (Phil 2:6), and speaks of the believers' "transformation" into the image of God's Son (Rom 8:29; 2 Cor 3:18; Phil 3:21; 1 Cor 15:49; cf. also Col 3:9).[67] "These passages are critical to understanding Paul's experience of conversion. They must be examined in close detail to understand their relationship to Jewish apocalypticism and mysticism, from which they derive their most complete significance for Paul" (p. 59). When we read 2 Cor 3:18–4:6 in the light of 12:1-10, we can conclude that "Paul's conversion experience involved his identification of Jesus as the image and Glory of God, as the human figure in heaven, and thereafter as Christ, son, and savior. At least this is how Paul construes it when he recalls it" (p. 61). Concomitant with this conception of Christ is the idea of "transformation." "Paul's conception of the risen body of Christ as the spiritual body (1 Cor 15:43) . . . and as the body of Glory (Phil 3:21) thus originates in Jewish apocalypticism and mysticism" (p. 64).[68] "Paul's imagery for the description of the coming resurrection in 1 Cor [15:42-51] fulfills the vocabulary of spiritual body and Glory of God that ultimately derives from his conversion" (p. 67).

67. Segal, "Paul's Thinking about Resurrection," 409, also affirms that the transformation is understood "as regaining the image of God which Adam lost."
68. In "Paul's Thinking about Resurrection," 418-19, Segal clearly states that the terms "spiritual body" and the "body of glory" also originate from Paul's experience of seeing the risen Christ in a vision.

So Segal concludes that

Paul's conversion experience and his mystical ascension form the basis of his theology. . . . This language of vision has informed his thought in a number of crucial respects. First, it has allowed him to develop a concept of the divinity of Christ or the messiah. . . . Second, he uses this Jewish mystical vocabulary to express the transformation experienced by believers. . . . Third, he uses the language of transformation, gained through contact with Jewish mystical-apocalypticism and presumably through ecstatic conversion, to discuss the ultimate salvation and fulfillment of the apocalypse, raising believers to immortality. (p. 69)

While basically confirming my main thesis on εἰκών-christology/soteriology (= transformation-soteriology), Segal's interpretation raises some problems in details. To mention only three, first of all, in spite of his strong emphasis on the origin of Paul's conception of Christ as the *eikon/morphe* of God and his transformation-soteriology from his conversion vision(s),[69] Segal also speaks about Paul learning the meaning of his experiences from "the gentile Christian community in which he lived."[70] He supports this view with the supposedly sociological finding that "converts learn the meanings of their experience in their new community."[71] In an argument whose logical flow is

---

69. Segal, *Paul the Convert,* thinks that Paul's conversion vision "need not have been one" (p. 37) but that "his conversion experience may have been a process involving several visions and the search for their meaning" (p. 66). I believe that this view is contrary to Paul's testimony in Gal 1:11-17. Indeed Paul may have had several visions (cf. 2 Cor 12:1, 7), but in the Galatians passage he gives the impression that he was converted and commissioned at the first revelatory vision of Christ as the Son of God (especially note the εὐθέως in v. 16). His subsequent visions would have confirmed and deepened the insights that he obtained from the first vision, but he apparently regarded his first vision as the decisive event for his conversion/commission. Segal himself seems to recognize this when he says in the end: "We shall never know Paul's experience. But we can see how Paul reconstructs it. In retrospect, Paul construes his first Christian experience as (ecstatic) conversion. Nor should we dispute Paul's own opinion" (*Paul the Convert,* 70). Segal, *Paul the Convert,* 314 nn. 9 and 10, erroneously attributes to me the views that the vision of 2 Cor 12:1-10 is the same as the vision of Acts 22:17-22, and that 2 Cor 12:1-10 recounts Paul's conversion vision. In contrast to this, Morray-Jones, "Paradise Revisited," 289 n. 82, criticizes me for viewing the Damascus Christophany as the origin of Paul's apostleship and underestimating the vision of Acts 22:17-22! Morray-Jones argues that the Damascus Christophany only brought about Paul's conversion, whereas the vision of 2 Cor 12:1-10, the *merkabah* vision, which he holds to be the same as the vision narrated in Acts 22:17-22, was the occasion in which Paul received his apostolic commission (see especially pp. 283-90). This view is unusual and unlikely in the face of Paul's clear testimonies to the contrary in Gal 1:11-17; 1 Cor 15:5-10.

70. Ibid., 37.

71. Ibid.

difficult to follow, Segal asks "why a Pharisee would have a vision of Christ" and says "a converted Pharisee who knew of mystical apocalyptic traditions would give these experiences Christian interpretations if that person had chosen to join a Christian community." Then, he immediately adds: "But it is clear that Paul had visions. He used these visions to interpret the consequences of his faith and to express the meaning of his conversion."[72] Later on, in connection with Paul's transformation-soteriology, Segal says: "It appears that Paul considers himself special in that the whole process of salvation has been revealed to him. Others have not had his visions, so his visions give him special powers to speak on the meaning of Christian life."[73] If so, for that reason as well as for the reason of their insufficient acquaintance with the Jewish throne-theophany vision tradition, "the gentile Christian community" could not have been in the position to teach him about the εἰκών-christology and his transformation-soteriology. So, then, did "the gentile Christian community" teach Paul only that "Christ was the figure on the throne"? For, as Segal says, "Only the identification of the Christ as the figure on the throne was novel by most Jewish standards."[74] But, then, does this mean that Paul saw a glorious figure in a vision and "wander[ed] about looking for someone to help him interpret it"?[75] Why did he not turn for help to a Jewish authority in apocalyptic mysticism instead of to the Christian heretics (and gentile ones at that!)?[76] As Carey C. Newman rightly asks, "Is it likely that Paul, the confessed persecutor of the church, would have joined a Christian community unless *before* his joining he was convinced that Jesus was the figure of Glory on the throne?"[77]

On the Damascus road Paul must have been convinced that the glorious figure on the divine throne whom he saw in the vision was Jesus Christ whose followers he was persecuting. The conviction must have confirmed in his mind that the Christians whom he was persecuting were right in their claims for Jesus. Only this can explain his *conversion* and his joining the Christian church. Once he joined the church, no doubt, he received *confirmation* from the church about his interpretation of the figure as Christ (cf. Acts 9:5, 17). This confirmation must soon have been followed by the church's teaching about the historical Jesus (the Jesus tradition) and by her more detailed

72. All these quotations from ibid., 37-38.

73. Ibid., 67.

74. Ibid., 320 n. 64.

75. Newman, *Glory-Christology*, 182.

76. Cf. Larry W. Hurtado, "Convert, Apostate or Apostle to the Nations: The 'Conversion' of Paul in Recent Scholarship," *Sciences in Religion* 22 (1993): 283, for a similar criticism.

77. Newman, *Glory-Christology*, 182 (his italics).

teaching on the confession of Jesus as Christ, Lord, and Son of God. Then, on the one hand, Paul must have appreciated these teachings as confirmed by his revelatory experience on the Damascus road, so that he was convinced that Jesus was indeed Christ, Lord, and Son of God. But, on the other hand, Paul must also have (re-)interpreted his revelatory experience ever more deeply in the light of this teaching. Therefore, as a new convert, Paul did learn from his new community the new faith, and it is not entirely wrong to say that with this new faith he interpreted his visionary experience, as Segal insists. However, in this reciprocal interaction between the revelatory vision on the Damascus road and the church's teaching (i.e., the tradition), the priority of the former has to be maintained not only because of the logical requirement, as we have tried to show here, but also because of Paul's insistence on it (Gal 1:11-17).[78]

Especially in the area of the εἰκών-christology and transformation-soteriology, the priority of the Damascus revelation has to be stressed. I think that what Segal himself says in connection with Paul's transformation-soteriology gives sufficient reason: "It appears that Paul considers himself special in that the whole process of salvation has been revealed to him. Others have not had his visions, so his visions give him special powers to speak on the meaning of Christian life."[79] As I have emphasized, the εἰκών-christology/ soteriology is a distinctive doctrine of Paul in the New Testament, with the *eikon/morphe/metamorphousthai* language appearing only in his epistles.[80] Therefore, when he derived his εἰκών-christology/soteriology from his interpretation of the Damascus vision of the exalted Christ in the light of the Old Testament-Jewish epiphanic tradition, especially the *merkabah* vision tradition of Ezek 1, we can hardly assume that any substantial role was played by the teaching of the church in this interpretation.

For this reason, second, Segal's confusing attempt to relate Paul's εἰκών-christology/soteriology with the pre-Pauline baptismal liturgy as well as the Damascus vision is also problematic. In spite of his strong emphasis on the origin of Paul's εἰκών-christology/soteriology from his conversion vision and on 2 Cor 3:18; 4:4-6 as reflecting that vision, Segal sees λάμπω, αὐγάζω, φωτισμός, and the idea of new creation in these verses as echoing a baptismal

---

78. Cf. also Newman, *Glory-Christology*, 182. On the relationship between the "gospel" that Paul received through the revelation of Christ on the Damascus road (Gal 1:11-17) and the "gospel" that he received from his Christian predecessors through a transmission process (1 Cor 15:1-11), see my *Origin*, 66-70.

79. Segal, *Paul the Convert*, 67.

80. For some material in Hebrews and the Johannine literature that bears a loose comparison with the Pauline ideas, see my *Origin*, 138-41.

liturgy and thinks: "it is quite possible that Paul is paraphrasing a baptismal liturgy to express this mystic identification. Paul's quotation might then indicate that it was specifically during baptism that the identification between the image of the savior and the believer was made."[81] Further, Segal sees Phil 2:6-11 as a fragment of primitive liturgy and Phil 3:10, 20-21; Rom 8:29; 12:2; 1 Cor 15:49; Gal 4:19 with their language of συμ-/μετα-μορφοῦσθαι and its synonyms as reflecting a baptismal liturgy.[82] He criticizes me for denying that Phil 2:6-11 and 3:20-21 are liturgical fragments in order to claim them as born of Paul's own revelatory experience.[83] According to Segal, "there is no need to decide whether the passage is originally Paul's (hence received directly through the Damascus revelation) since ecstatic language normally is derived from traditions current within the religious group."[84] I do not deny that Phil 2:6-11 may have been a hymn used as part of liturgy in the early church, but I deny its pre-Pauline origin alone, because its use of the distinctive Pauline term μορφή seems to tip the balance in favor of its Pauline authorship.[85] It is quite questionable whether one can really speak of Phil 3:20-21 as a liturgical fragment. The claim that the passage with its distinctive Pauline doctrine of transformation-soteriology is pre-Pauline is hardly justified.[86] However, in some of the other passages cited by Segal echoes of baptismal ideas may be present, although the future eschatological sense in Rom 8:29; 1 Cor 15:49; Phil 3:20-21 does not draw our attention to them. But here the real question is whether in passages such as 2 Cor 3:18; 4:4-6 we should see Paul applying the insights from his own conversion experience at the Damascus Christophany to other Christians' conversions, which are associated with baptism, or whether we should understand him as interpreting his conversion experience in the language of Christian baptismal liturgy that he learned from the church after his conversion. For the latter view, which seems to be Segal's, at least in the context of this argument, we must presuppose the existence of the εἰκών-christology/soteriology in the pre-Pauline baptismal liturgy. But then why did it leave no trace in the tradition of the New Testament outside the Pauline epistles? Further, if Paul learned the "ecstatic language" from the early church's "traditions" after his conversion, what be-

81. Segal, *Paul the Convert*, 61-62.
82. Ibid., 62-66.
83. Segal repeats the criticism three times over: *Paul the Convert*, 324 n. 102; "Paul and the Beginning of Jewish Mysticism," 122 n. 42; "Paul's Thinking about Resurrection," 412 n. 21.
84. Segal repeats this sentence in all three places listed in the above note.
85. See Kim, *Origin*, 147-49. Of course, I do not claim, either, that the hymn itself originated directly from the Damascus revelation.
86. Ibid., 150-56.

comes of Segal's assertion that Paul was acquainted with the Jewish apocalyptic-mystical vocabulary such as δόξα, εἰκών, μορφή, and συμ-/μετα-μορφοῦσθαι, and that he was the first-hand witness to the Jewish apocalyptic-mysticism of the *merkabah* vision tradition of Ezek 1? What becomes of his statement quoted above: "It appears that Paul considers himself special in that the whole process of salvation [i.e., the transformation-soteriology] has been revealed to him. Others have not had his visions, so his visions give him special powers to speak on the meaning of Christian life"?[87] What becomes of his efforts to prove that Paul's transformation-soteriology originated from Paul's vision of Christ as the glorious figure on the *merkabah*-throne? I believe this reveals a serious self-contradiction on the part of Segal.

Therefore, it is better to think that in some transformation-soteriology passages Paul generalizes the insights drawn from his own conversion experience and applies them to other Christians.[88] To paraphrase 2 Cor 3:18; 4:4-6, having beheld "the glory of God in the face of Christ" or Christ as the εἰκών of God, and having been commissioned to "enlighten" others with that "knowledge" on the Damascus road, Paul preaches "the gospel of the glory of Christ, who is the εἰκών of God," that is, "placards" Christ as crucified, risen, and exalted at the glorious throne of God (Gal 3:1). Those of his hearers who have not been blinded by Satan "behold the glory of the Lord" depicted by him in his gospel preaching and are "enlightened." Thus they behold the Lord of glory as Paul beheld him; they convert as he converted on the Damascus road; and they are transformed into the image of Christ as he was. Their conversion is made public and official at their baptism. Therefore, in their case, they can be said to experience all these in their baptism.

Finally, Segal's explanation of Paul's transformation-soteriology seems to require more demonstration than he has provided. I have explained it in terms of Paul's soteriological application of Adam-christology: from the Damascus Christophany Paul obtained the identification of Christ as the image of God; this led him to conceive of Christ in terms of the Adam of the eschaton who restored the image of God which had been lost by the first Adam; and, therefore, Paul began to think that those human beings who are incorporated into Christ by faith have the image of God restored to them or are transformed into his image which is God's image.[89] But Segal relates Paul's transformation-soteriology more directly to the Damascus Chris-

87. Segal, *Paul the Convert*, 67.

88. Cf. Segal, "Paul's Thinking about Resurrection," 409: "This transformation is accomplished . . . in *direct* visions as Paul apparently did, or *subsequently* by anyone through baptism" (my italics).

89. For details, see Kim, *Origin*, 319-26.

tophany than I have done. He does so because he interprets it in terms of the Jewish apocalyptic-mystical notion of certain heroes' transformation into the glorious figure on the *merkabah*-throne of God and of adepts' transformation into the glorious figure that they see in a vision.[90] So, Segal says, like *1 En.* 71 Paul understands that "the believer is subsumed into the body of [the] heavenly savior and becomes a kind of star or celestial immortal";[91] by gazing on the glorious Christ, Paul understands "he has been transformed into a more divine state" like Enoch in *1 En.* 70-71;[92] and "Paul's experience of the third heaven *may have* transformed him proleptically into an angelic creature, as Enoch was transformed in his heavenly journey."[93]

Second Corinthians 3:18 may indeed reflect the apocalyptic-mystical notion of adepts' transformation by gazing on the glorious figure on the *merkabah*-throne. However, whereas the examples cited by Segal from the Jewish literature mostly have the notion of the heroes' or adepts' being transformed into the glorious figure on the throne himself (e.g., in *1 En.* 71 Enoch is declared to be the Son of Man on the throne), in 2 Cor 3:18 Paul speaks of our transformation into τὴν αὐτὴν εἰκόνα, which in view of the analogy of Rom 8:29; 1 Cor 15:49; and Phil 3:21 must be interpreted in terms of our being conformed to the image of Christ or our bearing his image, rather than in terms of our becoming Christ himself or our being subsumed into his body. Paul may have found it difficult to have the apocalyptic-mystical notion of transformation serve the double duty of identifying Jesus Christ (the "hero") with the glorious figure *and* identifying himself (the "adept") with the same figure.[94] So he may have thought that Christ *is* the glorious figure on the throne and he and other Christians are transformed to become like the glorious Christ. At any rate, Segal's interpretation of Paul's understanding of his own transformation "into a more divine state" or "into an angelic creature" clearly goes beyond what Paul's own testimonies about his Damascus Christophany and his journey into Paradise

90. Segal, "Paul and the Beginning of Jewish Mysticism," 97, 101-8, 113-15. In this Segal is followed by C. R. A. Morray-Jones, "Transformational Mysticism in the Apocalyptic-Merkabah Tradition," *JJS* 43 (1992): 1-31.

91. Segal, *Paul the Convert*, 47.

92. Segal, "Paul and the Beginning of Jewish Mysticism," 104. See also his *Paul the Convert*, 47, 67; "Paul's Thinking about Resurrection," 409.

93. Segal, "Paul and the Beginning of Jewish Mysticism," 119 n. 23.

94. Segal's theory requires that Paul made both identifications. Is this likely? In this context, perhaps it is significant that in the tradition of the four rabbis entering the *Pardes*, which is often compared with Paul's account of his ascent to the *Paradise* (2 Cor 12:1-10), there is no idea of R. Elisha b. Abuyah (Acher) having been identified with or transformed into the Metatron whom he beheld (*b. Ḥag.* 15a).

(2 Cor 12:1-10) warrant.[95] On the contrary, in 2 Cor 12:1-10 Paul speaks about his suffering from a God-given "thorn in the flesh" and about his boasting of his weakness, "lest anyone should think more of me than he sees in me or hears from me" (v. 6).

Furthermore, Paul speaks not only about our being "conformed" to or "transformed" into the image of the glorious Christ but also about our being "conformed" to his death (Phil 3:10; cf. also Rom 6:5; 2 Cor 4:10-18). To explain this problem,[96] Segal generalizes it as a matter of the connection between suffering and resurrection, and then appeals to Jewish martyrology and Hellenistic mystery religions.[97] But this appeal appears strange as Segal does not explain how Jewish martyrology or Hellenistic mystery religions were related to Jewish apocalyptic-mysticism, which he has argued to have formed the background of Paul's idea of transformation. How was Paul's idea of "transformation" into the image of Christ that he obtained from his apocalyptic-mystic vision of the glorious Christ on the Damascus road related to his idea of "conforming" to Christ's death that he supposedly obtained from Jewish martyrology? To make his theory of the origin of Paul's transformation-soteriology more convincing, Segal will have to explain these questions adequately.[98]

In conclusion, for these three reasons, I find Segal's presentation of our common thesis about the origin of Paul's εἰκών-christology/soteriology (= transformation-soteriology) from his Damascus experience somewhat problematic in its details. Therefore, I continue to prefer my own version of the thesis.

The Origin of Adam-Christology

My version of the thesis includes the notion that Paul's εἰκών-christology gave rise to his Adam-christology, which is in turn applied to the transformation-soteriology: released from solidarity with the first Adam and joined in soli-

95. Segal, "Paul and the Beginning of Jewish Mysticism," 115, says: "Paul's letters are the very first witness to Jewish mysticism. . . . Paul tells us in his own language just what it feels like to be transformed into the Glory of God, to become a star, as it were." This conclusion is just fantastic!

96. Cf. Kim, *Origin*, 321-26, for my explanation of the problem in terms of Adam-christology/soteriology.

97. Segal, *Paul the Convert*, 68-69; "Paul and the Beginning of Jewish Mysticism," 114.

98. For my own explanation of the relationship between being "conformed" to Christ's death and being "conformed" to his glorious image, see my *Origin*, 321-26.

darity with the Last Adam through faith, we are transformed into the image of the Last Adam, the Son of God. Thus, for my whole thesis, it is important that Paul's Adam-christology developed from his εἰκών-christology and thus is rooted in the Damascus Christophany.

Recently, however, N. T. Wright has proposed an alternative theory on the origin of Paul's Adam-christology.[99] According to him, it is an exposition by Paul of the belief that Jesus is the Messiah. Paul retains " 'Messiahship' as a major category within his theology" and understands the Messiah to be the inclusive representative of Israel, the people of God.[100] Wright argues that in the Old Testament and in Second Temple Judaism, Israel was the heir of the role of Adam: "God's purposes for the human race in general have devolved on to, and will be fulfilled, in Israel in particular. Israel is, or will become God's true humanity. What God intended for Adam will be given to the seed of Abraham. . . . If there is a 'last Adam' in the relevant Jewish literature, he is not an individual. . . . He is the whole eschatological people of God."[101] With regard to Jewish messianic expectations, Wright argues: "Messianic expectations, where they occur, are best understood as a function of the fervent expectations of the covenant people. Thus a Messiah . . . draws on to himself the hope and destiny of the people itself."[102] With this background, according to Wright, Paul now sees that "Israel's role is taken by her anointed king, and this Messiah has acted out her victory in himself, being raised from the dead in advance of his people. That which Israel had expected for herself . . . has come true in the person of her representative, the Messiah."[103] Thus Jesus the Messiah has represented Israel who represented Adam. Therefore, Paul presents Jesus the Messiah in terms of Adam: "Paul's Adam-christology is basically an Israel-christology, and is predicated on the identification of Jesus as Messiah, in virtue of his resurrection."[104]

It is true that some elements of the Old Testament and the Jewish literature can be interpreted as meaning that Israel inherited the role of Adam. However, the understanding of Adam in Judaism was not so uniform as to provide Wright's theory with such a basis.[105] Furthermore, in Rom 1:18-32; 3:23; and 5:12, Paul is not thinking only of Israel but the whole of human-

---

99. N. T. Wright, "Adam, Israel and the Messiah," in *The Climax of the Covenant: Christ and the Law in Pauline Theology* (Minneapolis: Fortress, 1992), 18-40.

100. Ibid., 18, 28-29 (quotation on 18).

101. Ibid., 20-25 (quotation on 21).

102. Ibid., 25.

103. Ibid., 28.

104. Ibid., 29.

105. Cf. Kim, *Origin*, 187-90.

kind, as he interprets their fall in terms of Adam's fall. In the case of Rom 1:18-32, he is, in fact, thinking of gentile humanity, not Israel! Wright exposes serious vulnerability in his theory when, referring to but not discussing the above passages, he merely says: "We may simply notice that Paul argues, there and elsewhere, that Israel *too* is 'in Adam.'"[106] Doesn't his theory demand that in those passages Paul should think *only* of Israel?[107] With Paul not doing that, Wright's theory about the origin of Paul's Adam-christology fails to be convincing.

Discussing the Adam-christology in 1 Cor 15, however, Wright says:

> Paul's belief in Jesus' resurrection . . . went back to his vision on the road to Damascus (see 1 Corinthians 9.1, 15.8, etc. . . .). Paul believed Jesus to be alive as σῶμα πνευματικόν [1 Cor 15:44] because he had seen him with his own eyes. That is foundational to the whole chapter. This vision, with the new awareness of Jesus' identity that resulted from it, provides a better basis for Jesus' identification with, or representation of, his people than that offered by other theories.[108]

With this remark, Wright comes rather close to my theory about the origin of Paul's εἰκών-Christology and Adam-christology from the Damascus Christophany. Thus, I wonder whether, on the basis of my theory, Wright's view of Paul's understanding of Jesus the Messiah as the corporate representative of God's people, Israel, cannot perhaps be integrated with the notion of the exalted Christ on the *merkabah*-throne as the corporate representative of the true Israel[109] and the notion of Christ the Last Adam as the *Stammvater* of the new humanity.[110]

The "Son of Man" Christology Hidden

If Paul saw Christ as the Son of Man of Dan 7 and found confirmation of his vision in the Jesus tradition of the "Son of Man"–sayings, this integration would be easier. As I said above, as a secondary thesis in my *Origin,* I submitted that on the Damascus road Paul saw the exalted Christ on the *merkabah*-

---

106. Wright, "Adam, Israel and the Messiah," 26-27 (my italics).
107. Cf. ibid., 20: "Speculation about Adam [in the Jewish literature] is not about 'humankind in general.' It is about Israel, the people of God."
108. Ibid., 34.
109. Cf. Kim, *Origin,* 252-56. For an improved version of this notion, see below, pp. 211-13.
110. Ibid., 190-91, 263-64.

throne appearing אדם כמראה דמות or כבר אנש as well as "like God" or "like a son of God" according to the form and tradition of the epiphany visions of the Old Testament and Judaism, that then, seeing that the figure was Jesus, he designated him as the Son of God, and that it corresponded to Jesus' intention in his self-designation as "the 'Son of Man.'" I suggested that therefore those scholars who see an echo of "the Son of Man" in "the Son of God" in Gal 1:16 and 1 Thess 1:10 are correct:[111] Paul could well have said, in Gal 1:16, that on the Damascus road God revealed (proleptically) the Son of Man to him, and, in 1 Thess 1:10, that therefore we wait for the Son of Man from heaven.

There has been much debate as to whether there is any allusion to the Jesus tradition in 1 Thess 4:13-18 and 5:1-11. But I am convinced that in imparting some eschatological instructions "in the word of the Lord" in 1 Thess 4:15-17 Paul does echo Jesus' saying about the coming of the "Son of Man" (Mt 24:30-31 pars.) and his parable of virgins (Mt 25:1-13), and that in 1 Thess 5:1-7 likewise Paul echoes Jesus' parable of the Son of Man's coming like a thief and his other "Son of Man"–sayings (Lk 12:39-40/Mt 24:43-44; Lk 21:34-36/Mk 13:33-37; Lk 12:41-46/Mt 24:42-51).[112] If so, *it means not only that Paul knows Jesus' apocalyptic sayings about the coming of the Son of Man, but also that in writing 1 Thessalonians he is conscious of those sayings.* This then increases the likelihood that in 1 Thess 3:13 he also echoes "Son of Man"–sayings such as Mt 24:30-31/ Mk 13:26-27; Mk 8:38 pars.; Mt 25:31-33 (cf. Dan 7:9-14; also Zech 14:5), and 2 Thess 1:7, which parallels with 1 Thess 3:13, seems to confirm it. All this makes it reasonable to suppose that in 1 Thess 1:10, with the idea of our waiting for the Son of God from heaven for deliverance, Paul reflects the idea of the Son of Man coming from heaven for judgment and deliverance, as some have suspected.

If in his eschatological expectation for the parousia of Christ from heaven Paul reflects Jesus' teaching on the coming of "the Son of Man," we may also hear its echo in Phil 3:20-21, another passage in which Paul speaks about our "waiting [ἀπεκδεχόμεθα] for a Savior, the Lord Jesus Christ [from heaven]." In the Jesus

---

111. See n. 8 above.

112. See S. Kim, "Jesus, Sayings of," in *Dictionary of Paul and His Letters* (ed. G. F. Hawthorne, R. P. Martin and D. Reid; Downers Grove: InterVarsity, 1993), 475-77; in this volume pp. 261-64 below; also David Wenham, *Paul: Follower of Jesus or Founder of Christianity?* (Grand Rapids: Eerdmans, 1995), 305-16; P. Stuhlmacher, "Jesustradition im Römerbrief," *TBei* 14 (1983): 242-43; R. Riesner, "Paulus und die Jesus-Überlieferung," in *Evangelium, Schriftauslegung, Kirche* (P. Stuhlmacher FS; Göttingen: Vandenhoeck, 1997), 360; T. Holtz, *Der erste Brief an die Thessalonicher* (Neukirchener, 1990), 213-18; F. F. Bruce, *1 and 2 Thessalonians* (WBC 45; Waco: Word Books, 1982), 108-10; I. H. Marshall, *First and Second Thessalonians* (Grand Rapids: Eerdmans, 1983), 125-37; C. A. Wanamaker, *The Epistles to the Thessalonians* (Grand Rapids: Eerdmans, 1990), 170-84. See further S. Kim, "The Jesus-Tradition in 1 Thess 4:13–5:11," a paper presented at the SNTS meeting in Montreal, July 31–August 4, 2001.

tradition that reflects Dan 7:13, it is the Son of Man who is to come from heaven (e.g., Matt 24:30-31/Mark 13:26-27). When Paul goes on to say that the Lord Jesus Christ "will transform our lowly body to be like his glorious body κατὰ τὴν ἐνέργειαν τοῦ δύνασθαι αὐτὸν καὶ ὑποτάξαι αὐτῷ τὰ πάντα," he seems to be echoing Dan 7:14 as well as Ps 8:7.[113] The latter sings of God: "You made him (i.e., the "son of man" of v. 4) ruler over the works of your hands; you put everything under his feet [πάντα ὑπέταξας ὑποκάτω τῶν ποδῶν αὐτοῦ]." Being a song that celebrates God's creation of Adam as ruler of God's creation, in itself it naturally lacks the eschatological reference that is the main concern in Phil 3:20-21. Furthermore, although Ps 8:7b may have provided Paul with the vocabulary and idea of Christ "subjecting all things" to himself (καὶ ὑποτάξαι αὐτῷ τὰ πάντα) in Phil 3:21, Ps 8:7a seems to provide at most an indirect basis for the idea of Christ doing it by the power of God given to him (κατὰ τὴν ἐνέργειαν τοῦ δύνασθαι αὐτόν).[114] In contrast, in Dan 7:14 there is the idea of the figure "like a son of man" as invested by God with "authority [שׁלטן], glory and kingship" and all nations as subjected to worship him. And it is explicitly stated as a prophecy for the eschaton.[115] Finally, Ps 8 could not have provided the idea of the savior coming "from heaven." Thus in Phil 3:20-21 Paul seems to reflect Jesus' teaching on the coming of the Son of Man and its scriptural basis, Dan 7:13-14, as well as echoing Ps 8:7. As we have seen several times above, with the references to "heaven," Christ's "body of glory," and "transformation," Paul also reflects his Damascus vision of Christ appearing with the body of glory at God's right hand in heaven. Therefore, Phil 3:21 may be seen as resulting from an interplay of Paul's Damascus vision of the glorious Christ appearing "like a son of man," his interpretation of it in the light of Dan 7:13-14 and Ps 8:7 (a similar "son of man" passage), and Jesus' teaching about the coming of "the Son of Man."

Similar observations can also be made in 1 Cor 15:23-28. Psalm 8:7 is quoted in verse 27 and alluded to in verse 25 in combination with Ps 110:1. In the clause ὅταν καταργήσῃ πᾶσαν ἀρχὴν καὶ πᾶσαν ἐξουσίαν καὶ δύναμιν (v. 24), Martin Hengel sees an allusion to Dan 7:11-12, 26,[116] and Otto Betz

113. For an echo of Ps 8:7 here, cf. M. Hengel, "Sit at My Right Hand!" in *Studies in Early Christology* (Edinburgh: T & T Clark, 1995), 167; P. T. O'Brien, *The Epistle to the Philippians* (NIGTC; Grand Rapids: Eerdmans, 1991), 466.

114. ἐνέργεια here refers to divine power in action. Cf. Phil 2:13; also Col 2:12; Eph 1:9; 3:7.

115. May it be that there is yet a third "son of man" passage echoed here? Cf. Ps 80:18: "Let your hand rest on the man at your right hand, the son of man you have strengthened for yourself" (תְּהִי־יָדְךָ עַל־אִישׁ יְמִינֶךָ עַל־בֶּן־אָדָם אִמַּצְתָּ לָּךְ/γενηθήτω ἡ χείρ σου ἐπ' ἄνδρα δεξιᾶς σου καὶ ἐπὶ υἱὸν ἀνθρώπου ὃν ἐκραταίωσας σεαυτῷ) (cf. also v. 16)? Cf. Hengel, "Sit at My Right Hand!" 169.

116. Hengel, "Sit at My Right Hand!" 164 (cf. also p. 166); cf. also Wright, "Adam, Israel and the Messiah," 28.

finds an echo of Dan 7:14:[117] having received the "dominion and glory and kingship" from God, the "son of man" is to destroy "every dominion and every authority and every power" that the beasts of Dan 7:3-8 represent. With these allusions to the various verses of Dan 7 in our passage, Paul seems to be bringing out the thought of Dan 7 which is expressed more explicitly in the parallel passage in Daniel: "And in the days of those kings the God of heaven will set up a kingdom which shall never be destroyed. . . . It shall break in pieces all these kingdoms and bring them to an end" (Dan 2:44).[118] Then, the main idea of this passage, the temporary entrusting of God's kingly reign to Christ until he subjugates all those enemy forces, reflects Dan 7:13-14 as well as Ps 110:1 and 8:7. Concretely, the concept βασιλεία/βασιλεύειν here alludes to the βασιλεία/ מַלְכוּ which the "son of man" figure receives from God in Dan 7:14.[119] For that

117. O. Betz, *Jesus und das Danielbuch*, vol. 2, *Die Menschensohnworte Jesu und die Zukunftserwartung des Paulus (Daniel 7,13-14)* (Frankfurt: Peter Lang, 1985), 131-32. Betz (130-43) considers 1 Cor 15:23-28 as a virtual running commentary on Dan 7:13-14. Therefore, besides the concepts of Christ's "kingly rule" and his delivering the "Kingdom" to God and of his destruction of "every rule and every authority and power," Betz explains also the concepts παρουσία and "those who belong to Christ" in v. 23 as originating from Dan 7. Cf. F. Lang, *Die Briefe an die Korinther* (NTD; Göttingen: Vandenhoeck, 1986), 228.

118. Cf. the marginal reference to 1 Cor 15:24 in Nestle-Aland, *Novum Testamentum Graece*, 27th ed.

119. If there are these allusions to Dan 7 in our passage, the concepts of παρουσία and "those who belong to Christ" in v. 23 may also originate respectively from παρῆν of Dan 7:13 and from "the saints of the Most High" of Dan 7:18, 22, 27 whom the "son of man" represents, as Betz insists and Lang concurs (see n. 117 above). Paul uses the word παρουσία for the return of Christ only in 1 Cor 15:23; 1 Thess 2:19; 3:13; 4:15; 5:23. His more usual concept for it is "the day of the Lord/Christ" (e.g., 1 Cor 1:8; 5:5; 2 Cor 1:14; Phil 1:10; 2:16; 2 Thess 2:2), and in 1 Thess 5:2 he identifies the παρουσία of the Lord with "the day of the Lord." Matthew 24:27, 37, 39 have the phrase "the παρουσία of the Son of Man" while their Lukan parallels have "the day of the Son of Man" (Luke 17:24, 26, 30). Above I have argued that 1 Thess 3:13, 4:13-18 and 5:1-11 echo various "Son of Man"–sayings of Jesus, especially those of Matt 24 (p. 195), and here I am arguing that 1 Cor 15:23-28 echoes several elements of Dan 7. First Thessalonians 2:19 and 5:23 are similar to 1 Thess 3:13 in thought, so that if the latter echoes Jesus' "Son of Man"–sayings, the former may well echo them, too. Second Thessalonians 2:1 and 8 are clearly under the influence of 1 Thess 4:13-18 (cf. also 2 Thess 1:7). Thus, it is significant that Paul uses the word παρουσία only in the contexts where Jesus' "Son of Man"–sayings or their Danielic background is echoed. This finding seems to suggest that Paul derived the concept "παρουσία of the Lord/ Christ" from Dan 7:13. If the word παρουσία is not original in Matt 24:27, 37, 39, the idea of the coming of the Son of Man or the concept of "the day of the Son of Man" in the Jesus tradition may have led Paul to develop the concept "παρουσία of the Lord/Christ" from Dan 7:13 as an alternative for "the day of the Lord/Christ." If so, later Paul could have developed the imagery of the Lord's παρουσία and our ἀπάντησις in terms of the Hellenistic ceremony of a dignitary's visit (cf. 1 Thess 4:16-17).

concept is only implicit in Ps 110:1, and תְּמַשִׁילֵהוּ of Ps 8:7 is rendered καὶ κατέστησας αὐτόν in the LXX.[120] Since Dan 7:9-14 is a scene of enthronement of the "son of man" figure at the throne next to God's and his investiture with the kingly authority, glory, and rule,[121] it could easily be joined with Ps 110:1, which also speaks of the enthronement of God's Son at the right hand of God (cf. Ps 2:7).[122] So the "Son of Man"–saying of Mark 14:62 and parallels joins Dan 7:13-14 and Ps 110:1 in its scriptural allusion. Even if Paul did not know the saying of Mark 14:62, he himself could have taken the Danielic and Psalm passages together. They then could have drawn Ps 8:7 into a further combination, because the latter also speaks about the "son of man" being given dominion (= Dan 7:14) and God subjecting all things under his feet (= Ps 110:1//Dan 7:14).

The fact that Paul uses the concept of the kingdom of God eight times (Rom 14:17; 1 Cor 4:20; 6:9-10; 15:50; Gal 5:21; Col 4:10-11; 1 Thess 2:11-12; 2 Thess 1:5; cf. also 1 Cor 15:24; Col 1:13; 2 Tim 4:1, 18) and uses it basically in the same sense as Jesus is a strong indication that he knows that the kingdom of God was the central message of Jesus.[123] So our present passage, 1 Cor 15:23-28, may reflect Paul's knowledge of Jesus' kingdom gospel. In his kingdom proclamation, Jesus represented himself as one to whom God's kingly rule had been delegated (i.e., as God's "Son" in the biblical idiom), declaring forgiveness of sins on behalf of God, demonstrating God's saving power through healing, etc. This claim of Jesus is expressed especially clearly in the saying in Matt 11:27/Luke 10:22: "*All things* [πάντα] were *delivered* [παρεδόθη] to me by my *Father*, and no one knows the *Son* except the *Father*."

---

120. Hatch-Redpath, *A Concordance to the Septuagint*, 192-94, 194-96, does not cite a single case of rendering משל with βασιλεία/βασιλεύειν in the LXX.

121. For understanding the Danielic vision in terms of the "son of man's" enthronement and delegation with divine authority, see Segal, *Paul the Convert*, 57; "Paul and the Beginning of Jewish Mission," 99.

122. Cf. Wright, "Adam, Israel and the Messiah," 28.

123. Some critics like to say that Paul uses kingdom language "only" eight times. But I say that it is rather remarkable that Paul uses as many as eight times this language that is rare outside the Jesus tradition. For the similarities between Paul's kingdom references and Jesus' kingdom preaching, see G. Johnston, " 'Kingdom of God' Sayings in Paul's Letters," in *From Jesus to Paul* (F. W. Beare FS; ed. P. Richardson and J. C. Hurd; Waterloo, Ont.: Wilfrid Laurier University Press, 1984), 143-56; Kim, "Jesus, Sayings of," 479-80 (pp. 269-70 in this volume); cf. also E. Schweizer, "1. Korinther 15, 20-28 als Zeugnis paulinischer Eschatologie und ihrer Verwandtschaft mit der Verkündigung Jesu," in *Jesus und Paulus* (W. G. Kümmel FS; ed. E. E. Ellis and E. Grässer; Göttingen: Vandenhoeck, 1975), 301-14; and for the continuity between Jesus' gospel of the Kingdom and Paul's gospel of Christ's death and resurrection, see my "Jesus, Sayings of," 483-84, in this volume, pp. 275-77.

In saying that at the end (τὸ τέλος), "when *all things* [πάντα] are subjected to him, then the *Son*" "*delivers* [παραδιδῷ] the kingdom to the *Father*" and "will also be subjected to him" (vv. 24 + 28), Paul seems to echo specifically this saying of Jesus.[124] Paul would have seen that his Damascus vision of Christ appearing "like a son of God" and "like a son of man" enthroned next to God and invested with God's kingly authority was confirmed not only by the prophecies of Dan 7 and Pss 8 and 110 but also by the claim of the historical Jesus. So Paul is convinced that Christ reigns at present on behalf of God with God's kingly authority and that when his God-given mission as God's Son is completed with "all things" subjected to him, he will "deliver" the kingdom back to God the Father.

Our passage does not make it clear when Jesus Christ was delegated with God's kingly rule (cf. Rom 1:3-4), but it affirms only that the present is the period of Christ's reign, and that it is to last until the end (τὸ τέλος) when he returns the kingly rule to God the Father. The end will be the time when all the evil forces are subjugated to Christ. It has been disputed in our passage as to who Paul thinks does the work of subjugating the evil forces: Christ the Son or God the Father? Verses 27-28 make it unmistakably clear that it is God the Father. However, verses 24-25 make it equally plain that it is Christ the Son. It would be most awkward to read the latter two verses with God as the subject of the two subordinate clauses: "then the end, when he delivers the Kingdom to God the Father, after [God] destroys every rule and every authority and every power. For he must rule until [God] has put all the enemies under his feet." If God does the subjugating, what does Christ's "rule" consist of? Hengel prefers to take God as the subjugator throughout verses 24-28, but apparently he is uneasy about it, as he in the end suggests that we should recognize "the interchangeability or the unity of the action of God and Christ."[125] Indeed, the understanding that Christ subjugates the evil forces by the kingly power delegated to him by God the Father may be leading Paul to this way of apparent "double" talking. Christ rules and subjugates the evil forces to himself, but he does so on behalf of God and with the power of God delegated to him. Therefore, ultimately, God is to be seen as one who subjugates the evil forces through Christ.[126] When this work of subjugating all the evil forces is done by Christ with the power of God or by God through Christ, Christ is also to be subjected to God, "so that God may be all in all." To bring

124. So Wenham, *Paul*, 135-36. For the authenticity of the logion as well as its Danielic background, see W. Grimm, *Jesus und das Danielbuch*, Band I (Frankfurt: Peter Lang, 1984).

125. Hengel, "Sit at My Right Hand!" 165.

126. Compare this with the "double" talk about the "love of Christ" and the "love of God" in Rom 8:35 and 39.

out this relationship between God, the empowering commissioner, and Christ, the empowered agent, Paul uses the "Father-Son" language.

Now it is to be noted that the notion of Christ subjugating the evil forces by the power of God delegated to him which the "double" talk of our passage paradoxically makes clear is the same as what we have observed in Phil 3:21: at the parousia the Lord Jesus Christ "will transform our lowly body to be like his body of glory by the power [of God] which enables him also to subjugate all things to himself." Since Phil 3:21 reflects Paul's Damascus vision of Christ enthroned at the right hand of God to receive God's kingly power, we may ask whether in 1 Cor 15:23-28 also Paul may be conscious of his Damascus vision when he speaks about Christ exercising God's reign and power in the language of Dan 7 and Pss 8 and 110. With his description of Christ as the Last Adam "from heaven," "the heavenly man" who has a "spiritual body," and with his idea about our eventual transformation into "the image of the heavenly man," 1 Cor 15:44-49 suggests that there he alludes to his Damascus vision. Furthermore, 1 Cor 15:8-10 makes it clear that his whole argument for the resurrection of Christ and for the resurrection hope of believers in 1 Cor 15 is based on his Damascus experience of seeing the risen Christ as well as on the common kerygma (1 Cor 15:3-5).[127] Therefore, we may conclude that in writing 1 Cor 15:23-28 Paul is very much conscious of his Damascus vision of the risen, glorious Christ enthroned at the right hand of God in heaven.

Now could Paul have developed this notion of Christ as God's "Son," God's plenipotentiary, who reigns on behalf of God with the power of God, only and purely from an exegesis of Pss 8 and 110? With the echoes of Dan 7:9-14 and Jesus' kingdom preaching and filial self-understanding as well as the allusions to Pss 8 and 110, and with the allusions to the Damascus Christophany in the context, 1 Cor 15:23-28 seems to point rather to Paul's obtaining it from an interplay of the three elements: his Damascus vision of Christ enthroned at God's side, his interpretation of that experience in the light of the Scriptures (Dan 7; Pss 8; 110; etc.), and its confirmation by the Jesus tradition.

A similar interplay of those elements may also be seen in Rom 8:34. In concluding his exposition of the gospel of God's Son (Rom 1:3-4, 9) in terms of God's justification of believers (Rom 1:16-17), Paul presents God's love in Christ as the ground of the ultimate security of the justified believers in spite of tribulations (Rom 8:31-39). This love of God is supremely manifested in his giving up his own Son for us, as the eschatological atonement for our sins on the cross. As we have been justified by God on the basis of Christ's atone-

---

127. Cf. Wright, "Adam, Israel and the Messiah," 34.

ment, no one can bring any charge against us, God's elect. Furthermore, God has raised Jesus Christ to sit at his right hand so that he may intercede for us. Therefore, no one can condemn us. Thus, nothing can separate us from the love of Christ or the love of God in Christ. The central image of this passage, Christ sitting at the right hand of God as God's Son and interceding for us, has, quite naturally, drawn comparison with Stephen's vision of the Son of Man standing at the right side of God (Acts 7:56) and with the christology of Hebrews, which presents Christ as God's Son sitting at the right hand of God and interceding for us (Heb 1:13; 4:14-16; 5:5-6; 7:20-23; 8:1). In Hebrews, the idea of Christ as God's Son sitting at the right hand of God and performing his high priestly ministry of intercession is presented through an exegesis of Pss 2:7 and 110:1, 4. In view of the similarity of Rom 8:34 to this christology of Hebrews (cf. also 1 John 2:1-2), Martin Hengel rightly judges that "the connection between Ps 110:1 and 4 was not created by the author of this relatively late letter [Hebrews], but is much older and was already known to Paul."[128] Thus, echoes of Ps 110:1, 4 can be seen in Rom 8:34.

On the other hand, a comparison of Rom 8:34 with Acts 7:56 suggests that the former as well as the latter may well echo the first half of the "Son of Man"–saying of Luke 12:8-9 (/Matt 10:32-33): "And I tell you, every one who confesses me before human beings, the Son of Man also will confess before the angels of God, but he who denies me before human beings will be denied before the angels."[129] Mark 8:38 (/Luke 9:26/Matt 16:27) may be the Markan variant of the negative half of the Q saying: "For whoever is ashamed [ἐπαισχυνθῇ] of me and of my words . . . of him will the Son of Man also be ashamed, when he comes in the glory of his Father with the holy angels." In Rom 1:16a Paul seems to echo this saying: "For I am not ashamed [ἐπαισχύνομαι] of the gospel."[130]

Before coming to say this, Paul has already defined the gospel as concerning God's

---

128. Hengel, "Sit at My Right Hand!" 147.

129. So Stuhlmacher, "Jesustradition," 250; Wenham, *Paul*, 128; cf. also D. Crump, *Jesus the Intercessor: Prayer and Christology in Luke-Acts* (WUNT 2/49; Tübingen: Mohr-Siebeck, 1992; Grand Rapids: Baker, 1999), 196; D. M. Hay, *Glory at the Right Hand: Psalm 110 in Early Christianity* (SBLMS 18; Nashville: Abingdon, 1973), 130-31; J. Dupont, " 'Assis à la droite de Dieu': L'interprétation du Ps 110,1 dans le Nouveau Testament," in *Resurrexit: Actes du Symposium International sur la Résurrection de Jésus (Rome 1970)* (Rome, 1974), 380, cited from Crump, *Jesus the Intercessor*, 15. For an echo of Luke 12:8 (Matt 10:32) in Acts 7:56, see Crump, op. cit., 190-91, 200.

130. So Wenham, *Paul*, 163; cf. also C. E. B. Cranfield, *The Epistle to the Romans I* (ICC; Edinburgh: T & T Clark, 1975), 86; J. A. Fitzmyer, *Romans: A New Translation with Introduction and Commentary* (AB 33; New York: Doubleday, 1993), 255.

"Son, who was born of the seed of David according to the flesh
and was declared Son of God in power according to the Spirit of holiness
by his resurrection from the dead, Jesus Christ our Lord."

(Rom 1:3-4; also v. 9)

The second half of this confession is substantially the same as Rom 8:34: Christ, God's Son (Rom 8:32), "who was raised from the dead, who is at the right hand of God." By exalting Christ through his resurrection to his right hand to exercise his lordship ("Lord") on his behalf in fulfillment of Ps 110:1, God has declared Christ as his Son ("heir") in fulfillment of Ps 2:7 and 2 Sam 7:12-14. This is the thought at both Rom 1:3-4 and 8:34. The Son of God is the content of the gospel because his death was God's giving him up for our atonement (Rom 3:24-26; 4:25a; 8:32, 34b) and his resurrection was God's raising him up for our justification through his intercession at God's tribunal (Rom 4:25b; 8:34cd). In other words, the Son of God is the gospel because in the narrative of his story, the story of God's giving him up and raising him up, God's saving righteousness (δικαιοσύνη) for humankind is revealed (Rom 1:17).[131] This δικαιοσύνη of God is nothing but the ἀγάπη of God (Rom 8:35, 39). Thus, it seems that Paul is intending an *inclusio* between the introduction of the gospel of God's Son or God's righteousness in Rom 1:2-17 and its conclusion in Rom 8:31-39.

If so, we can see the connection between Paul's confession in Rom 1:16a and his confidence about Christ's intercession in Rom 8:34e *via* the logion of Luke 12:8-9/Matt 10:32-33 and Mark 8:38 and parallels: Paul is not ashamed (ἐπαισχύνομαι) of the Son of Man/Son of God and of his gospel before human beings, and so he is confident that the Son of Man/Son of God will not be ashamed of him but rather will intercede for him at the right hand of God. Paul is confident that so long as his readers go on believing in the gospel of Christ, the Son of God, the Son of God will intercede for them at the right hand of God so that they may overcome all the evil forces and obtain complete justification and salvation. This means that in Rom 8:34 Paul echoes Jesus' "Son of Man"–saying of Luke 12:8-9/Matt 10:32-33 and Mark 8:38 and parallels.

In echoing this saying, Paul may be conscious of its Danielic background, as Rom 8:31-39 reminds us of Dan 7, not only of its scene of the heavenly courtroom but also of its picture of the people of God being preserved and made triumphant over the beastly persecutions of the enemy forces. If so, in affirming Christ/Son of God as being "at the right hand of God" and interceding for us, Paul may be reflecting Dan 7:9-27 as much as Ps 110:1 and 4.

131. For the unity of the two definitions of the gospel in Rom 1:3-4, 9 and in Rom 1:16-17, see my *Origin*, 132-36.

Thus, at Rom 8:34 there seems to be an interplay of Pss 110:1 + 4, Jesus' "Son of Man"–saying of Luke 12:8/Matt 10:32-33, and Dan 7, and at Rom 1:16 an echo of Jesus' "Son of Man"–saying of Mark 8:38/Luke 9:26.

In Phil 1:19-20 Paul expresses basically the same thought as in Rom 1:16 and 8:34. At the impending trial that he faces on account of his preaching the gospel of Christ Jesus, he is fully confident that there will be "the support (ἐπιχορηγία) of the Spirit of Jesus Christ" and so he will have his deliverance, "because" (ὅτι)[132] he will not "be ashamed" (αἰσχυνθήσομαι) of the gospel under any circumstances but will "magnify" Christ "in all outspokenness" (ἐν πάσῃ παρρησίᾳ)[133] at the trial as he always has done (ὡς πάντοτε καὶ νῦν) (cf. Rom 1:16; 2 Cor 3:12). For Paul the intercession of the Spirit of Christ/God (Rom 8:9, 26-27) is the same as or corresponds to the intercession of Christ Jesus, the Son of God, at God's right hand (Rom 8:34). With the phrase "the support (ἐπιχορηγία) of the Spirit of Jesus Christ" in Phil 1:19, Paul apparently refers to the intercession of the Spirit of Christ, the Son of God, at the trial.[134] Thus, besides the keyword αἰσχυνθήσομαι,[135] the

132. Against the majority of the commentators, G. F. Hawthorne, *Philippians* (WBC 43; Waco: Word, 1983), 42, advances some good reasons for construing the phrase κατὰ τὴν ἀποκαραδοκίαν καὶ ἐλπίδα μου with what precedes it (so also Nestle-Aland 27th ed.): "For I know that through your prayers and the support of the Spirit of Jesus Christ this will turn out for my deliverance as I eagerly expect and hope." So he avoids the common mistake of taking the ὅτι-clause of v. 20 as the object of Paul's intense hope. However, missing the echo of Jesus' "Son of Man" saying here, Hawthorne takes the ὅτι-clause of v. 20 as the object of the main verb οἶδα like the ὅτι-clause of v. 19. But there is no καί before the ὅτι of v. 20 and the ὅτι-clause of v. 20 is no epexegesis of the earlier ὅτι-clause. In fact, the ὅτι-clause of v. 20 provides the ground for the ὅτι-clause of v. 19. Apparently no commentator has picked up the echo of Jesus' "Son of Man" saying here. Cf. P. T. O'Brien, *Commentary on Philippians* (NIGTC; Grand Rapids: Eerdmans, 1991), 114 n.40.

133. Cf. W. van Unnik, "The Christian's Freedom of Speech in the NT," *Sparsa Collecta* (Part Two; Leiden: Brill, 1980), 269-89, esp. 277-78; R. E. Brown, *The Epistles of John* (AB; Garden City: Doubleday, 1982), 381. When Hawthorne, *Philippians*, 43, connects the ἐν πάσῃ παρρησίᾳ of v. 20 both with the πολλῇ παρρησίᾳ of 2 Cor 3:12 (cf. also 1 Thess 2:2) and the εἰς ἀπολογίαν τοῦ εὐαγγελίου of Phil 1:16 as well as compares the ἐν οὐδενὶ αἰσχυνθήσομαι of v. 20 with the οὐκ ἐπαισχύνομαι of Rom 1:16, he comes rather close to my interpretation here.

134. Paul may be choosing this expression in order to combine the thought of Luke 12:8-9/ Matt 10:32-33 and Mark 8:38 pars with that of Mark 13:11; Luke 12:11-12; Matt 10:20, namely the assistance of the Spirit at the trial.

135. R. Bultmann, αἰσχύνω, κτλ., *TDNT* 1, 189-90, observes the full interchangeability of αἰσχύνω with ἐπαισχύνω as well as the difficulty of deciding whether αἰσχύνεσθαι is middle or passive. Then, seeing that αἰσχύνεσθαι is used as the opposite of παρρησία in 1 John 2:28, he interprets it as middle, meaning "'being ashamed of' . . . a dubious person or cause [as] in Mk. 8:38 and par." But strangely he interprets the αἰσχύνεσθαι in Phil 1:20 to mean "being disillusioned." Since the αἰσχύνεσθαι is used as the opposite of παρρησία in Phil 1:20 just as in 1 John

thought structure of Phil 1:19-20 exactly corresponds to Jesus' "Son of Man" saying of Luke 12:8-9/Matt 10:32-33 and Mark 8:38 pars. So, it is very likely that in Phil 1:19-20 as well as in Rom 1:16 and 8:34 Paul is echoing that saying of Jesus. By connecting directly his own determination not to be ashamed of the gospel with the intercession of the Spirit of Christ at the trial, Phil 1:19-20 seems to make this even clearer than Rom 1:16 and 8:34. At any rate, Phil 1:19-20 and Rom 1:16 and 8:34 (cf. also 1 John 2:28) support each other in providing the evidence that Paul is very much conscious of Jesus' "Son of Man" saying of Luke 12:8-9/Matt 10:32-33 and Mark 8:38 pars.

The words of the institution of the Lord's Supper (1 Cor 11:23-26) also seem to suggest that Paul knows Jesus' self-designation, "the Son of Man." In my monograph I have observed how in the Gospel traditions and the early church traditions the eucharistic words are associated with the title "the Son of Man."[136] In the Synoptic Gospels, Jesus presents the Last Supper as a symbolic dramatization of the meaning of the Son of Man's "departure" (ὑπάγει/ πορεύεται) or "being delivered" (παραδίδοται) (Matt 26:24/Mark 14:21/ Luke 22:22). Thereby he makes eating the bread and drinking the wine at the Last Supper in effect an eating of the body/flesh of the Son of Man and drinking his blood. This is well represented by the Johannine scene of the Last Supper (John 13:31-35) and the Johannine version of the eucharistic words: "Unless you eat the flesh of the Son of Man and drink his blood . . ." (John 6:53). Further, Mark 10:45 and parallels (cf. also 1 Tim 2:5-6) and Luke 22:28-30/Matt 19:28 show a firm connection of the title "the Son of Man" with the Last Supper.[137] This is probably the reason why in Ign. *Eph.* 20:2, *Acts John* 109, and *Gosp. Phil.* 15 the title is associated with the Lord's Supper.

2:28, should we not interpret it as in 1 John 2:28? In fact, in the exhortation of 1 John 2:28 for the believers to "remain" in Christ, i.e., to go on "confessing" (ὁμολογεῖν) Jesus as the Christ and the Son of God in spite of the antichrist's pressure to "deny" (ἀρνεῖσθαι) him (1 John 2:18-27, esp. 22-23), "so that when he appears we may have παρρησίαν and not αἰσχυνθῶμεν ἀπ' αὐτοῦ at his parousia," we should find an echo of Jesus' "Son of Man" saying of Luke 12:8-9/Matt 10:32-33 and Mark 8:38 pars as in Phil 1:19-20 (cf. S. S. Smalley, *1, 2, 3 John* [WBC 51; Waco: Word, 1984], 131). The three key words (ὁμολογεῖν; ἀρνεῖσθαι; αἰσχύνεσθαι) as well as the thought structure of 1 John 2:18-29 strongly suggest this. If this interpretation of Rom 1:16 and 8:34; Phil 1:19-20 and 1 John 2:28 (+ vv. 22-23) as echoing the saying of Jesus is correct, the three passages bear witness to the continuing vitality of the logion as well as to the unity of the Q logion (Luke 12:8-9/Matt 10:32-33) and the Markan logion (Mark 8:38 pars.).

136. Kim, *"The 'Son of Man,'"* 45-49.

137. For the view that Mark 10:45 pars. is to be seen within the context of the eucharistic words, see ibid., 43-52.

Now, if we look at the opening words of the institution: ὁ κύριος Ἰησοῦς ἐν τῇ νυκτὶ ᾗ παρεδίδετο (1 Cor 11:23) in the light of these Gospel traditions, we cannot help but wonder whether it may not be Paul's adaptation of the opening words of the Synoptic eucharistic tradition, ὁ υἱὸς τοῦ ἀνθρώπου παραδίδοται (Matt 26:24/Mark 14:21/Luke 22:22). In the Synoptic Gospels Jesus' passion announcements are firmly connected with "the Son of Man" (Mark 8:31/Luke 9:22; Mark 9:9/Matt 17:9; Mark 9:12/Matt 17:12; Mark 9:31 pars.; Mark 10:33 pars.; Mark 10:45/Matt 20:28; Mark 14:41/Matt 26:45; Matt 26:2; Luke 17:25; cf. also Matt 12:40/Luke 11:30), often in combination with the predicate παραδιδόναι (Mark 9:31 pars.; Mark 10:33 pars.; Matt 26:2; Mark 14:41/Matt 26:45; Luke 22:48; 24:7), and the eucharistic words are part of the passion announcements. John also represents this tradition rather faithfully, although he often interprets the passion of the Son of Man in his characteristic terms of being "lifted up" or glorified (3:14; 8:28; 12:23, 34; 13:31; cf. also 6:62). In the Synoptic Gospels, it is also "the Son of Man" who is to come in the future (Mark 8:38/Luke 9:26; Mark 13:26 pars.; Matt 24:27/Luke 17:24; Matt 24:37/Luke 17:26; Matt 24:39/Luke 17:30; Matt 24:44/Luke 12:40; Luke 21:36; Matt 25:31; Mark 14:62/Matt 26:64; Luke 17:22; 18:8; 21:36). For these reasons, I suspect that in the closing clause of 1 Cor 11:26 with the motifs of both the "Lord's" death and parousia (τὸν θάνατον τοῦ κυρίου καταγγέλλετε ἄχρις οὗ ἔλθῃ), Paul also replaces "the Son of Man" with "Lord."

In verse 23 Paul emphasizes the tradition character of the institution of the eucharist by using the technical term for transmission of tradition: παρέλαβον (קבל) — παρέδωκα (מסר).[138] When he received the tradition of the Lord's Supper, it must have had the title "the Son of Man" associated with the eucharistic words, since all the Gospel traditions bear witness to that association, as we have just seen. Along with the other post-Easter preachers of the gospel, however, Paul would not have found it expedient to use "the Son of Man," the misunderstanding-prone self-designation of Jesus, in confession and kerygma. So he normally connects the title "Christ" with death ("the death-formula": Christ died for us/our sins) and the title "Lord" with exaltation, worship, and the parousia,[139] although in the Jesus tradition the title "the Son of Man" is connected with both death and parousia. In 1 Cor 11:23 Paul replaces "the Son of Man" with "Lord" because the Lord's Supper is part of the activity of worshiping the "Lord" Jesus Christ. For this reason and for the additional reason of the reference to the parousia, Paul replaces "the Son of Man" with "Lord" also in verse 26.

---

138. Cf. also Paul's stress on "remembering" Jesus in the eucharist (vv. 24-25).

139. Cf. W. Kramer, *Christ, Lord, Son of God* (SBT 50; London: SCM, 1966), 65-84, 151-82.

Thus we have found probable echoes of various "Son of Man"–sayings of Jesus in many passages of Paul's letters (Rom 1:16; 8:34; 1 Cor 11:23-26; 1 Cor 15:23-28; Gal 1:16; Phil 1:19-21; 3:20-21; 1 Thess 1:10; 3:13; 4:13-18; 5:1-11). In Rom 8:32-34; 1 Cor 15:23-28; Gal 1:16; and 1 Thess 1:10, there seems to be equation, if not replacement, of "the Son of Man" with the Son of God. In 1 Cor 11:23-26 there are echoes of the sayings about "the Son of Man" παραδίδοται and about him ἔρχεσθαι. These three facts considered together lead me to wonder whether behind the sending formula (God sent his Son . . . : Rom 8:3; Gal 4:4) and the giving-up formula (God παρέδωκεν his Son . . . : Rom 8:32; Gal 2:20) also there may not stand the Jesuanic sayings of "the Son of Man [ἦλθεν]" (e.g., Matt 11:19/Luke 7:34; Mark 10:45 pars.) and of "the Son of Man [παραδίδοται]" (e.g., Mark 9:31 pars.; Mark 10:33 pars.; Matt 26:2; Mark 14:41/Matt 26:45; Luke 22:48; 24:7) respectively. The Johannine evidence supports this conjecture. John 3:13-14 and 16-17 equate "the Son of Man" who has come (or rather "descended") and is given up (or rather "lifted up") with the Son of God who has been "sent" and "given" (cf. John 1:49-51; 5:26-27). The sending formula in 1 John 4:10 ("And [God] sent his Son as expiation [ἱλασμός/כפרים] for our sins") looks very much like a paraphrase of Mark 10:45/Matt 20:28 ("The Son of Man came . . . to give his life as ransom [λύτρον/כפר] for many").

All these observations build a strong case for Paul's knowledge and use of Jesus' "Son of Man"–sayings. In at least one (1 Cor 15:23-28) of those Pauline passages which echo the sayings, there is also an echo of Jesus' kingdom preaching and filial claim. In three of the passages (Phil 3:21; 1 Cor 15:23-28; Rom 8:34), Paul also reflects Dan 7, combining it with Pss 8:7 and 110:1. Finally, in Phil 3:21 and 1 Cor 15:23-28 we have also seen an echo of Paul's Damascus experience of seeing Christ enthroned at the right hand of God (cf. also Gal 1:16; 2:20). Therefore, we have concluded that in the last two passages there is an interplay of the three elements: (1) Paul's experience of the Damascus Christophany, (2) Dan 7 and its related Scriptures Pss 8 and 110, and (3) the Jesus tradition, especially Jesus' teaching on the coming of "the Son of Man," and that in Rom 8:34 there is also a similar interplay of a "Son of Man"–saying of Jesus with Ps 110 and Dan 7.

These findings strongly suggest Paul's theologizing process or his theological method: *seeing Jesus' claim (and the early church's kerygma) confirmed by the Damascus revelation, he interpreted the revelation in the light of the Jesus tradition as well as the Scriptures, and vice versa.* His experience of the Damascus Christophany led Paul to accept the early church's kerygma of Jesus as Christ, Lord, and Son of God. For an interpretation of the Jesus Christ whom he saw in the vision, he went to Dan 7, which described a vision similar to his

Damascus vision.[140] When he learned of Jesus' "Son of Man"–sayings (together with his filial claim and "kingdom" preaching) from Christians, he understood that Jesus had designated himself as "*the* 'Son of Man'" in reference to the figure appearing "like a son of man" in Dan 7:13. So he became convinced that Jesus whom he saw appearing "like a son of man" or "like a son of God" was indeed the Son of God who had appeared "like a son of man" in the Danielic vision and who had been exalted to the throne next to God's and delegated with God's "dominion, glory and kingdom" (Dan 7:14). Therefore Paul could designate Jesus "the 'Son of Man'" as "Son of God" and "Lord" who sits at the right hand of God, who, having "inherited" God's kingship, rules as "Lord" over all on God's behalf and with God's power. He could readily accept Christians' references to Pss 2:7; 110:1; and 8:7, and so on, which he could see as having prophesied the Messiah's enthronement just as Dan 7 did, and so he joined the Psalm texts together with Dan 7 to interpret the exalted Christ. In the case of Ps 8, the common keyword "son of man" was an additional reason for him to join it with Dan 7. So it was natural for him to teach about the work of the exalted Christ, reflecting all these elements — his Damascus Christophany, Jesus' sayings of "the 'Son of Man'" and the kingdom, and Dan 7 and its related texts (Pss 8; 110; etc.) — intermixed in such passages as those we have surveyed here.

I believe this is the only way we can account for what Andrew Chester calls the "astounding" fact "that Paul can apply these terms and traditions [of heavenly mediatorial figures] to a human figure not from the remote past (or biblical tradition) but from contemporary history and experience."[141] Chester affirms that "this is something that is unique to the New Testament, in the context of Jewish usage." Then, referring to Paul's Damascus experience as a starting point for explaining the phenomenon, Chester says: "one reason that Paul can so readily apply to Christ the terminology used of exalted mediator concepts and heavenly figures may be because this corresponds, as much as any verbal description or tradition available to him could, to what he has himself experienced."[142] I appreciate this conclusion, as it confirms the thesis that I propounded in my *Origin*. However, it affirms only half the truth, and I would like to supplement it: Paul's knowledge of Jesus' self-designation as

---

140. The fact that the echoes of the Damascus Christophany, of Dan 7, and of Jesus' "Son of Man"–sayings are found combined in 1 Cor 15:23-28 and Phil 3:20-21 suggests that his experience of the Damascus Christophany led Paul to the similar vision in Dan 7 as well as to the Jesus tradition for its interpretation.

141. Chester, "Jewish Messianic Expectations," 76. M. Hengel, "Sit at My Right Hand!" 203, calls it an "unspeakably audacious and at the same time provocative step" (see also p. 201).

142. Chester, "Jewish Messianic Expectations," 76-77.

"the 'Son of Man,'" his filial consciousness, and his kingdom preaching was an element as essential as the two elements, Paul's own Damascus experience and the Old Testament-Jewish tradition of heavenly mediator figures. From the latter two elements alone, the "astounding" fact cannot adequately be explained. Without having the interpretation of Christ derived from those two elements properly confirmed by what Jesus actually claimed to be and what he actually did (i.e., the Jesus tradition), Paul could hardly have proclaimed that the Jesus crucified only a few years ago was the "Lord" and "Son of God" enthroned at God's right hand.[143]

Christ, the Last Adam, and the Wisdom of God

Now it is significant that in 1 Cor 15:23-28 and Phil 3:20-21 the combined echoes of the Damascus Christophany, Ps 8, Dan 7, and Jesus' "Son of Man"–sayings are further combined with the motif of Adam-christology/soteriology. First Corinthians 15:23-28 follows directly on the contrast between Adam and Christ in the preceding verses 21-22: "For as through an ἄνθρωπος came death, through an ἄνθρωπος has come also the resurrection of the dead. For as in Adam all die, so also in Christ shall all be made alive." In Phil 3:21, the idea of the Lord Jesus Christ coming to "transform our lowly body to be conformed to his body of glory" is an expression of Adam-soteriology. Therefore, 1 Cor 15:23-28 and Phil 3:20-21, on the one hand, help confirm my thesis that Paul derived his Adam-christology from the Damascus Christophany, and, on the other hand, suggest that the Adam-christology is also related to Jesus' self-designation, "the Son of Man." Having developed the conception of Christ in terms of Adam from the Damascus Christophany, apparently Paul found it confirmed by Jesus' self-designation as "the 'Son of Man.'"

In the light of the form- and tradition-history of the epiphany visions of

---

143. A mythologization of an ancient hero like Enoch, Jacob, or Moses did happen in Judaism (e.g., *1 En.* 71; *Pr. Jos.*; the Exagoge of Ezekiel, 68-82). But a mythologization of the crucified Jesus by his contemporaries purely on the basis of a vision or a scriptural exegesis without any reference to what he was and did is scarcely imaginable. See further Hengel, "Sit at My Right Hand!" 185-214, who argues that in pre-Christian Judaism there was a general aversion to the idea of any human being enthroned on God's throne, except Enoch, and that the idea of enthronement of heroes and martyrs arose only in some post-Christian Jewish traditions, probably under the Christian influence. Hengel says that the "unspeakably audacious and . . . provocative step" the primitive church took in proclaiming the crucified Jesus as God's throne-companion must have had "a basis in the teaching and the bearing of Jesus himself" (p. 203).

the Old Testament and Judaism, I have repeatedly affirmed that Paul could have thought that on the Damascus road he had seen the glorious Christ appearing "like a son of God" or "in the image of God" or "like a son of man." This experience led Paul, on the one hand, to Gen 1:26-27, where Adam is said to have been created in the image of God, and, on the other hand, to Dan 7, where a heavenly figure appears "like a son of man" in a vision similar to the one he had. From the former Paul developed the conception of Christ in terms of Adam: Christ is the Last Adam, the Adam of the eschaton, who has restored the image of God lost by (the first) Adam. From the latter Paul found the primitive church's kerygma of Jesus as the Son of God enthroned at God's right hand confirmed. Later he found it further confirmed by the Jesus tradition, that is, Jesus' self-designation as "the 'Son of Man,'" his kingdom-preaching, and his filial claim, which he could understand all very well in the light of Dan 7: Jesus was *the* 'Son of Man'" of Dan 7:13-14, the Son of God who had appeared "like a son of man" and been entrusted with God's kingship in the Danielic vision. Then, Paul also found his new conception of Christ as the Last Adam confirmed by this self-designation of Jesus as seen in the light of Dan 7. Since Jesus used to designate himself as "the 'Son of Man,'" meaning the Son of God who had "inherited" God's kingship to exercise it on his behalf according to the prophecy of Dan 7 (cf., e.g., Mark 2:10 pars.; Matt 19:28/Luke 22:29-30),[144] this Jesus, "the 'Son of Man,'" fulfilled the mandate that God gave to Adam according to the creation narrative (Gen 1:26-28). Paul further found this interpretation of the Jesus tradition in the light of Dan 7 confirmed by Ps 8:4-8, which celebrates God's mandating Adam to rule over the whole creation: "What is man [אֱנוֹשׁ/ἄνθρωπος] that you are mindful of him, or son of man [בֶן אָדָם/υἱὸς ἀνθρώπου] that you care for him? You made him a little lower than the heavenly beings and crowned him with glory and honor. You made him rule over the works of your hands; you put everything under his feet." Therefore, Paul could equate Jesus "the 'Son of Man'" with Christ the Last Adam. For all this interpretation the fact that בַּר אֱנָשׁ/בֶן אָדָם was equivalent to אָדָם helped Paul, so that he could well understand the בַּר אֱנָשׁ of Dan 7:13-14 as well as the בֶן אָדָם/אֱנוֹשׁ of Ps 8:4-8 in terms of Adam; to the "son of man" figure was restored the divine mandate to rule over all on God's behalf which Adam originally had received but then lost. Then the "son of man" was the Adam of the eschaton, the Last Adam. Therefore, Jesus, "the 'Son of Man,'" was the Last Adam. Hence, on the Damascus road he appeared as a glorious heavenly figure "in the image of God," as the Adam of the eschaton, who has restored the image of God that had been lost

144. Cf. Kim, *"The 'Son of Man,' "* 15-81.

by (the first) Adam. Thus the circle was closed. All this consideration makes it quite plausible to suppose that Paul found his Adam-christology derived from his conception of Christ as the εἰκών of God as confirmed by Jesus' self-designation, "the "Son of Man,'" as it was seen in the light of Dan 7:13-14 and Ps 8:4-8.[145]

With this new explanation of the origin of Paul's Adam-christology, I modify my earlier thesis. In *The Origin of Paul's Gospel*, in my enthusiasm for what I considered to be a new discovery, namely, that Paul developed his distinctive Adam-christology from his experience of seeing the exalted Christ appearing in the εἰκών of God on the Damascus road, I rejected the attempts made by various scholars to derive Paul's Adam-christology directly from Jesus' self-designation or Dan 7.[146] I still believe that those attempts in themselves are not convincing. Any attempt to derive Paul's Adam-christology directly from Jesus' self-designation or Dan 7 without any recourse to Paul's experience of the Damascus Christophany is not convincing. So I still uphold my original view that Paul's Adam-christology developed from his εἰκών-christology which he had derived from the Damascus Christophany. I still regard passages such as 1 Cor 15:42-49; 2 Cor 3:18; 4:4-6; and Phil 3:20-21 as evidencing this by displaying the εἰκών- and Adam-christology/soteriology in the midst of their clear allusion to the Damascus Christophany. But now, realizing that it is only half of the truth, I would like to affirm also that the Jesus tradition, especially Jesus' self-designation as "the 'Son of Man,'"[147] played an important role in its development together with Dan 7 and Ps 8, as shown above. Therefore, I modify my thesis in this way: *Paul developed his Adam-christology from his Damascus experience of seeing the exalted Christ appearing in the image of God* and *by confirming it by Jesus' self-designation as "the 'Son of Man' "* and *by Dan 7 and Ps 8*.

Here once more we see Paul's theological method that we have observed above: the development of a new theological insight out of the interplay of

145. Therefore the efforts of Dunn, *Christology in the Making*, 107-13, to explain the origin of Paul's Adam-christology only from an exegesis of Pss 8 and 110 are inadequate.

146. Kim, *Origin*, 180-86, 192.

147. It is a question whether, alongside Jesus' self-designation and Kingdom-preaching, some other elements of the Jesus tradition such as the temptation narrative (Mark 1:12-13/Matt 4:1-11/Luke 4:1-13) and the parable of the prodigal son (Luke 15:11-32) may also have played a role, since in the temptation narrative there seems to be an implicit contrast between Jesus and Adam as well as Israel, and the parable of the prodigal son looks very much like a retelling of the story of the fall of Adam (Gen 3). In that parable Jesus put himself on the side of the father and identified his hearers as Adamic and as needing to return to God, the loving father, for forgiveness and abundant life. But Paul could have seen the representation by Christ of human beings as including even this aspect.

the Damascus revelation, the Jesus tradition, and the Scriptures for mutual interpretation and confirmation.

The same theological method may be observed in Paul's Wisdom-christology. When explaining in my *Origin* that Paul developed the conception of Christ as the Wisdom of God from his experience of seeing him as the εἰκών of God in the light of the Wisdom literature of the Old Testament and Judaism and from his insight that Christ was the end of the law (Rom 10:4), I inadequately acknowledged the role played by Jesus' Wisdom-sayings (Matt 11:16-19/Luke 7:31-35; Matt 11:25-27/Luke 10:21-22; Matt 11:28-30; Matt 23:34-36/Luke 11:49-51).[148] But seeing that the saying of Matt 11:25-27/Luke 10:21-22 is probably reflected in 1 Cor 15:24-28 and still more profusely in Paul's contrast between Christ the Wisdom of God and the wisdom of the world (1 Cor 1–4),[149] I am now inclined to think that the Jesus tradition played a substantial role in the development of Paul's Wisdom-christology as well. In analogy to his Adam-christology, I would say that *Paul found his conception of Christ as the Wisdom of God obtained from his Damascus experience confirmed by the Wisdom sayings of Jesus* in which Jesus identified himself with the final representative of divine Wisdom. Thus, with regard to Paul's Wisdom-christology also, we can see the interplay of the Damascus revelation, the Old Testament-Jewish background, and the Jesus tradition.[150]

Now, if, as has been argued here, Paul perceived Christ as "*the* 'Son of Man'" of Dan 7 in accordance with his Damascus vision and Jesus' self-designation, and if that perception contributed to the development of his Adam-christology, then we can see that that perception could well have contributed also to the rise of Paul's conceptions of the church as the true Israel and the body of Christ, as well as his conception of solidarity in Adam and in Christ. Since the "son of man" figure appears as the inclusive representative of "the saints of the Most High" in Dan 7:18, 22, 27, we can see how Paul could have conceived of Christ, "the Son of Man," as the inclusive representative of

---

148. See Kim, *Origin,* 123-36, 258-60.

149. See Wenham, *Paul,* 129-37; also P. Richardson, "The Thunderbolt in Q and the Wise Man in Corinth," in *From Jesus to Paul* (F. W. Beare FS; ed. P. Richardson and J. C. Hurd; Waterloo, Ont.: Wilfrid Laurier University Press, 1984), 91-111.

150. Dunn, "A Light to the Gentiles," 97, considers that Paul's Wisdom-christology was stimulated more by the Corinthians' mistaken speculation about wisdom than by the Damascus revelation. Indeed, their misunderstanding of the gospel in terms of wisdom may well have led Paul to contrast the crucified Christ as the Wisdom of God to the worldly conception of wisdom and echo some of Jesus' Wisdom-sayings in the course of it in 1 Cor 1–4. But it is scarcely possible to think that Paul's Wisdom-christology, which is visible also in Gal 4:4-6; Rom 8:3, etc., originated from the Corinthian controversy.

the true Israel, the eschatological Israel, and of Christians as being in solidarity with or included in Christ, the Son of Man, their inclusive representative.[151] Equating the Son of Man with the Adam of the eschaton (i.e., the Last Adam) for the reasons suggested above, Paul could then conceive of the eschatological people of God as being in solidarity with the Last Adam or included in him. Together with the general Jewish way of thinking in terms of the *Stammvater* incorporating his whole descendants in himself, this perspective led Paul to conceive of the old humanity as being "in Adam," as sharing in his sin and death in solidarity with him (1 Cor 15:22), and to develop the contrast "Adam — the Last Adam" as the inclusive head of the old fallen humanity and that of the new redeemed humanity, respectively (Rom 5:12-19; 1 Cor 15:21-22). From this perspective we can well understand how Paul developed his distinctive theologoumenon ἐν Χριστῷ/σὺν Χριστῷ to explain redemption through our inclusion or participation in or our solidarity with Christ, the Last Adam, our inclusive head, in his representative death and resurrection (see especially Rom 6:1-11). The new humanity redeemed "in Christ," the Last Adam, is the church. When it is seen in terms of the particularistic salvation-history of Israel, it is called the "Israel of God," in the sense of the true people of God in contradistinction from the Jewish nation (Gal 6:16; cf. also Phil 3:3), and when it is seen in terms of universal salvation-history, it is called the "new creation" (2 Cor 5:17; 6:15; cf. also Gal 3:28; Col 3:10-11). Surely the thought of Christ, the Last Adam, incorporating the eschatological people of God, or the church being incorporated in Christ, the Last Adam, must have been an element in the distinctive Pauline conception of the church as the "body of Christ." Therefore, this Pauline metaphor for the church, too, is at least indirectly connected with the Damascus Christophany. The concept of שעור קומה in the later Jewish *merkabah* mysticism may help derive the metaphor more directly from the Christophany.[152]

---

151. If Paul reflected on another "son of man" passage, namely Ps 80:18 (above n. 113), with its identification of the "son of man" with Israel, it could also have helped Paul in this. In my *Origin*, 254-56, I tried to derive Paul's conception of Christ as the inclusive representative of God's people from the Damascus Christophany by interpreting it in the light of the Targumic/rabbinic tradition on Gen 28:12, which thought of Jacob-Israel as sitting on the divine throne. But the Targumic/rabbinic tradition is part of the *merkabah* vision tradition that developed the "son of man" figure in Dan 7; *1 En.* 46-71; etc. Now that I have come to see that Paul appreciated Jesus' self-designation in reference to the "son of man" figure in Dan 7, I do not need to appeal to the later tradition.

152. Cf. G. Quispel, "Ezekiel 1:26 in Jewish Mysticism and Gnosis," *VC* 34 (1980): 11; G. G. Stroumsa, "Form(s) of God: Some Notes on Metatron and Christ," *HTR* 76 (1983): 281-82; J. E. Fossum, *The Image of the Invisible God*, 9-10, 32.

But the problem of dating the Jewish concept stands in the way of obtaining any certainty about this.

Conclusion

Thus I reaffirm my theses on Paul's εἰκών-, Adam- and Wisdom-christology/ soteriology as having originated from the Damascus Christophany. Interactions with Alan F. Segal and some other scholars who recently have stressed the importance of the tradition of the throne-theophany of Ezek 1 have strengthened those theses. However, it has been discovered that in several passages Paul echoes Jesus' "Son of Man"–sayings and that the Jesus tradition, especially Jesus' self-designation as "the 'Son of Man'" and his Wisdom-sayings, has made a substantial contribution to the development of Paul's Adam-christology and Wisdom-christology by confirming them as they were derived from his experience of seeing the exalted Christ appearing in the image of God on the Damascus road. This new discovery has led me to have a glimpse into Paul's theological method of developing new theological insights by using the Damascus revelation, the Jesus tradition, and the Scriptures (especially Gen 1 and 3; Pss 8 and 110; Dan 7) for mutual interpretation and confirmation. So this new discovery has led me also to clarify further my theses on the origin of Paul's Adam-christology and Wisdom-christology from the Damascus Christophany.

CHAPTER 6

2 Corinthians 5:11-21 and the Origin of Paul's Concept of Reconciliation

In my doctoral dissertation[1] I put forward the thesis that "reconciliation," the unique Pauline metaphor for God's saving act in Christ, originated from Paul's personal experience of God's reconciliation of him to himself on the Damascus road. The thesis was developed mainly from an exegesis of 2 Cor 5:11-21. Subsequently, I came to know that some earlier commentators had hinted at that probability[2] and also that a couple of more recent writers came close to affirming it.[3]

---

1. Submitted to the University of Manchester in 1977 and subsequently published as *The Origin of Paul's Gospel* (Tübingen: Mohr-Siebeck, 1981; Grand Rapids: Eerdmans, 1982; 2nd & enlarged edition: Tübingen: Mohr-Siebeck, 1984), 13-20, 311-15.

2. E.g., A. Klöpper, *Kommentar über das zweite Sendschreiben des Apostels Paulus an die Gemeinde zu Korinth* (Berlin: Reimer, 1874), 302; A. Menzies, *The Second Epistle of the Apostle Paul to the Corinthians* (London: Macmillan, 1912), 43.

3. E.g., O. Hofius, "Erwägungen zur Gestalt und Herkunft des paulinischen Versöhnungs-gedankens," originally in *ZThK* 77 (1980), now reprinted in his *Paulusstudien* (Tübingen: Mohr-Siebeck, 1989), 14; A. De Oliveira, *Die Diakonie der Gerechtigkeit und der Versöhnung in der Apologie des 2. Korintherbriefes* (Münster: Aschendorff, 1990), 371, 379.

A simplified version of this essay was presented at the 2nd H. H. Bingham Colloquium in New Testament held at McMaster Divinity College, Hamilton, Ontario, Canada, June 17-18, 1996, and subsequently published as "2 Cor. 5:11-21 and the Origin of Paul's Concept of 'Reconciliation,'" *Novum Testamentum* 39 (1997): 360-84. I am grateful to Prof. Richard N. Longenecker for inviting me to the Colloquium and for encouraging me to publish this fuller version separately, and I am grateful to Brill Academic Publishers for permission to use material from the previously published version.

Commentators regularly note that (1) the καταλλάσσειν-terminology is unique to Paul in the New Testament, (2) its usage in Paul is quite different from that in Hellenistic or Hellenistic Jewish literature, and (3) Paul's Damascus experience of conversion/call is reflected in several points in 2 Cor 5:11-21, one of the two passages in the Pauline *Hauptbriefe* (the other being Rom 5:1-11) where "reconciliation" is a key term. Then, is it not naturally suggested that these three points should be considered in a mutual connection? It is, therefore, rather strange that in scholarship Paul's doctrine of "reconciliation" has not been discussed more often in connection with his Damascus experience of divine "reconciliation" and call.

Linguistic Background

Recently, in his thorough study of the linguistic background of the καταλλάσσειν-terminology, C. Breytenbach points out that in the Hellenistic literature the terminology for "reconciliation" in interpersonal relationships is used most prominently for peace-treaty processes in the politico-military context, but not for the relationship between God and human beings or in a religious context.[4] Noting the parallelism between the Hellenistic conception of the "ambassadors" (πρέσβεις) who are sent to "petition" (δέομαι) or "appeal" (παρακαλεῖν) to warring parties for reconciliation, and the same set of vocabulary in 2 Cor 5:20, Breytenbach explains this Hellenistic usage of the καταλλάσσειν-terminology in the diplomatic context to be the background of Paul's concept of "reconciliation."[5]

However, I. H. Marshall points to some passages in 2 Maccabees where the καταλλαγή- terminology is used for God being reconciled to his people.[6] When their apostasy has aroused the wrath of God, the people may pray to God "to be reconciled with his servants" (καταλλαγῆναι τοῖς αὐτοῦ δούλοις) (2 Macc 8:29; similarly 1:5). Or, when God has vented his wrath upon them or their representatives, God will be reconciled with his people (2 Macc 5:20; 7:32-33).

4. C. Breytenbach, *Versöhnung* (Neukirchen: Neukirchener, 1989), 40-83; cf. now also S. E. Porter, *Καταλλάσσω in Ancient Greek Literature, with Reference to the Pauline Writings* (Cordoba: Ediciones El Almendro, 1994), 39-76.

5. For references to the literature where these words appear, see Breytenbach, *Versöhnung*, esp. 64f.

6. I. Howard Marshall, "The Meaning of 'Reconciliation,' " in *Unity and Diversity in NT Theology* (G. E. Ladd FS; ed. R. Guelich; Grand Rapids: Eerdmans, 1978), 120f., 129f.; cf. Porter, *Καταλλάσσω*, 61f.

Breytenbach himself points out that, like 2 Maccabees, both Philo (*VitMos.* 2.166) and Josephus (*Bell.* 5.415; *Ant.* 7.153) also apply, though not frequently, the originally diplomatic terminology of καταλλάσσειν to the relationship between God and human beings: God's being "reconciled" to Israel or David at their repentance or prayer (cf. also *Jos. Asen.* 11.18). However, impressed by the difference between the Hellenistic Jewish usage of the terminology (God is reconciled to human beings) and Pauline usage (God reconciles human beings to himself) as much as by the close parallelism between the profane Hellenistic diplomatic usage and Pauline usage in 2 Cor 5:18-20, Breytenbach insists that only the profane Hellenistic usage is the background of Paul's usage.[7]

However, surely the application of the originally diplomatic terminology to the religious usage for the relationship between God and human beings itself is, at least formally, a significant contact point between Paul and the Hellenistic Jewish literature, especially since, as Breytenbach himself stresses, there is no evidence of a religious usage of the terminology in the profane Hellenistic literature. Further, P. Stuhlmacher is clearly justified in criticizing Breytenbach for neglecting to consider whether the conception in both Philo (*VitMos.* 2.166; *QuestEx.* 2.49) and Josephus (*Ant.* 3.315) of Moses as μεσίτης and καταλλάκτης between God and Israel may not be reflected in 2 Cor 5:18–6:2, in view of Paul's comparison/contrast between his ministry of the new covenant and Moses' ministry of the old covenant in 2 Cor 3.[8]

So it seems necessary to affirm that Paul does reflect the Hellenistic Jewish usage of the καταλλάσσειν-terminology, even if eventually he has to make a fundamental correction of it. And as we shall see, Paul reflects also the profane Hellenistic usage of it in the politico-military context.

Uniquely Pauline Terminology within the New Testament

It is well known that within the New Testament the καταλλάσσειν-terminology is used for the relationship between God and human beings only in the Pauline corpus: (a) καταλλάσσειν: Rom 5:10 (x2); 2 Cor 5:18, 19, 20; (b) καταλλαγή: Rom 5:11; 11:15; 2 Cor 5:18, 19; and (c) ἀποκαταλλάσσειν: Eph 2:16; Col 1:20, 22.[9]

---

7. Breytenbach, *Versöhnung,* 70-81.

8. P. Stuhlmacher, *Biblische Theologie des Neuen Testaments,* vol. 1, *Grundlegung von Jesus zu Paulus* (Göttingen: Vandenhoeck, 1992), 319.

9. In 1 Cor 7:11, Paul uses it for a wife-husband relationship, and in Mt 5:24 a similar verb διαλλάσσειν is used for a relationship between human beings.

It is also well known that the Pauline usage of the language is unique: Paul uses the terminology never to imply that God is reconciled (or God reconciles himself) to human beings, but always to suggest that God reconciles human beings to himself or human beings are reconciled to God. These two (both the negative and the positive) points distinguish Paul's usage of the terminology from the Hellenistic Jewish as well as the profane Hellenistic usage. This distinctive usage of the terminology seems to suggest that Paul deliberately makes a fundamental correction of the Hellenistic Jewish conception of reconciliation between God and human beings: it is not God who needs to be reconciled to human beings, but it is human beings who need to be reconciled to God; and it is not by repentance, prayers, or other good works on the part of human beings that reconciliation is brought about between God and human beings, but it is by his grace that God reconciles human beings to himself.

Both the unique appearance and the unique usage of the καταλλάσσειν-terminology in Paul within the New Testament have led many scholars to affirm that the "reconciliation" motif is a uniquely Pauline category of interpretation of God's saving act in Christ.[10] But some other scholars think that Paul took over a pre-Pauline Hellenistic Christian conception. However, nowadays there are hardly any supporters of E. Käsemann's view of 2 Cor 5:18-21 as "a pre-Pauline hymnic fragment" or R. P. Martin's conception of it (minus vv. 19b and 20c) as a pre-Pauline "confessional statement."[11] A few scholars have made a more serious attempt to see only 2 Cor 5:19ab as a quotation of a pre-Pauline formulation.[12] But since it has also been quite soundly repudiated by R. Bieringer and M. E. Thrall,[13] in view of the limited space

10. E.g., L. Goppelt, *Christologie und Ethik* (Göttingen: Vandenhoeck, 1969), 148-53; also his *Theologie des NT* (Göttingen:Vandenhoeck, 1976), 467-70; Marshall, "Reconciliation," 129; Hofius, "Erwägungen," 11; J. Lambrecht, " 'Reconcile Yourselves . . .': A Reading of 2 Corinthians 5:11-21," in *Studies on 2 Corinthians* (ed. R. Bieringer and J. Lambrecht; Louvain: Louvain University Press, 1994), 391, 393; R. Bieringer, "2 Korinther 5:19a und die Versöhnung der Welt," *ibid.*, 453f. (citing J. Dupont, *La réconciliation dans la théologie de Saint Paul* (Louvain: Louvain University Press, 1953), 255-302); Stuhlmacher, *Biblische Theologie*, 318; Porter, *Καταλλάσσω*, 16, 128, 143.

11. E. Käsemann, "Erwägungen zum Stichwort 'Versöhnungslehre im NT,' " in *Zeit und Geschichte* (Bultmann FS; ed. E. Dinkler; Tübingen: Mohr-Siebeck, 1964), 48-50; R. P. Martin, *Reconciliation* (Atlanta: Knox, 1981), 94f.

12. E.g. P. Stuhlmacher, *Gerechtigkeit Gottes bei Paulus* (Göttingen: Vandenhoeck, 1966), 77f.; V. Furnish, *II Corinthians* (Garden City: Doubleday, 1984), 334; H. J. Findeis, *Versöhnung-Apostolat-Kirche* (Würzburg: Echter, 1983), 244f.; Breytenbach, *Versöhnung*, 118-20.

13. Bieringer, "2 Korinther 5:19a," 429-59; and M. E. Thrall, *The Second Epistle to the Corinthians,* vol. 1 (ICC; Edinburgh: T & T Clark, 1994), 445-49. See also Hofius, "Erwägungen," 2; Lambrecht, "Reconcile," 390; Marshall, "Reconciliation," 129.

here, we may abbreviate the discussion. So we would like to reaffirm the conclusions (1) that the καταλλάσσειν-terminology is uniquely Pauline within the New Testament and (2) that the Pauline usage of the terminology represents a real innovation in *Religionsgeschichte*.

Various Suggestions about Its Origin

The conclusions naturally lead to the question how then Paul came to develop that metaphor for God's saving work in Christ. L. Goppelt has proposed to see its "material *Ansatz*" in Jesus-tradition (his offer of forgiveness to sinners on God's behalf and his teaching expressed, e.g., in the parable of the prodigal son) and in the early Christian confession of Jesus' death as vicarious atonement.[14] As one who has come to appreciate more and more Paul's knowledge of and dependence upon Jesus-tradition,[15] I would agree with this view. However, it is insufficient for explaining how Paul came to use the *terminology*.

According to O. Hofius, Paul has developed the "reconciliation"-motif chiefly from the fourth Servant Song of Dt-Isa. (Isa 52:13–53:12). The concepts καταλλάσσειν and καταλλαγή had been given to him in Hellenistic Judaism; "but Paul found in Dt-Isa. the *material content (Sache)* witnessed to, which he appropriately brings to expression with these concepts."[16] Hofius points to the parallelism between Isa 52:13–53:12, where the "sinless" Servant's vicarious suffering and death "for many" makes them righteous and gives them "peace," and 2 Cor 5:11-21, where the sinless Christ's vicarious death is affirmed as the ground for God's justification of human beings and his reconciliation of them to himself. Emphasizing the "peace" of Isa 53:5 to be a material equivalent to Paul's concept of reconciliation in 2 Cor 5:19, Hofius points to Rom 10:15, 16, which witnesses to Paul's appreciation of the concepts of "peace" and "gospel" in Isa 52:6-10. According to Hofius, the combination of Isa 52:13–53:12 and 52:6-10 led Paul to affirm in 2 Cor 5:18-21 "that God's saving act includes *both:* the cross-event as the *act* of creating the universal 'peace' and the cross-preaching as the *word* that proclaims 'peace' worldwide."[17] Hofius's impressive demonstration of Paul's reflection of Isa 52–53 in 2 Cor 5:11-21 has been further strengthened by O. Betz's study

14. Goppelt, *Christologie*, 152f.

15. See S. Kim, "Jesus, Sayings of," in *The Dictionary of Paul and His Letters* (Downers Grove: InterVarsity Press, 1993), 474-92; reprinted in this volume as ch. 8.

16. Hofius, "Erwägungen," 11 (his italics).

17. Ibid., 11-13 (quotation from 13; his italics).

on 2 Cor 5:16 which also convincingly demonstrates Paul's reflection of the fourth Servant Song in that verse.[18]

However, it is a question whether it is adequate just to point to the concept of "peace" in Isa 53:5 and 52:7 to explain how Paul could have come to designate God's saving act in Christ's death and his apostolic ministry in terms of his καταλλάσσειν/καταλλαγή while interpreting them in the light of Isa 52–53, when the terminology is lacking in the Isaianic passage.[19]

I. H. Marshall speculates that the Jewish martyr tradition represented in 2 Maccabees probably acted as the catalyst for Paul's development of the category of "reconciliation": that is, while interpreting Jesus' death as an atoning sacrifice in the light of the martyr tradition of 2 and 4 Maccabees, Paul could have formulated his "reconciliation" doctrine in deliberate contrast to the Jewish view of martyr's death as moving an angry God to "be reconciled" to his people.[20]

It is possible that in Paul's development of the "reconciliation"-motif the Hellenistic Jewish tradition represented in 2 Maccabees exerted some influence. But a theory about the origin of the motif must be able to explain not only how Paul came to apply the καταλλάσσειν-terminology to God's saving act in Christ's death but also how he came to designate his own ministry as a διακονία τῆς καταλλαγῆς (2 Cor 5:18). Marshall's conjecture seems to fall short of doing the latter.

According to Bieringer, the conflict situation between the Corinthian church and Paul himself has led Paul to use the "reconciliation" category for interpretation of Christ's death in 2 Cor 5.[21] But this view is unlikely, as in 2 Cor 5 Paul speaks only of God's reconciliation of human beings to himself and not of a reconciliation between himself and the Corinthian church.

---

18. O. Betz, "Fleischliche und 'geistliche' Christuserkenntnis nach 2 Korinther 5:16," *ThBeitr* 14 (1983), 167-79, now in his *Jesus — der Herr der Kirche* (Tübingen: Mohr-Siebeck, 1990), 114-28.

19. Cf. Breytenbach, *Versöhnung*, 25; H. Merkel, καταλλάσσω κτλ., *EDNT* 2:262. Noting Paul's allusion to Isa 43:18f. in 2 Cor 5:17b, and finding the themes in Isa 40–66 such as God's wrath over Israel's sins, God's redemption of them and his restoration of peace for them through the sacrificial death of his Servant, his restoration of them to their homeland which is described as a new creation, etc. as paralleling those in 2 Cor 5:14-21, G. K. Beale, "The Old Testament Background of Reconciliation in 2 Corinthians 5–7 and Its Bearing on the Literary Problem of 2 Corinthians 6:14–7:1," *NTS* 35 (1989): 550-81, proposes to see Isa 40–66 as the background for Paul's ideas of reconciliation and new creation in 2 Cor 5:14-21. Along with the more focused proposal of Hofius and Betz, this proposal is also helpful as a delineation of the broad ideological background. But just like the former, it falls short of explaining the origin of the "reconciliation"-terminology.

20. Marshall, "Reconciliation," 129f.

21. Bieringer, "2 Kor. 5:19a," 454f.

This brief review of the various suggestions put forward of the origin of Paul's category of "reconciliation" shows that while in Paul's doctrine of "reconciliation" various elements — the primitive Christian confession of Christ's death as vicarious atonement, Jesus-Tradition, the Servant Song of Isa 53, the Hellenistic Jewish tradition of reconciliation represented in 2 Macc, and the Hellenistic diplomatic terminology of reconciliation — may be seen as reflected, none of them can be claimed as the decisive catalyst for its development.

Perhaps it is out of his intuitive awareness of this situation that Hofius concludes his study on the origin of the Pauline doctrine of "reconciliation" as follows:

> The Pauline idea of "reconciliation" is . . . shaped decisively by the message of Dt-Isa. Its *foundation* lies, however, elsewhere: in the encounter with the Risen One, in which God disclosed to the persecutor the cross as his *act* of reconciliation and called him to be the envoy of the *word* of reconciliation. What had been revealed to Paul in this event, he then found confirmed and interpreted through the prophetic witness of Scripture. Thus he obtained from the OT the language in which he was able to express the saving act of God in Jesus Christ.[22]

This is an excellent thesis. But Hofius has not substantiated it at all. So, in this essay we make it our task to substantiate it.

2 Corinthians 5:11-21

Of the five passages in the Pauline corpus where the "reconciliation" doctrine appears, 2 Cor 5:11-21 is the earliest and seems to provide the best access to the origin of the doctrine.

(1) The Structure

Within 2 Cor 5:18-21, where the καταλλάσσειν-terminology is concentrated, verse 19 is clearly a disturbing element. Among the various problems pre-

---

22. Hofius, "Erwägungen," 14. Similarly, Beale, "OT Background," 579f. also ends up suggesting Paul's Damascus experience as the catalyst for his interpreting the Christ-event in terms of "reconciliation" in the light of Isa. 40–66. But his effort to substantiate the view is rather circuitous.

sented by the verse, we are concerned here with the uncertainty of the meaning of ὡς ὅτι and with the mutual relationship of the three participles: καταλλάσσων, λογιζόμενος and θέμενος. Some commentators take the two participial phrases in verse 19b and 19c led respectively by λογιζόμενος and θέμενος as coordinated to each other and together subordinated to the main sentence of verse 19a. But a μή . . . καί construction would be strange, and a parallel coordination of a present participle (λογιζόμενος) and an aorist participle (θέμενος) would produce an illogical sense, making "the entrusting of the 'word of reconciliation' prior in time to the reconciling act itself."[23] So, most commentators take ἦν . . . καταλλάσσων as periphrastic, λογιζόμενος as subordinate to the main sentence, and θέμενος as equivalent to the finite form ἔθετο. But this analysis has also a difficulty in the unnatural combination of the periphrastic imperfect (ἦν . . . καταλλάσσων) and the aorist (θέμενος).[24]

Some commentators take this incongruity between verse 19ab and 19c to be a sign that verse 19ab is a citation of a pre-Pauline formulation and verse 19c Paul's own addition. They further point out that (a) the change from the aorist in verse 18 to the imperfect in 19ab is equally uneven; (b) the transition from αὐτοῖς in 19b to ἐν ἡμῖν in 19c is not smooth; (c) the content of 19ab has the function of elaborating and substantiating the statement of 18; (d) the ὡς ὅτι can be well understood as an introductory formula for a citation; and (e) there is a logical consistency if we take verses 18bc and 19c together, leaving 19ab out.[25]

All these points clearly suggest that verse 19ab is indeed an insertion. However, since there is little valid reason to regard it as pre-Pauline,[26] we propose once more[27] that it is best to take it as a (Pauline) parenthesis. As Furnish now also thinks,[28] the aorist participle θέμενος in verse 19c clearly belongs together with those in 18bc, καταλλάξαντος and δόντος, and the three participial phrases together make up a logically coherent statement.

---

23. Thrall, *Second Epistle to the Corinthians*, 435; also O. Hofius, " 'Gott hat unter uns aufgerichtet das Wort von der Versöhnung' (2 Kor. 5:19)," *ZNW* 71 (1980), now in his *Paulusstudien*, 18; *pace* Porter, *Καταλλάσσω*, 135-37.

24. Cf. Breytenbach, *Versöhnung*, 118.

25. E.g., ibid., 118f.; Furnish, *Second Corinthians*, 320.

26. See above n. 13.

27. See Kim, *Origin*, 19 (n. 2).

28. Furnish, *Second Corinthians*, 320. He rightly says: "Although the nominative case of *themenos* has been determined by *Theos* in . . . (v. 19a), the participle is coordinate in meaning as well as in tense with the participles in v. 18." While dictating the long statement of vv. 18f., Paul could have pronounced θέμενος instead of θεμένου under the influence of θεός or the -ος endings of καταλλάξαντος and δόντος. I only regret that Furnish regards v. 19ab as a citation of a pre-Pauline material.

18 Τὰ πάντα ἐκ τοῦ Θεοῦ

          τοῦ <u>καταλλάξαντος</u> ἡμᾶς ἑαυτῷ διὰ Χριστοῦ

    καὶ   <u>δόντος</u> ἡμῖν τὴν διακονίαν τῆς καταλλαγῆς

(19ab ὡς ὅτι θεὸς <u>ἦν</u> ἐν Χριστῷ κόσμον καταλλάσσων ἑαυτῷ

          μὴ λογιζόμενος αὐτοῖς τὰ παραπτώματα αὐτῶν)

19c   καὶ   <u>θέμενος</u> ἐν ἡμῖν τὸν λόγον τῆς καταλλαγῆς

Here ὡς ὅτι should probably be seen as a combination of the comparative ὡς and the causal ὅτι and as introducing a parenthetical statement that provides the ground for what Paul has said in verse 18.[29]

So, in this passage Paul is talking about God's reconciliation of Paul to God himself, God's giving him the ministry of reconciliation, and God's entrusting him with the word of reconciliation, pointing to God's (objective) reconciliation work in the Christ-event as the ground for this statement.

(2) Allusions to the Damascus Event

The three aorist participles of verses 18bc and 19c (καταλλάξαντος, δόντος, and θέμενος) clearly allude to Paul's experience of God's forgiveness/reconciliation, his call to apostleship, and his revelation or entrusting of the gospel for him to preach.[30] Hofius observes well (1) that verse 19c corresponds to Paul's testimony about his Damascus experience of God's revelation of the gospel in Gal 1:12, 15-16a, and (2) that verse 18c corresponds to his testimony of God's apostolic commission in Gal 1:16b.[31] We may add (3) the correspondence of verse 18ab to what is implicit in Paul's emphasis on God's grace to him over against his past as a persecutor of the church in Gal 1:13-14. These close cor-

29. I still think that A. Schlatter, *Paulus der Bote Jesu* (Stuttgart: Calwer, 1962), 566, offers the best explanation: "Paul begins the sentence of v. 19 with ὡς because he compares his own experience with what God has done for the world. However, since the particle alone does not adequately express the relation between the two as the latter is the ground of the former, he adds ὅτι to ὡς" (cited by Kim, *Origin*, 19, n. 2). Similarly also P. Bachmann, *Der zweite Brief des Paulus an die Korinther* (Leipzig: Werner Scholl, 1922), 266: "*as could and did happen, because . . .*"; A. Plummer, *The Second Epistle of St. Paul to the Corinthians* (Edinburgh: T & T Clark, 1925), 183: "as was the case, because . . ."; further, Lambrecht, "Reconcile," 386; Bieringer, "2 Kor. 5:19a," 445.

30. So, C. Wolff, "True Apostolic Knowledge of Christ: Exegetical Reflections on 2 Corinthians 5:14ff.," in *Paul and Jesus* (ed. A. J. M. Wedderburn; Sheffield: Sheffield Academic, 1989), 92-94.

31. Hofius, "Gott hat . . . ," 29 (n. 66). Cf. also De Oliveira, *Diakonie,* 371, 379.

respondences between Gal 1:13-16 and 2 Cor 5:18-19 make even clearer that the three participial phrases in the latter allude to Paul's Damascus experience.

This is, of course, extremely significant for the thesis that we are propounding here. However, they are not the only allusions to Paul's Damascus experience within 2 Cor 5:11-21, the passage in which Paul defends his apostolic ministry over against both "those who boast in what is external rather than what is in the heart" (v. 12c) and "you," the Corinthians who are apparently under their influence (vv. 11-13, 20).[32]

Verse 16 is almost universally recognized as alluding to it.[33] The ἀπὸ τοῦ νῦν signals a fundamental turning-point. The turning-point took place as a consequence (ὥστε) of Paul's proper recognition of the eschatological saving event of Christ's death and resurrection (vv. 14f.). The recognition has resulted in a fundamental change in his perspective or his way of estimating Christ or any other person. There is no doubt that Paul is here speaking of his Damascus experience of abandoning his prior "fleshly" estimate of Christ in the face of divine revelation of Christ as the one who had died for humankind and been raised from the dead. So, as also widely recognized, the aorist participle κρίναντας in verse 14 also clearly alludes to Paul's Damascus experience.[34]

Verse 17 also alludes to Paul's Damascus experience. The "new creation" (καινὴ κτίσις) certainly took place in the eschatological event of the death and resurrection of Christ. However, as the individualizing τις makes it clear,

32. So, the "we/us" in this section (except those in the general confessional statement of v. 21) should be taken throughout as a stylistic plural referring primarily to Paul himself. So, e.g. K. Dick, *Der schriftstellerische Plural bei Paulus* (Halle: Niemeyer, 1900), 167ff.; Plummer, *Second Epistle of Paul to the Corinthians*, 182; Schlatter, *Bote*, 565ff.; Findeis, *Versöhnung*, 173; Breytenbach, *Versöhnung*, 114f. This is not to deny that they are potentially capable of including those who are in the same situation as Paul himself (Christians, or apostles in vv. 18c, 19c, 20), but in this apologetic argument Paul has primarily his own case in mind. With a statement like v. 18b surely Paul would not mean that God reconciled *only* him to himself, but the juxtaposition of "we" and "you" in v. 20 suggests that in v. 18b Paul is consciously making a statement only about himself. Some commentators try to see ἡμῖν in v. 18c and ἐν ἡμῖν in v. 19c as referring to the apostles as a whole or even to the church (e.g. Hofius, "Gott hat . . . ," 25ff.). But as C. K. Barrett, *A Commentary on the Second Epistle to the Corinthians* (London: Black, 1973), 176, recognizes, it is difficult to give ἡμῖν in v. 18c (so also that in v. 19c) a meaning different from that given to ἡμᾶς in v. 18b. It is not easy to understand why Hofius, despite emphasizing the correspondence between vv. 18c and 19c and Paul's "own testimony" in Gal 1:12, 15-16 (see above n. 31), nevertheless tries to interpret the ἡμῖν in vv. 18c and 19c to refer not just to Paul but to all the apostles. Cf. Wolff, "Knowledge," 93f.

33. See the recent articles of Betz, "Fleischliche," and Wolff, "Knowledge."

34. See, e.g., Thrall, *Second Epistle to the Corinthians*, 409.

Paul is here thinking of an individual person's participation in it through coming to be "in Christ." Although verse 17 is formulated gnomically in general terms (τις), in view of the context in which Paul speaks mainly of himself in his apostolic defense, the verse must be taken to refer to Paul's own case. So, he is speaking of his own experience of having been made a "new creature." On the Damascus road, he came to a correct perception of Christ and of his vicarious death for him and he came to be "in Christ" by faith in him. In 2 Cor 4:6 he spoke of his encounter with the risen Christ appearing in the shining light of divine glory on the Damascus road in terms of God's letting light shine in his heart just as he had let light shine at the first creation, and so Paul has already implied that on the Damascus road God's act of new creation took place in respect of him.[35] The fact that he speaks of "new creation," on the one hand, in connection with what may safely be called his "conversion" experience (vv. 13-16),[36] reminds us of a similar language in the Hellenistic Jewish work *Joseph and Aseneth* (8.10f.),[37] and the fact that he does it, on the other hand, in connection with his "reconciliation" to God (vv. 18-21) reminds us of the rabbinic tradition that compares forgiveness and atonement on the New Year's Day or on the Day of Atonement with a new creation (בריאה חדשה).[38]

We would like to suggest that in verse 14 not just κρίναντας but also the strong word συνέχει allude to Paul's Damascus experience. That Paul came to a new and correct "judgment" about Christ's death as a vicarious death on the Damascus road is beyond doubt. There he realized the magnitude of Christ's love for him and for humankind. Since then, the love of God "impels" him to devote himself wholeheartedly to the service of God/Christ and others like the Corinthians (vv. 13, 15; cf. Gal 2:20). This strong language of συνέχει,[39] used in the context of speaking about his apostolic ministry and in associa-

35. See Kim, *Origin,* 5-13, 229-33, where reference is also given to the widespread recognition of the verse as an allusion to the Damascus event. See also, among more recent commentators, e.g., Thrall, *Second Epistle to the Corinthians,* 316-20; R. P. Martin, *2 Corinthians* (Waco: Word, 1986), 80. C. Wolff, *Der zweite Brief des Paulus an die Korinther* (Berlin: Evangelische Verlagsanstalt, 1989), 87.

36. For the appropriateness of the term "conversion" for Paul's Damascus experience, cf. A. F. Segal, *Paul the Convert* (New Haven: Yale University Press, 1990).

37. Cf. P. Stuhlmacher, "Erwägungen zum ontologischen Charakter der καινὴ κτίσις bei Paulus," *EvTh* 27 (1967): 18.

38. Cf. Hermann Strack and Paul Billerbeck, *Kommentar zum Neuen Testament,* 7 vols. in 6 (Munich: Beck, 1922-61), II.421f.; III.519; Stuhlmacher, "καινὴ κτίσις," 15; Wolff, "Knowledge," 92.

39. Cf. Walter Bauer et al., *Greek-English Lexicon of the New Testament and Other Early Christian Literature,* 2nd ed. (Chicago: University of Chicago Press, 1979), *s.v.* 7.

tion with other allusions to his Damascus experience, is clearly reminiscent of similarly strong words Paul uses in connection with his apostolic call on the Damascus road: he was "enlisted" (κατελήμφθην) by Christ (Phil 3:12); he was saved and called to preach the gospel in order that he might preach the gospel to the gentiles (Gal 1:15f.), so that he is a "debtor" (ὀφειλέτης) to the gentiles (Rom 1:14); and a "fateful necessity" (ἀνάγκη) is laid on him to preach the gospel (1 Cor 9:16).[40]

Finally, we would like to suggest that ἐξέστημεν in verse 13 also alludes to Paul's Damascus experience. Many commentators agree that the word here refers to religious ecstasy and also that here Paul responds to a criticism of his opponents in the Corinthian church. However, they are divided as to whether Paul was criticized for appealing to his ecstatic experiences to recommend his apostolic ministry[41] or whether, on the contrary, he was criticized for a deficiency of such ecstatic experiences as those on which his rivals apparently based part of their "apostolic" claim (cf. 2 Cor. 10–13).[42] Those who support the latter view are, of course, motivated by the fact that Paul's opponents who themselves prized highly ecstatic religious experiences would not have criticized Paul for appealing to such experiences. However, the natural reading of verse 14 clearly suggests that here Paul is defensive of his ἐκστῆναι. So, one of the champions of the latter view, M. E. Thrall, thinks that, in verse 14, against the criticism about his deficiency of ecstatic experiences, Paul responds in effect that his ecstatic experiences (which he does have) "are no concern of his readers but concern God only."[43]

However, juxtaposed to σωφρονοῦμεν, here the ἐξέστημεν seems to carry with it a pejorative undertone of "madness," and Paul seems to be defensive of it. Further, the juxtaposition of the aorist ἐξέστημεν and the present σωφρονοῦμεν seems to suggest that with the former Paul refers to a single event in his past.[44] What might then be the single ecstatic experience in Paul's life that was disputed by his opponents? The context of 2 Cor 5:11-21, which is Paul's apostolic *apologia*, clearly points to his Damascus experience of conversion and call. The most natural interpretation of verse 13a, therefore, seems to be that Paul is responding to his opponents' criticism of his basing his apostolic claim on his visionary experience of Christ on the Damascus

40. Cf. Kim, *Origin*, 288-96.

41. E.g., Plummer, *Second Epistle of Paul to the Corinthians,* 172; P. E. Hughes, *Paul's Second Epistle to the Corinthians* (Grand Rapids: Eerdmans, 1962), 191f.

42. E.g., Furnish, *Second Corinthians,* 324; Thrall, *Second Epistle to the Corinthians,* 407.

43. Thrall, *Second Epistle to the Corinthians,* 407.

44. So E. B. Allo, *Saint Paul: Seconde Épître aux Corinthiens* (Paris: Libraire Lecoffre, 1956), cited by Martin, *2 Corinthians,* 127.

road (cf. 1 Cor 9:1; 15:8-10), rather than on a proper appointment by Jesus and on the proper doctrine of Christ and his salvation that his apostles taught.[45] Perhaps they ridiculed his Damascus vision as nothing but "madness."[46] So, in 2 Cor 5:11-21 Paul defends his conversion/call experience as genuine by pointing to the true recognition of Christ and his salvation which that experience has brought to him.

(3) The Context

Thus, 2 Cor 5:11-21 abounds with allusions to the Damascus experience of Paul and the various allusions corroborate one another. But why were these allusions called for? They were clearly in response to his opponents' attempts to discredit his apostolic ministry. Then, who were the opponents? If we know their identity and their criticism of Paul accurately, we will be able to interpret Paul's defense also much more precisely. It is, of course, impossible for us to deal adequately here with this most thorny issue of Paul's opponents in 2 Corinthians. We can only refer to some of their salient features presented in 2 Corinthians.

They came to Corinth from outside (11:4), claiming to be "apostles/ministers [διάκονοι] of Christ" and "ministers of righteousness" (11:13, 15, 23). They boasted of being Hebrews, Israelites, and descendants of Abraham (11:22). What had motivated them to infiltrate (improperly, in Paul's eyes) into Paul's gentile mission field (10:12-18) was apparently their desire to correct his (deficient, in their eyes) gospel or doctrine of Jesus Christ, his doctrine of the Spirit, and his understanding of the ministry (11:4-12; 5:11-21). They apparently gloried in the Mosaic covenant and Torah (3:1–4:6). But they also boasted of their visions and revelations, their signs, wonders and miracles, and their knowledge and rhetorical power (ch. 10–12).

These apparently double characteristics, the Palestinian Jewish or even Judaizing characteristic on the one hand and the more Hellenistic characteristic on the other, of the opponents have led to two rival types of views in identifying them. One type affirms that they were the Judaizers who, as in the Galatian church, sought to bring the gentile christians in Corinth under

45. Plummer, Second Epistle of Paul to the Corinthians, 172, thinks of a charge made by some Jews that Paul went mad at his Damascus conversion. But the charge must have been from the Judaizing Christian opponents who infiltrated into Corinth.

46. Cf. Acts 26:24-25: to Paul's testimony of his Damascus vision, Festus reacts, "You are mad [μαίνῃ], Paul!" and Paul replies, "I am not mad [οὐ μαίνομαι]."

47. E.g., E. Käsemann, "Die Legitimität des Apostels," ZNW 41 (1942): 33-71; C. K. Barrett, "Paul's Opponents in 2 Corinthians," NTS 17 (1970/71): 233-54.

the Mosaic covenant and Torah.[47] One of the difficulties for this view has been how to account for what appear to be Hellenistic features of the opponents.[48] But recently P. Barnett has sought to do it by showing that during the political upheaval of A.D. 44-66 Judea, which had been considerably Hellenized anyway, had a religious milieu of prophetic inspiration and miraculous signs such as that the opponents apparently represented.[49] The other type affirms that the opponents were Hellenistic pneumatics or Hellenistic Jewish Christians.[50] Among the representatives of this view, G. Friedrich seems to have produced the most plausible explanation. Struck by the many similarities between the characteristics of the party of Stephen and Philip in Acts and those of Paul's opponents in 2 Corinthians, Friedrich suggests that the opponents were the Hellenistic Jewish Christians of Stephen's party.[51] Actually, this group, which was driven out of Judea back into the diaspora, might explain what appear to be the double characteristics of the opponents in 2 Corinthians.[52]

In spite of the uncertainty in making an exact identification of the opponents, we can ascertain, to some extent, what might have been their criticisms of Paul. Clearly they took issue with Paul's "qualification" (ἱκανότης) to be an apostle (3:5f.; cf. also 2:6, 16; 1 Cor 15:9). His external signs of weakness such

48. Another objection to this view has been that unlike Galatians, 2 Corinthians shows no sign that the opponents demand circumcision. But this difference may be due to the fact that in Corinth their operation is after the Apostolic Council whereas in Galatia it was before the Council. So, although in Corinth they emphasize the Torah and Jewish Christian superiority generally (esp. ch. 3), they are not demanding circumcision because at the Apostolic Council it was agreed not to impose circumcision on gentile Christians. Cf. G. Lüdemann, *Paulus, der Heidenapostel*, vol. 2, *Antipaulinismus im frühen Christentum* (Göttingen: Vandenhoeck, 1983), 141-43; M. Hengel, "Der Jakobusbrief als antipaulinische Polemik," in *Tradition and Interpretation* (E. E. Ellis FS; ed. G. F. Hawthorne; Grand Rapids: Eerdmans, 1987), 252f.

49. P. Barnett, "Opposition in Corinth," *JSNT* 22 (1984): 3-17.

50. E.g., R. Bultmann, *The Second Letter to the Corinthians* (Minneapolis: Augsburg, 1985); D. Georgi, *Die Gegner des Paulus im 2 Korintherbrief* (Neukirchen: Neukirchener, 1964).

51. G. Friedrich, "Die Gegner des Paulus im 2. Korintherbrief," in *Abraham unser Vater* (O. Michel FS, ed. O. Betz et al.; Leiden: Brill, 1963), 181-215. Cf. R. P. Martin, "The Opponents of Paul in 2 Corinthians," in *Tradition and Interpretation in the New Testament* (ed. G. F. Hawthorne and O. Betz; Grand Rapids: Eerdmans, 1987), 284-87. A difficulty for this view is that the opponents in 2 Cor claim to be Ἑβραῖοι, whereas Stephen's party in Acts are called Ἑλληνισταί. However, the fact that Paul, a "Hellenist" from Tarsus, claims to be a "Hebrew" in order to match the boasting of his opponents (11:22) makes it possible to think that though they were "Hellenists" in Jerusalem (Acts 6:1), in the diaspora they claimed to be "Hebrews" (2 Cor 11:22), emphasizing their recent move from Palestine and also their ability to speak Aramaic (as well as Greek). Cf. Kim, *Origin*, 37.

52. See below, n. 65.

as an unimpressive physical presence, an unimpressive rhetorical power and physical suffering, his apparent lack of spiritual experiences such as visions and revelations, as well as his apparent lack of spiritual power such as signs and wonders and miracles, and his humble demeanor of making a living with his own hands rather than claiming the privilege the Lord had given to his apostles to live on the church's support, all seem to have been used by the opponents as arguments against Paul's apostolic qualification (ch. 10–13). They also pointed to the fact that Paul had no "letter of recommendation" (3:1ff.). To them, this meant that, unlike themselves, who had such a document, he was not made an apostle in a proper way and was not recognized as an apostle in the church (of Jerusalem?). Instead, he was a self-made apostle who, therefore, was engaged in self-commendation (3:5; 3:1; 4:2; 5:12; 6:4; 10:12, 18; 12:11).

The opponents took issue also with Paul's gospel. They criticized that his gospel was "veiled" (4:3). Paul acknowledges that their "gospel" was indeed different from his and that they preached "a Jesus other than the one [he] preached" (11:4). To him, however, "Jesus" is the Christ who died and was raised for us, and the meaning of "Jesus" is determined entirely by his death (and resurrection) (4:10-14; 5:14-16, 21). This recognition came to him through the revelation of Jesus Christ on the Damascus road (5:14). Here two points are immediately striking. One is Paul's stress on Christ's vicarious death for our redemption, of which the vivid phrase νέκρωσις τοῦ Ἰησοῦ (4:10) and the starkest sentence τὸν μὴ γνόντα ἁμαρτίαν ὑπὲρ ἡμῶν ἁμαρτίαν ἐποίησεν (5:21) belong to the most powerful formulations of Paul about Christ's death. The other is the repeated use of "Jesus" in 4:10-14 (six times; once more in 4:5). The use of the name without combination of a title is unusual,[53] but its use in the "death-formula" where the title Χριστός is normally used is even more unusual. The comparison of these verses with Gal 6:17 and 1 Thess 4:14 where "Jesus" also appears unaccompanied by a title in the "death-formula" clearly suggests that in such usage Paul is thinking of the historical Jesus and the historical event of his death.[54] The stress on Christ's death must surely have been in conscious contrast to the picture of "another Jesus" which the opponents were preaching (11:4). The phrase "another Jesus" in 11:4 seems to suggest that with the unusual use of the name "Jesus" alone Paul partly reflects their own language. What kind of christology might they have had when they referred to "Jesus" without laying any particular emphasis on his death of vicarious atonement?

53. So Friedrich, "Gegner," 189. Of the six appearances, only once at 4:14 the title κύριος is combined according to the readings of ℵ C D F etc., but not according to the readings of P^46B etc.

54. So Friedrich, "Gegner," 189; K. Kleinknecht, Der leidende Gerechtfertigte (Tübingen: Mohr-Siebeck, 1984), 274; Wolff, "Knowledge," 90.

In 5:16 Paul seems implicitly to criticize that christology as "knowing Christ κατὰ σάρκα." It is now commonly agreed that the phrase κατὰ σάρκα in 5:16 is an adverbial phrase modifying the verbs in that verse and that Paul is here talking about knowing or estimating Christ according to the "fleshly" criterion or from a "fleshly" perspective. What then is meant by this "fleshly" criterion or perspective? Since the phrase "to boast κατὰ σάρκα" in 11:18 seems to correspond to the phrase "to boast ἐν προσώπῳ rather than ἐν καρδίᾳ" in 5:12 and κατὰ σάρκα in 5:16 also seems to be related to the latter, first of all, it probably has to do with an emphasis on outward appearance. In 11:18ff. Paul specifies what he means by their "boasting κατὰ σάρκα." He refers to their boasting of their being Hebrews, Israelites and Abraham's descendants (11:22), their apostolic accomplishments (11:23) and their visions, miracles, etc. (12:1ff.). The last of the three suggests that the phrase κατὰ σάρκα in 5:16 like the phrase ἐν προσώπῳ in 5:12 refers to a perspective that values an impressive outward appearance of a person with spectacular charismatic manifestations. But Paul's understanding of the opponents' boasting of their being Hebrews, Israelites, and so on also as being κατὰ σάρκα reminds us of Phil 3:2-10, where he also accuses his opponents of having their "confidence ἐν σαρκί" on the ground of their being Israelites and Hebrews. Just as in our passage, so also in the Philippians passage, he contrasts the "fleshly" perspective with one that is determined by the knowledge of Christ as one who died and was raised again (cf. also Gal 6:12-16). So, it seems that the phrase κατὰ σάρκα in 5:16 also refers to a perspective that values the Jewish particularistic *Heilsgeschichte,* that is, to a Jewish nationalistic perspective (cf. also Rom 4:1; 9:3-5; 1 Cor 10:18; Gal 4:21ff.). The opponents' apparent boasting of the Mosaic covenant, against which Paul has just argued in chapter 3, seems to support this reading. Of course, from Paul's point of view, this element is also part of valuing the outward appearance rather than "the heart" (cf. Rom 2:28-29). So, it seems that the phrase κατὰ σάρκα in 5:16 refers to a perspective that appreciates an impressive outward appearance and concretely both the Jewish salvation-historical connection and the powerful charismatic manifestations.

What was, then, the christology of the opponents which Paul implicitly designates as christology κατὰ σάρκα, from a "fleshly" perspective? First of all, their emphasis on the name "Jesus" rather than on his atoning death seems to suggest that they focused on the historical Jesus. Then, in view of their stress on the charismatic gifts of visions and miracles, one possibility is that they presented Jesus mainly as a powerful miracle-worker.[55] In view of

55. Cf. Georgi, *Gegner,* 254-57, 290ff.

their probable emphasis on the glory of the Mosaic ministry (3:7-18), they may have presented Jesus more specifically as the second Moses or the eschatological prophet like Moses (cf. Deut 18:15).[56] Or, in view of their Jewish nationalistic emphasis, they may even have presented Jesus as the Davidic national messiah.[57]

Whichever of these may have been the case, it was basically the same as Paul's pre-conversion estimation of "Christ" in so far as it was from a "fleshly" perspective. For the opponents, a christology from this "fleshly" perspective may still have made sense, but for him, it was impossible. For, seen from the "fleshly" perspective that had made Paul and his contemporaries expect a powerful messiah like David or Moses who could redeem the Jews, Jesus could not possibly have been the Messiah. On the contrary, seen from that perspective, his death by crucifixion only indicated that he had been accursed by God (Gal 3:13; 1 Cor 12:3; Deut 21:23). Paul admits that in his pre-conversion days he had this negative estimation of Jesus from the "fleshly" perspective (5:16b). In 5:16 he does not specify the correct view of Christ to which he eventually came, because he has already made that clear in 5:14: Jesus' messianic work consisted in his vicarious death for all. But in 5:21, by way of a recapitulation, Paul states it most succinctly again: Jesus' *Christ-act* consisted in his bearing the sins of all humankind and dying vicariously to make the eschatological atonement for them all.

While with the real conditional sentence εἰ καί[58] in 5:16b Paul admits his wrong perspective of Christ during his pre-conversion days, with the emphatic ἡμεῖς in 5:16a he implicitly contrasts himself with his opponents: he has his "fleshly" perspective changed, but they persist in it.[59] So, in this apologetic section, Paul not only defends his gospel (christology and soteriology) but also attacks his opponents' still defective christological perspective.

What might have led Paul to do this?[60] Was it called for just because he had to counter his opponents' "glory"-christology on which they not only based their own understanding of "glory"-apostleship but also discredited Paul's gospel of Christ crucified and his apostleship of weakness and suffering? But if it was just for that, did he need to admit his mistaken perspective

56. So Friedrich, "Gegner," 191, 204.

57. Cf. O. Michel, " 'Erkennen dem Fleisch nach' (2 Kor. 5:16)," *EvTh* 14 (1954): 26f.; Schlatter, *Bote*, 561-63; Barrett, *A Commentary*, 171; F. F. Bruce, *Paul and Jesus* (Grand Rapids: Eerdmans, 1974), 22-25.

58. Cf. Wolff, "Knowledge," 82f.; Thrall, *Second Epistle to the Corinthians*, 415f.

59. Cf. Thrall, *Second Epistle to the Corinthians*, 414, 418; Wolff, "Knowledge," 87.

60. Thrall, *Second Epistle to the Cornthians*, 420, raises this pertinent question often ignored by commentators, but her answer seems to be inadequate.

in his pre-conversion days?[61] Why did he need to go on recounting his Damascus experience of having been made a new creature, "reconciled" to God and commissioned with the "ministry/word of reconciliation"? This consideration seems to suggest that what really led Paul to this line of apologetic in 5:11-21 was the opponents' insinuation of his past as a persecutor of the church and as an enemy of Jesus Christ and God as well as their rejection of his claim to his apostleship on the basis of the Damascus revelation of Christ (cf. 1 Cor 9:1; 15:8-10).[62]

Above we surmised from the issue of no "recommendation letter" (3:1ff.) and from Paul's apologetic reference to his ecstatic experience (εἴτε γὰρ ἐξέστημεν . . .) (5:13) that his opponents discredited his claim to apostleship on the basis of his Damascus experience. Now, it seems that as part of their dispute of his apostleship they also referred to his past as a persecutor of the church. So we may reconstruct the opponents' criticism as the context of his *apologia* in this way: Paul is not an apostle properly "qualified." His appeal to his experience of the revelation of Christ and his commission on the Damascus road is invalid because it was nothing but "madness." Instead of being a follower of Jesus, actually he used to be extremely opposed to him, and, instead of being associated with Jesus' original disciples and apostles, he used to be a fierce persecutor of the church. So he is not recognized as an apostle by the Jerusalem church, and his inability to produce a "letter of recommendation" confirms this. That his apostleship is defective is shown also in the fact that his "gospel" is "veiled" or incomprehensible as he ignores the Mosaic covenant and Torah, concentrating only on Jesus' death. His feeble appearance, without a proper apostolic authority and power, is a clear sign of his being no genuine apostle.

It is most interesting to observe these arguments against Paul's apostleship reappearing in the Pseudo-Clementine *The Kerygmata Petrou*.[63] In H. XVII.13-19 Peter's dispute with Simon *alias* Paul is reported. There Peter re-

---

61. Cf. Breytenbach, *Versöhnung*, 130 (n. 165).

62. So Friedrich, "Gegner," 214; Breytenbach, *Versöhnung*, 130 (n. 165). If the opponents belonged to Stephen's party, their criticism of Paul's past as a persecutor of the church would be all the more understandable, since they seem to have borne the brunt of Paul's persecution (Acts 7:58–8:1) (so Friedrich, "Gegner," 209f.). When Paul, their persecutor, was converted on the Damascus road, they had accepted him into their fellowship. But later when they and he became estranged from each other for theological and other reasons, they may have devalued his conversion, disputing the genuineness of his christophanic vision and highlighting his persecution activities.

63. G. Strecker in Hennecke-Schneemelcher, *NT Apocrypha*, vol. 2 (London: SCM, 1972), 111, dates it ca. A.D. 200.

jects Paul's appeal to vision (ὀπτασία) as a means of valid revelation of God or his Son, attributing it rather to a demon. His own experience of God's revelation of his Son (Matt 16:13-17) was a revelation between friends and was from mouth to mouth, but through visions God's wrath is revealed because they are means of revelation to an "enemy" (cf. Num 12:6-9). He goes on:

> And if our Jesus appeared to you also and became known in a vision and met you as angry with an enemy, yet he has spoken only through visions and dreams or through external revelations. But can any one be made competent to teach through a vision? And if your opinion is, "That is possible," why then did our teacher spend a whole year with us who were awake? . . . But if you were visited by (the Lord Jesus) for a space of an hour and were instructed by him, and thereby have become an apostle, then proclaim his words, expound what he has taught, be a friend to his apostles and do not contend with me, who am his confidant. But if you really desire to cooperate with the truth, then learn first from us what we have learned from him and, as a learner of the truth, become a fellow-worker with us.[64]

If the opponents of Paul in 2 Corinthians were somehow connected with Peter,[65] and if *KerygPetr.* reflects the Petrine tradition, this parallelism would be seen as a confirmation of our reconstruction of the context of 2 Cor 5:11-21. Even if we cannot be certain in both of these cases, the material from *KerygPetr.* may still be taken as lending some weight to our reconstruction with its suggestion that such a disputing of Paul's apostleship as we have reconstructed did arise within the Jewish Christian community.[66]

Seen in this light, 1 Cor 9:1-3 and 15:8-10 appear to imply that already at the time of writing 1 Corinthians Paul's opponents had disputed his claim to apostleship on the basis of the Damascus revelation of the Lord Jesus Christ and insinuated, in that context, about his past as a persecutor of the church. Both passages seem to imply that the opponents were not willing to grant his

64. Ibid., 122f. Cf. G. Strecker, *Das Judenchristentum in den Pseudoklementinen* (Berlin: Akademie, 1981), 191-96.

65. So, e.g. Barrett, "Paul's Opponents"; M. E. Thrall, "Super-Apostles, Servants of Christ, and Servants of Satan," *JSNT* 6 (1980): 42-57; M. Hengel, *Zur urchristlichen Geschichtsschreibung* (Stuttgart: Calwer, 1979), 83. Even if originally they were those of Stephen's party, later on they could still have been connected with Peter. For it is quite probable that Peter joined them in the diaspora (e.g. Antioch) when he was driven out of Palestine in ca. A.D. 42 (cf. Hengel, *Geschichtsschreibung*, 79-84).

66. O. Cullmann, *Petrus: Jünger, Apostel, Märtyrer* (Munich: Siebenstern, 1967), 67f., and Lüdemann, *Antipaulinismus*, 257, see some continuity between the transmitters of the anti-Pauline tradition in *KerygPetr.* and Paul's contemporary opponents. Cf. also Strecker, *Judenchristentum*, 196.

Damascus vision of the risen Lord as being equal to the resurrection appearances of the risen Lord to his (true) apostles, and that they were not willing to recognize his claim to apostleship on the basis of that vision as equal in validity to that of his (true) apostles. Of all the references to the Damascus event, 1 Cor 15:8-10 is rather distinctive in that only here does Paul *apologetically* refer to his past persecution of the church, *explicitly* admitting it *as his guilt*,[67] and at the same time emphatically claim his apostleship by appealing to God's grace shown in his revelation of the risen Christ to him on the Damascus road and in his subsequent enabling in Paul's ministry (cf. 1 Tim 1:12-14). So the opponents' dispute about Paul's apostleship, as seen in 2 Cor 2:14–7:4, seems to have been a continuation of that which had already arisen at the time of writing 1 Corinthians, and had both the elements of rejecting Paul's appeal to his Damascus vision of the risen Lord Jesus Christ and of criticizing his past as a persecutor of the church.[68]

Thus a consideration of 1 Cor 9:1-3; 15:8-10 with an illustration drawn from *KerygPetr.* appears to confirm our interpretation of the context of Paul's *apologia* in 2 Cor 5:11-21.

(4) Paul's Reply

Once this context of 2 Cor 5:11-21 is established, it is not difficult to discern the logical sequence of Paul's *apologia* in that passage[69] and to appreciate the function of the metaphor "reconciliation" in that *apologia*.

---

67. Contrast Gal 1:13 and Phil 3:6, where his reference to his past persecution of the church functions primarily to stress his success in Judaism against his Judaizing opponents (cf. also Acts 22:3-5; 26:9-11).

68. The parallelism between 1 Cor 9:1-3 and 15:8-10 on the one hand and 2 Cor 3:1–4:6 and 5:11-21 on the other is considerable: the question of Paul's apostolic "competence/qualification" (ἱκανότης); the Corinthian church as evidence of Paul's genuine apostleship; reference to the Damascus vision of the risen Lord; etc. If our exegesis here is correct, 1 Cor 15:8-10 and 2 Cor 5:16-20 have the same structure of Paul's admitting the guilt of his pre-conversion past and yet emphatically claiming his apostolic commission by God's grace. In order to show that the dispute about his apostleship in 2 Corinthians started already in 1 Corinthians, we may point out further Paul's defense on his position about the financial matters, which is common to 1 Cor 9:4-18 and 2 Cor 11:7-11, and his appeal to his apostolic labor as greater than that of his opponents', which is common to 1 Cor 15:10 and 2 Cor 11:23-33.

69. The failure to perceive this context leads many commentators to a perplexity about the logical sequence in the passage, especially about the connection between vv. 18ff. and the foregoing: e.g., H. Lietzmann–W. G. Kümmel, *An die Korinther I/II* (Tübingen: Mohr-Siebeck, 1969), 126; Barrett, *A Commentary*, 175. See E. Güttgemanns, *Der leidende Apostel und sein Herr* (Göttingen: Vandenhoeck, 1966), 312ff.

First of all, Paul admits his past hostility to Jesus Christ and his past persecution of the church. Then he explains that they were due to his misjudgment of Jesus Christ (v. 16b). Like his contemporary Jewish colleagues, he, as a zealous Pharisee (Phil 3:5), had expected a powerful nationalistic Messiah like David or Moses. Seen from this perspective, Jesus could not be the Messiah; on the contrary, his death by crucifixion only indicated that he had been cursed by God (Deut 21:23; Gal 3:13; 1 Cor 12:3). So he was hostile to Jesus and persecuted his followers. But on the road to Damascus God revealed to him the crucified Jesus as Christ and Lord, and this experience led Paul to a new "judgment" (κρίναντας v. 14) about Jesus Christ, that he died vicariously for humankind, bearing their sins, and was raised by God from the dead (vv. 14f., 21). So he came to a new, correct knowledge about Jesus Christ, that his messianic act or Christ-act consisted in his atoning death and resurrection.

At this "conversion" experience, Paul himself appropriated Christ's atonement by faith in him so that he came to be "in Christ" and received God's forgiveness of his sins. This was an experience of being made a "new creation." Unlike the Jewish conception of "new creation" that had been thought to be brought about on the New Year's Day or the Day of Atonement, this was an individual application to Paul of God's eschatological act of new creation through his Messiah. The point of Paul's recounting his Damascus experience in terms of being made a "new creation" in this context is clearly to underscore his having been liberated from the burden of his past hostility to Christ and his church through God's forgiveness and to indicate that his opponents' insinuation of his past is therefore quite futile. This point is made abundantly clear by Paul's allusion in verse 17b to Isa 43:18-19 (LXX): "Do not remember the former things, and do not discuss *the old things. Behold* I make *new things*" (cf. also Isa 42:9; 48:6; 66:17), which is an exhortation for Israel to forget its past sin and judgment, and look to God's work of restoration/new creation.[70] So Paul was told by God on the Damascus road to forget his past sin of acting in hostility to Christ and persecuting his church, and to rejoice in God's new creation of him in Christ! What then is the point of his opponents' insinuating of his past sin?

In this context Paul introduces the metaphor "reconciliation" along with the metaphor "new creation." The Jewish tradition of applying the metaphor "new creation" for atonement on the New Year's Day or the Day of Atonement may stand in the background. But what directly leads him to introduce the metaphor "reconciliation" here is his opponents' criticism of his past enmity to Christ and his church as part of their repudiation of his apostolic

---

70. Cf. Beale, "OT Background," 553f. See p. 106 above.

claim. Against it, he says, God's forgiveness on the Damascus road was his "reconciliation" of him to himself. True, Paul was hostile to Christ and his church. Indeed, he was an "enemy" of Christ and therefore of God. But God "reconciled" his angry "enemy" Paul to himself.

Paul regards sinners as "enemies" of God (Rom 5:10). So, the Jews who reject the gospel are "enemies" of God (11:28), and those who live in a manner not consistent with the gospel are "enemies of the cross of Christ" (Phil 3:18). In view of such conception, it is quite likely that he also viewed his own past hostility to the gospel of the crucified Christ in terms of an "enemy" of God. That he took the word quite realistically seems to be suggested by the imagery of θριαμβεύεσθαι in 2 Cor 2:14. In his thorough study on the imagery, S. J. Hafemann stresses that the imagery comes from the Roman institution of triumphal procession and that it refers to being led in the triumphal procession of a conqueror general as a conquered enemy and slave, usually to one's death. So, according to Hafemann, in Paul's use of the word in 2 Cor 2:14 his having been defeated as an "enemy" of God and his having been taken as a "slave" of Christ on the Damascus road is presupposed. So, in 2 Cor 2:14, with a view to his Damascus conversion/call on the one hand and to his present ministry of suffering on the other hand, Paul is speaking of his apostolic ministry in terms of his being led by God as a conquered "enemy" and slave in his triumphal procession in order to display the majesty and power of his conqueror God.[71]

Thus the imagery θριαμβεύεσθαι in 2 Cor 2:14 clearly suggests both that Paul generally looks upon his pre-Damascus past in very realistic terms of his having been an "enemy" of God, and that in speaking of God's "reconciliation" of him to himself in 2 Cor 5:11-21 (continuation of his apostolic defense started off by that 2 Cor 2:14), he is very much conscious of his having been an "enemy" of God on the Damascus road. Further, the imagery of θριαμβεύεσθαι makes it highly likely that in his use of the καταλλάσσειν-terminology in 2 Cor 5:18-20 Paul is conscious of its usual military-diplomatic usage in Hellenism, as C. Breytenbach insists.[72]

Against this background Paul's statements in 5:18-20 make perfect sense: God conquered his "enemy" Paul and "reconciled" him to himself. A further miracle of divine grace was that God went on to appoint him as his "ambassador" (πρέσβυς) and send him to the rebellious world to "petition" (δέομαι) and "appeal" (παρακαλεῖν) for it to be "reconciled" to God. Thus he gave him

---

71. S. J. Hafemann, *Suffering and Ministry in the Spirit* (Grand Rapids: Eerdmans, 1990), esp. 31f.

72. See above, nn. 4 and 5.

the "ministry of reconciliation" and entrusted him with the "message of reconciliation." From the references to his conversion on the significance of Christ (v. 16) and to God's forgiveness and new creation of him (v. 17), this is an advance in his polemical defense against his opponents who referred to his past in order to dispute his claim to apostleship on the basis of God's Damascus call. Could they go on insinuating his past when he showed that God had conquered him as an "enemy" and "reconciled" him to himself? Could they go on disputing his apostleship when he showed how perfectly God's "reconciliation" of him to himself and his appointment of him as his "ambassador of reconciliation" illustrated the gospel, the message of God's work of reconciling the world to himself through Christ's atoning death (v. 19ab)?[73]

Conclusion: Origin and Development of the Doctrine of Reconciliation

The four facts we have ascertained so far are:

1. The "reconciliation" language is uniquely Pauline in the New Testament;
2. Paul's use of the "reconciliation" terminology reflects both the Hellenistic and Hellenistic Jewish background, but his consistent formulation of God "reconciling" human beings to himself is unique and it represents a fundamental innovation in *Religionsgeschichte;*
3. 2 Cor 5:11-21 is full of allusions to Paul's Damascus experience of conversion/call: what he is talking about in that passage is *what happened to him on the Damascus road;* and
4. Paul's emphasis on God's "reconciliation" of him to himself and his commissioning him as a minister of "reconciliation" in his polemical defense of his apostleship in 2 Cor 5:11-21 was in response to his opponents who criticized his past as an enemy of Christ and his church in order to discredit his apostolic claim based on the Damascus event.

---

73. Since Paul's antithetical comparison of his ministry of the new covenant and the gospel and Moses' ministry of the old covenant and the Torah in 2 Cor 3 is in the same context as his apostolic *apologia* (2 Cor 5:18-20), it is just possible that Paul is aware of the Jewish conception of Moses as καταλλάκτης and μεσίτης between God and his people (Philo, *VitMos.* 2.166; *QuaestEx.* 2.49; Josephus, *Ant.* 3.315). Against his opponents who were glorying in Moses and criticizing Paul for neglecting the Mosaic Torah, in 5:18-20 Paul may be implicitly arguing that his ministry of the new covenant as the ministry of God's reconciliation in Christ is incomparably more glorious than the Mosaic ministry of reconciling God to his people through his intercession (Exod 32) (so Stuhlmacher, *Biblische Theologie,* 319).

These facts together make it reasonable to conclude that Paul developed his soteriological metaphor "reconciliation" from his own Damascus experience.

We cannot say whether Paul developed it for the first time at the time of writing 2 Cor 5 or whether he had developed it before and then used it in his apostolic defense in 2 Cor 5. In any case, he developed it out of his theological reflection on his personal experience on the Damascus road. In our judgment, it is this supposition rather than anything else that can explain convincingly the fundamental innovation he wrought in the Jewish idea of reconciliation: it is not human beings who reconcile an angry God to themselves through their prayer, repentance or good works; but rather it is God who has reconciled human beings to himself and still brings them to reconciliation to himself through the atoning death of Jesus Christ.[74] For on the Damascus road Paul himself experienced God's reconciling him, a hostile enemy, to himself, forgiving his sins and making him a new creature by his grace.[75]

This overwhelming experience came together with his new understanding of Jesus Christ's death as God's provision for atonement for humankind: "Christ died for our sins," that is, God "made him who knew no sin sin for us, so that we might become God's righteousness in him" (2 Cor 5:21). It was God who provided the means of atonement for us, so that we might be restored to the right relationship to himself. So his personal experience of God's overwhelming grace in his reconciliation of him to himself led Paul to interpret Christ's death as God's provision of the means of atonement and as God's work of *reconciliation* of the world to himself. Thus arose the unique Pauline formulation of the doctrine of *reconciliation*.

Once through his personal revelatory experience he came to a new understanding of God's work, he, as a well-trained rabbinic scholar, had to substantiate it through the Scriptures. For this, he found Deutero-Isaiah, especially the fourth Servant Song in Isa 53, a marvelous prophecy of God's work of reconciliation of sinners through the vicarious death of Christ. So, as O. Hofius, O. Betz, and G. K. Beale have clearly demonstrated,[76] Paul's presentation in 2 Cor 5:11-21 bears all the marks of his reflection on Christ and God's work in him in the light of Deutero-Isaiah, especially around Isa 53.

---

74. This innovation in the doctrine of "reconciliation," which unlike that in the doctrine of "justification" is not disputed, seems to hold a great significance for the current debate on Paul's relationship to Judaism, especially on his juxtaposition of grace/faith and the "works of the law."

75. In the formulation in Rom 5:10a: εἰ ἐχθροὶ ὄντες κατηλλάγημεν τῷ θεῷ διὰ τοῦ θανάτου τοῦ υἱοῦ αὐτοῦ . . . Paul may be consciously reflecting his own Damascus experience.

76. See above notes 16-18, and 22.

Then, Paul must have come to a firm conviction of the truth of his doctrine of God's reconciliation in Christ when he found, alongside the Scriptures, also much of the material from Jesus-tradition such as Jesus' offer of forgiveness to sinners on God's behalf, his teaching like the parable of the prodigal son, and his logia like the cup-saying at the Last Supper,[77] as confirming that doctrine or "gospel" that he received through God's revelation of Christ and his reconciliation of him to himself on the Damascus road.

In this way, "reconciliation," one of the most significant categories of preaching the gospel of Christ, came into being. How its effectiveness as a soteriological category has been rediscovered in recent theology is a topic for another study. However, we may point out that if our thesis here propounded is correct, the way Paul developed the doctrine has a paradigmatic significance for our theologizing today: as a personal experience of being encountered by Christ leads us to confirm the truth of the apostolic kerygma, we may interpret the kerygma with a new category drawn from that experience in order to make it more relevant to our situation today; but then we will have to secure a quality of objective truth with substantiation not only from the Scriptures but also from the historical Jesus, from what he was and what he did.

CHAPTER 7

The "Mystery" of
Romans 11:25-26 Once More

One of the theses submitted in my book, *The Origin of Paul's Gospel*, was that Paul obtained the "mystery" of Rom 11:25-26 from an interpretation of his Damascus revelation chiefly in the light of Isa 6 and 49. Some critics have objected to it by pointing to 1 Thess 2:14-16 or Rom 9:2-3; 10:1, and others have attempted to explain the origin of the "mystery" solely in terms of Paul's scriptural exegesis in the light of his actual missionary situation. However, I find neither these attempts adequate nor the objections to my thesis substantial. Hence this new attempt to strengthen my thesis and develop it further.

My Original Thesis in Brief[1]

The καὶ οὕτως of Rom 11:26 is inferential ("and so/therefore"). So the "mystery" proper is the ὅτι-clause of Rom 11:25c, and the next clause of 26a is an inference from it.[2] However, with the conjunction καί Paul binds the mystery proper and the inference closely together, so that the "mystery" is: "Partial

---

1. For details, see Seyoon Kim, *The Origin of Paul's Gospel* (Tübingen: Mohr-Siebeck, 1981, 1984; Grand Rapids: Eerdmans, 1982), 74-99.

2. So also H. Hübner, *Gottes Ich und Israel* (Göttingen: Vandenhoeck, 1984), 109; J. M. Gundry-Volf, *Paul and Perseverance* (Tübingen: Mohr-Siebeck, 1990), 179-80.

The substance of this chapter was originally presented at the fifty-first general meeting of *Studiorum Novi Testamenti Societas* in Strasbourg in August 1996 and was subsequently published as "The 'Mystery' of Rom 11.25-26 Once More," *New Testament Studies* 43 (1997): 474-92. It is reprinted here with the permission of Cambridge University Press.

hardening has come upon Israel until the full number of the gentiles have come in, and so all Israel will be saved." Καθὼς γέγραπται introduces a scriptural support for the foregoing statement, "all Israel will be saved" (v. 26a).

With the doxology in Rom 11:33-36 (cf. 1 Cor 2:6-16), Paul clearly suggests that the "mystery" is not a human speculation but the νοῦς κυρίου, the divine counsel revealed to him by the Spirit. Then, when and how did the revelation take place? I started my inquiry with an interpretation of 1 Cor 2:1-16 (esp. vv. 6-10) as alluding to Paul's Damascus experience of divine revelation and call.[3] Then I established the parallelism between 1 Cor 2:6-10 (with 2:1 and 4:1) on the one hand and Col 1:23c-29 and Eph 3:1-13 on the other: (1) the allusion to Paul's Damascus experience; (2) the "revelation-schema": the mystery which existed from eternity in concealment is now revealed; (3) Paul is the οἰκονόμος of the mystery; and (4) the mystery designates Christ and God's plan of salvation that Christ embodies. In the three passages, however, a shift of emphasis or a gradual concretization was also observable: (a) in 1 Cor 2, "the mystery of God" or "God's wisdom in mystery" designates Christ or God's plan of salvation embodied in Christ; (b) in Col 1:23c-29, the mystery is "Christ among you," the Christ who is preached among the gentiles, that is, God's plan of salvation that includes the gentiles in salvation; and (c) in Eph 3, "the mystery of Christ" is that "the gentiles are fellow heirs, members of the same body, and fellow partakers in the promise in Christ Jesus through the gospel" (v. 6).[4] Thus, at least the latter two passages make explicit what is implicit in Paul's testimony in Gal 1:11-16 that at the Damascus "revelation of Christ" he received his apostolic call and the gospel meant *for the gentiles.*

From this it was natural to ask whether the "mystery" of Rom 11:25-26 was also to be understood in the same context. For, on the one hand, the common concern for God's secret and wise plan of salvation which is expressed through the common language of μυστήριον and νοῦς κυρίου/χριστοῦ, connects Rom 11:25-26 (and vv. 33-36) to 1 Cor 2, and, on the other hand, the common language of μυστήριον and the common concern for the divine *Heilsplan* for the gentiles and the Jews also connect Rom 11:25-26 to Col 1/ Eph 3. This web of interrelationship among Rom 11:25-26; 1 Cor 2; Gal 1:11-

---

3. So also K. O. Sandness, *Paul — One of the Prophets?* (Tübingen: Mohr-Siebeck, 1991), 86f.; P. Stuhlmacher, "The Hermeneutic Significance of 1 Cor 2:6-16," in *Tradition and Interpretation* (E. E. Ellis FS; ed. G. Hawthorne; Grand Rapids: Eerdmans, 1987), 334.

4. If Colossians and Ephesians are deutero-Pauline, in view of their parallelism to 1 Cor 2 and Gal 1, Col 1:23-29 and Eph 3 are to be seen as legitimate interpretations or developments of Pauline understanding, and so their evidence can be used in support of our thesis here.

16; Col 1:23c-29; and Eph 3 increased the probability that like the other passages Rom 11:25-26 was also related to the Damascus revelation.

For this hypothesis, O. Betz's insight about Paul's interpretation of his Damascus call in the light of Isa 6 was seminal.[5] Then W. Zimmerli's study of the "Form- und Traditionsgeschichte der prophetischen Berufungserzählung," which H. Wildberger adopts for his analysis of Isa 6,[6] was helpful, although contrary to their view that only Luke narrated Paul's call in the form of Isa 6 (Acts 9:3-19; 22:6-16; 26:12-18) I had to show that Paul's language of ἀποκαλύπτειν/ἀποκάλυψις (Gal 1:12, 16) and his testimonies in 1 Cor 9:1; 15:8; 2 Cor 4:6 suggested that he had a vision of Christophany at the Damascus call rather like the theophany vision at Isaiah's call.

So, taking into account the known fact of Paul's interpreting his Damascus call in the light of Isa 49 (Gal 1:15-16), I formulated the hypothesis more specifically that Paul derived the "mystery" of Rom 11:25-26 by interpreting the Damascus revelation in the light of Isa 6 and 49. For this hypothesis, I first drew parallels between the reports of Paul's call and Isaiah's call: (1) both Isaiah and Paul saw the κύριος (Isa 6:1//1 Cor 9:1) in glory (Isa 6:1//2 Cor 4:6); (2) they both received divine forgiveness and atonement at their call (Isa 6:7// 2 Cor 5:16-21; 1 Cor 15:8-10; etc.); (3) they both were "sent" (ἀποστέλλειν) at the theophany/Christophany (Isa 6:8//1 Cor 9:1; etc.); and (4) just as Isaiah describes that in the vision he was let into the council before God's throne and heard God's counsels (6:8-13), so Paul also implies with the concepts ἀποκαλύπτειν/ἀποκάλυψις (Gal 1:12, 16; Eph 3:3) and μυστήριον (1 Cor 2:1, 6-10; Col 1:26-29; Eph 3:4-13) that he received the gospel and God's counsel from the enthroned Lord in vision (cf. Acts 9; 22; 26).[7]

Then I showed how smoothly Paul's gentile apostleship and the "mystery" of Rom 11:25-26 could be explained in the combined light of Isa 6 and 49: (1) the divine hardening of the heart of Israel (Isa 6:10 LXX; cf. John 12:40). (2) The ἄχρι οὗ of Rom 11:25 formally corresponds to Isaiah's question, "ἕως πότε, O, Lord?" and the divine answer, "ἕως ἄν . . ." (Isa 6:11). (3) Paul's call to the gentile apostleship is logically connected with the hardening of Israel. God has hardened them, as it were, in order to create room for a gentile mission in time (Rom 11:11-12, 15, 28-32). Since Israel is hardened and while she remains so, Paul is to proclaim the gospel to the gentiles and thus be a "light" to them (cf. 2 Cor 4:4-6), so "that [God's] salvation may

5. O. Betz, "Die Vision des Paulus im Tempel von Jerusalem" (1970), now in his *Jesus der Herr der Kirche* (Tübingen: Mohr-Siebeck, 1990), 91-102.

6. W. Zimmerli, *Ezechiel 1* (Neukirchen: Neukirchener, 1969), 16-21; H. Wildberger, *Jesaja 1* (Neukirchen: Neukirchener, 1972), 234-38.

7. Cf. Wildberger, *Jesaja*, 236.

reach to the end of the earth" (Isa 49:6; cf. Acts 26:18 = Isa 42:6-7, 16). (4) The hope for the eventual salvation of Israel can also be explained in the combined light of Isa 6:13 (MT and Tg) and Isa 49:5-6. (5) When the "mystery" is taken together with Rom 11:11, 13-14 and 15:15-16, 19, 23, it appears to involve a self-understanding on Paul's part as the gentiles' apostle who was, first, responsible to bring in "the full number of the gentiles" but then also responsible to bring about the eventual salvation of Israel thereby. This implication is illuminated by Isa 49:5-6 where the *Ebed* is called both to be "the light to the gentiles" and to restore Israel. (6) In Acts 28:25-28, Luke reports Paul as quoting Isa 6:9-10 to explain Israel's rejection of the gospel and as claiming that because of their obduracy the gospel of salvation has been sent to the gentiles, and thus Luke supports the thesis here propounded.

All this complicated argument was only to confirm what seemed, from the beginning, to be implied in the fundamental testimony of Paul that he was called to preach the gospel to the gentiles at the Damascus Christophany. For it was hard to believe that Paul, the former "zealous" Pharisee (Gal 1:13-14; Phil 3:5-6), could have been conscious of a divine call to the gentile apostleship without, at the same time, an understanding of divine *Heilsplan* about the Jews and the gentiles such as the "mystery."

From Scriptural Exegesis Alone?

However, various scholars have proposed to explain the origin of the "mystery" simply in terms of Paul's scriptural exegesis. Certainly Paul could have obtained the "mystery" from a scriptural exegesis, as the Teacher of Righteousness did (e.g., 1QpHab 7.4-5; cf. Eph 5:32). The Scriptures cited in 11:26b-27 (Isa 59:20-21; 27:9; Jer 31:33-34) are clearly designed to substantiate the inference from the "mystery" proper, namely, that "all Israel will be saved" (v. 26a), though not quite the "mystery" proper in verse 25c. In the inference of verse 26a, many have also recognized a reflection of Isa 45:17, 25,[8] and O. Hofius considers also the possible reflection of Isa 6:11-13 (LXX/Tg).[9] In the idea of divine "hardening" of Israel in the "mystery" proper of verse 25c, some[10] have recognized an echo of Isa 6:9-10. Sandness

8. E.g., O. Hofius, "Das Evangelium und Israel," in *Paulusstudien* (Tübingen: Mohr-Siebeck, 1989), 202; Hübner, *Gottes Ich,* 113, 121-22; F. Mussner, " 'Ganz Israel wird gerettet werden' (Röm 11,26)," *Kairos* 18 (1976): 254-55.

9. Hofius, "Evangelium," 201; cf. Kim, *Origin,* 97.

10. Hübner, *Gottes Ich,* 113-14 (n. 405); Hofius, "Evangelium," 201. This is quite probable especially because Rom 11:7-8, the verses related to Rom 11:25, almost certainly echo Isa 6:9-10:

also sees the ἄχρι οὗ of Rom 11:25 as corresponding to Isaiah's question in Isa 6:11.[11]

However, Hübner, who finds Isa 6:9-10 reflected in the "mystery" proper, recognizes that in contrast to the inference in verse 26a, the "mystery" proper in 25c "is not formulated in so close dependence upon an OT statement."[12] This is in line with his fine observation that from Rom 11:11 on, while the supplementary ideas of God's will for Israel's hardening and for making them jealous of the gentiles' salvation are substantiated with scriptural references, the "main idea that the *Unheil* of Israel has been caused for the sake of the salvation of the gentiles is not."[13] So, for the characteristic idea of the "mystery" that *first* the gentiles are to come into the Kingdom of God or the *Heilsgemeinde* and *only thereafter* will all Israel be saved, and its implication that God has hardened Israel in order to save the gentiles first, Paul apparently does not provide a scriptural substantiation. If the "mystery" was obtained only through a scriptural exegesis, is this not a strange state of affair?

Hofius[14] has attempted to show that Paul's reversing the order of salvation (Israel first — the gentiles later) usual in the tradition of the nations' eschatological pilgrimage to Zion is based on some Old Testament passages where first the salvation of the gentiles and then that of Israel are spoken of: Isa 59:19a + 20; Isa 45:14-16 + 17; Isa 45:20-24 + 25; and Micah 4:1-5 + 6-8. Since Isa 59:20 is actually cited in Rom 11:26b and Isa 45:17, 25 are often seen to be reflected in the inference from the "mystery" (Rom 11:26a), we can see that Paul could have been aware of the verses in their neighborhood and that these passages could have helped him to discern the order of salvation in God's *Heilsplan*.

But is this attempt adequate? The order of salvation of Israel first and the gentiles later is, as Hofius[15] himself recognizes, "characteristic" in the tradition of the nations' eschatological pilgrimage to Zion. So, then, from what we know of Paul's usual practice, should we not expect him to cite those rare scriptural texts explicitly in order to justify his "forceful remoulding" of the usual conception?[16] Is it not strange that Paul explicitly substantiates the inference from the "mystery" proper with the Scriptures but does not do the same for the "mystery" proper itself? Had he obtained the "mystery" from an

---

so B. Lindars, *New Testament Apologetic* (London: SCM, 1961), 164; J. D. G. Dunn, *Romans 9–16* (Waco: Word, 1988), 640-41, 679.

11. Sandness, *Paul*, 178; cf. Dunn, *Romans 9–16*, 679.
12. Hübner, *Gottes Ich*, 113. He also considers whether Isa 49:22-26 is reflected in vv. 25-26.
13. Ibid., 107-8; cf. also 122. So also Sandness, *Paul*, 181.
14. Hofius, "Evangelium," 202.
15. Ibid.
16. Cf. E. Käsemann, *An die Römer* (Tübingen: Mohr-Siebeck, 1974), 299.

exegesis of the Scriptures, is it not to be expected of him to substantiate it with reference to those Scriptures?

Further, even if all those passages cited by Hofius are granted to have influenced Paul's formulation of the "mystery,"[17] the fundamental problem still remains: what caused Paul to look at those passages, setting aside the more numerous texts which support the "characteristic" order of salvation for Israel first and the gentiles later?

Since U. B. Müller's suggestion, it has become popular to see the "mystery" as a prophetic saying which Paul received from God as the answer to his intercessory prayer for Israel (Rom 10:1; cf. 9:2-3). It is supposed that in his anguish over the shocking revelation of God's eschatological rejection of Israel in another prophetic saying, namely, 1 Thess 2:14-16, Paul interceded for Israel and, through scriptural exegesis, he obtained the "mystery" as the "comforting" answer from God.[18] The hypothesis, if substantiated, could explain how Paul could have been led to those rare texts that could be interpreted as teaching the order of salvation as the gentiles first and Israel later.

But if Paul had received the "mystery" as the divine answer to his anguish about Israel's rejection and his prayer for her salvation, why does he say that he is *still* in anguish for Israel's rejection in Rom 9:2-3 and he is *still* praying for her salvation in Rom 10:1?[19] According to the hypothesis, has he not *already* received the "mystery" *specifically* as the divine answer *to that particular prayer* and has he not *already* been comforted *thereby?* One can avoid this problem only when one can show that Paul obtained the "mystery" while actually dictating Rom 11:25-26. But this is impossible because its content has been intimated since 11:11 on.[20] Or shall we say that as Paul came to dictate

---

17. His suggestion is not without problems: e.g., (1) what about Isa 45:13? (2) Does Isa 59:19a really have the *salvation* of the gentiles in view? Cf. also Sandness, *Paul,* 181, n. 40.

18. U. B. Müller, *Prophetie und Predigt im Neuen Testament* (Gütersloh: Gütersloher, 1975), 229-32; D. Zeller, *Juden und Heiden in der Mission des Paulus* (Stuttgart: KBW, 1976), 252-53; U. Wilckens, *Der Brief an die Römer (6–11)* (Zürich: Benziger/Neukirchen: Neukirchener, 1980), 254.

19. Note the present tense of the verbs in Rom 9:2-3 and of the implied verb in 10:1. On ηὐχόμην in 9:3, cf. C. E. B. Cranfield, *The Epistle to the Romans II* (ICC; Edinburgh: T & T Clark, 1979), 455-56. In the interest of his thesis, Müller, *Prophetie,* 229, says: "In 10,1; vgl. 9,2f., spricht Paulus von seinem Gebet zu Gott, in dem er für die Erretung Israels *gebeten hat*" (my emphasis). But is there any justification for this distortion?

20. Cf. D. Sänger, *Die Verkündigung des Gekreuzigten und Israel* (Tübingen: Mohr-Siebeck, 1994), 182-83. However, Sänger's denial of the revelational or "mystery" character of the "mystery" of Rom 11:25-26 on the ground that its content is already imbedded in Rom 11:11ff. (180-81, 192-93), betrays a confusion. The state of affairs which he refers to indicates rather that at the climax of his argument Paul solemnly discloses the "mystery," something previously known

the section from 11:11 on he was gradually made to speculate on the divine *Heilsplan* until he could finally formulate it in the "mystery"? So, then, should we think that the "mystery" was given to Paul between Rom 10:1 and 11:11 or 11:25-26? We need not speculate along this unpromising line, because the proponents of the hypothesis themselves insist for its own sake that Paul received the "mystery" some time before writing Romans.[21]

Finally, we may mention J. Jeremias' view[22] that the word of Deut 32:21 (cf. Rom 10:19; 11:11, 14) about God's will to "make Israel jealous by those who are no people" led Paul to perceiving God's *Heilsplan* embodied in the "mystery." But we may ask again: what caused Paul to look at the texts like Deut 32:21?

The usual answer would be the actual missionary situation that Paul

---

to him, as the basis on which his argument so far has rested, than that while dictating Rom 11, he summarizes his argument so far under the novel concept of "mystery" for the first time. Against Sänger, cf. also Dunn, *Rom 9–16*, 679. I am glad that Dunn has now come to affirm that "Paul rooted [the conviction which he calls 'mystery'] back in his conversion revelation — that God's Son had to be preached among the Gentiles (Gal. 1.16)" (*The Theology of Paul the Apostle* [Grand Rapids: Eerdmans, 1998], 526-27). However, this does not prevent him from arguing that my thesis here propounded "largely ignores the dramatic function of 11:25-26 as the climactic resolution of the dilemma posed at the beginning of the section (9.6); that is, the problem to which 11.25-26 was the answer only emerged with the continuing failure of the bulk of Israel to hear and believe/obey the gospel (10.14-21)" (ibid., 526). In view of what I have written on these pages (pp. 244-46; see also below, pp. 250-51), the first sentence of Dunn's criticism is strange. Further, it is not clear how exactly the two sentences of the criticism here cited are related to each other. Apparently Dunn means that quite a long period after his apostolic call to the gentiles, faced with the continuing obduracy of Israel *vis-à-vis* the gospel, Paul began to reflect on his Damascus revelation afresh and found the "mystery" already contained in it. It is a pity that Dunn does not ask how long after his Damascus call Paul could have done this. But still, with this view, Dunn has the difficult task of explaining how Paul, the "zealotic" Pharisee, could be so "immediately" convinced of his call to gentile mission (but not to Jewish mission), as Dunn repeatedly insists he was (see ch. 1 above), when the prevailing view in Judaism and in the Jewish church was that Israel must first be saved. Is Dunn's attempt to explain Paul's gentile mission as a corollary of the crucified Christ (as interpreted by Dunn himself) convincing (see above, pp. 9-10, 18-21, 131-34)?

21. Dunn, *Rom 9–16*, 679; Sandness, *Paul*, 180; Müller, *Prophetie*, 229-31: wary of the possible criticism of his hypothesis from the fact that the "mystery" actually does not function as a "comforting assurance of salvation" in the context of Rom 11 but rather finds itself within a paraenetic context addressed to the *gentile Christians* (cf. Sänger, *Verkündigung*, 182), Müller insists that the "mystery" "has an independent character over against its immediate context" (p. 229), and says that "the mystery of Rom 11.25f. is the original answer to Paul's intercession on which he reports in 10.1" (p. 231).

22. J. Jeremias, "Einige vorwiegend sprachliche Beobachtungen zu Röm 11,25-36," in *Die Israelfrage nach Römer 9–11* (ed. L. De Lorenzi; Rome: Abtei von St Paul von den Mauern, 1977), 201.

faced: the gentiles' positive response to the gospel in contrast to the Jews' negative response.[23] This could have caused Paul to turn to passages like Deut 32:21; Isa 45:14-17, 20-25; 59:19-20; and Micah 4:1-8. To be sure, the actual missionary situation must have, at least, confirmed the truth of the "mystery" in Paul's mind.

However, the question is whether it is an adequate explanation for the origin of the "mystery." It involves an assumption that at first Paul followed the standard view about the order of salvation, Israel first and the gentiles later, or at least that he believed in a simultaneous salvation of the Jews and the gentiles. For the assumption, however, it is most strange why there is, then, little evidence for Paul's ever having concentrated on a mission to the Jews, or, at least, for his having worked for the Jewish mission as much as for the gentile mission. There are indeed some who assert that Paul must have started his mission among the Jews first and turned to the gentiles only after its failure. But they cannot bring any concrete evidence for that apparently psychologically comfortable conjecture. Rather, the evidence is overwhelmingly in favor of the view that from the beginning of his apostleship Paul concentrated on the gentile mission, although he never hesitated to preach the gospel to the Jews on the way or use their synagogues as useful bases for his gentile mission. Is it not significant that he reviews his apostolic ministry from Jerusalem to Illyricum as work "for the obedience of the gentiles" (Rom 15:18-19)?[24]

23. Cf., e.g., M. N. A. Bockmuehl, *Revelation and Mystery* (Tübingen: Mohr-Siebeck, 1990), 174-75.

24. See p. 252 below. Cf. G. Lüdemann, *Paulus, der Heidenapostel,* vol. 1, *Studien zur Chronologie* (Göttingen: Vandenhoeck, 1980), 96. According to R. Riesner, *Die Frühzeit des Apostels Paulus* (Tübingen: Mohr-Siebeck, 1994), 217-38, Paul started his mission among the Jews and only later, during his first visit to Jerusalem (Gal 1:18; Acts 9:26-30), did he come to an understanding of his apostolic call as intended for the gentiles (cf. Acts 22:17-21). For this thesis, Riesner rejects the often suggested view (most recently by J. Murphy-O'Connor, "Paul in Arabia," *CBQ* 55 [1993]: 732-37), that Paul's reference to "Arabia" in Gal 1:17 implies his missionary work among the Nabateans, on the grounds that (1) "while in the transition from the mission to the pure Jews to that to the Samaritans there was a contact-point not only of blood but also of religion, in connection with the Nabateans this factor was completely absent," (2) "in no other place does Paul mention churches in Arabia," and (3) in Rom 15:19 Paul mentions Jerusalem as the starting point of his gentile mission (230-31). But should Riesner's first ground be valid, Paul would never have been able to start a gentile mission! If on that ground Riesner cannot believe that Paul could have started it after the Damascus call vision, how can he believe that Paul could start it after the temple vision (Acts 22:17-21), or under the Hellenists' influence in Jerusalem? Was there any reason why that ground was not valid for the Hellenists or for a later Paul, whereas it was valid for an earlier Paul? As for Riesner's second ground: should, then, Paul's failure to mention a church in Damascus also be construed as denying his missionary work in that city? (In fact, Paul's stay in Arabia may have been brief and his mission there not

How could, then, Paul, the former Pharisee "zealous" for Judaism, concentrate on the gentile mission, to the relative neglect of the Jewish mission? Could he have done this without having thought through the theological and salvation-historical implications? Is it plausible to think that his gentile mission was at first driven by his situation of having started his Christian life in the company of Hellenistic Jewish Christians around Damascus who were engaged in a gentile mission and so he could carry it on without much theological and salvation-historical reflection? For a well-trained Jewish theologian like Paul who was in the habit of substantiating a theological conviction or religious act from the Scriptures, is it not much more plausible to think that for the truly revolutionary decision to participate in the gentile mission he began immediately to think through its theological and salvation-historical implications and to seek its scriptural justification?

So it seems that a simple appeal to the actual missionary situation as the *Anlass* for Paul's search of the Scriptures for the "mystery" is inadequate. Then, is there an alternative to the Damascus revelation and call as the actual *Anlass* for the "mystery"?

The Damascus Revelation and Call

As said above, originally the studies of Zimmerli and Wildberger about the "form- and tradition-history of prophetic call narratives" were useful in establishing the likelihood that Paul viewed and narrated his experience of divine revelation and call at the Damascus Christophany in the form and tradition of Isaiah's experience of those at the theophany in Isa 6. This view can be further supported with a study of W. Stenger. He extends to Paul's autobiographical report in Gal 1:15-16 K. Baltzer's application of E. Otto's concept of "ideal biography" to the Old Testament prophetic and Jewish apocalyptic *Gattung* of *Einsetzungsbericht*, and shows Gal 1:15-16a as containing the essential elements of the *Gattung*.[25] As the *Gattung* normally involves a *Thron-*

---

very successful — so Murphy-O'Connor). And regarding Riesner's third ground: in Rom 15:19, Paul mentions Jerusalem first not necessarily because he started his gentile mission from there but rather, as most commentators think, because Jerusalem was understood to be the salvation-historical center from which the gospel was to go out to the whole world and possibly also because she was the southernmost location of his preaching to the gentiles, while Illyricum represented the northwesternmost location of his gentile mission so far. See pp. 103-4 above.

25. W. Stenger, "Biographisches und Idealbiographisches in Gal 1,11–12,14," in *Kontinuität und Einheit* (F. Mussner FS; ed. P.-G. Müller and W. Stenger; Freiburg: Herder, 1981), 132-40. Cf. K. Baltzer, *Biographie der Propheten* (Neukirchen: Neukirchener, 1975).

saalvision in which divine revelation and installation take place, Stenger sees the sentence of Gal 1:15-16a as "an abbreviated apocalyptic formula for *Thronsaalvision*."[26] So he confirms my earlier suggestion from Gal 1:12, 16 and other texts that Paul implies his having received the gospel, the apostolic call, and the divine *Heilsplan* in a vision of the council before God's throne rather like Isaiah in Isa 6.[27]

So, (1) the studies of Zimmerli/Wildberger and Baltzer/Stenger make it highly likely that Paul saw and narrated his Damascus Christophany vision in the form of Isaiah's theophany vision. Then, (2) the substantial parallelism between Isa 6 and Paul's reports of his Damascus experience, as shown above, must be taken as strongly suggesting that Isa 6 was actually one of the texts in the light of which he interpreted his Damascus experience. To these, now add (3) the fact noted above, that various scholars also see Isa 6:9-10 and 6:11-13 as reflected in the ideas in the "mystery" of Israel's hardening, of its limitedness in time, and of her eventual salvation, as I suggested.[28] Then, is it not reasonable to consider whether the "mystery" originated from Paul's interpretation of his Damascus Christophany in the light of Isa 6?

From Gal 1:15-16 (//Isa 49:1, 5, 6) and the subsequent verses (Gal 1:24// Isa 49:3; Gal 2:2//Isa 49:4; cf. also 2 Cor 4:4-6//Isa 42:6-7; 49:6),[29] it is well known that Paul interpreted his apostolic call at the Damascus Christophany in the light of Isa 49:1-6. This being so, the fact that the "mystery" is neatly explained in the combined light of Isa 49 and Isa 6[30] also does contribute to my thesis that Paul indeed interpreted his Damascus experience in the light of Isa

26. Stenger, "Biographisches," 136.

27. Kim, *Origin*, 94. Cf. Sandness, *Paul*, 59, 143-44. In connection with the uniquely Pauline title "image of God" for Christ, I worked out the thesis much more broadly — see my *Origin*, 205-56. It must be noted, however, that Stenger's strange contrast between the form of *Einsetzungsbericht* and Christophany and his attempt to see in Gal 1:15-16 only the former ("Biographisches," 138) are not justified.

28. T. L. Donaldson, " 'Riches for the Gentiles' (Rom 11:12): Israel's Rejection and Paul's Gentile Mission," *JBL* 112 (1993): 88 (n. 29), wonders "how the conception of the *failure* of the gospel within Israel could have made sense to the one who had been driven to zealous persecution of the Jewish church because of its *success*" (his emphasis). But (1) did Paul really persecute the Jewish church because of the *success* of her mission? (2) Even at the time of his Damascus experience, in view of his own hardening, Paul would have understood the hardening of Israel against the gospel only too well! Cf. Rom 10:2-4 with Phil 3:4-11, and cf. 2 Cor 3:12-18; also W. Grundmann, "Paulus, aus dem Volke Israel, Apostel der Völker," *NovT* 4 (1960): 268; B. Longenecker, "Different Answers to Different Issues: Israel, the Gentiles and Salvation History in Romans 9–11," *JSNT* 36 (1989): 100-101.

29. Most recently Sandness, *Paul*, 61-62, appealing, e.g., to L. Cerfaux, "Saint Paul et la 'Serviteur de Dieu' d'Isaie," *Recueil Lucien Cerfaux II* (Gembloux: Duculot, 1954), 439-54.

30. See pp. 241-42 above.

6 as well as Isa 49 and obtained the "mystery" thereby. Once Paul realized God's call and sending to the gentiles and God's *Heilsplan* about the temporary hardening of Israel and about the order of salvation (the gentiles first and Israel at the end), by interpreting his experience in the light of the call narratives of Isaiah (Isa 6) and the *Ebed* (Isa 49), he could have been drawn to the passages like Isa 45:14-17, 20-25, and 59:19-20 as well as Deut 32:21, seeing them confirm that understanding of God's *Heilsplan*.[31]

At this point, the autobiographical report by Josephus of a revelatory experience and its interpretation provides an illuminating illustration.[32] At Jotapata, Josephus received from God a revelation in dreams about the impending fate of the Jews and the future of the Roman emperors. But the words of God in the dreams remained ambiguous until Josephus interpreted them through meditation on the Scriptures. Upon interpretation of the divine will, Josephus became conscious of divine election and sending to announce the divine plan (*Bell.* 3.352-54).

Above we observed that had Paul obtained the "mystery" only through an exegesis of the Scriptures he would have referred to those Scriptures to substantiate it. In terms of my thesis, however, the absence of an explicit scriptural substantiation for the "mystery" proper is quite understandable. Paul did not explicitly refer to Isa 6 and 49 or any other passage to substantiate the "mystery" proper, because they were not the primary sources of the "mystery," but only confirmation of it which he had received through his special revelation. Josephus's neglect to refer to the Scriptures which had helped him for the interpretation of the divine revelation in dreams again illustrates the point here well.[33] But, for the inference from the "mystery" — the eventual salvation of all Israel, Paul provided a scriptural substantiation, precisely because he needed to show that it was the *right* inference, as well as because in the context the inference had to be strongly affirmed. However, Isa 6:11-13, taken alone, was less than transparent, and a citation of Isa 45:17, 25 would have had only the effect

31. Hübner, *Gottes Ich,* 127-29 also (1) recognizes the priority of the Damascus revelation and call, (2) agrees that from the beginning of his apostolic career Paul was convinced of his call to a gentile apostleship, and (3) grants that my attempt to explain the "mystery" in terms of Isa 6 is "äusserst erwägenswert." Yet Hübner rejects my thesis, pointing to 1 Thess 2:14-16 and also arguing that Paul could not have seen his call in the light of Isa 6 because there Isaiah was sent to Israel. On 1 Thess 2:14-16, see below. But apropos his second objection, couldn't Paul have overcome the problem by combining the relevant elements of Isa 6 and 49? Overall, given the above three factors, is it not more reasonable than "speculative" to posit a thesis like mine?

32. See Betz, *Jesus,* 100, for a parallelism between the conversion/call of Paul and that of Josephus.

33. Sandness, "Vision," 180-81, recognizes this, and yet, in a confusing manner, insists that Paul obtained the "mystery" only through a scriptural exegesis.

of confirming what was axiomatic in Judaism. So, in order to prove *how*, in spite of everything (Israel's hardening and God's apparent rejection), *God* will save them, beyond confirming the certainty of Israel's eventual salvation, Paul cited, instead, Isa 59:20-21 (Ps 14:7); 27:9; Jer 31:33-34, the texts which emphasize divine action in Israel's eventual salvation.

For an Early Dating

Now, even if it is granted in principle that Paul derived the "mystery" ultimately from an interpretation of his Damascus experience of divine revelation and call mainly in the light of Isa 6 and 49, it may be argued that the development took place rather late, in connection with his experiences of the actual missionary situation.

In fact, against my thesis, especially against my early dating of the "mystery," objections have been raised by some scholars on the basis of 1 Thess 2:14-16 and/or Rom 9:2-3; 10:1: the prophetic declaration about God's eschatological judgment upon Israel in 1 Thess 2:14-16 could not have been made, had Paul already known of God's *Heilsplan* as in the "mystery." So the latter must have been a development subsequent to the former.[34] Further, had he already known of the eventual salvation of Israel as in the "mystery," Paul's emotional prayer in Rom 9:2-3; 10:1 would be a "riddle."[35]

But if 1 Thess 2:14-16 is to be taken *in the sense of these critics,* then, it would indeed be a riddle why Paul made efforts to win the Jews (1 Cor 9:20; 2 Cor 11:24; Rom 11:13-14) and also why he prayed for them in Rom 9:2-3; 10:1. Would they not have been useless?[36] This consideration clearly suggests that 1 Thess 2:14-16 was not meant in so absolute a sense as the critics interpret and that it must be taken as a prophetic hyperbole.[37] On the other hand, if one becomes a little realistic, one would find no difficulty in understanding how even with a conviction about Israel's eventual salvation, Paul could have anxiously prayed for their salvation. Is it so strange for one to be convinced of God's deliverance and, at the same time, earnestly to pray for it? Is it not exactly in line with what Paul does with regard to his Philippian converts (Phil

---

34. Hübner, *Gottes Ich,* 129-30, citing Wilckens, *Römer (6–11),* 184-85.

35. Sandness, *Paul,* 180; Sänger, *Verkündigung,* 182.

36. See above, pp. 244-45, against the attempt to see Paul's prayer in Rom 9:2-3; 10:1 as his response to the prophetic pronouncement in 1 Thess 2:16 and the "mystery" of Rom 11:25-26 as divine answer to that prayer.

37. Cf. C. J. Schlueter, *Filling Up the Measure: Polemical Hyperbole in 1 Thessalonians 2:14-16* (Sheffield: JSOT, 1994).

1:6, 9-11)? Moreover, as the "mystery" meant God's judgment upon Israel and his rejection of them until the uncertain date when the "full number of the gentiles come in," Paul quite naturally would have had anguish about this most unexpected and shocking fate of his people. He would naturally have prayed and worked anxiously for salvation of "some" of them now (Rom 11:13-14) and for that of "all Israel" at the end, through his gentile mission. This would be a "riddle" only to those who are so unrealistically rationalistic.

So since 1 Thess 2:14-16 does not stand in the way of an early dating of the "mystery," I would like to make several considerations in justification of it. (1) First is the fact that in Gal 1–2 Paul emphasizes the *Zuständigkeitsbereich* of his apostolic call to have been the gentiles "without even a glance at the Jews"[38] and elsewhere also consistently defines his apostleship in terms of the gentiles: Rom 1:5; 11:13; 15:15-16; 2 Cor 10:13; Col 1:24-29; Eph 3:7-9; 1 Thess 2:16.

J. D. G. Dunn properly appreciates its significance:

[The sending to the gentiles] was clearly integral to Paul's sense of apostleship . . . and cannot be separated from it. . . . According to Paul, this was his conviction *from the start.* . . . Indeed . . . this was for Paul the main point of and *reason for* the revelation of Christ to him — "in order that I might preach him among the gentiles."[39]

---

38. Sandness, *Paul*, 65.

39. James D. G. Dunn, *The Epistle to the Galatians* (Peabody: Hendrickson, 1993), 66 (his emphasis). He states this view even more strongly in his " 'A Light to the Gentiles,' or 'The End of the Law'? The Significance of the Damascus Road Christophany to Paul," in *Jesus, Paul and the Law* (London: SCM, 1990), 89-107. However, it is astonishing that Dunn denies that in Gal 1–2 Paul testifies to the immediacy of the revelation of the *gospel* as well as that of the call to gentile apostleship at the Damascus christophany. Actually in Gal 1–2 Paul's primary concern is to defend his *gospel*, his law-free gospel which has come into trouble in Galatia at the moment, by appealing, above all, to its divine revelation on the Damascus road (ἀποκάλυψις in Gal 1.12, 16!), and he mentions his apostolic call to the gentiles along with the revelation of the gospel only because it is inseparable from the latter (cf. my *Origin*, 68-69; B. Lategan, "Is Paul Defending His Apostleship in Galatians?" *NTS* 34 [1988]: 411-30). Fortunately, in his essay "The Relationship between Paul and Jerusalem according to Galatians 1 and 2," which immediately follows the essay "Light" in his volume (pp. 108-29), Dunn appropriately speaks of the Damascus event in terms both of revelation of the gospel and of the apostolic call (see, e.g., p. 118), and by doing so, he at least implicitly turns against his own attempt to separate the two elements of the Damascus event and play one off against the other. This is no occasion to make a comprehensive response to Dunn's critique of my *Origin* in his essay "Light," 93-100 (see ch. 1 in this volume). While appreciating some helpful remarks of his, however, I am not persuaded by much of his argument, especially when he fails to take evidence fairly. In connection with the εἰκών-christology, readers will have to judge whether his critique of my thesis is justified (see ch. 5 in this volume). Here I would only like to point out that his argument for the presence of only

(2) Note again how Paul connects his apostleship with a "mystery": 1 Cor 1:17 + 2:6-10 + 4:1; Col 1:23-29; Eph 3:1-13, in the latter two of which the "mystery" clearly concerns God's saving plan for the gentiles and so is materially connected with the "mystery" of Rom 11:25, as we have seen.[40]

(3) Note the passionate nature of the language Paul employs for his apostleship: he is not just "enlisted" (κατελήμφθην) by Christ into his service, but he is a "debtor" (ὀφειλέτης) to all the gentiles (Rom 1:14) and so "a fateful necessity" (ἀνάγκη) is laid upon him to preach the gospel (1 Cor 9:16): Since God saved and called Paul, an "enemy" of God (cf. Rom 5:10; 2 Cor 5:16-21), "in order that [he] might preach the gospel to the gentiles" (Gal 1:16), to some extent Paul owes his salvation as well as his apostolic call to the gentiles. So it is a fateful necessity for him to preach the gospel to them, and by preaching to them he shares in salvation together with those who come to salvation through his preaching (1 Cor 9:23).[41] The gentile world is "the sphere of service [τὸ μέτρον τοῦ κανόνος] which God assigned [ἐμέρισεν] to [Paul] as [his] sphere [μέτρου]" (2 Cor 10:13).[42]

Should we not take this "fate/lot" language Paul uses for his gentile apostleship as an indication of its association with the fateful event on the Damascus road?[43] Is it credible that such apostolic self-consciousness developed slowly over a long period of time? Is it easier to imagine that Paul began to reflect on the soul-shattering experience of the Damascus Christophany in the light of the Old Testament accounts of prophetic calls immediately or only years later?

(4) As observed above, there is little evidence for a period in which Paul worked among the Jews at least as much as among the gentiles. From all the

---

the Adam-motif in 2 Cor 4:4, 6, consistent as it is with his argument for taking the evidence of Gal 1–2 only for the Damascus origin of Paul's gentile apostleship (cf. pp. 97-98), is just as one-sided as the latter. In fact, his argument represents a failure to understand Paul's emphasis in both places. For, while in 2 Cor 3:18; 4:4, 6 both the Adam-motif and the Wisdom-motif are present, the revelational language of 2 Cor 4:4, 6 clearly indicates that the latter is the primary concern of the two in 2 Cor 4:4, 6 (cf. my *Origin*, 267), just as in Gal 1–2, while the Damascus origin of both Paul's gospel and gentile apostleship is testified to, the former is the primary concern of the two.

40. Dunn, "Light," 90, also connects the μυστήριον motif of Rom 11:25; 16:25-26; Col 1:26-27; and Eph 3:1-13 with Paul's Damascus experience of divine ἀποκάλυψις and call (Gal 1:12, 15), although in his *Romans 9–16*, 678-79, he forgets this completely. See above, n. 20.

41. See Kim, *Origin*, 288-96.

42. Rendering of R. P. Martin, *2 Corinthians* (Waco: Word, 1986), 351-52. In view of his association of μερίζειν and καλεῖν in 1 Cor 7:17-20, here Paul seems to have in view God's allotment of gentile apostleship to him at his Damascus call which was confirmed at the apostolic conference of Jerusalem in Gal 2:7. So F. Lang, *Die Briefe an die Korinther* (Göttingen: Vandenhoeck, 1986), 333.

43. Cf. J. C. Beker, *Paul the Apostle* (Philadelphia: Fortress, 1980), 7.

available data, on the contrary, one could even speak of Paul systematically avoiding Jerusalem and Judea while concentrating on the mainly gentile world.[44] How could he, a former "zealous" Pharisee, do this?

(5) If the πεπληρωκέναι in Rom 15:19 is connected with the πλήρωμα of Rom 11:25,[45] it implies that Paul carried out his missionary work from Jerusalem to Illyricum in accordance with the "mystery" from early on, in the hope of offering up the "full number of the gentiles" as the προσφορὰ τῶν ἐθνῶν (Rom 15:16), so that there may also be an "offering" of all Israel (cf. Isa 66:19-20).[46]

May we not take these five points as suggesting a high probability (1) that soon after his Damascus experience he was aware of God's call to gentile apostleship and (2) that concurrently with that self-consciousness he developed an understanding of God's *Heilsplan* as involving the salvation of the gentiles first, by reflecting on the Damascus revelation and call in the light of the Old Testament accounts of prophetic revelations and calls?

Paul's Visit with Peter the *Terminus ad Quem?*

But then how soon after the Damascus revelation and call could Paul have obtained the "mystery"? Would it be possible to set a *terminus ad quem* for the development of the "mystery"? Recently, improving upon the original view of E. Dinkler,[47] G. Lüdemann and A. Schmidt have made an interesting suggestion that Gal 2:7-8 represents an agreement Paul reached with Peter *on his first Jerusalem visit* (Gal 1:18) and Gal 2:9 an official resolution (an endorsement of the former) at the apostolic council on his second Jerusalem visit.[48]

This hypothesis may be supported through several considerations. (1) If

44. See above, pp. 245-46. In Rom 15:19, he indeed refers to his mission in Jerusalem, but it is doubtful whether Paul had in mind anything more than the occasional preachings he must have done during his visits in the city (Gal 1:18; 2:1-10).

45. So P. Stuhlmacher, "Erwägungen zum Problem von Gegenwart und Zukunft in der paulinischen Eschatologie," *ZThK* 64 (1967): 430-31; Dunn, *Romans 9–16*, 864.

46. Cf. Riesner, *Frühzeit*, 219.

47. *Signum Crucis* (Tübingen: Mohr-Siebeck, 1967), 278-82.

48. Lüdemann, *Paulus*, 91-96; Schmidt, "Das Missionsdekret in Galater 2.7-8 als Vereinbarung vom ersten Besuch Pauli in Jerusalem," *NTS* 38 (1992): 149-52. Their suggestions are based chiefly on the differences between vv. 7-8 and v. 9: (1) whereas in vv. 7-8 only Peter and Paul are mentioned as representing the mission to the Jews and that to the gentiles respectively, in v. 9 "James, Cephas and John" on the one hand and Paul and Barnabas on the other hand are mentioned as representing the two branches of mission respectively. (2) Whereas in vv. 7-8 the name Πέτρος is used, in v. 9 Κηφᾶς is used.

the agreement of vv. 7-8 was reached at Paul's second visit to Jerusalem (Gal 2:1), it would have been "fourteen" or seventeen ("three" plus "fourteen") years since his Damascus call (ca. A.D. 32) and so some time between A.D. 45 and 48. If R. Riesner is to be followed in dating Peter's departure from Jerusalem in the wake of the persecution by Herod Agrippa I in A.D. 41 (or at the latest 42), it was then at least a few years after the departure.[49] Finding the causes for Herod's persecution in the first steps taken by the church or at least a wing of it represented by Peter and the Zebedaic James for gentile mission and in Herod Agrippa's desire to impress the zealotically inclined Jews, Riesner says:

> When now Peter as the leader of the Twelve left . . . the holy land . . . , it marked a clear interruption in the work for Israel. The neglect of making up the circle of the Twelve [filling James' place — contrast Acts 1:15-26] suggests the consciousness of living in a new era in which the missionary struggle for the old people of God in Jerusalem and the holy land was no longer the sole task.[50]

If so, the question is whether even a few years after that point Peter's commission for the Jewish mission with the "gospel for the circumcision" would still be so emphasized as in Gal 2:7. Would it not have been more natural if it was affirmed in the 30s (ca. A.D. 34 — Gal 1:18) while Peter was still active in the Jewish mission in Jerusalem? Further, is it at all easy to imagine that in the situation where the Jerusalem church and the Jewish mission had been led by James for some time[51] Peter could be singled out as the unique representative of the Jewish mission as in Gal 2:7-8?

(2) N. Walter explains that in view of the context of Gal 1:16 and 2:2 the phrase ἱστορῆσαι Κηφᾶν in Gal 1:18 should be taken in the sense that Paul wanted "to discover the view of Cephas" or "to take counsel with Cephas on the question" about his gentile mission.[52] This helpful explanation supports Lüdemann's linking the phrase ἱστορῆσαι Κηφᾶν with the agreement in Gal 2:7-8.[53]

(3) This seems to be confirmed by the parallelisms between Gal 1:12, 15-16 and 2:7-9a and between Gal 1:12, 15-16 and Matt 16:16-20. In Gal 2:7-9a, the construction ἐνήργησεν . . . εἰς, the phrase τὴν χάριν τὴν δοθεῖσάν μοι (cf.

---

49. Riesner, *Frühzeit*, 105-8.

50. Ibid., 104-10, quotation from 107-8. Similarly already F. F. Bruce, *Paul the Apostle of the Heart Set Free* (Grand Rapids: Eerdmans, 1977), 174.

51. This is correctly reflected in the list with James at the head in Gal 2:9.

52. N. Walter, "Paul and the Early Christian Jesus-Tradition," in *Paul and Jesus* (ed. A. J. M. Wedderburn and C. Wolff; Sheffield: JSOT, 1989), 65-66.

53. Lüdemann, *Paulus*, 93.

Rom 12:3; 15:15; 1 Cor 3:10; Eph 3:2, 7, 8), and the close parallelism between the passage and Gal 1:12, 15-16[54] clearly indicate that Paul has his Damascus call in view.[55] This means that he draws out an exact parallelism between his Damascus commission and Peter's commission. Then, it is interesting to observe another close parallelism between Gal 1:12, 15-16 and Matt 16:16-20.[56] It seems to suggest that Paul saw and narrated his Damascus call in conscious parallelism to that of Peter at Caesarea Philippi. Where and when would Paul, then, have learnt the tradition of Peter's commission to draw the parallelism between it and his own commission? Is there a better candidate for this than the fortnight visit which Paul paid to Peter "to get to know/to consult Cephas" (Gal 1:18)? If so, it requires only a little imagination to think that on that occasion they could have come to confirm the similarity of their commission experiences and so to agree on the mutual recognition of each other's commission along the lines suggested in Gal 2:7-8.[57]

Then, at the apostolic conference during Paul's second visit to Jerusalem (Gal 2:2), the representatives of the Jerusalem church may have officially endorsed the agreement between Paul and Peter, making especially a point implicit in it, namely, the division of mission field, a contractual agreement be-

---

54. πεπίστευμαι τὸ εὐαγγέλιον τῆς ἀκροβυστίας (2:7)
τὴν χάριν τὴν δοθεῖσάν μοι (2:9)
ὁ . . . ἐνεργήσας Πέτρῳ . . . ἐνήργησεν καὶ ἐμοί (2:8)

ἵνα εὐαγγελίζωμαι αὐτὸν ἐν τοῖς ἔθνεσιν (1:16)
καὶ καλέσας διὰ τῆς χάριτος αὐτοῦ (1:15)
ὁ ἀφορίσας με . . . καὶ καλέσας (1:15)

Cf. Stenger, "Biographisches," 130.

55. Kim, *Origin*, 25-27.

56. See the parallelism chart in D. Wenham, "Paul's Use of the Jesus Tradition," in *Gospel Perspectives* 5 (ed. D. Wenham; Sheffield: JSOT, 1989), 26-27; cf. also Riesner, *Frühzeit*, 212-13.

57. As D. Wenham, *Paul: Follower of Jesus or Founder of Christianity?* (Grand Rapids: Eerdmans, 1995), 202-3, suggests, the unusual Greek designation Πέτρος in Gal 2:7-8 instead of Paul's usual Aramaic designation Κηφᾶς may represent Paul's desire to remind his Greek readers of Jesus' wordplay on "rock" in Matt 16:18. If so, it is an evidence that in Gal 2:7-8 Paul has the tradition in Matt 16:16-20 in mind. This would then strengthen the attempt to see in Gal 1:15-16 an allusion to the tradition in Matt 16:16-20 and also to see the agreement in Gal 2:7-8 as reached during Paul's private fellowship with Peter. Apparently during this time Peter and Paul agreed that they both had the "rock" position for the Jewish and the gentile mission respectively. With the exact parallelism between Peter's commission and his own and with Πέτρος in Gal 2:7-8, Paul tries to remind his Greek readers of this fact. Cf. A. Oepke, *Galatians* (5th ed.; ed. J. Rohde; Berlin: Evangelisches, 1984), 81, against the attempt to see in the absence of the title "apostle" with regard to Paul in Gal 2:8 a significance more than a grammatical nicety. Further, if the original agreement had really lent itself to construing as a denial of apostleship to Paul, how could he cite it here when it would only have nullified his whole argument in Gal 1–2? Would he not have cited it with ἀπόστολος prominently inserted?

tween themselves on the one hand and Paul and Barnabas on the other (Gal 2:7-9). Paul may have just hinted at his agreement with Peter in Gal 1:18 with the phrase ἱστορῆσαι Κηφᾶν, postponing an explicit reference to its content to the context of Gal 2:1-9 for the following reasons: (a) he was shy of making an explicit reference to it in Gal 1:18, immediately after his strong assertion that he did not consult any "flesh and blood" or the Jerusalem apostles (Gal 1:16-17); (b) since it was discussed and endorsed at the later apostolic conference, he had to refer to it in the context of Gal 2:1-9 anyway; and (c) moreover, mentioning it in the context of the more official apostolic conference rather than in that of a private fellowship with Peter gave Paul an advantage of emphasizing that his independent gospel and apostleship were nevertheless recognized *officially* by the "pillars" of the Jerusalem church.

If our argument so far is sound, then Gal 2:7-8 reflects the agreement reached between Paul and Peter about A.D. 34/35. The agreement was not the starting-point of Paul's gentile mission. It was rather a confirmation of his self-understanding as the gentiles' apostle and of his gentile mission up to that point. Nevertheless, it clearly marked a decisive point in his career as the gentiles' apostle, and this may be reflected in the tradition of Acts 22:17-21.[58]

Now it must be noted that the agreement between Paul and Peter contained an element in which they agreed to differ: Peter was for Jewish mission but Paul was for gentile mission. What might have been involved in the discussion leading up to it? Surely their understandings of divine *Heilsplan* must have been an element involved. Then, Paul must have had a conviction different from the usual view of divine *Heilsplan* and must have presented an argument worthy of a serious consideration even for Peter to consent for his gentile mission now, instead of urging him to join in his and the other apostles' Jewish mission. Doesn't this consideration suggest that at least by this time Paul must have had an understanding of divine *Heilsplan* as represented in the "mystery"? It was one thing for Paul to make Peter nod at the plausibility of his understanding, but quite another to persuade him to abandon his own view strongly supported by tradition and by the majority of the church and adopt Paul's novel view. Hence, they just agreed to respect each other's conviction.

58. Cf. Betz, "Vision"; Riesner, *Frühzeit*, 234.

256

Conclusion

Thus it seems reasonable to suppose that *by about* A.D. *34/35 Paul had the "mystery" of Rom 11:25-26 as his conviction of divine* Heilsplan *and began to design his apostolic mission in accordance with it.* Just as Paul's agreement with Peter on his personal visit with him was not the starting point but rather a confirmation of his gentile mission up to that moment, so was it not the birthday but rather a confirmation of the "mystery." Probably we are to suppose that soon after his Damascus experience of divine revelation and call Paul searched the Scriptures (esp. Isa 6 and 49; but also Isa 45:14-25; 59:19-20; Deut 32:21; etc.) to interpret the most unexpected revelation and call and came to an understanding of divine *Heilsplan* as embodied in the "mystery." His experience of a favorable acceptance among the gentiles but resistance among the Jews in his actual mission field confirmed it. So, he went to Peter of whose call to the "rock" position within the church he had probably heard, discussed with him his experience of divine revelation (the gospel and the *Heilsplan*) and of divine call for the gentile apostleship, and obtained Peter's consent to his interpretation of that divine revelation and call.[59]

---

59. If Peter consented to Paul's gospel, his understanding of the divine *Heilsplan,* and his gentile apostleship at their fortnight meeting, he may have done so recalling Jesus' welcome of the outcasts, his disregard of some aspects of the law, and his words like Matt 8:11-12/Luke 13:28-29 and Luke 21:23-24. Such Jesus traditions as these would have made Paul further convinced of his understanding of the divine *Heilsplan* embodied in the "mystery" as well as of his gospel and gentile apostleship which he had developed by interpreting the Damascus revelation and call in the light of the Scriptures. So we may see in the "mystery" also an interplay of the Damascus revelation, the Scriptures, and the Jesus tradition.

CHAPTER 8

The Jesus Tradition in Paul

When one moves from the Gospels to the Pauline letters one is immediately struck by the virtual absence of quotations of sayings of Jesus. While Paul makes Jesus Christ and his work of salvation the center of his preaching, he hardly ever quotes actual sayings of this Jesus or refers to his deeds, except to his death and resurrection. In his paraenesis, or teaching, he gives instructions similar to those of Jesus, and yet he seldom cites the latter. There may be some references to or echoes of Jesus' sayings in the Pauline letters, but they are very allusive, a phenomenon which raises the question of a proper criterion for correctly discerning them. In any case, these allusions do not seem to be numerous. This state of affairs is puzzling when contrasted with the often observed continuity in theology and attitude between Jesus and Paul. This paucity and allusive character of Paul's references to sayings of Jesus has led some critics to conclude that Paul did not know much of Jesus tradition or that he was not at all interested in the tradition or in the historical Jesus. So our topic constitutes a central element in the "Jesus-Paul debate."

Certain or Probable References

There are six explicit references to "words of the Lord" in Paul's letters: 1 Cor 7:10-11; 9:14; 11:23-25; 14:37; 2 Cor 12:9; 1 Thess 4:15-17. Among them 2 Cor 12:9 obviously refers to the word of the risen Lord, and the "command of the

This chapter originally appeared in 1993 as an article entitled "Jesus, Sayings of," in the *Dictionary of Paul and His Letters,* ed. Gerald F. Hawthorne, Ralph P. Martin, and Daniel G. Reid. It is reprinted here by permission of InterVarsity Press, P.O. Box 1400, Downers Grove, IL 60515. www.ivpress.com

Lord" in 1 Cor 14:37 is probably a "prophetic" teaching of Paul who has "the mind of Christ" (1 Cor 2:16). The "minimalists" who allow a minimum number of references, allusions, or echoes of the sayings of Jesus in Paul deny a reference to the historical Jesus in 1 Thess 4:15-17, understanding the phrase "in the word of the Lord" exclusively in terms of the Old Testament idiom which the prophets used in order to indicate in whose commission and authority they spoke. They discount also 1 Cor 11:23-25, arguing that Paul received and transmitted it as a liturgical tradition. So, for the "minimalists" like F. Neirynck and N. Walter, there are only two explicit references to sayings of Jesus in Paul.

(1) 1 Corinthians 7:10-11

In 1 Cor 7:10-11 Paul cites the "command" of the Lord, emphasizing that it is the Lord's and not his own. It is fairly clear that it is a reformulation of Jesus' teaching on divorce preserved in Mark 10:9-12 (par. Matt 19:6, 9); Matt 5:32 (par. Luke 16:18). The parenthetical remark in 1 Cor 7:11a is often thought to be Paul's "free" modification of Jesus' teaching. But it is more a faithful representation of Jesus' teaching in Mark 10:11 (cf. Matt 19:9) than a "free modification" of it. As D. Wenham has shown, there are two indications that Paul knew Jesus' teaching on divorce in its Synoptic context: (1) In Matt 19 (par. Mark 10) Jesus bases his teaching on the "one flesh" principle drawn from Gen 2:24, and precisely this principle is used by Paul in the passage immediately preceding his teaching on marriage and divorce (1 Cor 6:12-20), for his teaching that a Christian, being a member of the body of Christ, cannot join himself to a prostitute; and (2) in Matt 19 Jesus' teaching on divorce is followed by his sayings about those who are eunuchs for the kingdom of God (Matt 19:10-12). These latter sayings are often seen to be echoed in 1 Cor 7:7, 32-35 in Paul's teaching on celibacy as a special gift from God for more effective service of the Lord. Thus it seems that Paul knew not just an isolated saying of Jesus on divorce but rather his teaching on marriage as a whole, including its "one flesh" principle and its relationship to the service of the kingdom of God.

(2) 1 Corinthians 9:14

In 1 Cor 9:14 Paul also cites a "command" of the Lord, in this case "for those who preach the gospel to get their living from the gospel." Again, this is a faithful representation of Jesus' saying in Luke 10:7 (par. Matt 10:10), though not a verbatim quotation of it. D. L Dungan has shown that just as in 1 Cor 7 Paul reflects his knowledge both of Jesus' divorce saying and of its interpretation in the tradition behind the Synoptics, so also in 1 Cor 9 he reflects his knowledge both of Jesus' missionary charge itself and its interpretation in the Q tradition. However, Paul's practice of forgoing the apostolic right tends to be viewed by some critics as if it reflected his freedom from Jesus' command or evidenced his disregard for Jesus' sayings in general. But surely Jesus' "command" in this case was intended as a "permission" from the beginning, so that Paul's failure to avail himself of it is hardly a "disobedience" to it (Bruce, 107-8). In fact, Jesus' intention in the "command" was probably for the effective preaching of the gospel. The apostles might concentrate on preaching the gospel without having to divert themselves to securing their living. In that case Paul's refusal to avail himself of the privilege "in order not to burden" any of his churches, but to preach the gospel more effectively, causing no worldly misunderstanding in the Hellenistic cities where wandering Cynics peddled their doctrines (1 Thess 2:1-12; 1 Cor 9), is paradoxically a real obedience to his Lord Jesus. Clearly Paul sought to obey the "spirit" of Jesus' teaching rather than its letter.

(3) 1 Corinthians 11:23-25

The fact that 1 Cor 11:23-25 is a liturgical tradition does not necessarily mean that Paul is unconscious of his transmitting actual sayings of Jesus, or that it is no indication of Paul's interest in the sayings of Jesus. On the contrary, the concrete reference to "the night" and the use of the word *paradidosthai* ("to be delivered up"), which is so characteristic of Jesus' passion announcements (Mark 9:31 par.; Mark 10:33 par.; Mark 14:18; Matt 26:21; John 13:21; Mark 14:21 par.) and so prominent in the Synoptic passion narratives, could hardly have failed to make Paul conscious of the historical reality of the event of the Last Supper and of the words spoken by the man who was to be delivered up and crucified. If nothing else, then, at least the word "Do this in remembrance of me" (1 Cor 11:25) must have reminded Paul of the importance of remembering those sayings of Jesus as well as his acts.

(4) 1 Thessalonians 4:15-17

Concerning 1 Thess 4:15-17, the Old Testament prophetic idiom of "in the word of the Lord" is now widely recognized. It has been noted that there is a

261

substantial similarity between 1 Thess 4:15-17 and 1 Cor 15:51-52, and that in the latter Paul speaks of a "mystery," a revelation by the risen Lord. However, there is also a wide recognition of an echo here of Jesus' eschatological saying in Matt 24:30-31 and parallels. In addition D. Wenham sees here several echoes of the parable of virgins (Matt 25:1-13, e.g.: "with him/the Lord" in 1 Thess 4:14, 17 and the "shout of command"/the "voice of the archangel" in 1 Thess 4:16 are matched by "with him" in Matt 25:10 and the "cry" in Matt 25:6 respectively, and the phrase *eis apantēsin,* "to meet," appears both in 1 Thess 4:17 and Matt 25:6). Recently R. H. Gundry has argued that in 1 Thess 4:15-17 Paul is drawing on Jesus' saying (whose original form may have been: "The one who has died will rise, and the one who is alive will never die") embedded in John 11:25-26 and that, prompted by the pre-Johannine tradition of the raising of Lazarus (cf. John 12:13-18) and intending to console the grief-stricken Thessalonians more effectively, Paul portrays the future coming of the Lord and the believers' meeting him in terms of the imperial visit *(parousia)* and the citizens' going out to meet the approaching emperor *(apantēsis)* in the Hellenistic world. In view of the undeniable echoes of various sayings of Jesus here, P. Stuhlmacher thinks that Paul is presenting his own prophetic reapplication of Synoptic tradition. However, in arguing that it is uncertain whether Paul is conscious of applying Jesus-tradition, N. Walter suggests that 1 Thess 4:15-17 should be regarded merely as containing Christian insights (Walter, 66). But the several and clear echoes of Jesus' sayings in the passage seem to suggest that Paul must be conscious of the material he is using as Jesus material and therefore that with "the word of the Lord" here Paul is referring to the word(s) of the historical Jesus he is using (cf. Wenham; Gundry; Holtz), rather than a prophetic oracle spoken in the name of the Lord.

(5) 1 Thessalonians 5:1-7

The formulation "You yourselves know accurately . . ." *(autoi . . . akribōs oidate . . .)* in 1 Thess 5:2 may also be an indication that allusions to Jesus' sayings are to be found in 1 Thess 5:1-7. It is widely recognized that verses 2 and 4 echo Jesus' parable of the thief (Matt 24:43 par. Luke 12:39), especially as the metaphor of thief is not applied in an eschatological context in the Old Testament and Jewish literature. Then, as Wenham has shown, there is a close parallelism in vocabulary, structure, and meaning between 1 Thess 5:3 and Luke 21:34-35.

1 Thessalonians 5:3:
"come upon them suddenly as birthpangs . . . escape"
(aiphnidios autois ephistatai . . . hōsper hē ōdin . . . ekphygōsin)

Luke 21:34-36:
"come upon you suddenly as snare . . . escape
(epistē eph' hymas aiphnidios . . . hōs pagis . . . ekphygein)

(*Pagis* ["snare"] and *ōdin* ["birthpangs"] may be translation variants of an original *ḥbl/ḥbl'*, caused by different pointings of the word or, as Wenham argues, the original *pagis* may have been replaced by Paul with *ōdin* under the influence of Isa 13:6-7 and Jer 6:14-21.) Paul's exhortation in the 1 Thessalonians passage to be awake and sober, not asleep nor drunk, represents the general tenor of Matt 24:42-51 (par. Luke 12:41-46) and Luke 21:34-36 (par. Mark 13:33-37).

In view of these clear echoes of Jesus' eschatological sayings, how are we to understand the introductory formula "you yourselves know accurately . . ."? With that unusual introductory formula Paul cannot possibly refer so simply to anything that was taught by anybody other than himself and his coworkers, even if there had been such an occurrence within the short interval between his founding the church at Thessalonica and his writing of 1 Thessalonians. Nor can he refer to what was simply his own teaching based on the Old Testament-Jewish tradition. For what the Thessalonians are supposed to "know accurately" in 1 Thess 5:2-10 has already been shown, in part, according to the criteria of dissimilarity and coherence, to contain clear echoes of Jesus' sayings. Nor can he refer to his teaching that was based simply on a common Christian tradition, without any consciousness of the teachings of Jesus himself. Some of the parallels between our passage and the dominical sayings recorded in the Gospels seem too striking for that to be correct. It also is hard to believe that Paul was unaware that the Christian tradition was based on Jesus' own teachings, especially in view of the presence of Silvanus, who surely bore tradition from Jerusalem and was with Paul both at the time of founding the church and of writing 1 Thessalonians.

It may be helpful to compare our passage with 1 Thess 4:2 ("For you know what instructions we gave you through the Lord Jesus"). Here the phrase "through the Lord Jesus" *(dia kyriou Iēsou)* may in itself refer to the origin or inspiration of the instructions. What the Thessalonians are supposed to "know accurately" (1 Thess 5:2) is probably part of the "instructions" Paul gave them *dia kyriou Iēsou*. In giving them that instruction *dia kyriou Iēsou*, was Paul conscious only of being inspired by the Lord Jesus, or was he conscious also of it originating from the actual teaching of the Lord

Jesus recorded in the tradition? The clear echoes of Jesus' sayings in 1 Thess 5:2-7 suggest the latter as the more likely case. Paul must have given at least this part of the instruction on the basis of the actual sayings of Jesus, even if he interpreted and adapted them as one standing under the inspiration of the Lord.

The conclusion seems unavoidable: with the introductory formula "you yourselves know accurately . . .," Paul is trying to remind the Thessalonians of the teaching that he delivered to them at the time of founding their church (cf. 2 Thess 2:15; 3:6) on the basis of Jesus' eschatological sayings.

This further strengthens our previous conclusion with regard to the formula "in the word of the Lord" (1 Thess 4:15). For by way of an analogy it points to the following conclusion: just as Paul based the instruction now recalled in 1 Thess 5:2-7 ("through the Lord Jesus") on Jesus' teaching, recognized by its many echoes of that teaching, so also in giving a new instruction in 1 Thess 4:13-18 on the fate of the Christian dead "in the word of the Lord," he bases it on Jesus' teaching so that it too contains many echoes of that teaching.

So the formulas "in the word of the Lord" and "you yourselves know accurately . . .," which follow each other so closely in the wake of Paul's reminder of his previous instructions "through the Lord Jesus" (1 Thess 4:2), both indicate that in 1 Thess 4:15–5:7 Paul is alluding to the eschatological teachings of Jesus.

(6) Romans 14:14

There is a general consensus that Rom 14:14a ("I know and am convinced by the Lord Jesus that nothing is unclean in itself") is an allusion to a saying of Jesus recorded in Mark 7:15 (par. Matt 15:11) and that Rom 14:20 ("all [foods] are clean") corresponds to the editorial remark of Mark ("he declared all foods clean," Mark 7:19). Between Rom 14:14a and Mark 7:15 there is not only an exact material correspondence, but also a verbal agreement: *ouden koinon/ouden . . . koinōsai*. For this reason some think that with the phrase "by the Lord Jesus" Paul refers to the historical Jesus and seeks to indicate that he is alluding to Jesus' teaching. However, others think that in Rom 14:14a, 20 Paul is giving a general Christian maxim or an insight from his gospel (cf. 1 Cor 6:13; 8:8a), and that the phrase "by the Lord Jesus" is not necessarily a reference to the historical Jesus (cf. Phil 2:19).

This negative judgment is supported by the recent argument of H. Räisänen that Paul's failure to refer to the logion of Mark 7:15 in his controversy with Peter at Antioch (Gal 2:11-21) and Luke's failure to refer to it in Acts 10–11; 15:7-9 indicate that Mark 7:15 is inauthentic. But this argument has justly been rejected by H. Merkel and M. Thompson (see below). Furthermore, Thompson appropriately asks how it is possible for Paul simply to declare "Nothing is unclean in itself" and "All [foods] are clean" to an unknown church containing a number of Jewish Christians, to whom he is concerned to show that he is upholding the Law (Rom 7:12) and whose support he is soliciting for his mission to Spain. Unless he knows that a teaching like Mark 7:15 has already been delivered to the church he is treading on dangerous ground. Given the apparent dispute between the "strong" and the "weak" in the Roman church, it would hardly do for Paul to utter a mere declaration without any accompanying theological justification of what would be taken as simply a corollary of his (disputed) gospel or an opinion ("maxim") of a certain party. So with the phrase "by the Lord Jesus" in Rom 14:14a Paul seems to be alluding to a saying of Jesus (Mark 7:15 par.) in the hope that the Romans would recognize its authority.

(7) Romans 12:14-21 and 1 Corinthians 4:11-13

There is broad agreement that in Rom 12:14-21 and 1 Cor 4:11-13 there are a number of clear echoes of the sayings of Jesus. Even N. Walter, a "minimalist," grants this and notes particularly the following sets of correspondences:

Rom 12:14	Luke 6:28a (Matt 5:44b)
Rom 12:17a (1 Thess 5:15a)	Luke 6:29 par. Matt 5:39b-41
Rom 12:18	Mark 9:50 par. Matt 5:9
Rom 12:19-21	Luke 6:27a + 35 par. Matt 5:44a
1 Cor 4:11a	Luke 6:21a par. Matt 5:6; 10:9-10; 11:19
1 Cor 4:12b-13	Luke 6:22-23 par. Matt 5:11-12;
	Luke 6:27-28 (Matt 5:44)

Of course, there are some who doubt one or another of these sets. But there is virtual consensus that Rom 12:14 echoes Matt 5:44 (par. Luke 6:27-28). J. Piper's conclusion on the basis of the criterion of dissimilarity is entirely convincing: "There need be no doubt that Jesus commanded 'Love your enemies,' . . . we found nothing so explicit and unequivocal in our survey of Jesus' environment; nor is it thinkable that the early church should invent the saying and thus impose upon themselves such a troublesome requirement" (Piper, 56). So Thompson considers Rom 12:14 to be "a virtually certain echo" or "possibly even an allusion" to a teaching of Jesus. Related to this observation is the often observed fact that the series of Paul's exhortations in Rom 12:14-21 is matched by a series of Jesus' sayings that appear in the central section of Luke's Sermon on the Plain (Allison) or Matthew's Sermon on the Mount (Wenham). This provides a strong argument for the view that the Pauline exhortations as a whole are echoes of those sayings of Jesus and therefore that the similar autobiographical remarks in 1 Cor 4:11-13 also are echoes of them (Walter; Thompson).

Granting all these points, however, Walter thinks that the question might be left open as to "whether Paul, in using these sayings, did so in the consciousness that these were sayings *of Jesus*" (Walter, 56). He maintains there is no indication that Paul considered them as sayings of Jesus but, of course, neither can he give any evidence that Paul did *not* so regard them. Some have seen the imperative *eulogeite* ("bless," Rom 12:14) in a section where Paul otherwise gives his exhortations mostly using participles, infinitives or adjectives in verbless clauses, as evidence of Paul's using Jesus' saying without adapting it to the grammatical style of the context. Having represented a saying of Jesus by "bless *[eulogeite]* those who persecute [you]" (cf. Matt 5:44), Paul may be adding "bless *[eulogeite]* and do not curse [them]," repeating the word *eulogeite* because the use of *eulogeite* in Rom 12:14a "has instantly recalled a more familiar logion" recorded in Luke 6:28. If so, the repetition of *eulogeite* may be an indicator that here Paul deliberately alludes to a saying of Jesus (Thompson). However, whether or not Paul was conscious of the echoes of Jesus' sayings will have to be decided after examining all those passages and considering a number of other factors.

(8) Romans 13:8-10 and Galatians 5:14

The majority of scholars also see in Rom 13:8-10 and Gal 5:14 echoes of Jesus' sayings, especially that of Mark 12:28-34 and parallels. Thompson observes them well, and in the following we give a summary of his observations (with our supplement starting with point 5).

(1) Paul's linking of love and "debt" in Rom 13:8a may reflect Jesus' teaching represented, for example, in his parables of the unforgiving servant (Matt 18:23-35) and of the debtor (Luke 7:36-50) as well as his sayings like Luke 6:36; Matt 6:12, and so on (cf. Rom 15:1-3; Col 3:13): the recipient of love from God owes a debt of love to others.

(2) The article *to* introducing "love one another" in Rom 13:8a indicates it to be "the well-known command" that the readers are expected to recognize immediately. In view of John 13:34-35; 15:12-13, 17 and 1 John 3:11;

2 John 5; 1 Pet 1:22, it is probable that they are expected to recognize it as a dominical command.

(3) The expression "fulfilling [*plēroō*] the Law" in Rom 13:8b (also Rom 13:10b) and in Gal 5:14 (especially with its eschatological nuance), while being rare in Jewish literature, is paralleled by Matt 5:17.

(4) Paul's exhortation "Bear one another's burdens, and so fulfill the law of Christ" in Gal 6:2 (cf. also 1 Cor 9:21) should be taken with Gal 5:14: "For the whole law is fulfilled in one word, 'You shall love your neighbor as yourself' " (Lev 19:18).

(5) In a very similar formulation to Gal 5:14, Rom 13:9 also cites Lev 19:18 as the epitome of the whole Law. This corresponds to Jesus' answer to the question about the greatest commandment (Mark 12:28-34 par. Matt 22:34-40 and Luke 10:25-28). Scholars have debated the authenticity of the Synoptic logion. Was there a similar practice of summing up the Law in first-century Judaism? If so, the principle of dissimilarity (i.e., that sayings of Jesus that are dissimilar to his environment are more likely to be authentic) would reduce its claim to authenticity. But even if scholars are correct in noting the presence of such summaries of the Law in Judaism, the fundamental difference between the Jewish practice on the one hand and the Pauline and the Synoptic summaries on the other is to be noted. The Jewish practice aims at stating the Law that is logically prior and therefore includes by implication all the rest, in order to facilitate learning and keeping all the stipulations of the law. The Pauline and Synoptic summaries seek to stress "that love is what *really* matters, more so than legal scruples" (Thompson). Further, the combination of Deut 6:5 and Lev 19:18, as in Mark 12:28-34 and parallels, has no analogy in Judaism (Neirynck). So the summary of the Law in terms of love for God (Deut 6:5) and love for the neighbor (Lev 19:18) must be accepted as an authentic teaching of Jesus. If so, in view of the material connection between Gal 5:14 and 6:2 as observed above (4), the striking formulation "the law of Christ" in Gal 6:2 should be seen not as merely including a reference to Gal 5:14, but as concretely designating the summary of the Law in Gal 5:14 *as the teaching of (Jesus) Christ on the Law* or *as the Law given by (Jesus) Christ.* If this is so, as in Gal 5:14; 6:2, so also in Rom 13:8-10 Paul is clearly alluding to Jesus' teaching on the Law.

An objection has been raised against this conclusion from the fact that while Jesus summarized the Law in two commandments, Paul does it in only one. Here Thompson answers well: in Rom 13:8-10 (and also Gal 5:14) Paul refers only to the second commandment because in the context(s) he is concerned with giving his readers ethical exhortations for proper behavior toward one another, rather than giving an instruction in Jesus tradition.

Romans 12:17 shows how Paul is capable of using only half of a tradition: citing Prov 3:4 ("Take care to do what is noble in the sight of the Lord and people"), he leaves out the reference to the Lord because it does not suit his immediate purpose. Furthermore, he has already stated in the opening verses the believers' duty to love God (Rom 12:1-2) as the foundation for the whole paraenetical section of Rom 12–15. In fact it is quite probable that Rom 12:1-2 echoes the first part of Jesus' double summary of the Law.

(9) Romans 13:7

The conclusion that Rom 13:8-10 alludes to Jesus' saying in Mark 12:28-34 (and pars.) strengthens the view that Rom 13:7 echoes the saying of Jesus in Mark 12:17 (and pars.). Those who hold this view derive support not only from the material correspondence between the Pauline injunction and the dominical saying, but also from the fact that the dominical sayings that are echoed in Paul's successive exhortations of Rom 13:7 and 13:8-10 also stand closely connected and in the same order in the conflict stories of Mark 12:13-17, 28-31 and Matt 22:15-22, 34-40. Those who reject this view, however, point to the uncertainty as to whether the two Synoptic narratives stood together in the pre-Markan collection of conflict stories, and also to the difficulty of the generalizing phrases "Pay *[apodote] all of them [pasin]* what you owe. . . . Let not any debt to *anyone [mēdeni]* remain unpaid" (Rom 13:7a and 8a). They also point to the absence of anything in Rom 13:7 that corresponds to the second part of Jesus' double saying ("Render unto God the things that are God's"), which is the real point of the whole saying. There is, however, discussion as to whether the phrase in Rom 13:7, "[render] fear to whom fear is due" *(tō ton phobon ton phobon),* refers to that second part of the Jesus logion (Cranfield). It is uncertain. However, Paul's omission of the second part of Jesus' double saying here can be understood exactly the same way as that in Rom 13:8-10: having already stated in the principial declaration of Rom 12:1-2 the duty of rendering unto God what is God's (our whole being), he omits repetition of that in Rom 13, as it does not suit his immediate purpose of instructing his readers about their proper attitude to the civil authorities. (While in Jesus' original saying the second part is stressed, by omitting it in the context of Rom 13 Paul undoubtedly makes the first part prominent. This is probably conditioned by the situation of the Roman Christians or that of the church as a whole at that critical period in its history.) Once this is recognized, the generalizing phrases in Rom 13:7-8 pose no problem. They just indicate that here Paul is applying a generalized form of Jesus' teaching ("Render unto Caesar the things that are Caesar's") to different authorities. Even if Mark 12:13-17 and parallels, and Mark 12:28-34 and its parallels did not stand together in the *pre-Markan* collection of conflict stories, their present connection in Mark and Matthew, corresponding to the connection of Paul's two exhortations in Rom 13:7 and 8–10, is significant. So it is highly likely that Rom 13:7 is an echo of Jesus' saying found in Mark 12:17 and parallels.

(10) Romans 8:15 and Galatians 4:6

The *abba* address for God to which Paul refers twice (Rom 8:15; Gal 4:6) is universally recognized as originating in Jesus' teaching. But we should note also the unique formulas: "the Spirit of his Son" (Gal 4:6) and "the Spirit of adoption" (Rom 8:15). Is Paul not referring to the Holy Spirit with these formulas as the Spirit who indwelt Jesus, attesting (making?) him as the Son of God and so enabling him to use this unique form of address for God? If so, when Paul says that this Spirit sent by God into our hearts cries "*Abba* Father!" (Gal 4:6), he may have in mind the fact that Jesus taught his disciples to use that same unique form of address. The Spirit of Jesus the Son of God indwells the hearts of those who by faith and baptism unite with the Son of God, Jesus Christ, and who participate in his divine sonship. It is this indwelling Spirit that enables them to use the same form of address for God as Jesus the Son of God used. Thus Rom 8:15 and Gal 4:6 seem to show Paul's awareness of the full significance of Jesus' *abba* address.

Further, some commentators wonder whether with "*Abba* Father!" Paul may not actually be referring to the Lord's Prayer, which opens with "*Pater!*" ('*abbā*', Luke 11:2). But the context of Rom 8:12-27 seems to remind us rather of Jesus' prayer at Gethsemane (Mark 14:32-42 pars.; cf. Thompson). Paul introduces the cry "*Abba!*" in the context of describing the reality of Christians' participation in Christ's suffering in order for them to participate in his glory. Furthermore, the "groanings" of Christians and the idea of the Spirit's helping them make the right prayer according to God's will are reminiscent respectively of Jesus' anxiety and sorrow, and of his prayer at Gethsemane, "Remove this cup from me; yet not what I will, but what you will."

(11) Kingdom of God

Finally, Paul's references to the "kingdom of God" (Rom 14:17; 1 Cor 4:20; 6:9-10; 15:50; Gal 5:21; Col 4:10-11; 1 Thess 2:11-12; 2 Thess 1:5; cf. 1 Cor

15:24; Col 1:13; 2 Tim 4:1, 18) must be considered. In view of the fact that in the Synoptics the kingdom of God is the center of Jesus' preaching, while the death (and resurrection) of Jesus Christ is the center of Paul's preaching, critics tend to emphasize the infrequency with which Paul uses that characteristic expression of Jesus. However, while the thought expressed by the "kingdom of God" was central to contemporary Judaism, the term itself was by no means common in Judaism (let alone to Hellenism). This observation, considered together with the fact that the total number of occurrences of "the kingdom of God" in the non-Pauline writings of the New Testament outside the Synoptics is hardly more than those within the Pauline corpus, points out that the eight Pauline references to the kingdom of God are by no means insignificant.

Among the many similarities between Paul's concept of the kingdom of God and that of Jesus (see below), Paul's language of "inheriting the kingdom of God" may be singled out as a sign of his adoption of the characteristic language of Jesus. The phrase "inherit the kingdom of God" is not frequent in the Synoptics (Matt 25:34; cf. 5:5; 19:29), yet it is practically synonymous with the characteristic phrase of Jesus, "enter the kingdom of God" (Mark 10:15 pars.; 10:23-27 pars.; etc.). Both phrases were formed after the Old Testament model of "inheriting" or "entering" the promised land of Canaan (e.g., Deut 4:1; 6:17-18; 16:20; cf. also the phrases reflecting God's "giving" the kingdom (Luke 12:32; cf. 22:29; Mark 4:11 pars.) and the believers' "receiving" it (Mark 10:15 pars.; Luke 18:17). In the cluster of the synonymous expressions of Jesus (to "enter," "inherit" and "receive" the kingdom of God), Paul seems to have chosen the one of "inheriting the kingdom of God" (1 Cor 6:9; 15:50; Gal 5:21) under the influence of the common Jewish turn of speech, to "inherit" the age to come or eternal life. So it is fairly certain that Paul knew about Jesus' kingdom preaching and that he reflects it in his letters.

Possible Echoes

There are also a large number of Pauline texts which may be seen, with a varying degree of probability, as echoing sayings of Jesus. They do not show any direct indication for it, and they are more disputed than those that have hitherto been treated. As space does not allow them to be discussed and evaluated here, they are simply presented in tabular form (see chart on pp. 272-73). However, some of them will be drawn into discussion in the subsequent sections.

(1) 1 Corinthians

First Corinthians is distinguished among Paul's letters by the unique presence of three explicit references to the word/command of the Lord (1 Cor 7:10; 9:14; 11:23-26) and by the relative frequency of echoes of Jesus' sayings. It is also distinguished by Paul's explicit statement that on certain issues he has no *Herrenwort* ("word of the Lord," 1 Cor 7:12, 25, 40) and by the tenfold "Do you not know that . . . ?" formula. These characteristics raise several interesting questions concerning Paul's attitude to and transmission of the dominical logia on the one hand, and the Corinthian problems and the nature of 1 Corinthians on the other. (In this article the former question will be taken up at relevant places.)

Paul's use of the "Do you not know that . . . ?" formula is quite suggestive and has not received adequate attention in scholarly discussions of Jesus' sayings in Paul. Among its ten occurrences, 1 Cor 5:6; 6:2 and 6:3; 6:9 have often been cited as echoes of Jesus' sayings in Mark 8:15-16 and parallels; in Matt 19:28 (par. Luke 22:29-30); and in Matt 5:20 respectively. First Corinthians 9:13, 24, however, refer to Old Testament practice or common sense. The other four cases remain to be explained:

> 1 Cor 3:16 ("that you are the temple of God")
> 1 Cor 6:15 ("that your members are members of Christ")
> 1 Cor 6:16 ("that he who joins himself to a prostitute becomes one body with her")
> 1 Cor 6:19 ("that your body is a temple of the Holy Spirit within you")

E. E. Ellis has sought to demonstrate that they refer to Paul's previous teaching to the Corinthians on "body" and "temple," which was based on Jesus' own teaching. To summarize his argument briefly: 1 Cor 10:16 and 11:23-24 show that Paul's theology of the body of Christ is partly rooted in the eucharistic sayings of Jesus. First Corinthians 6:15 as well as 1 Cor 12:12, 27 reflect the same theology of the "body of Christ." Ephesians 5:30, which also speaks of Christians as "members of Christ's body," grounds the conception in an exposition of Gen 2:24: "The two shall be one flesh." Precisely this same passage is in Paul's mind in 1 Cor 6:15-17. This shows that the Corinthians' knowledge of their being "members of Christ" or of his "body" is based both on the Last Supper teaching of Jesus and on an exposition of Gen 2:24, which the Corinthians had learned from Paul. It is most interesting then that Gen 2:24 forms a part of the Synoptic tradition of Jesus' teaching on divorce, to which Paul alludes in 1 Cor 7:10-11. This means that Paul's conception of the

Possible Echoes of Sayings of Jesus

Romans

1.	Rom 12:1-2	Mark 12:17 par.; Mark 12:29-30 par.
2.	Rom 12:9-13	Mark 7:6 par. Matt 15:7; Mark 12:15 par. Matt 22:18; Luke 12:56; Matt 7:5 par. Luke 6:42
3.	Rom 13:11-14	Luke 21:28, 31, 34 (cf. 1 Thess 5; Eph 6)
4.	Rom 14:1-13a	Matt 7:1 par. Luke 6:37 (cf. Rom 2:1-5; 1 Cor 4:3-5)
5.	Rom 14:13b	Mark 9:42 par. (cf 1 Cor 8:13)
6.	Rom 15:8-9	Matt 15:24; 8:11; Mark 10:45 par. (cf. 1 Cor 9:19; 10:33; 11:1 and Mark 10:44-45 par. Matt 20:27-28)
7.	Rom 16:19	Matt 10:16

1 Corinthians

8.	1 Cor 1:18–2:16	Luke 10:21-24 par. Matt 11:25, 27; 13:16-17
	1 Cor 1:23	Matt 11:6 par. Luke 7:23
	1 Cor 2:8	Luke 23:13, 35; 24:20
9.	1 Cor 4:1-5	Luke 12:41-46 par. Matt 24:45-51; Matt 25:14-30 par. Luke 19:12-27; Luke 12:37; Matt 7:1 par. Luke 6:37a
10.	1 Cor 7:7	Matt 19:12
11.	1 Cor 8:13	Mark 9:42 par.
12.	1 Cor 9:19; 10:33; 11:1	Mark 10:45 par.
13.	1 Cor 10:27	Luke 20:8
14.	1 Cor 13:2b	Matt 17:20; Mark 11:22-23 par. Matt 21:21
15.	1 Cor 3:16; 5:6; 6:2, 3, 9, 15, 16, 19 containing the "Do you not know that?" formula (see below)	

2 Corinthians

16.	2 Cor 4:10	Mark 9:31 par.; Mark 10:33 par.; Mark 14:21, 41 par.; etc. (cf. Rom 4:25; 8:32; Gal 1:4; 2:20)
17.	2 Cor 5:1	Mark 14:58 par. (see below)
18.	2 Cor 6:16	Mark 14:58 par. (see below)
19.	2 Cor 12:12	Mark 6:7 par. (cf. Mark 16:17-18)

Galatians

20.	Gal 1:4; 2:20	see 16 above
21.	Gal 1:1, 12-16; 2:7-9	Matt 16:16-17 (cf. 1 Cor 3:11; Wenham)

Ephesians

22. Eph 2:19-21	Mark 14:58 par. (cf. 1 Cor 3:11, 16; 2 Cor 6:16; Gal 2:9; see below)
23. Eph 6:10-18	Luke 21:28, 31, 34-36

Philippians

24. Phil 1:27–2:11	Mark 10:43-45 par.; Luke 14:11; Matt 23:12 par. Luke 18:14

Colossians

25. Col 3:5	Mark 9:43-48 (cf. Matt 5:29; 18:8-9)
26. Col 3:13	Matt 6:12 par. Luke 11:4

1 Thessalonians

27. 1 Thess 2:2-9	Matt 10:10 par. Luke 10:7
28. 1 Thess 2:16	Matt 23:32-33
29. 1 Thess 4:8	Luke 10:16 (cf. Matt 10:14; John 13:20)
30. 1 Thess 5:15	Matt 5:39-40 par. Luke 6:27-29 (cf. Rom 12:17)

2 Thessalonians

31. 2 Thess 2:1-12	Mark 13 par.

church as the "body of Christ" is rooted, partly, both in Jesus' Supper teaching and in his marriage/divorce teaching based on Gen 2:24. The formula "Do you not know that . . . ?" in 1 Cor 6:15, 16 as well as the references to the Last Supper tradition in 1 Cor 11:23-24; 10:16 (perhaps a variant form of the formula "Do you not know that . . . ?") then indicate that Paul had previously taught the Corinthians about the church being the "body of Christ" and about divorce on the basis of Jesus' teachings (cf. above).

For an explanation of the origin of the temple typology in 1 Cor 3:16 and 6:19 it is helpful to consider 1 Cor 3:11 and 2 Cor 5:1. The statement "you are the temple of God" (1 Cor 3:16) must somehow be related to the earlier statement that the "foundation" which the apostle Paul has laid is Jesus Christ (1 Cor 3:11). The use of "foundation" *(themelion)* here may reflect the influence of Isa 28:16, which is alluded to in Eph 2:20-22 and explicitly cited in 1 Pet 2:4-10 in connection with the conception of the church as the temple of God in both passages. In 1 Pet 2:4-10, Isa 28:16 is cited together with Ps 118:22 (the "rejected stone" becoming the "head of the corner"), which Jesus used in his explanation of the meaning of his sign-act at the temple of Jerusalem (Mark 11:27–12:11 par.; cf. Kim). May it not be that in 1 Cor 3:11, 16 Paul reflects Jesus' teaching on the temple and, in echoing Isa 28:16 (cf. Rom 9:33), he has also Ps 118:22 in mind? (Cf. *kephalē gōnias* in Ps 118:22 and *lithos . . .*

akrogōniaios in Isa 28:16.) The several verbal affinities between 2 Cor 5:1 and the temple saying attributed to Jesus (Mark 14:58 par. Matt 26:61) suggest that 2 Cor 5:1 echoes the saying and reflects an interpretation of it which, as in John 2:21-22, identifies Jesus' resurrection body as the new temple. Paul's introductory formula in 2 Cor 5:1, "for we know that . . ." indicates that he had previously taught the Corinthians the temple typology on the basis of Jesus' temple saying. So they "know" that they are the "temple of God" (1 Cor 3:16) or "that your body is the temple of the Holy Spirit" (1 Cor 6:19).

At this point Ellis's argument needs much supplementing. Elsewhere I have attempted to show that Jesus did predict the destruction of the Jerusalem temple and promise to build a new temple, and that by the new "temple" he meant the community of the new people of God he was to create through his vicariously atoning and covenant-establishing death and resurrection. So the new "temple" was the people of God whom he, as their substitute and representative, embodied, as it were, and it was to come into being with his resurrection. Therefore it was interpreted in terms of the resurrection "body" of Christ in John 2:21-22, where the "body" concept is perhaps both individual and collective (in its latter aspect, approaching the Pauline concept of the church as the "body of Christ"). Many Qumran documents illustrate the Jewish background for Jesus' metaphorical or "spiritual" interpretation of temple, and passages like 1QH 7:4, that use for the community the language of body as well as that of building, illustrate the interpretation of "temple" as "body". Paul seems to reflect both the collective interpretation of the "temple" (1 Cor 3:16) and its individual interpretation (6:19). The resurrection "body" which believers are to put on as a "building from God, a house not made with hands, eternal in the heavens" (2 Cor 5:1) is the resurrection body like that of the Last Adam, the "man from heaven" (1 Cor 15:42-49). But this resurrection body has already begun to take on reality in believers, insofar as they have died and risen with Christ through faith-baptism, and as the Holy Spirit has already taken residence in them and they are being transformed into the glorious image of the risen Lord (2 Cor 3:18). Hence we find the statement of 1 Cor 6:19! Space forbids a substantiation of the thesis in greater detail, but at any rate Paul's "temple" typology (cf. also 2 Cor 6:16–7:1) is undoubtedly based on Jesus' unique teaching on the temple which is closely bound up with his kingdom preaching. First Corinthians 3:16; 6:19 and 2 Cor 5:1 clearly suggest that Paul had previously taught the Corinthians about it.

If this is so, all the cases of the formula "Do you not know that . . . ?" in 1 Corinthians (except 9:13, 24) and its variant forms in 1 Cor 10:16 and 2 Cor 5:1 suggest that Paul transmitted Jesus' teachings to the Corinthian church at the time of his founding the church.

Continuity/Similarity in Theology and Attitude

We have seen that in only a few cases does Paul clearly indicate his reference to a saying of Jesus, and even in those cases, as 1 Cor 7:10-11 and 9:14 show, he does not quote them verbatim but *re-presents* them in his own language, sometimes using one or two words and/or the form drawn from them. This suggests that verbal parallelism cannot be made the sole criterion for judging whether a Pauline statement reflects a dominical saying or not. The presence of a parallel content or meaning must also be considered. The instances of allusions and echoes listed above in this chapter are the result of critical comparisons of the vocabulary, form and/or content of Pauline statements with those of dominical logia preserved in the Synoptics. The critical criteria used are the principle of dissimilarity (i.e., a Pauline statement that is similar to a saying of Jesus could have come only from the latter, since the latter is unique, being dissimilar to Old Testament-Judaism and Hellenism) and the principle of coherence (i.e., a Pauline statement should be both similar to and cohere well with a saying of Jesus). (The limited space, however, has prevented the actual display of comparisons for the instances tabulated in section 2.) Undoubtedly this investigation involves a fair degree of subjectivity. Some may wonder whether there may not be more allusions or echoes that have gone undetected, while others may reject many of the above cases. Even where a Pauline statement clearly seems to reflect a saying of Jesus, minimalists will wish to question whether Paul was conscious that it originated with Jesus when he made the statement.

In such a situation can there not be another criterion to provide a more reliable judgment? It is submitted here that the continuity or similarity between Paul and Jesus both in theology and in attitude must be considered as a factor, if not a criterion.

It is widely recognized that there is a real continuity between Jesus' kingdom preaching and Paul's doctrine of justification (Bultmann; Jüngel). As noted above, the fact that the specific Jesuanic term *kingdom of God* is used by Paul at all (and over eight times, when elsewhere in the New Testament outside the Gospels it is rarely used) is significant. Like Jesus, Paul teaches that the kingdom of God is both present (Rom 14:17; 1 Cor 4:20; Col 1:13; 4:11) and future (all other instances). It presents its saving power through the Spirit (1 Cor 4:20; cf. Matt 12:28; Luke 11:20). It will be "inherited" not by natural, sinful people (1 Cor 15:50; Gal 5:21) but only by the righteous or those who are worthy of the kingdom (1 Cor 6:9; 1 Thess 2:12; 2 Thess 1:5; Gal 5:21; cf. Matt 5:20, 10) or by those who have been made God's children and are so privileged to call God *abba* (Rom 8:15-17; Gal 4:6-7; cf. Mark 10:15 par.).

Paul's emphasis on divine grace corresponds to Jesus' emphasis on the kingdom's transcendental and grace character exhibited in his language of the kingdom "coming," and of God's "giving" it and people's "receiving" or "inheriting" it. It is also seen in Jesus' parables of the kingdom (Matt 20:1-16; Luke 7:36-50; 15:11-32; 18:9-14; Mark 1:40-45). Jesus' summary of the Law in terms of the double commandments of love for God and for one's neighbor, his critique of the contemporary Jewish understanding of the Law, and his disregard for the laws of the Sabbath, fasting, purity, table-fellowship, and so on, find their close correspondence in Paul's teaching on the Law and his criticism of the "works of the Law" as the means of justification. Jesus' blessing the poor and helping the outcasts — the "sinners" according to the Law — who respond to his kingdom preaching is not only continuous with Paul's outreach to the gentiles but also with his doctrine of the "justification of the ungodly" *sola gratia* (Dahl, 115).

It is more true to say that there is a close correspondence between Jesus' teaching centered upon the kingdom of God and Paul's theology as a whole, rather than specifically between the former and Paul's doctrine of justification. For the post-Easter church in general, what Jesus had *promised* through his kingdom preaching, namely to create a people (or children) of God to live in his love and wealth, has been *realized* in his atoning and covenant-establishing death, and this has been confirmed by God through his resurrecting Jesus. So the post-Easter church naturally concentrates on preaching the good news of salvation *already wrought* in Christ's death (and resurrection) rather than on simply repeating Jesus' kingdom preaching which had basically the character of a promise and an invitation (see Kim). So also Paul makes Jesus' death on the cross the center of his preaching. He expounds the meaning of salvation wrought in it by various categories or metaphors such as justification, reconciliation, adoption, new creation, life in the Spirit, and transformation. He explains its blessings in terms of righteousness, peace, joy, freedom, hope, life, and so on. These categoties/metaphors and these blessings are those that were explicitly or implicitly promised in Jesus' kingdom preaching. They have now been made available by Jesus' death. Thus *the fact that Jesus' gospel of the kingdom is replaced with Paul's gospel of the death and resurrection of Jesus Christ means no discontinuity between Jesus and Paul*. Rather, the reverse is true: *it had to be so replaced.*

However, in explaining the salvation promised in Jesus' preaching of the kingdom and accomplished by his death and resurrection, could Paul not have continued using the "kingdom" language? If so, why does he do so only on a few occasions? Among the various categories/metaphors which Paul uses in place of kingdom language, justification is the most prominent. At least, those who maintain that the notion of justification is not merely a "subsidiary crater" or something that developed later out of polemical necessity, but rather is the central category of Paul's soteriology, owe an explanation as to why Paul replaced the language of kingdom chiefly with the language of justification. Certainly the reason must be seen against the background of "righteousness" being a central concern of the Jews, whether they were trying to earn salvation or remain in a saving covenant relationship with God by keeping the Law. It may also have something to do with Paul's attempt to avoid a political misunderstanding of his gospel in the Roman world. Further, it is connected also with his own conversion from a zeal for Law-righteousness to receiving God's righteousness in Jesus Christ (Gal 1:13-16; Phil 3:4-11). From that experience, Paul saw clearly God's saving act in Jesus Christ as God's righteousness, and he realized also that righteousness/justification was the best category for bringing out the *grace* character of salvation over against the Jewish conception of Law-righteousness-salvation.

The main reason, however, must lie in his understanding of Jesus' death as the atoning and covenant-establishing sacrifice that has wrought the salvation promised by Jesus in his kingdom preaching (Rom 3:24-26; 2 Cor 5:21; etc.). Since this *saving event* was the atoning and covenant-establishing *sacrifice* and, furthermore, since Jesus indicated that his death was to bear such meaning and he portrayed it in terms of the '*Ebed Yahweh* ("Servant of the Lord") who was to "pour out his soul to death" as '*āšām* ("guilt offering"), "making many accounted *righteous*" (Isa 53:10-12; Mark 14:17-25 par.), Paul naturally interpreted the salvation wrought through Jesus' death chiefly through the category of righteousness/justification. This category of righteousness/justification, which expresses the concerns of atonement, the forgiveness of sins, and the restoration of the proper, or covenantal, relationship to God, had the additional advantage of perfectly bringing out the intention of Jesus' kingdom preaching and his conduct in receiving sinners.

Thus not only the close material connection between Jesus' gospel of the kingdom of God and Paul's gospel of Jesus Christ's death and resurrection, but also Paul's choice of righteousness/justification as the main category of interpretation of salvation in Jesus Christ betrays his intimate knowledge of Jesus' kingdom preaching and Jesus' view of his own death.

We have already noted how Paul echoes Jesus' unique teaching on the temple as well as his unique address for God as *abba,* and his teaching on the adoption of believers into God's family. These teachings of Jesus are in fact closely associated with his kingdom preaching. Jesus' association with sinners, which is seen by many as a basis for Paul's outreach to the Gentiles, is in fact granted as a foretaste and pledge of salvation, of entrance into the kingdom of God. The close similarity between Paul and Jesus in their eschatological teachings is also often noted (see esp. E. Schweizer on the Pauline kingdom passage of 1 Cor 15:20-28). Jesus' eschatological teaching is given in terms of the kingdom of God. Here the continuity between Jesus' intention of gathering the people of God in solidarity with him in the kingdom and Paul's conception of the church as the people of God and the body of Christ is instructive. These parallels also indicate Paul's intimate knowledge of Jesus' kingdom preaching.

C. Wolff has conveniently surveyed the Jesus and Pauline evidence to compare the conduct of Jesus and Paul under the four headings of deprivation, renunciation of marriage, humble service and suffering persecution. In this area Wolff affirms "some remarkable correspondences" between the two figures, and concludes that Paul as an apostle, a representative of Jesus Christ, "displays himself as a true follower" of him. May we not then take this as evidence that Paul knew of Jesus' life and teaching quite well?

Some try to see the similarities between Paul and Jesus in theology and in attitude and conduct as mediated by the *Hellenists* (Wedderburn, 117-43; cf. Hengel; Dunn). Indeed, the Hellenists may have been the first tradents of the dominical tradition. However, it is very unrealistic to suppose that Paul would have been satisfied merely with knowing their teaching and attitude. Since he preached none other than Jesus Christ and God's saving work in him, he would have demanded to know that what the Hellenists claimed to represent about Jesus Christ and his teaching was accurate. For example, if Paul had heard the Hellenists justify their outreach to the Gentiles on the basis of Jesus' attitude to the outcasts, would he not have felt the urge to know how Jesus justified his attitude, especially since it would have been unacceptable to him in his preconversion days? For Paul, Jesus was no legendary ancient hero, but a contemporary of his who had been only recently crucified as a false messiah. Given this fact, it is impossible to think that Paul did not try to learn of Jesus, his life and teaching, more accurately from the primary witnesses like Peter as well as others from Jerusalem such as Barnabas, Silvanus, and John Mark. Nor is it easy to think that the close correspondences between the teaching and conduct of Jesus, and the teaching and conduct of Paul, could have come about if there was anything less than an earnest desire on Paul's part to learn of Jesus.

Therefore, we conclude that the remarkable similarities between Paul and Jesus in theology and attitude may be taken as evidence for Paul's intimate knowledge of Jesus' teaching and attitude. They must be counted then as Paul's reflections of Jesus' sayings, since it is chiefly by means of one's sayings that one's teaching is imparted. If Paul's theology, especially his doctrine of justification, closely represents Jesus' kingdom preaching, we must conclude that he knew it well, and this conclusion implies that he knew well Jesus' sayings (including the parables) about the kingdom of God.

This consideration of the theological continuity between Jesus and Paul should tip the balance in favor of a positive judgment in the cases (like those considered in 2 above) where there is a dispute about a possible echo of a saying of Jesus in a Pauline statement. A thesis may now be submitted, one analogous to that of J. Jeremias on the question of authenticity of dominical logia in the Synoptics: *When in the Pauline letters an echo of a dominical logion is disputed, the burden of proof lies more heavily on those who would deny it, than on those who would accept it.*

Theological Loci and Sayings of Jesus

The sayings of Jesus that we have discerned, whether they be allusions or echoes, are diverse and appear in various contexts of Paul's teaching. The majority of them, however, may be classified as connected with Paul's *ethical* and *eschatological teaching*. It is especially noteworthy that in a number of places Paul echoes the sayings of Jesus which are compiled by Matthew and Luke in the Sermon on the Mount/Plain. D. C. Allison infers from this that Paul knew an early collection of Jesus' logia now preserved in Luke 6:27-38, the central section of the Sermon on the Plain (cf. Matt 5:38-48; 7:12). Ascertaining Paul's "heavy dependence" on the pre-Synoptic eschatological traditions of Jesus, D. Wenham even uses the Pauline echoes as important pieces of evidence in elucidating the history of those Gospel traditions.

One of Paul's explicit references to Jesus' sayings is about the apostolic privilege to "get their living by the gospel" (1 Cor 9:14; cf. 1 Thess 2:2-9), and several of Paul's echoes of Jesus' sayings are concerned with *apostleship* and *mission* (Rom 15:8-9; 16:19; 1 Cor 4:1-5; 7:7; 2 Cor 12:12; Gal 1:12-16; 2:7-8; 1 Thess 4:8; etc.). Here one must consider also Paul's close "following" (or imitation) of Jesus in his apostolic existence of deprivation, unmarried life, humble service, and suffering, which, as argued above, implies his knowledge of Jesus' life and of his teaching about such a life. Clearly, as an apostle and missionary, Paul cherished his Lord's teaching on apostleship and mission and his example (cf. 1 Cor 11:1).

Since the words of Jesus at the Last Supper are explicitly referred to by Paul, their influence on Paul's doctrine of the *eucharist* needs no further substantiation. We have also seen some intimations of the influence of Jesus' teachings on the temple and on marriage/divorce as well as his eucharistic sayings, as they shaped Paul's conception of the *church as the body of Christ.*

Now we turn to the question of whether Paul's christology and soteriology also echo Jesus' teaching. Walter claims that precisely in "expounding the central content of his gospel, in making his important christological or soteriological statements . . . Paul adduces no Jesus-tradition" (Walter, 74). Moreover, he also maintains that "in expounding the gospel of Christ Paul shows no trace of the influence of the theologically central affirmations of Jesus' preaching, in particular of his characteristic 'Jesuanic' interpretation of the kingdom of God" (Walter, 63). Walter concludes that Paul was either not very familiar with Jesus' message or not able "to understand and assimilate these central ingredients of the Jesus-tradition" (Walter, 64).

However, this sort of statement can be made only by the "minimalists" who accept exclusively those few passages in Paul where there is an explicit reference to sayings of Jesus. But as we have seen, there is a strong continuity between Jesus' kingdom preaching and Paul's gospel of God's salvation through the death and resurrection of Jesus Christ and his interpretation of this salvation chiefly through the category of justification. We have tried to show that the replacement of the former by the latter was not only expedient but also logically required. We have argued that this continuity or unity presupposes Paul's intimate knowledge of Jesus' kingdom preaching and Jesus' view of his own death. Otherwise we cannot explain the theological unity between Paul and Jesus.

In addition to this fundamental consideration, we may, *contra* Walter, point to Paul's references to the kingdom of God, which with similarities to Jesus' kingdom preaching are significant in themselves. We may also point to his citation of the eucharistic words of Jesus, which could hardly have failed to influence his soteriology; to his allusion to Jesus' *abba* address to God, which forms a basis of his Son christology and his adoption soteriology as well as his teaching on the testimony of the Spirit in Rom 8; to his use of the language of *paradidomai* ("to be given up," 2 Cor 4:10-11; Rom 4:25; 8:32; Gal 1:4; 2:20), which echoes Jesus' passion announcements; and to his christological and soteriological argument in 1 Cor 1:18–2:16, which is full of echoes of Jesus' shout of praise (Luke 10:21-24 par.) and passion. There is no space here to examine whether behind his *kyrios* christology, reconciliation and new creation soteriology, and so on, there may not stand some concrete teachings of Jesus. However, enough has been shown to indicate that in his christological and soteriological statements also there are clear echoes of Jesus' teachings.

Certainly it is true that he does not cite any saying of Jesus as a proof-text

280

for his christological or soteriological statement. But except for 1 Cor 7:10-11 and 9:14, he does not use Jesus tradition in that manner for other kinds of theological statements either. In comparison with his ethical and eschatological teachings, Paul shows a greater freedom in interpreting Jesus' teaching as he incorporates it into his christology and soteriology, where he more frequently replaces Jesus' language with his own. This is quite understandable. Our earlier consideration (see 3 above) goes some way toward explaining the reason for this.

So in his christology and soteriology as well as in all the other areas of his theology, Paul echoes Jesus' sayings. That is, *Jesus' teaching provides Paul with a basis for his theology as a whole.*

Narrative Tradition

According to Walter, there is "no hint that Paul knew of the narrative tradition about Jesus." But again this is a positivistic statement by a minimalist. With M. Hengel, one must realistically consider the *Sitz im Leben* of Paul's missionary preaching: "It was simply impossible in the antiquities to proclaim a man crucified a few years ago, as Kyrios, Son of God and Redeemer, without saying something about who this man was, what he taught and did, and why he died" (Hengel 1971, 34). This consideration should prevent interpreters from dealing cavalierly with various indications in Paul's letters of his knowledge of the narrative tradition about Jesus, simply because they are mere indications and not extended narratives of Jesus' life and deeds such as those found in the Gospels.

In Gal 3:1 Paul reminds the Galatians of his having "portrayed Jesus Christ as crucified before your eyes" at his first preaching to them. In Gal 6:17 and 2 Cor 4:10 he speaks of his apostolic life in terms of both carrying about the "marks [*stigmata*] of Jesus" in his body and the "putting to death [*nekrōsis*] of Jesus" in his body. Here his use of the name *Jesus* (instead of the more familiar "death of Christ [Jesus]") as well as the terms *stigmata* and *nekrōsis* clearly indicate his consideration of the concrete process of Jesus' crucifixion (Wolff). From this Kleinknecht rightly infers that Paul "must have had a certain visual image" of Jesus' death. We receive the same impressions from Phil 3:10, where Paul speaks of his resolution to "participate in [Christ's] sufferings, being conformed to his death."

Further, we have already suggested that Paul's use of the *paradidomai* language (2 Cor 4:11; Rom 4:25; 8:32; Gal 2:20; cf. 1 Cor 11:23; Gal 1:4) indicates his knowledge of the passion tradition. First Corinthians 2:8 alludes to the

Jewish and Roman rulers' crucifying Jesus, and Rom 15:3 probably refers to the "insults" Jesus suffered on the cross (cf. also 2 Cor 13:4). Of course, it would be most arbitrary if the direct and concrete data provided by 1 Cor 11:23-25 and 15:3-5 were excluded from consideration of Paul's knowledge of a version of the passion narrative on the ground that they are a liturgical and a kerygmatic formula (*pace* Walter). Walter tries to argue against this overwhelming evidence by granting that Paul "certainly knew something about the event of the passion of Jesus," but at the same time by denying "Paul's knowledge of the passion narrative in the (or a) pre-Synoptic version" (Walter, 63). But this distinction is quite arbitrary. If Paul knew something about the passion of Jesus, then he knew *a* version of the passion narrative. How could it have been otherwise?

Since Paul makes the death and resurrection of Jesus Christ the center of his preaching, it is natural that his allusions to the narrative tradition about Jesus would also be concentrated on the passion narrative. However, indications of his knowledge of other kinds of the narrative tradition are not lacking. Walter asserts again confidently that "Jesus' actions played no role" in Paul's picture of him, "and certainly not his actions as a performer of miracles." However, when Paul speaks of "the signs of the apostle" in terms of "signs and wonders and mighty works" (2 Cor 12:12; Rom 15:18-19; Gal 3:5; 1 Cor 2:4; 1 Thess 1:5), he seems to reflect Jesus' word of apostolic commission (Mark 6:7-8 par.; cf. Mark 16:17-18). But does not the fact that he regards miracles as a sign of an apostle, as the representative and revealer of Jesus Christ, imply that he knows that Jesus demonstrated the salvation of the kingdom of God through his miracles? Does not precisely this knowledge stand behind Paul's summary description in Rom 15:18-19 of his apostolic ministry: "I will not venture to speak of anything except what *Christ* has wrought *through me* to bring about the obedience of the Gentiles, by word and deed, by the power of signs and wonders, by the power of the Spirit" (cf. 1 Cor 2:4; 1 Thess 1:5)? So Christ *is* a performer of miracles, and the miracles Paul the apostle has performed are in fact the works *of Christ* done *through him*. Unless Paul knew that Jesus was a miracle worker, how could he speak like this (see below)?

In fact, one of Paul's kingdom sayings (1 Cor 4:20) seems to betray his knowledge of Jesus' kingdom preaching as accompanied by miracles (cf. Luke 11:20 par.; G. Haufe). As Jesus actualized through miracles the salvation of the kingdom he preached, so also Paul, his apostle, has actualized through miracles the salvation of the gospel he has preached. But Paul did it in the name of his Lord Jesus Christ, and he was conscious that in this work of his the risen Lord Jesus Christ carried on his work of salvation as during his earthly ministry. Thus Paul reveals, though allusively, his knowledge of a narrative tradition about Jesus as a miracle worker.

Passages such as Rom 15:3, 8-9; 1 Cor 10:33–11:1; 2 Cor 4:5; 8:9; 10:1; Phil 2:6-8 clearly reveal Paul's knowledge of Jesus' life as one of poverty and humble service. The lists of qualities set forth for the Christian life in 1 Cor 13:4-7 and Gal 5:22-23 are "character sketches" of Jesus (Dunn; Wedderburn). Paul exhorts Christians to "put on Christ" (Rom 13:14; Gal 3:27) and speaks of "imitating" him (1 Cor 11:1; 1 Thess 1:6). In these and other instances of his ethical instruction he often thinks of the *example* of Christ, and the exemplary "character of Jesus as Paul understood it is consistent with the character of Jesus as portrayed in the Gospels" (Bruce, 96; cf. also H. Schürmann).

To be sure, when Paul speaks of Christ's example of self-renunciation, service, love, humility, and meekness, he has in view not just Jesus' actions during his earthly days but his total existence from his preexistence through the incarnation and the earthly life to his post-exaltation present status. But the actions and character of Christ in his supra-historical existence are affirmed in the light of those of the earthly Jesus (or as Wedderburn, 188, puts it, they are "projections backwards and forwards of the patterns of action and the attitudes of the earthly Jesus"). It may be conceivable that without actually knowing anything about the life and character of the historical Jesus, Paul simply attributed those nice qualities to his "Christ." But, as noted above, the "remarkable correspondences" between Jesus and Paul in a life of suffering and humble service suggest that it is more realistic to think that having actually learned of the life and character of the historical Jesus, Paul as his apostle tried to imitate him. This is far more likely than that he gave himself up so totally to deprivation, service, and persecution solely for a figment of his own imagination (note well the use of the name "Jesus" in 2 Cor 4:5 as well as in 2 Cor 4:10; Gal 6:17). So we must assume on Paul's part an extensive knowledge of a narrative tradition of Jesus' life, ministry and character as standing behind those passages where Paul refers to Christ's example (though the term *example* as an example to be imitated is debated; see Käsemann, Martin).

The continuity between Jesus' welcoming sinners and Paul's mission to the Gentiles also suggests Paul's knowledge of a narrative tradition about the former. As argued above, this cannot be denied by appealing to a theory of the Hellenists' mediating this aspect of Jesus' ministry as a justification for their outreach to Gentiles. In fact, Rom 12:16b (cf. Rom 15:7) seems to indicate that Paul was conscious of the model character of Jesus' association with the humble (Käsemann 1980, 347; Thompson).

Finally, Rom 1:3-4; 9:5 and Gal 4:4 (cf. also Gal 1:19: "James the brother of the Lord") hint that Paul would not have been totally ignorant of or un- interested in the family origin of Jesus.

Paucity and Allusive Character of References

If our argument so far is sound, in the Pauline corpus there are a considerable number of references to or echoes of the sayings of Jesus and the narrative tradition about him. They are found in all the letters of Paul, and are con- nected with all the major themes of his theology. However, critics regularly comment that they are "strikingly" few. But the question of whether they are to be evaluated as many or few depends on the terms of comparison. Cer- tainly they are strikingly few and indirect in comparison with Paul's refer- ences to the Old Testament or with the habits of the contemporary rabbis and Hellenistic philosophers in their references to the teachings of their masters. However, as is often noted, in comparison to the references to the actions and teachings of Jesus in other New Testament writings, such as Acts, 1 Peter, the Johannine letters, and James, those in Paul's writings are by no means few.

A. J. M. Wedderburn (117-18) lists some issues in connection with which Paul might be expected to refer to Jesus' teaching but, in fact, he does not: (1) the controversies over observance of certain days (Gal 4:10; Rom 14:5-6); (2) the advice for the "virgins" (1 Cor 7:25-28; cf. Matt 19:10-12?); (3) the at- titude toward the authorities (Rom 13:1-7); (4) the question about food and table fellowship (Rom 14; 1 Cor 8–10; Gal 2:11-14; cf. Mark 7:15, 18-19 par.); and (5) the doctrine of salvation by grace and not by works (cf., e.g., the para- ble of the workers in the vineyard, Matt 20:1-16).

However, it has already been argued (1) that in Rom 13:1-7 Paul does echo Jesus' teaching in Mark 12:17 and (2) that in Rom 14:14a, 20 he does al- lude to Jesus' saying in Mark 7:15, 19. In 1 Cor 8–10, he may have avoided re- ferring to Jesus' saying in Mark 7 because the saying was known to the Corin- thians and precisely its right interpretation was part of the controversy between the strong and the weak at Corinth. Similarly, in Gal 2:11-14 Paul may also have been conscious of the different interpretation of the saying by the Jerusalemites as well as of the fact that he could hardly speak as authorita- tively on the Jesus tradition as could Peter.

(3) It has been noted that in 1 Cor 7:7 Paul probably echoes the saying of Jesus recorded in Matt 19:12. Then, when he regrets that he has "no com- mand of the Lord concerning the virgins" in 1 Cor 7:25, he must have found Jesus' saying in Matt 19:10-12 irrelevant to the "virgins."

(4) The reason why Paul did not cite the examples of Jesus' working on the Sabbath days in connection with the controversies over observance of certain holy days may be that he had already taught the Galatians about the real meaning of the Sabbath, citing Jesus' healings on Sabbath days as tokens of his eschatological fulfillment of its true intention (note Paul's reference to his previous "labor" for them in Gal 4:11) or, in the case of Rom 14:5-6, that he regards the Sabbath observance (like dietary observance) as an *adiaphoron* ("a matter of indifference"), so long as it is properly understood as fulfilled in Jesus and not elevated to a meritorious work for salvation.

(5) For us it would have been natural and most effective if he had cited Jesus' parables, such as that of the workers in the vineyard or the prodigal son (Luke 15), in support of his argument for the doctrine of salvation by grace and not by works. The reason he did not do it, however, lies probably in the more thorough interpretation and re-presentation of Jesus' teaching that Paul gave in his own language in the areas of christology and soteriology. Apparently, in his argument for the doctrine of salvation by grace, he judged it to be far more effective to refer to the actual revelation of God's grace in Christ's vicarious death than to refer to his parabolic teaching about it.

Taking all of this into consideration, it becomes evident that the number of places in which Paul fails to echo a saying of Jesus are, in fact, but few, and the instances are all naturally understandable. Nevertheless, when one compares these with Paul's references to the Old Testament Scriptures and with the practices of the contemporary rabbis and philosophers as they referred to the words of their teachers, it becomes clear that Paul's references to the sayings of Jesus are incomparably few. Furthermore, while his references to the Old Testament Scriptures are very often explicit and verbatim, although some are allusive, his references to the sayings of Jesus are mostly allusive, often hardly more than an echo and seldom verbatim.

Now the reason(s) for these phenomena must be found. Certainly the great reverence Paul shows for the "command" of the Lord in 1 Cor 7:10-11, distinguishing it from his own instruction, and his regret in 1 Cor 7:25 not to have a "command" of the Lord for the "virgins" clearly indicate that his lack of interest in or reverence for the sayings of Jesus does not explain the phenomena.

Some try to explain this paucity in terms of a hypothesis in which Paul's opponents play a significant role. Wedderburn suggests that Paul saw the teaching of Jesus largely held "in enemy hands" and misused in a legalistic way by his Judaizing opponents (Wedderburn, 100). As we have seen, this hypothesis may explain Paul's failure to refer to some sayings of Jesus (cf. Mark 7:15 par.) in a few exceptional cases like Gal 2:11-14 or 1 Cor 8–10. But it is hardly adequate to explain the problem as a whole. H. W. Kuhn speculates that it is a result of Paul's using his theology of the cross to counter the two groups of his opponents at Corinth: one, the Jewish-Christian opponents who concentrated on a Q-type collection of Jesus' sayings, presenting him as a wisdom teacher, and the other, the "enthusiasts," who transmitted the miracle stories of Jesus, presenting him in the style of a Hellenistic "divine man" *(theios anēr)*. But Kuhn is then left to explain Paul's reticence about Jesus tradition in his other letters. Why precisely in 1 Corinthians and only there does Paul cite explicitly the sayings of Jesus three times over and refer to the kingdom of God more frequently than in any of the other letters? Ultimately, the "opponents hypotheses" are inadequate for solving our problem.

The only viable solution seems to be one that starts by noticing that Paul's attitude to Jesus tradition is exactly in line with the general phenomenon observable in the New Testament writings outside the Gospels. Luke in Acts hardly ever refers to the Jesus traditions of his Gospel, and 1 John contains few references to the traditions found in the Gospel of John. In the other non-Pauline letters and Revelation the situation is the same. So the scarcity of Paul's explicit reference to Jesus tradition can hardly mean his lack of knowledge of or interest in it. In this vein B. Gerhardsson has argued that the concrete Jesus tradition was treated as an independent entity and transmitted separately as a unique tradition within the early church (Gerhardsson). This argument is persuasive when one observes the general phenomenon of the Epistles, Acts, and Revelation in contrast with the Gospels. Explicit recountings of Jesus tradition are found only in the Gospels, and the Gospels contain only Jesus tradition. On the other hand, James may be taken as an illustration of an early Christian author who works out many of his motifs, phrases and words from the Jesus tradition and yet does not cite sayings of Jesus.

It is also to be observed that like Acts 20:35, the only case of citation of a saying of Jesus in Acts (an *agraphon,* i.e., not found in the Gospels), so also Paul's citation of Jesus' words in 1 Cor 11:23-25 has the character of reminding the Corinthian church of the words that they already know. There, using the Jewish technical terms for the faithful transmission of a tradition, *parelabon* (Heb *qbl*) and *paredōka* (Heb *msr*), Paul indicates that he had faithfully transmitted the eucharistic tradition to the Corinthians. Similarly, in several other places Paul refers to the "tradition" he transmitted or taught to his churches (1 Cor 11:2; 15:3; Phil 4:9; Col 2:7; 1 Thess 4:1-2; 2 Thess 2:15; 3:6; cf. also Rom 6:17), and to the knowledge they already have about various teachings in the tradition (1 Cor 3:16; 5:6; 6:2, 3, 9, 15, 16, 19; 2 Cor 4:14; 5:1; Gal 2:16; 1 Thess 2:11-12; 3:3-4; 5:2). We have already seen that several of these passages echo sayings of Jesus.

So it is very probable that his initial preaching at each place included a separate transmission of Jesus tradition (the Antiochian tradition?) as well as the christological and soteriological exposition of the Christ-event and paraenesis based on both the Christ-event and Jesus tradition. Then, in his letters to his converts to whom he had already delivered Jesus tradition, Paul did not have to transmit it again. He needed only to refer to it, if necessary.

Thus the fundamental reason why in Paul's letters, as well as in other New Testament writings outside the Gospels, the references are fewer in number and more allusive in nature than we might expect may well be that Paul and the other representatives of the early church treated Jesus tradition *separately* as a unique and sacred tradition.

Nevertheless we could imagine that Paul's references to Jesus' teaching would have been more numerous and would have taken the form of an exact citation, had he used it in his argument to *prove* the truth of his gospel or of his paraenesis. But Paul bases his argument for the truth of his gospel on the Christ-event, that is, not on Jesus' teaching but on his *Christ-act,* which is the fulfillment of the promise contained in his teaching (see above). For Paul, Jesus is significant primarily not as a teacher but as the *Christ* who died and rose again for the salvation of humankind! Hence the meaning of Jesus as the risen Lord for Paul is essentially and fundamentally different from that of a rabbinic or a philosophic teacher for his pupil. Therefore the manner in which Paul refers to Jesus' teaching in his letters cannot be compared to that of a rabbi's or a philosopher's references to his teacher in the rabbinic or philosophical tractates.

Considering the realistic logic of Hengel's statement cited above, we can well imagine that in his initial preaching at each place, Paul expounded the meaning of the death (and resurrection) of Jesus Christ in relation to Jesus' teaching, which Paul transmitted separately, indicating how the former had fulfilled the promise contained in the latter. In his letters he did not need to repeat this. Since his opponents were not denying the character of Jesus' death as the eschatological atonement or as the accomplishment of salvation promised in Jesus' teaching, Paul was not required to cite elements of Jesus' teaching to prove these points. The "Judaizers" in Antioch, Galatia, Philippi and elsewhere, took issue with him only because of their insistence that the Gentiles must receive circumcision and take upon themselves the yoke of the Law of the covenant in order to avail themselves of the salvation effected by the death and resurrection of Jesus Christ, the fulfillment of the old covenant. The "enthusiasts" in Corinth irritated Paul with their misunderstanding of the gospel, interpreting it in terms of Hellenistic wisdom, and with their overconfident belief that they had already obtained full salvation.

Paul would have found few concrete sayings of Jesus that were directly relevant to his struggle against the "Judaizers" and the "enthusiasts" in his Gentile churches. For Jesus it had been largely a case of welcoming Israelite "sinners," not Gentiles, to table fellowship as a token of their entry into the kingdom of God. So instead of *citing* any concrete saying of Jesus, Paul concentrated on expounding the full significance of Jesus' death for his people (its vicarious character), guided by the general spirit of Jesus' teaching (hence the theological continuity between Jesus and Paul), in order to prove the truth of his gospel of *sola gratia* and *sola fide*, or that of his theology of the cross against a theology of glory. He backed up his arguments with citations of the Scriptures, which he had come to understand anew in light of the Christ-event.

In paraenesis, unlike in theological argument, one normally does not *prove* the truth of one's teaching, and so is not required to cite its sources. So, as an apostle of Christ who had the mind of Christ (1 Cor 2:16) and spoke under the inspiration of his Spirit (7:40), Paul usually imparted his authoritative apostolic teaching. However, when he was conscious of the opinions or attitudes contrary to his own teachings, he *did* refer or allude to Jesus' teachings in order to support his apostolic teachings with the Lord's authority. Romans 14:14; 1 Cor 7:10-11; 9:14; Gal 5:14 (+ 6:2) and other passages (discussed in 1 above) well illustrate this point. With Paul's eschatological teaching also a similar phenomenon is observable, and 1 Thess 4:15-17; 5:1-7 illustrate this. Thus, Paul *did* use Jesus' sayings in support of his own teaching when he found himself in the situation where he had to *prove* its veracity. In the usual situations, however, he did not need to make any *explicit citation* of the sayings of Jesus. Nevertheless, since as an apostle he had to represent his Lord's teaching, he *re*-presented it in his own language, sometimes alluding to or echoing some of his concrete sayings. This *re*-presentation was necessary in order to make Jesus' teaching more suitable to Paul's changed, post-Easter situation (Goppelt, 42-46), or to his audience in the Hellenistic world. Furthermore, it is to be noted that even in paraenesis he tends to concentrate on the cross and resurrection of Christ as a motivating force rather than on his concrete sayings and deeds. About this, Thompson puts it well: "Why should Paul point to an act [or a command — we may add] of love, humility, or compassion during Jesus' ministry when he could cite his example of total commitment on the cross? Why should he cite a healing act of power, when he could refer to the resurrection? Everything Jesus said and did before his death and vindication paled in significance by comparison to the Christ-Event."

Thus, the "paucity" and allusive character of Paul's references to Jesus' sayings turn out, partly, to have been necessitated by Paul's living in the post-Easter period, and partly to have been natural. In any case they turn out to be quite understandable. They should no longer be used as evidence for Paul's lack of knowledge of or interest in the Jesus tradition or in the historical Jesus.

Summary and Conclusion

We have ascertained over twenty-five instances where Paul certainly or probably makes reference or allusion to a saying of Jesus. In addition, we have tabulated over forty possible echoes of a saying of Jesus. These are distributed throughout all of the Pauline letters, though 1 Corinthians and Romans contain the most.

There is a real continuity between Jesus' teaching centered on the kingdom of God and Paul's theology as a whole. The replacement of Jesus' gospel of the kingdom with the apostolic gospel of the death and resurrection of Jesus Christ was logically necessitated by the salvation promised in Jesus' kingdom preaching having been realized in his death and resurrection. In Paul's central soteriological category of justification, he accurately expressed the intention of Jesus' gospel of the kingdom. The theological continuity between Jesus and Paul is further supported by Paul's concrete echoes of the "kingdom of God" and *"abba,"* by his teachings on the Law, the temple and eschatology, by his welcoming sinners, and by other aspects of his attitude and conduct such as renunciation of privilege and humble service.

The close similarities between Jesus and Paul in theology and attitude may be taken as evidence of Paul's intimate knowledge of Jesus' teaching and attitude. This consideration should incline interpreters toward a more positive judgment in those cases where there is a dispute over the presence of an echo of a saying of Jesus, placing the burden of proof more heavily on those who would deny it than on those who would accept it.

Echoes of Jesus' sayings are discernible in all the major themes of Paul's theology. His christology and soteriology are conditioned by Jesus' teaching as much as are his other theological *loci,* leading to the conclusion that Jesus' teaching provides Paul with a basis for his theology as a whole.

Paul also provides hints of his knowledge of the narrative tradition of Jesus' passion, his healing ministry, his welcoming sinners, his life of poverty and humble service, his character, and other aspects.

The number of contexts in which Paul fails to refer to a saying of Jesus against our expectation is in fact few and explainable. Nevertheless, the fact that Paul's references to Jesus' sayings are not numerous and they are all allusive, a characteristic shared by other New Testament writings outside the Gospels, requires an explanation. Paul, like the other New Testament writers, probably treated Jesus tradition as an independent entity and transmitted it separately to his churches at their foundation (cf. Gerhardsson). However, for Paul, as for the post-Easter church as a whole,

Jesus was significant primarily not as a teacher but as the Christ who had died and risen. Hence Paul concentrated on the Christ event. He cannot be compared to a rabbi or a Hellenistic philosopher who diligently cites his teacher.

In his letters Paul was called upon not to prove the character of Jesus' death as the fulfillment of Jesus' ministry, but the availability of that salvation to Gentiles apart from works of the Law. So Paul did not need to cite Jesus' kingdom preaching to prove its fulfillment in his death, and he would have found few concrete sayings from the Jewish context of Jesus' ministry that were directly relevant to his conflict with Judaizers and enthusiasts in his Gentile churches. Paul, therefore, concentrated on expounding the full significance of Jesus' death, guided by the general spirit of Jesus' teaching, in order to prove the truth of his gospel of the cross, *sola gratia* and *sola fide*.

In paraenesis and eschatology, in order to support his teaching with the Lord's authority in the face of a contrary opinion, Paul occasionally referred explicitly to Jesus' sayings. But usually he did not need to *prove* the truth of his teaching. As an apostle of Christ who had the mind of Christ and spoke under the inspiration of his Spirit, he could simply impart his authoritative apostolic teaching. In this he seldom cited Jesus' sayings explicitly, but *represented* them, echoing them in his own language. Although he shows a great reverence for Jesus' sayings and shapes his theology as a whole according to them, he does not use them in a literalistic or legalistic way, but adapts them to the new post-Easter situations and to his Hellenistic audiences, modifying their letter while respecting their spirit.

Against this background the "paucity" and allusive character of Paul's references to Jesus' sayings should no longer be used as evidence for Paul's reputed lack of knowledge of or interest in the Jesus tradition or in the historical Jesus. On the contrary, we are led to search for echoes of Jesus' sayings woven into Paul's statements. Once these echoes as well as Paul's allusions to Jesus' sayings are established, we can study in detail the actual method by which Paul used them (cf. Gundry; Ellis) and their relationship to the history of the Synoptic tradition (cf. Dungan; Allison; Kuhn; esp. Wenham).

Bibliography

D. C. Allison, "The Pauline Epistles and the Synoptic Gospels: The Pattern of the Parallels," *NTS* 28 (1982): 1-32.

F. F. Bruce, *Paul: Apostle of the Heart Set Free* (Grand Rapids: Eerdmans, 1977), 95-112.

C. E. B. Cranfield, *A Critical and Exegetical Commentary on the Epistle to the Romans*, vol. 2 (ICC; Edinburgh: T & T Clark, 1979).

N. Dahl, "The Doctrine of Justification: Its Social Function and Implications," in *Studies in Paul: Theology for the Early Christian Mission* (Minneapolis: Augsburg, 1977), 95-120.

D. L. Dungan, *The Sayings of Jesus in the Churches of Paul* (Philadelphia: Fortress, 1971).

J. D. G. Dunn, "Mark 2.1–3.6: A Bridge between Jesus and Paul on the Question of the Law," in *Jesus, Paul and the Law* (Louisville: Westminster/John Knox, 1990), 10-31.

E. E. Ellis, "Traditions in 1 Corinthians," *NTS* 32 (1982): 481-502.

B. Gerhardsson, "The Path of the Gospel Tradition," in *The Gospel and the Gospels* (ed. P. Stuhlmacher; Grand Rapids: Eerdmans, 1991), 75-96.

L. Goppelt, *Theology of the New Testament*, vol. 2 (Grand Rapids: Eerdmans, 1982).

R. H. Gundry, "The Hellenization of Dominical Tradition and Christianization of Jewish Tradition in the Eschatology of 1-2 Thessalonians," *NTS* 33 (1987): 161-78.

G. Haufe, "Reich Gottes bei Paulus und in der Jesustradition," *NTS* 31 (1985): 467-72.

M. Hengel, "Between Jesus and Paul: The 'Hellenists,' the 'Seven' and Stephen (Acts 6.1-15; 7.54–8.3)," in *Between Jesus and Paul* (Philadelphia: Fortress, 1983), 1-29.

————, "Die Ursprünge der christliche Mission," *NTS* 18 (1971): 15-38 (= "The Origins of the Christian Mission," in *Between Jesus and Paul* [Philadelphia: Fortress, 1983], 48-64).

T. Holtz, "Tradition im 1. Thessalonicherbrief," in *Die Mitte des NT* (ed. U. Luz and H. Weder; Göttingen: Vandenhoeck & Ruprecht, 1983).

E. Jüngel, *Paulus und Jesus: Eine Untersuchung zur Präzisierung der Frage nach dem Ursprung der Christologie* (HUT 2; Tübingen: J. C. B. Mohr, 1962).

E. Käsemann, *Commentary on Romans* (Grand Rapids: Eerdmans, 1980).

————, "A Critical Analysis of Philippians 2:5-11," in *God and Christ* (New York: Harper & Row, 1968), 45-88.

S. Kim, "Jesus — the Son of God, the Stone, the Son of Man and the Servant: The Role of Zechariah in the Self-Identification of Jesus," in *Tradition and Interpretation* (E. E. Ellis FS; ed. G. F. Hawthorne with O. Betz; Grand Rapids: Eerdmans, 1987), 134-48.

————, "Jesus' Kingdom Preaching and Christian Politics," *Presbyterian Theological Quarterly* 222 (1989): 6-49 (in Korean).

K. T. Kleinknecht, *Der leidende Gerechtfertigte: Die alttestamentlich-jüdische Tradition vom 'leidenden Gerechten' und ihre Rezeption bei Paulus* (WUNT 2.13; Tübingen: J. C. B. Mohr, 1984).

H. W. Kuhn, "Der irdische Jesus bei Paulus als traditionsgeschichtliches und theologisches Problem," *ZTK* 67 (1970): 295-320.

R. P. Martin, *Carmen Christi: Philippians ii.5-11 in Recent Interpretation and in the Setting of Early Christian Worship* (SNTSMS 4; Cambridge: University Press, 1967).

H. Merkel, "Die Gottesherrschaft in der Verkündigung Jesu," in *Königsherrschaft Gottes und himmlischer Kult* (ed. M. Hengel and A. M. Schwemer; Tübingen: J. C. B. Mohr, 1991).

F. Neirynck, "Paul and the Sayings of Jesus," in *Apôtre Paul* (ed. A. Vanhoye; Leuven: Leuven University Press, 1986), 265-321.

J. Piper, *"Love Your Enemies": Jesus' Love Command in the Synoptic Gospels and the Early Christian Paraenesis* (SNTSMS 38; Cambridge: University Press, 1979).

H. Räisänen, "Zur Herkunft von Markus 7,15," in *The Torah and Christ* (Helsinki: Finnish Exegetical Society, 1986), 209-18.

P. Richardson, "The Thunderbolt in Q and the Wise Man in Corinth," in *From Jesus to Paul: Studies in Honour of F. W. Beare* (Waterloo: W. Laurier University, 1984), 91-111.

P. Richardson and P. Gooch, "Logia of Jesus in 1 Corinthians," in *Gospels Perspectives 5: The Jesus Tradition outside the Gospels* (ed. D. Wenham; Sheffield: JSOT, 1985), 39-62.

H. Schürmann, " 'Das Gesetz des Christus' (Gal 6,2): Jesu Verhalten und Wort als letztgültige sittliche Norm nach Paulus," in *Neues Testament und Kirche* (ed. J. Gnilka; Freiburg: Herder, 1974), 282-300.

E. Schweizer, "1. Korinther 15,20-28 als Zeugnis paulinischer Eschatologie und ihrer Verwandtschaft mit der Verkündigung Jesu," in *Jesus und Paulus* (ed. E. E. Ellis and E. Grässer; Göttingen: Vandenhoeck & Ruprecht, 1975), 301-14.

P. Stuhlmacher, "Jesustradition im Romerbrief?" *Theologische Beiträge* 14 (1983): 240-50.

M. Thompson, *Clothed with Christ* (JSNTSS 59; Sheffield: JSOT, 1991).

N. Walter, "Paul and the Early Christian Jesus-Tradition," in *Paul and Jesus* (ed. A. J. M. Wedderburn and C. Wolff; JSNTSS 37; Sheffield: JSOT, 1989), 51-80.

A. J. M. Wedderburn, "Paul and Jesus: The Problem of Continuity," in *Paul and Jesus* (ed. A. J. M. Wedderburn and C. Wolff; JSNTSS 37; Sheffield: JSOT, 1989), 99-115.

————, "Paul and Jesus: Similarity and Continuity," in *Paul and Jesus* (ed. A. J. M. Wedderburn and C. Wolff; JSNTSS 37; Sheffield: JSOT, 1989), 117-43.

————, "Paul and the Story of Jesus," in *Paul and Jesus*, 161-89.

D. Wenham, *Gospel Perspectives 4: The Rediscovery of Jesus' Eschatological Discourse* (Sheffield: JSOT, 1984).

————, "Paul's Use of the Jesus Tradition: Three Samples," in *Gospel Perspectives 5: The Jesus Tradition outside the Gospels* (ed. D. Wenham; Sheffield: JSOT, 1985), 7-37.

C. Wolff, "Humility and Self-Denial in Jesus' Life and Message and in the Apostolic Existence of Paul," in *Paul and Jesus* (ed. A. J. M. Wedderburn and C. Wolff; JSNTSS 37; Sheffield: JSOT, 1989), 145-60.

Conclusion

These second thoughts on the origin of Paul's gospel have yielded two results. On the one hand, they have confirmed and strengthened my original theses in their essentials. On the other hand, they have clarified them throughout and supplemented them in some parts. Therefore, I submit once more that Paul's εἰκών-, Adam- and Wisdom-christology and its soteriological application, transformation-soteriology, originated from the revelation of the exalted Christ as the image of God, that his soteriology of justification and reconciliation originated from his experience of his own justification and reconciliation through God's grace on the Damascus road while persecuting Christians out of his zeal for the law, and that he obtained the "mystery" of Rom 11:25-26, that is, his understanding of God's plan to save the gentiles now and Israel as a whole at the eschaton, by interpreting the revelation and his apostolic call on the Damascus road in the light of the Scriptures, especially Isa 6 and 49. So once more I appreciate Paul's testimony that he received his gospel as well as his apostleship through the revelation of Jesus Christ on the Damascus road (Gal 1:11-17).

The new discovery that Paul interpreted his apostolic call in the light of Isa 42 as well as Isa 49 provides an answer to the curious question of why Paul started his mission in Arabia (Gal 1:17). Further, it leads me to supplement my original thesis with the belief that in Paul's obtaining the "mystery" of Rom 11:25-26, Isa 42 played as much a role as Isa 49. But the more important implication of the new discovery is that Paul was conscious of his having been endowed with the Holy Spirit at his apostolic call on the Damascus road. Of course, this has a great implication for explaining his apostolic self-understanding and ministry. However, in this book, I have appreciated its implication especially for his doctrine of justification. It enables us to explain how he developed his distinctive antitheses, the Spirit-the law and the Spirit-the flesh, by inter-

293

preting his experience of the Holy Spirit in the light of Scriptures such as Ezek 36–37 and Jer 31. This in turn explains how he came to the conviction that by the (works of the) law no one is justified (Gal 3:10-11). Thus, this consideration not only strengthens the thesis that his gospel of justification by grace and through faith without works of the law originated from his Damascus experience, but also makes his radical reassessment of the law understandable.

This extensive reexamination of Paul's conversion/call experience in a critical interaction with the New Perspective as represented especially by James D. G. Dunn has confirmed the thesis that Paul obtained his gospel of justification *sola gratia/fide* from his Damascus experience and that he preached it also in Thessalonica and Corinth, where there was no controversy with the Judaizers. The study on the Damascus origin of Paul's distinctive doctrine of reconciliation, which is parallel to his doctrine of justification, supports this conclusion. This conclusion contradicts the New Perspective School's view that he did not develop the doctrine of justification until fifteen to seventeen years after his conversion, in the wake of the Antiochian or Galatian controversy with the Judaizers, for the strategic purpose of defending the gentile believers' right to membership in God's people.

Furthermore, the studies in chapters 1 and 4 on Paul's doctrines of the law and of justification have set a large question mark beside the fundamental assumption of the New Perspective School concerning Second Temple Judaism. They have shown rather that Paul is an extremely important witness to the presence of the element of works-righteousness within the overall covenantal nomism of first-century Judaism. But the New Perspective School nevertheless elevates E. P. Sanders's definition of Second Temple Judaism as covenantal nomism to the status of a dogma and insists on interpreting Paul only in terms of that dogma. The result has been to make Paul totally arbitrary, hardly addressing the Judaism of his time (E. P. Sanders)[1] or willfully distorting it (H. Räisänen). Dunn thinks that with his sociological approach to Paul's phrase of "works of the law" he can avoid such an unreal conclusion and show how Paul in fact criticizes contemporary Judaism for making its covenantal nomism an ethnocentric barrier to the gentiles' membership in the people of God. But our examination of his two chosen "test cases," Paul's conversion/call and Gal 3:10-14, and his key concepts such as "works of the law" and "my/their own righteousness" has shown that his exegesis of them is faulty and that they do in fact point to an element of works-righteousness in Judaism. Thus, Paul simply cannot be brought in line with the dogma of the

---

1. Dunn himself criticizes Sanders thus ("The New Perspective on Paul," in *Jesus, Paul and the Law* [Louisville: Westminster/John Knox, 1990], 202).

New Perspective School. Therefore, I suggest here that we should first strive to interpret Paul without allowing any dogma, whether that of the New Perspective or of the Old Perspective, to predetermine our exegesis, and see what picture of Judaism he provides. It is a call to take Paul seriously as a first-hand witness to the Judaism of the first century, at least as seriously as other Jewish documents.[2]

The general conclusion to be drawn here concerning the doctrine of justification is that the traditional understanding of the doctrine is essentially correct. The New Perspective School seems to make a contribution only by leading the upholders of the Old Perspective to appreciate better the doctrine's overall covenantal framework and its sociological or missiological implications.

It is a curious fact that in spite of all its emphasis on the importance of Paul's gentile mission as the *Ansatz* for his theologizing, the New Perspective School does not take the "mystery" of Rom 11:25-26 seriously. For me, without an understanding of God's *Heilsplan* such as embodied in the "mystery," Paul, the "zealot" for the law and Judaism, could hardly have carried out his systematic, worldwide gentile mission, and without his doctrine of justification *sola gratia/fide* without works of the law, he could scarcely have started his gentile mission. Therefore, I reaffirm that (1) the revelation of the gospel of the Son of God, the Lord over all, and of justification *sola gratia/fide*; (2) the apostolic call to the gentiles; (3) the endowment of the Holy Spirit; and (4) the revelation of the "mystery" of Rom 11:25-26 all belong together as the four essential elements of the Damascus event as interpreted by Paul, and that they together made a passionate apostle to the gentiles out of a Pharisee and "zealot" for the law and Judaism.

The recent emphasis of Alan F. Segal and others on the importance of the Old Testament-Jewish apocalyptic-mystical vision tradition of Ezek 1 as a background for Paul strengthens my thesis on the Damascus origin of Paul's Image-, Adam- and Wisdom-christology/soteriology. However, I have discovered that Paul echoes Jesus' "Son of Man"-sayings in several places and that Jesus' self-designation as "the 'Son of Man' " and its scriptural background,

2. The picture of Judaism found in Paul's writings comports well with that which M. A. Elliott, *The Survivors of Israel: A Reconsideration of the Theology of Pre-Christian Judaism* (Grand Rapids: Eerdmans, 2000), has read out of pre-Christian Jewish literature. I regret that I came upon this fundamentally important book of Elliot too late to utilize its findings effectively. As it in effect destroys the very basis of the New Perspective School, the fundamental assumption of Second Temple Judaism as "covenantal nomism" (as defined by E. P. Sanders), it could have greatly helped my arguments against the School's interpretation of Paul. In summary, Elliot's study of Jewish literature and this study of Pauline literature corroborate each other to a large extent.

Dan 7, also contributed to the development of Paul's Adam-christology/ soteriology. Similarly Jesus' Wisdom-sayings contributed to the development of Paul's Wisdom-christology. So I modify my thesis: Paul developed his Adam-christology/soteriology from his Damascus experience of seeing the exalted Christ as the image of God and from his confirmation of that experience by Jesus' self-designation as "the 'Son of Man' " and by Dan 7 and Ps 8. Paul likewise developed his Wisdom-christology from seeing the exalted Christ as the image of God and as the end of the law on the Damascus road and from his confirming this understanding by Jesus' identification with (the representative of) Wisdom and by the Wisdom theology of the Old Testament and Judaism.

Paul also found Jesus' gospel of the kingdom of God, his critique of the contemporary Jewish understanding of the law, and his welcoming the outcasts while criticizing the unresponsive Jews, to be confirmation of his doctrines of justification and reconciliation and his conviction about the gentile mission, all of which he developed from his revelatory experience on the road to Damascus. Perhaps it is more appropriate to state this fact the other way around: in the light of the Damascus revelation, Paul accepted the post-Easter church's gospel of Christ's death and resurrection as the proper representation of Jesus' gospel of God's kingdom. Then, in the light of his Damascus experience, Paul interpreted and re-presented the gospel in terms of the soteriology of justification, reconciliation, adoption, transformation, and new creation as well as the christology of Jesus as Christ, Lord, Son of God, Last Adam, and so on. By means of his doctrine of justification, Paul represented especially well Jesus' intent in his preaching of God's kingdom, in his ministry for sinners, and in his death of atoning and covenant-establishing sacrifice.

The new appreciation of the Jesus tradition in Paul's theology as a whole and some concrete examples of Paul's use of Jesus' "Son of Man"-sayings in his Son-christology and Adam-christology have given me a glimpse into Paul's theological method of developing new theological insights and conceptions by using the Damascus revelation, the Jesus tradition, the Scriptures, and the early church kerygma for mutual interpretation and confirmation. From this perspective, I would like to modify my fundamental thesis: Paul's gospel originated from both the Damascus revelation and the Jesus tradition. It needs a further, more comprehensive study to determine more precisely how the Damascus revelation, the Jesus tradition, the Scriptures, and the early church kerygma were brought into an interplay to produce various Pauline theological conceptions. But still the present study, though no more than a preliminary study on this question, leads me to submit the above thesis for further discussion.

Conclusion

The best metaphor that I can think of to illustrate this double origin of Paul's gospel is that it is the child of two parents, the Damascus revelation being the father and the Jesus tradition the mother. Just as a child resembles both parents, so that from one perspective it looks very much like the father while from another perspective very much like the mother, Paul's gospel appears stamped with the Damascus revelation throughout when seen from the perspective of the Damascus revelation, while it appears as a reinterpretation and reapplication of Jesus' gospel in the new salvation-historical and missiological contexts when viewed from the perspective of the Jesus tradition. To continue with the metaphor, we may see the Old Testament as a grandparent of Paul's theology and the pre-Pauline Christian kerygma as an older sibling.

As I observed at the end of chapter 6, Paul's theological method of developing new theological insights for new situations by using the Damascus revelation, the Jesus tradition, the Scriptures, and the early church kerygma for mutual interpretation and confirmation has a paradigmatic significance for our theologizing for our situations today.

Bibliography

1. The Texts

The Aramaic Bible: The Targums, ed. Martin McNamara et al. Wilmington: Michael Glazier, 1987-89; Collegeville: Liturgical Press, 1991-.

Biblia Hebraica Stuttgartensia, ed. Karl Elliger and Wilhelm Rudolph et al., 5th ed. Stuttgart: Deutsche Bibelgesellschaft, 1997.

The Dead Sea Scrolls: Hebrew, Aramaic, and Greek Texts with English Translations, ed. James H. Charlesworth, 10 vols. The Princeton Theological Seminary Dead Sea Scrolls Project. Tübingen: Mohr-Siebeck; Louisville: Westminster/John Knox, 1994-.

The Dead Sea Scrolls Translated: The Qumran Texts in English, ed. Florentino García Martínez, 2d ed. Leiden: E. J. Brill; Grand Rapids: Eerdmans, 1996.

Josephus, *Works,* 10 vols., Loeb Classical Library. Cambridge, Mass.: Harvard University Press, 1926-65.

New Testament Apocrypha, ed. W. Hennecke and W. Schneemelcher, English edition by R. McL. Wilson, 2 vols. London: SCM, 1965.

Novum Testamentum Graece, ed. Eberhard Nestle and Kurt Aland, 27th ed. Stuttgart: Deutsche Bibelgesellschaft, 1993.

The Old Testament Pseudepigrapha, ed. James H. Charlesworth, 2 vols. Garden City: Doubleday, 1983, 1985.

Philo, *Works,* 10 vols., Loeb Classical Library. Cambridge, Mass.: Harvard University Press, 1929-62.

Septuaginta, ed. Alfred Rahlfs, 2 vols., 8th ed. Stuttgart: Württembergische Bibelanstalt, 1965.

Septuaginta: Vetus Testamentum Graecum Auctoritate Academiae Scientiarum Gottingensis editum. Göttingen: Vandenhoeck & Ruprecht, 1931.

The Targum of Isaiah, ed. John F. Stenning. Oxford: Clarendon, 1949, 1953.

Bibliography

2. References

Aland, Kurt. *Vollständige Konkordanz zum griechischen Neuen Testament.* Berlin: de Gruyter, 1975.

Bauer, Walter. *Griechisch-deutsches Wörterbuch zu den Schriften des Neuen Testaments und der frühchristlichen Literatur.* 6th ed., Kurt Aland and B. Aland. Berlin: de Gruyter, 1988.

Bauer, Walter, William F. Arndt, F. Wilbur Gingrich, and Frederick W. Danker. *Greek-English Lexicon of the New Testament and Other Early Christian Literature.* 2nd rev. and augmented ed. Chicago: University of Chicago Press, 1979.

Blass, Friedrich W., Albert Debrunner, and Friedrich Rehkopf. *Grammatik des neutestamentlichen Griechisch.* 14th ed. Göttingen: Vandenhoeck & Ruprecht, 1975.

Brown, Francis, S. R. Driver, and C. A. Briggs. *A Hebrew and English Lexicon of the Old Testament.* Oxford: Clarendon Press, 1976.

Hatch, Edwin, and Henry A. Redpath. *A Concordance to the Septuagint and Other Greek Versions of the Old Testament.* 3 vols. Oxford: Clarendon, 1897-1906. Repr., Graz: Akademische Druck- u. Verlaganstalt, 1954.

3. Secondary Literature

Allison, Dale C. "The Pauline Epistles and the Synoptic Gospels: The Pattern of the Parallels." *New Testament Studies* 28 (1982): 1-32.

Allo, Ernest B. *Saint Paul: Seconde Épître aux Corinthiens.* Paris: Libraire Lecoffre, 1956.

Avemarie, Friedrich. "Erwählung und Vergeltung: Zur Optionalen Struktur Rabbinischer Soteriologie." *New Testament Studies* 45 (1999): 108-26.

Bachmann, Philipp. *Der zweite Brief des Paulus an die Korinther.* 3d ed. Leipzig: Deichertsche, 1922.

Baltzer, Klaus. *Biographie der Propheten.* Neukirchen-Vluyn: Neukirchener, 1975.

―――. *Deutero-Jesaja.* Kommentar zum Alten Testament 10/2. Gütersloh: Gütersloher Verlagshaus, 1999.

Balz, Horst R., and Gerhard Schneider, eds. *Exegetical Dictionary of the New Testament.* Grand Rapids: Eerdmans, 1990-1993.

Barclay, John M. G. *Obeying the Truth: Paul's Ethics in Galatians.* Edinburgh: T & T Clark, 1988; Minneapolis: Fortress, 1991.

―――. "Paul and the Law: Observations on Some Recent Debates." *Themelios* 12 (1987): 5-15.

Barnett, Paul. "Opposition in Corinth." *Journal for the Study of the New Testament* 22 (1984): 3-17.

―――. *The Second Epistle to the Corinthians.* New International Commentary. Grand Rapids: Eerdmans, 1997.

Barrett, Charles K. *Commentary on the First Epistle to the Corinthians.* 2d ed. Black's New Testament Commentaries. London: Black, 1971.

299

———. *A Commentary on the Second Epistle to the Corinthians.* Black's New Testament Commentaries. London: Black, 1973.

———. *Freedom and Obligation.* Philadelphia: Westminster, 1985.

———. *Paul: An Introduction to His Thought.* Louisville: Westminster/John Knox, 1994.

———. Paul's Opponents in 2 Corinthians." *New Testament Studies* 17 (1970/71): 233-54.: An Introduction to His Thought. Louisville: Westminster/John Knox, 1994.

Beale, Gregory K. "The Old Testament Background of 2 Corinthians 6:14–7:1." *New Testament Studies* 35 (1989): 550-81.

Becker, Jürgen. *Paulus: Der Apostel der Völker.* Tübingen: Mohr-Siebeck, 1989.

Beet, Joseph A. *A Commentary on St. Paul's Epistles to the Corinthians.* 5th ed. London: Hodder and Stoughton, 1892.

Beker, Johan C. "Echoes and Intertextuality: On the Role of Scripture in Paul's Theology." Pages 64-69 in *Paul and the Scriptures of Israel.* Edited by Craig A. Evans and James A. Sanders. Journal for the Study of the New Testament Supplement Series 83. Sheffield: Academic Press, 1993.

———. *Paul the Apostle.* Philadelphia: Fortress, 1980.

Bell, Richard H. *Provoked to Jealousy.* Wissenschaftliche Untersuchungen zum Neuen Testament 2/63. Tübingen: Mohr-Siebeck, 1994.

Best, Ernest. *The First and Second Epistles to the Thessalonians.* Black's New Testament Commentaries. London: Black, 1972.

Betz, Hans Dieter. "The Concept of the 'Inner Human Being' in Paul's Anthropology." *New Testament Studies* 46 (2000): 315-42.

———. *Galatians: A Commentary on Paul's Letter to the Churches in Galatia.* Philadelphia: Fortress, 1979.

Betz, Otto. "'Fleischliche' und 'geistliche' Christuserkenntnis nach 2. Korinther 5,16." *Theologische Beiträge* 14 (1983): 167-79. Repr. pages 114-28 in *Jesus: der Herr der Kirche: Aufsätze zur biblischen Theologie, 2.* Wissenschaftliche Untersuchungen zum Neuen Testament 52. Tübingen: Mohr-Siebeck, 1990.

———. *Jesus und das Danielbuch,* vol. 2. *Die Menschensohnworte Jesu und die Zukunftserwartung des Paulus (Daniel 7,13-14).* Frankfurt: Peter Lang, 1985.

———. "Jesu Evangelium vom Gottesreich." Pages 232-54 in *Jesus: der Messias Israels: Aufsätze zur biblischen Theologie.* Wissenschaftliche Untersuchungen zum Neuen Testament 42. Tübingen: Mohr-Siebeck, 1987.

———. "Jesus und Jesaja 53." Pages 3-19 in *Geschichte — Tradition — Reflexion: Festschrift für Martin Hengel zum 70. Geburtstag,* vol. 3. *Frühes Christentum.* Edited by Hubert Cancik, Hermann Lichtenberger, and Peter Schäfer. Tübingen: Mohr-Siebeck, 1996.

———. "Paulus als Pharisäer nach dem Gesetz: Phil. 3,5-6 als Beitrag zur Frage des frühen Pharisäismus." In *Treue zur Thora: Beiträge zur Mitte des christlich-jüdischen Gesprächs,* G. Harder FS. Edited by P. von der Osten-Sacken. Berlin: Institut Kirche und Judentum, Selbstverlag, 1977. Repr. pages 103-13 in *Jesus: der Herr der Kirche.*

———. "Die Vision des Paulus im Tempel von Jerusalem." Pages 113-23 in *Verborum*

Veritas. Wuppertal: R Brockhaus Verlag, 1970. Repr. pages 91-102 in *Jesus: der Herr der Kirche*.

Bieringer, Reimund. "2 Korinther 5:19a und die Versöhnung der Welt." Pages 429-59 in Reimund Bieringer and Jan Lambrecht, *Studies on 2 Corinthians*. Bibliotheca Ephemeridum Theologicarum Lovaniensium 112. Leuven: Leuven University Press, 1994.

Billerbeck, Paul (H. L. Strack). *Kommentar zum Neuen Testament aus Talmud und Midrasch*. 6 vols. München: C. H. Beck, 1922-61.

Black, Matthew. "Pauline Doctrine of the Second Adam." *Scottish Journal of Theology* 7 (1954): 170-79.

Blank, Josef. *Paulus und Jesus: Eine theologische Grundlegung*. Munich: Kösel, 1968.

Bockmuehl, Markus N. A. " 'The Form of God' (Phil. 2:6): Variations on a Theme of Jewish Mysticism." *Journal of Theological Studies* n.s. 48 (1997): 1-23.

———. *Revelation and Mystery in Ancient Judaism and Pauline Christianity*. Tübingen: Mohr-Siebeck, 1990.

Botterweck, G. Johannes, and Helmer Ringgren, eds. *Theologisches Wörterbuch zum Alten Testament*. Stuttgart: W. Kohlhammer, 1973-1977. (Or Botterweck, G. Johannes, and Helmer Ringgren, eds. *Theological Dictionary of the Old Testament*. Rev. ed. Translated by John T. Willis. Grand Rapids: Eerdmans, 1977-.)

Bowker, John W. " 'Merkabah' Visions and the Visions of Paul." *Journal of Semitic Studies* 16 (1971): 157-73.

Braswell, Joseph P. " 'The Blessing of Abraham' versus 'The Curse of the Law': Another Look at Gal 3:10-13." *Westminster Theological Journal* 53 (1991): 73-91.

Breytenbach, Cilliers. *Versöhnung*. Neukirchen-Vluyn: Neukirchener, 1989.

Brown, Raymond E. *The Epistles of John*. Anchor Bible 30. Garden City, N.Y.: Doubleday, 1982.

Bruce, Frederick F. *The Epistle to the Galatians*. New International Greek Testament Commentary. Grand Rapids: Eerdmans, 1982.

———. *1 and 2 Thessalonians*. Word Biblical Commentary 45. Waco: Word Books, 1982.

———. *Paul and Jesus*. Grand Rapids: Eerdmans, 1974.

———. *Paul the Apostle of the Heart Set Free*. Grand Rapids: Eerdmans, 1977.

———. *This Is That*. Exeter: Paternoster, 1968.

Bultmann, Rudolf. αἰσχύνω, κτλ. Pages 189-91 in *Theological Dictionary of the New Testament*, vol. 1, ed. Gerhard Kittel. Grand Rapids: Eerdmans, 1964.

———. *The Second Letter to the Corinthians*. Minneapolis: Augsburg, 1985.

———. *Theology of the New Testament*. Vol. 1. London: SCM; New York: Scribner, 1952.

Burchard, Christoph. *Der dreizehnte Zeuge: Traditions- u. kompositionsgeschichtl. Untersuchungen zu Lukas' Darstellung d. Frühzeit d. Paulus*. Forschungen zur Religion und Literatur des Alten und Neuen Testaments 103. Göttingen: Vandenhoeck & Ruprecht, 1970.

Buttrick, George A. ed. *The Interpreter's Dictionary of the Bible*. 4 vols. New York: Abingdon, 1962.

BIBLIOGRAPHY

Campbell, David A., "The ΔΙΑΘΗΚΗ from Durham: Professor Dunn's *The Theology of Paul the Apostle.*" *Journal for the Study of the New Testament* 72 (1998): 91-111.

Cerfaux, Lucien. *Christ in the Theology of St. Paul.* Translated by G. Webb and A. Walker. New York: Herder & Herder, 1959.

———. "Saint Paul et le 'Serviteur de Dieu' d'Isaie." Pages 439-54 in *Recueil Lucien Cerfaux: Études d'exégèse et d'histoire religieuse, réunies à l'occasion de son soixante-dixième anniversaire.* Vol. 2. Gembloux: Duculot, 1954.

Chae, D. J-S. *Paul as Apostle to the Gentiles.* Carlisle: Paternoster, 1997.

Chester, Andrew. "Jewish Messianic Expectations and Mediatorial Figures and Pauline Christology." Pages 17-89 in *Paulus und das antike Judentum: Tübingen-Durham-Symposium.* Edited by Martin Hengel and Ulrich Heckel. Wissenschaftliche Untersuchungen zum Neuen Testament 58. Tübingen: Mohr-Siebeck, 1991.

Ciampa, Roy E. *The Presence and Function of Scripture in Galatians 1 and 2.* Wissenschaftliche Untersuchungen zum Neuen Testament 2/102. Tübingen: Mohr-Siebeck, 1998.

Collange, Jean-François. *Énigmes de la deuxième Épître de Paul aux Corinthiens.* Cambridge: Cambridge University Press, 1972.

Cranfield, Charles E. B. *The Epistle to the Romans.* 2 vols. International Critical Commentary. Edinburgh: T & T Clark, 1975-86.

———. "'The Works of the Law' in the Epistle to the Romans." *Journal for the Study of the New Testament* 43 (1991): 89-101.

Cranford, Michael. "The Possibility of Perfect Obedience: Paul and an Implied Premise in Galatians 3:10 and 5:3." *Novum Testamentum* 36 (1994): 242-58.

Crump, David M. *Jesus the Intercessor: Prayer and Christology in Luke-Acts.* Wissenschaftliche Untersuchungen zum Neuen Testament 2/49. Tübingen: Mohr-Siebeck, 1992.

Cullmann, Oscar. *Petrus: Jünger, Apostel, Märtyrer.* Munich: Siebenstern, 1967.

Dahl, Niels A. "The Doctrine of Justification: Its Social Function and Implications." Pages 95-120 in *Studies in Paul: Theology for the Early Christian Mission.* Minneapolis: Augsburg, 1977.

Deines, Roland. *Die Pharisäer: Ihr Verständnis im Spiegel der christlichen und jüdischen Forschung seit Wellhausen und Graetz.* Wissenschaftliche Untersuchungen zum Neuen Testament 101. Tübingen: Mohr-Siebeck, 1997.

Denney, James. *The Second Epistle to the Corinthians.* London: Hodder, 1894.

Dick, K. *Der schriftstellerische Plural bei Paulus.* Halle: Niemeyer, 1900.

Dietzfelbinger, Christian. *Die Berufung des Paulus als Ursprung seiner Theologie.* Wissenschaftliche Monographien zum Alten und Neuen Testament 58. Neukirchen-Vluyn: Neukirchener, 1985.

Dinkler, Erich. "Die Taufterminologie in 2Kor 1,21f." Pages 99-107 in *Signum Crucis: Aufsätze zum Neuen Testament zur christlichen Archäologie.* Tübingen: Mohr-Siebeck, 1967.

Dodd, Charles H. *According to the Scriptures.* London: Nisbet, 1952.

Donaldson, Terence L. "Israelite, Convert, Apostle to the Gentiles: The Origin of Paul's Gentile Mission." Pages 62-83 in *The Road from Damascus: The Impact of*

Paul's Conversion on His Life, Thought and Ministry. Edited by Richard N. Longenecker. Grand Rapids: Eerdmans, 1997.

———. *Paul and the Gentiles: Remapping the Apostle's Convictional World.* Minneapolis: Fortress, 1997.

———. "'Riches for the Gentiles' (Rom 11:12): Israel's Rejection and Paul's Gentile Mission." *Journal of Biblical Literature* 112 (1993): 81-98.

———. "Zealot and Convert: The Origin of Paul's Christ-Torah Antithesis." *Catholic Biblical Quarterly* 51 (1989): 655-82.

Donfried, Karl P., ed. *The Romans Debate.* Rev. and expanded ed. Peabody: Hendrickson, 1991.

Dungan, David L. *The Sayings of Jesus in the Churches of Paul.* Philadelphia: Fortress, 1971.

Dunn, James D. G. *Christology in the Making: A New Testament Inquiry into the Origins of the Doctrine of the Incarnation.* 2nd ed. London: SCM, 1989; Grand Rapids: Eerdmans, 1996.

———. *The Epistle to the Galatians.* Black's New Testament Commentary. London: Black; Peabody: Hendrickson, 1993.

———. *Jesus, Paul and the Law: Studies in Mark and Galatians.* Louisville: Westminster/John Knox, 1990.

———. "Jesus and Ritual Purity: A Study of the Tradition-History of Mark 7.15." Pages 37-60 in *Jesus, Paul and the Law: Studies in Mark and Galatians.*

———. *Jesus and the Spirit.* London: SCM, 1975.

———. "'A Light to the Gentiles,' or 'The End of the Law'? The Significance of the Damascus Road Christophany for Paul." Pages 251-66 in *The Glory of Christ in the New Testament: Studies in Christology in Memory of George Bradford Caird.* Edited by Lincoln D. Hurst and Nicholas T. Wright. Oxford: Clarendon, 1987. Repr. pages 89-107 in *Jesus, Paul and the Law: Studies in Mark and Galatians.* Louisville: Westminster/John Knox, 1990.

———. "Mark 2.1–3.6: A Bridge between Jesus and Paul on the Question of the Law." Pages 10-31 in *Jesus, Paul and the Law: Studies in Mark and Galatians.*

———. "The New Perspective on Paul." *Bulletin of the John Rylands University Library of Manchester* 65 (1983): 95-122. Repr. pages 183-214 in *Jesus, Paul and the Law: Studies in Mark and Galatians.*

———. *The Partings of the Ways between Christianity and Judaism.* Philadelphia: Trinity, 1991.

———. "Paul and Justification by Faith." Pages 85-101 in *The Road from Damascus.* Edited by Richard N. Longenecker. Grand Rapids: Eerdmans, 1997.

———. "Paul's Conversion — A Light to Twentieth Century Disputes." Pages 77-93 in *Evangelium, Schriftauslegung, Kirche.* P. Stuhlmacher Festschrift. Edited by J. Ådna, S. J. Hafemann, and Otto Hofius. Göttingen: Vandenhoeck & Ruprecht, 1997.

———. "The Relationship between Paul and Jerusalem according to Galatians 1 and 2." Pages 108-29 in *Jesus, Paul and the Law.*

———. *Romans 1–8.* Word Biblical Commentary 38A. Waco: Word, 1988.

———. *Romans 9–16.* Word Biblical Commentary 38B. Waco: Word, 1988.

———. *The Theology of Paul the Apostle.* Grand Rapids: Eerdmans, 1998.

———. "Works of the Law and the Curse of the Law (Gal 3.10-14)." Pages 215-41 in *Jesus, Paul and the Law: Studies in Mark and Galatians.*

Dupont, Jacques. "'Assis à la droite de Dieu': L'interprétation du Ps 110,1 dans le Nouveau Testament." *Resurrexit: Actes du Symposium International sur la Résurrection de Jesus (Rome 1970).* Edited by E. Dhanis. Rome: Libreria Editrice Vaticana, 1974.

———. "Filius meus est tu." *Recherches de science religieuse* 35 (1948): 522-43.

Eckstein, Hans-Joachim. *Verheissung und Gesetz: Eine exegetische Untersuchung zu Galater 2,15–4,7.* Wissenschaftliche Untersuchungen zum Neuen Testament 86. Tübingen: Mohr-Siebeck, 1996.

Elliger, Karl. *Jesaja 40,1–45,7.* Vol. 1 of *Deuterojesaja.* Biblischer Kommentar: Altes Testament 11/1. Neukirchen-Vluyn: Neukirchener, 1978, 1989.

Elliott, Mark A. *The Survivors of Israel: A Reconsideration of the Theology of Pre-Christian Judaism.* Grand Rapids: Eerdmans, 2000.

Ellis, Edward Earle. "Traditions in 1 Corinthians." *New Testament Studies* 32 (1982): 481-502.

Eskola, Timo. "Paul, Predestination and 'Covenantal Nomism' — Re-Assessing Paul and Palestinian Judaism." *Journal for the Study of Judaism in the Persian, Hellenistic, and Roman Periods* 28 (1997): 390-412.

———. *Theodicy and Predestination in Pauline Soteriology.* Wissenschaftliche Untersuchungen zum Neuen Testament 2/100. Tübingen: Mohr-Siebeck, 1998.

Fee, Gordon D. *God's Empowering Presence: The Holy Spirit in the Letters of Paul.* Peabody: Hendrickson, 1994.

———. "Paul's Conversion as Key to His Understanding of the Spirit." Pages 167-83 in *The Road from Damascus.* Edited by Richard N. Longenecker. Grand Rapids: Eerdmans, 1997.

Findeis, Hans-Jürgen. *Versöhnung, Apostolat, Kirche: Eine exegetisch-theologische und rezeptionsgeschichtliche Studie zu den Versöhnungsaussagen des Neuen Testaments (2 Kor, Röm, Kol, Eph).* Würzburg: Echter, 1983.

Fitzmyer, Joseph A. *Romans: A New Translation with Introduction and Commentary.* Anchor Bible 33. New York: Doubleday, 1993.

Fossum, Jarl E. *The Image of the Invisible God: Essays on the Influence of Jewish Mysticism on Early Christianity.* Novum Testamentum et Orbis Antiquus 30. Freiburg, Switz.: Universitätsverlag Freiburg/Göttingen: Vandenhoeck & Ruprecht, 1995.

———. *The Name of God and the Angel of the Lord.* Wissenschaftliche Untersuchungen zum Neuen Testament 36. Tübingen: Mohr-Siebeck, 1985.

Fredricksen, Paula. "Paul and Augustine: Conversion Narratives, Orthodox Traditions, and the Retrospective Self." *Journal of Theological Studies* n.s. 37 (1986): 3-34.

Frey, Jörg. "Die paulinische Antithese von 'Fleisch' und 'Geist' und die palästinisch-jüdische Weisheitstradition." *Zeitschrift für die neutestamentliche Wissenschaft und die Kunde der älteren Kirche* 90 (1999): 53-73.

Friedrich, Gerhard. "Die Gegner des Paulus im 2. Korintherbrief." Pages 181-215 in *Abraham unser Vater: Juden und Christen im Gespräch über die Bibel. Festschrift für Otto Michel zum 60. Geburtstag.* Edited by Otto Betz, Martin Hengel, and Peter Schmidt. Arbeiten zur Geschichte des Spätjudentums und Urchristentums 5. Leiden: E. J. Brill, 1963.

—————. "Ein Tauflied hellenistischer Judenchristen: 1 Thess 1:9f." *Theologische Zeitschrift* 21 (1965): 502-16.

Fuller, Daniel F. "Paul and 'the Works of the Law.'" *Westminster Theological Journal* 38 (1975): 28-42.

Fung, Ronald Y. K. *The Epistle to the Galatians.* New International Commentary on the New Testament. Grand Rapids: Eerdmans, 1988.

Furnish, Victor P. *II Corinthians.* Anchor Bible 35. Garden City: Doubleday, 1984.

Gager, John G. *The Origins of Anti-Semitism: Attitudes toward Judaism in Pagan and Christian Antiquity.* New York: Oxford University Press, 1983.

Gaston, Lloyd. *Paul and the Torah.* Vancouver: University of British Columbia, 1987.

Gaventa, Beverly R. "Galatians 1 and 2: Autobiography as Paradigm." *Novum Testamentum* 28 (1986): 310-26.

Georgi, Dieter. *Die Gegner des Paulus im 2 Korintherbrief.* Neukirchen-Vluyn: Neukirchener, 1964.

Gerhardsson. Birger. "The Path of the Gospel Tradition." Pages 75-96 in *The Gospel and the Gospels.* Edited by Peter Stuhlmacher. Grand Rapids: Eerdmans, 1991.

Gieschen, Charles A. *Angelomorphic Christology: Antecedents and Early Evidence.* Arbeiten zur Geschichte des antiken Judentums und des Urchristentums 62. Leiden: E. J. Brill, 1998.

Goodman, Martin. *Mission and Conversion: Proselytizing in the Religious History of the Roman Empire.* Oxford: Clarendon, 1994.

Goppelt, Leonhard. *Christologie und Ethik.* Göttingen: Vandenhoeck & Ruprecht, 1969.

—————. *Theologie des Neuen Testaments.* Göttingen: Vandenhoeck & Ruprecht, 1976.

—————. *Theology of the New Testament.* Vol. 2. Grand Rapids: Eerdmans, 1982.

Grimm, Werner. *Jesus und das Danielbuch.* Vol. 1. Frankfurt am Main: Peter Lang, 1984.

Gruenwald, Ithamar. *Apocalyptic and Merkavah Mysticism.* Arbeiten zur Geschichte des antiken Judentums und des Urchristentums 14. Leiden: E. J. Brill, 1980.

Grundmann, Walter. "Paulus, aus dem Volke Israel, Apostel der Völker." *Novum Testamentum* 4 (1960): 267-91.

Gundry, Robert H. "Grace, Works, and Staying Saved." *Biblica* 60 (1985): 1-38.

—————. "The Hellenization of Dominical Tradition and Christianization of Jewish Tradition in the Eschatology of 1–2 Thessalonians." *New Testament Studies* 33 (1987): 161-78.

Gundry-Volf, J. M. *Paul and Perseverance.* Tübingen: Mohr-Siebeck, 1990.

Güttgemanns, Erhardt. *Der leidende Apostel und sein Herr.* Göttingen: Vandenhoeck & Ruprecht, 1966.

Haacker, Klaus. "Die Berufung des Verfolgers und die Rechtfertigung des Gottlosen." *Theologische Beiträge* 6 (1975): 1-19.

————. *Der Brief des Paulus an die Römer.* Theologischer Handkommentar zum Neuen Testament. Leipzig: Evangelische Verlagsanstalt, 1999.

————. *Paulus: Der Werdegang eines Apostels.* Stuttgarter Bibelstudien 171. Stuttgart: Katholisches Bibelwerk, 1997.

Hafemann, Scott J. *Paul, Moses, and the History of Israel.* Wissenschaftliche Untersuchungen zum Neuen Testament 81. Tübingen: Mohr-Siebeck, 1995.

————. *Suffering and Ministry in the Spirit.* Grand Rapids: Eerdmans, 1990.

Hagner, Donald A. "Paul and Judaism. The Jewish Matrix of Early Christianity: Issues in the Current Debate." *Bulletin for Biblical Research* 3 (1993): 111-30.

Hammer, Paul L. "Canon and Theological Variety: A Study in the Pauline Tradition." *Zeitschrift für die neutestamentliche Wissenschaft und die Kunde der älteren Kirche* 67 (1976): 83-89.

Haufe, Günter. "Reich Gottes bei Paulus und in der Jerusalemtradition." *New Testament Studies* 31 (1985): 467-72.

Hawthorne, G. F. *Philippians.* Word Bible Commentary 43. Waco: Word, 1983.

Hay, David M. *Glory at the Right Hand: Psalm 110 in Early Christianity.* Society of Biblical Literature Monograph Series 18. Nashville: Abingdon, 1973.

Hegermann, Harald. *Die Vorstellung vom Schöpfungsmittler im hellenistischen Judentum und Christentum.* Texte und Untersuchungen 82. Berlin: Akademie-Verlag, 1961.

Heininger, Bernhard. *Paulus als Visionär: Eine religionsgeschichtliche Studie.* Herders biblische Studien 9. Freiburg: Herder, 1996.

Hengel, Martin. *The Atonement.* London: SCM, 1981.

————. "Between Jesus and Paul: The 'Hellenists,' the 'Seven' and Stephen (Acts 6.1-15; 7.54–8.3)." Pages 1-29 in *Between Jesus and Paul.* Philadelphia: Fortress, 1983.

————. "Der Jakobusbrief als antipaulinische Polemik." Pages 248-78 in *Tradition and Interpretation in the New Testament: Essays in Honor of E. Earle Ellis for His Sixtieth Birthday.* Edited by Gerald F. Hawthorne and Otto Betz. Grand Rapids: Eerdmans; Tübingen: Mohr-Siebeck, 1987.

————. "E. P. Sanders' 'Common Judaism', Jesus und die Pharisäer." Pages 392-479 in *Judaica et Hellenistica: Kleine Schriften.* Vol. 1. Wissenschaftliche Untersuchungen zum Neuen Testament 90. Tübingen: Mohr-Siebeck, 1996.

————. "'Sit at My Right Hand!' The Enthronement of Christ at the Right Hand of God and Psalm 110:1." Pages 119-225 in *Studies in Early Christology.* Edinburgh: T & T Clark, 1995.

————. "Die Ursprünge der christliche Mission." *New Testament Studies* 18 (1971): 15-38. Repr. "The Origins of the Christian Mission." Pages 48-64 in *Between Jesus and Paul.*

————. "Der vorchristliche Paulus." Pages 268-91 in *Paulus und das antike Judentum.* Wissenschaftliche Untersuchungen zum Neuen Testament 58. Tübingen: Mohr-Siebeck, 1991.

————. *Zur urchristlichen Geschichtsschreibung.* Stuttgart: Calwer, 1979.

Hengel, Martin, and Anna M. Schwemer. *Paul between Damascus and Antioch: The Unknown Years.* Translated by John Bowden. Louisville: Westminster/John Knox, 1997.

————. *Paulus zwischen Damaskus und Antiochien*. Wissenschaftliche Untersuchungen zum Neuen Testament 108. Tübingen: Mohr-Siebeck, 1998.

Hofius, Otto. "Das Evangelium und Israel." Pages 197-262 in *Paulusstudien*. Wissenschaftliche Untersuchungen zum Neuen Testament 51. Tübingen: Mohr-Siebeck, 1989.

————. "Erwägungen zur Gestalt und Herkunft des paulinischen Versöhnungsgedankens." Pages 11-14 in *Paulusstudien*.

————. "Das Gesetz des Mose und das Gesetz Christi." Pages 50-74 in *Paulusstudien*.

————. "'Gott hat unter uns aufgerichtet das Wort von der Versöhnung' (2 Kor 5,19)." *Zeitschrift für die neutestamentliche Wissenschaft und die Kunde der älteren Kirche* 71 (1980): 3-20. Repr. pages 15-32 in *Paulusstudien*.

Holtz, Traugott. *Der erste Brief an die Thessalonicher*. Evangelisch-katholischer Kommentar zum Neuen Testament. Zürich: Benziger; Neukirchen-Vluyn: Neukirchener, 1990.

————. "Tradition im 1. Thessalonicherbrief." Pages 55-78 in *Die Mitte des Neuen Testaments*. Edited by U. Luz and H. Weder. Göttingen: Vandenhoeck & Ruprecht, 1983.

————. "Zum Selbstverständnis des Apostels Paulus." *Theologische Literaturzeitung* 91 (1966). Reprinted in *Geschichte und Theologie des Urchristentums*. Wissenschaftliche Untersuchungen zum Neuen Testament 57. Tübingen: Mohr-Siebeck, 1991.

Hong, I. G. *The Law in Galatians*. Sheffield: JSOT, 1993.

Hooker, Morna D. "Paul and Covenantal Nomism." Pages 47-56 in *Paul and Paulinism: Essays in Honour of Charles K. Barrett*. Edited by Morna D. Hooker and S. G. Wilson. London: SPCK, 1982.

Hübner, Hans. *Biblische Theologie des Neuen Testaments*, vol. 2. *Die Theologie des Paulus und ihre neutestamentliche Wirkungsgeschichte*. Göttingen: Vandenhoeck & Ruprecht, 1993.

————. *Gottes Ich und Israel*. Göttingen: Vandenhoeck & Ruprecht, 1990.

Hughes, Philip E. *Paul's Second Epistle to the Corinthians*. Grand Rapids: Eerdmans, 1962.

Hurtado, Larry W. "Convert, Apostate or Apostle to the Nations: The 'Conversion' of Paul in Recent Scholarship." *Sciences in Religion* 22 (1993): 273-84.

————. *One God, One Lord: Early Christian Devotion and Ancient Jewish Monotheism*. Philadelphia: Fortress, 1988.

Jeremias, Joachim. "Einige vorwiegend sprachliche Beobachtungen zu Röm 11,25-36." Pages 193-203 in *Die Israelfrage nach Römer 9–11*. Edited by L. De Lorenzi. Rome: Abtei von St Paul von den Mauern, 1977.

————. *Der Schlüssel zur Theologie des Paulus*. Stuttgart: Calwer, 1971.

Jeremias, Jörg. "מִשְׁפָּט im ersten Gottesknechtslied." *Vetus Testamentum* 22 (1972): 31-42.

Jervell, Jacob. "Die Zeichen des Apostels: Die Wunder beim lukanischen und paulinischen Paulus." *Studien zum Neuen Testament und seiner Umwelt* 4 (1979): 54-75.

Johnston, G. "'Kingdom of God' Sayings in Paul's Letters." Pages 143-56 in *From Jesus to Paul: Studies in Honor of Francis Wright Beare*. Edited by Peter Richardson and John C. Hurd. Waterloo: Wilfrid Laurier University Press, 1984.

Jones, Peter. *La deuxième Épître de Paul aux Corinthiens: Chapitres 18–21*. Vaux-sur-Seine: Edifac, 1992.

Jüngel, Eberhard. *Paulus und Jesus: Eine Untersuchung zur Präzisierung der Frage nach dem Ursprung der Christologie*. Hermeneutische Untersuchungen zur Theologie 2. Tübingen: Mohr-Siebeck, 1962.

Käsemann, Ernst. *An die Römer*. 2nd ed. Handbuch zum Neuen Testament 8a. Tübingen: Mohr-Siebeck, 1974.

————. *Commentary on Romans*. Grand Rapids: Eerdmans, 1980.

————. "A Critical Analysis of Philippians 2:5-11." Pages 45-88 in *God and Christ*. New York: Harper & Row, 1968.

————. "Erwägungen zum Stichwort 'Versöhnungslehre im NT.'" Pages 47-59 in *Zeit und Geschichte: Dankesgabe an Rudolf Bultmann zum 80. Geburtstag*. Edited by Erich Dinkler. Tübingen: Mohr-Siebeck, 1964.

————. "Gottesgerechtigkeit bei Paulus," *Exegetische Versuche und Besinnungen*. 2d ed. Göttingen: Vandenhoeck & Ruprecht, 1965.

————. "Die Legitimität des Apostels." *Zeitschrift für die neutestamentliche Wissenschaft und die Kunde der älteren Kirche* 41 (1942): 33-71.

Kim, Seyoon. "2 Cor 5:11-21 and the Origin of Paul's Concept of 'Reconciliation.'" *Novum Testamentum* 39 (1997): 360-84.

————. "Jesus' Kingdom Preaching and Christian Politics." *Presbyterian Theological Quarterly* 222 (1989): 6-49 (in Korean).

————. "Jesus, Sayings of." Pages 474-92 in *Dictionary of Paul and His Letters*. Edited by G. F. Hawthorne, R. P. Martin, and D. Reid. Downers Grove: InterVarsity Press, 1993.

————. "Jesus — the Son of God, the Stone, the Son of Man and the Servant: The Role of Zechariah in the Self-Identification of Jesus." Pages 134-48 in *Tradition and Interpretation in the New Testament: Essays in Honor of E. Earle Ellis for His Sixtieth Birthday*. Edited by Gerald F. Hawthorne and Otto Betz. Grand Rapids: Eerdmans; Tübingen: Mohr-Siebeck, 1987.

————. "The Jesus-Tradition in 1 Thess 4:13-5:11," a paper presented at the SNTS meeing in Montreal, July 31–August 4, 2001.

————. "The 'Mystery' of Rom 11.25-26 Once More." *New Testament Studies* 43 (1997): 412-29.

————. *The Origin of Paul's Gospel*. Wissenschaftliche Untersuchungen zum Neuen Testament 2/4. Tübingen: Mohr-Siebeck, 1981. Grand Rapids: Eerdmans, 1982. 2nd ed. Tübingen: Mohr-Siebeck, 1984.

————. *"The 'Son of Man'" as the Son of God*. Wissenschaftliche Untersuchungen zum Neuen Testament 30. Tübingen: Mohr-Siebeck, 1983. Grand Rapids: Eerdmans, 1985.

Kittel, Gerhard, and Gerhard Friedrich, eds. *Theological Dictionary of the New Testa-*

ment. Translated by Geoffrey W. Bromiley. 10 vols. Grand Rapids: Eerdmans, 1964-1976.

Kleinknecht, Karl T. *Der leidende Gerechtfertigte: Die alttestamentlich-jüdische Tradition vom 'leidenden Gerechten' und ihre Rezeption bei Paulus.* Wissenschaftliche Untersuchungen zum Neuen Testament 2/13. Tübingen: Mohr-Siebeck, 1984.

Klöpper, Albert. *Kommentar über das zweite Sendschreiben des Apostels Paulus an die Gemeinde zu Korinth.* Berlin: Reimer, 1874.

Koch, Dietrich-Alex. *Die Schrift als Zeuge des Evangeliums: Untersuchungen zur Verwendung und zum Verständnis der Schrift bei Paulus.* Beiträge zur historischen Theologie 69. Tübingen: Mohr-Siebeck, 1986.

Kramer, Werner. *Christ, Lord, Son of God.* Studies in Biblical Theology 50. London: SCM, 1966.

Kuhn, Heinz-Wolfgang. "Der iridische Jesus bei Paulus als traditionsgeschichtliches und theologisches Problem." *Zeitschrift für die Theologie und Kirche* 67 (1970): 295-320.

Laato, T. *Paul and Judaism: An Anthropological Approach.* Atlanta: Scholars Press, 1995.

Lambrecht, Jan. "'Reconcile Yourselves . . .': A Reading of 2 Corinthians 5:11-21." Pages 363-412 in Reimund Bieringer and Jan Lambrecht, *Studies on 2 Corinthians.* Leuven: University Press, 1994.

Lang, Friedrich. *Die Briefe an die Korinther.* Das Neue Testament Deutsch. Göttingen: Vandenhoeck & Ruprecht, 1986.

Lategan, Bernard C. "Is Paul Defending His Apostleship in Galatians?" *New Testament Studies* 34 (1988): 411-30.

Lietzmann, Hans, and Werner G. Kümmel. *An die Korinther I, II.* 5th and expanded ed. Tübingen: Mohr-Siebeck, 1969.

Lindars, Barnabas. *New Testament Apologetic.* London: SCM, 1961.

Longenecker, Bruce W. "Different Answers to Different Issues: Israel, the Gentiles and Salvation History in Romans 9–11." *Journal for the Study of the New Testament* 36 (1989): 95-123.

———. *The Triumph of Abraham's God.* Nashville: Abingdon, 1998.

Longenecker, Richard N. "The Focus of Romans: The Central Role of 5:1–8:39 in the Argument of the Letter." Pages 49-69 in *Romans and the People of God: Essays in Honor of Gordon D. Fee on the Occasion of His Sixty-fifth Birthday.* Edited by Sven K. Soderlund and Nicholas T. Wright. Grand Rapids: Eerdmans, 1999.

———. *Galatians.* Word Biblical Commentary 41. Dallas: Word, 1990.

Lüdemann, Gerd. *Paulus, der Heidenapostel.* Vol. 1: *Studien zur Chronologie.* Göttingen: Vandenbeck, 1980.

———. *Paulus, der Heidenapostel.* Vol. 2: *Antipaulinismus im frühen Christentum.* Göttingen: Vandenhoeck & Ruprecht, 1983.

Lyons, George. *Pauline Autobiography: Toward a New Understanding.* Society of Biblical Literature Dissertation Series 73. Atlanta: Scholars Press, 1986.

Marshall, I. Howard. *First and Second Thessalonians.* New Century Bible Commentary. Grand Rapids: Eerdmans, 1983.

————. "The Meaning of 'Reconciliation.'" Pages 117-32 in *Unity and Diversity in New Testament Theology: Essays in Honor of George E. Ladd*. Edited by Robert Guelich. Grand Rapids: Eerdmans, 1978.

————. "Salvation, Grace and Works in the Later Writings in the Pauline Corpus." *New Testament Studies* 42 (1996): 339-58.

Martin, Ralph P. *2 Corinthians*. Word Biblical Commentary 40. Waco: Word, 1986.

————. *Carmen Christi: Philippians ii.5-11 in Recent Interpretation and in the Setting of Early Christian Worship*. Society for New Testament Studies Monograph Series 4. Cambridge: Cambridge University Press, 1967. Grand Rapids: Eerdmans, 1983.

————. "The Opponents of Paul in 2 Corinthians: An Old Issue Revisited." Pages 279-89 in *Tradition and Interpretation in the New Testament: Essays in Honor of E. Earle Ellis for His Sixtieth Birthday*. Edited by Gerald F. Hawthorne and Otto Betz. Grand Rapids: Eerdmans; Tübingen: Mohr-Siebeck, 1987.

————. *Reconciliation: A Study of Paul's Theology*. Atlanta: John Knox, 1981.

Martini, Carlo M. "Alcuni Temi Letterari di 2 Cor 4,6 e i racconti della conversione di San Paolo negli Atti." Pages 461-74 in *Studiorum Paulinorum Congressus Internationalis Catholicus 1961*. Vol. 1. Analecta biblica 17-18. Rome: Editrice Pontificio Istituto Biblico, 1963.

Matlock, R. Barry. "Sins of the Flesh and Suspicious Minds: Dunn's New Theology of Paul." *Journal for the Study of the New Testament* 72 (1998): 67-90.

McKnight, Scot. *A Light among the Gentiles: Jewish Missionary Activity in the Second Temple Period*. Minneapolis: Fortress, 1991.

Meissner, Stefan. *Die Heimholung des Ketzers: Studien zur jüdischen Auseinandersetzung mit Paulus*. Wissenschaftliche Untersuchungen zum Neuen Testament 2/87. Tübingen: Mohr-Siebeck, 1996.

Menoud, Philippe H. "Revelation and Tradition: The Influence of Paul's Conversion on His Theology." *Interpretation* 7 (1953): 131-41.

Menzies, Allan. *The Second Epistle of the Apostle Paul to the Corinthians*. London: Macmillan, 1912.

Merkel, Helmut. "Die Gottesherrschaft in der Verkündigung Jesu." Pages 119-61 in *Königsherrschaft Gottes und himmlischer Kult*. Edited by Martin Hengel and Anna M. Schwemer. Tübingen: Mohr-Siebeck, 1991.

————. "καταλλάσσω κτλ." Pages 261-63 in *Exegetical Dictionary of the New Testament*. Vol. 2. Edited by Horst Balz and Gerhard Schneider. Grand Rapids: Eerdmans, 1991.

Meyer, Heinrich A. W. *Kritisch-exegetisches Handbuch über den zweiten Brief an die Korinther*. Göttingen: Vandenhoeck & Ruprecht, 1870.

Michel, Otto. "Christologische Überlegungen." *Theologische Beiträge* 21 (1990): 32-34.

————. "'Erkennen dem Fleisch nach' (II. Kor. 5,16)." *Evangelische Theologie* 14 (1954): 22-29.

Moo, Douglas J. *The Epistle to the Romans*. New International Commentary on the New Testament. Grand Rapids: Eerdmans, 1996.

————. "Israel and Paul in Romans 7.7-12." *New Testament Studies* 32 (1986): 122-35.

————. "'Law,' 'Works of the Law,' and Legalism in Paul." *Westminster Theological Journal* 45 (1983): 73-100.

Moore, George F. *Judaism in the First Centuries of the Christian Era.* 3 vols. Cambridge, Mass.: Harvard University Press, 1927-30.

Morray-Jones, C. R. A. "Paradise Revisited (2 Cor 12:1-12): The Jewish Mystical Background of Paul's Apostolate. Part 1: The Jewish Sources." *Harvard Theological Review* 86 (1993): 177-217.

————. "Paradise Revisited (2 Cor 12:1-12): The Jewish Mystical Background of Paul's Apostolate. Part 2: Paul's Heavenly Ascent and Its Significance." *Harvard Theological Review* 86 (1993): 265-92.

————. "Transformational Mysticism in the Apocalyptic-Merkabah Tradition." *Journal of Jewish Studies* 43 (1992): 1-31.

Moule, Charles F. D. "Jesus, Judaism, and Paul." Pages 43-52 in *Tradition and Interpretation in the New Testament: Essays in Honor of E. Earle Ellis for His Sixtieth Birthday.* Edited by Gerald F. Hawthorne and Otto Betz. Grand Rapids: Eerdmans; Tübingen: Mohr-Siebeck, 1987.

Müller, Ulrich B. *Prophetie und Predigt im Neuen Testament.* Gütersloh: Gütersloher, 1975.

Munck, Johannes. *Christ and Israel: An Interpretation of Romans 9–11.* Translated by Ingeborg Nixon. Philadelphia: Fortress, 1967.

————. *Paul and the Salvation of Mankind.* Translated by Frank Clarke. Richmond: John Knox Press, 1959.

Murphy-O'Conner, Jerome. "Paul in Arabia." *Catholic Biblical Quarterly* 55 (1993): 732-37.

Mussner, Franz. *Der Galaterbrief.* Freiburg: Herder, 1974.

————. "'Ganz Israel wird gerettet werden' (Röm. 11,26). Versuch einer Auslegung." *Kairos* 18 (1976): 245-53.

Neirynck, Frans. "Paul and the Sayings of Jesus." Pages 265-321 in *Apôtre Paul: personnalité, style et conception du ministère.* Edited by Albert Vanhoye. Bibliotheca ephemeridum theologicarum lovaniensium 73. Leuven: Leuven University Press, 1986.

Newman, Carey C. *Paul's Glory-Christology: Tradition and Rhetoric.* Supplements to Novum Testamentum 69. Leiden: E. J. Brill, 1992.

Niebuhr, Karl-Wilhelm. *Heidenapostel aus Israel.* Wissenschaftliche Untersuchungen zum Neuen Testament 62. Tübingen: Mohr-Siebeck, 1992.

O'Brien, P. T. *The Epistle to the Philippians.* New International Greek Testament Commentary. Grand Rapids: Eerdmans, 1991.

Oepke, Albrecht, and Joachim Rohde. *Der Brief des Paulus an die Galater.* 5th ed. Berlin: Evangelisches, 1984.

Oliveira, Anacleto de. *Die Diakonie der Gerechtigkeit und der Versöhnung in der Apologie des 2. Korintherbriefes: Analyse und Auslegung von 2 Kor 2,14–4,6; 5,11–6,10.* Münster: Aschendorff, 1990.

Piper, John. *'Love Your Enemies': Jesus' Love Command in the Synoptic Gospels and the*

Early Christian Paraenesis. Society for New Testament Studies Monograph Series 38. Cambridge: Cambridge University Press, 1979.

Plaq, Christoph. *Israels Weg zum Heil: Eine Untersuchung zu Römer 9 bis 11*. Stuttgart: Calwer, 1969.

Plummer, Alfred. *The Second Epistle of Paul to the Corinthians*. Edinburgh: T & T Clark, 1925.

Porter, Stanley E. καταλλάσσω *in Ancient Greek Literature, with Reference to the Pauline Writings*. Cordoba: Ediciones El Almendro, 1994.

Quarles, Charles L. "The Soteriology of R. Akiba and E. P. Sanders' *Paul and Palestinian Judaism*." *New Testament Studies* 42 (1996): 185-95.

Quispel, Gilles. "Ezekiel 1:26 in Jewish Mysticism and Gnosis." *Vigiliae christianae* 34 (1980): 1-13.

———. "Hermetism and the New Testament, Especially Paul." *ANRW* Part 2, Principat, 22. Edited by H. Temporini and W. Haase. New York: de Gruyter, forthcoming.

———. *Things Unutterable: Paul's Ascent to Paradise in Its Greco-Roman, Judaic and Early Christian Contexts*. Lanham: University Press of America, 1986.

Rabens, Volker. "The Development of Pauline Pneumatology: A Response to F. W. Horn." *Biblische Zeitschrift* 43 (1999): 161-79.

Rad, Gerhard von. *Old Testament Theology*. 2 vols. Translated by D. M. G. Stalker. New York: Harper, 1962-1965.

Räisänen, Heikki. *Paul and the Law*. Wissenschaftliche Untersuchungen zum Neuen Testament 29. Tübingen: Mohr-Siebeck, 1983. Philadelphia: Fortress, 1986. 2nd ed. Tübingen: Mohr-Siebeck, 1987.

———. "Paul's Conversion and the Development of His View of the Law." *New Testament Studies* 33 (1987): 404-19.

———. "Zur Herkunft von Markus 7,15." Pages 209-18 in *The Torah and Christ: Essays in German and English on the Problem of the Law in Early Christianity*. Helsinki: Finnish Exegetical Society, 1986.

Richardson, Peter. "The Thunderbolt in Q and the Wise Man in Corinth." Pages 91-111 in *From Jesus to Paul: Studies in Honor of Francis Wright Beare*. Edited by Peter Richardson and John C. Hurd. Waterloo: Wilfrid Laurier University Press, 1984.

Richardson, Peter, and P. Gooch. "Logia of Jesus in 1 Corinthians." Pages 39-62 in *The Jesus Tradition outside the Gospels*. Vol. 5 of *Gospel Perspectives*, ed. David Wenham. Sheffield: JSOT Press, 1989.

Riesner, Rainer. *Paul's Early Period: Chronology, Mission Strategy, Theology*. Translated by Doug Stott. Grand Rapids: Eerdmans, 1998.

———. "Paulus und die Jesus-Überlieferung." Pages 347-65 in *Evangelium, Schriftauslegung, Kirche*, Peter Stuhlmacher Festschrift. Edited by J. Adna, S. J. Hafemann, and O. Hofius. Göttingen: Vandenhoeck & Ruprecht, 1997.

Roo, Jacqueline C. de. "The Concept of 'Works of the Law' in Jewish and Christian Literature." Pages 116-47 in *Christian-Jewish Relations through the Centuries*. Edited by S. E. Porter and B. W. R. Pearson. Journal for the Study of the New Testament Supplement Series 192. Sheffield: Academic Press, 2000.

Bibliography

Rowland, Christopher C. "The Influence of the First Chapter of Ezekiel on Judaism and Early Christianity." Ph.D. diss., Cambridge University, 1974.

———. *The Open Heaven: A Study of Apocalyptic in Judaism and Early Christianity.* New York: Crossroad, 1982.

Rylaarsdam, John C. "Atonement, Day of." Pages 313-16 in *Interpreter's Dictionary of the Bible,* vol. 1. Edited by George A. Buttrick. New York: Abingdon, 1962.

Sanders, Ed P. *Jesus and Judaism.* Philadelphia: Fortress, 1985.

———. *Paul and Palestinian Judaism.* London: SCM; Philadelphia: Fortress, 1977.

———. *Paul, the Law, and the Jewish People.* Philadelphia: Fortress, 1983.

Sandness, K. O. *Paul — One of the Prophets? A Contribution to the Apostle's Self-Understanding.* Wissenschaftliche Untersuchungen zum Neuen Testament 2/43. Tübingen: Mohr-Siebeck, 1991.

Sänger, Dieter. *Die Verkündigung des Gekreuzigten und Israel: Studien zum Verhältnis von Kirche und Israel bei Paulus und im frühen Christentum.* Tübingen: Mohr-Siebeck, 1994.

Schlatter, Adolf von. *Paulus der Bote Jesu.* Stuttgart: Calwer, 1962 (originally in 1934).

———. *Theologie des Apostels.* Stuttgart: Calwer, 1922.

Schlier, Heinrich. *Der Brief an die Galater.* Göttingen: Vandenhoeck & Ruprecht, 1971.

Schlueter, Carol J. *Filling Up the Measure: Polemical Hyperbole in 1 Thessalonians 2.14-16.* Sheffield: JSOT Press, 1994.

Schmidt, A. "Die Missionsdekret in Galater 2.7-8 als Vereinbarung vom ersten Besuch Pauli in Jerusalem." *New Testament Studies* 38 (1992): 149-52.

Schnelle, Udo. "Der erste Thessalonicherbrief und die Entstehung der paulinischen Anthropologie." *New Testament Studies* 32 (1986): 207-24.

Schoeps, Hans J. *Paul: The Theology of the Apostle in the Light of Jewish Religious History.* Philadelphia: Westminster, 1959.

Scholem, Gershom G. *Jewish Gnosticism, Merkabah Mysticism, and Talmudic Tradition.* 2d ed. New York: The Jewish Theological Seminary of America, 1965.

———. *Major Trends in Jewish Mysticism.* New York: Schocken, 1941.

———. *On the Mystical Shape of the Godhead.* New York: Schocken, 1991.

Schrage, Wolfgang. *Der erste Brief an die Korinther,* vol. 1, *Teil. 1 Kor 1:1–6:11.* Evangelisch-katholischer Kommentar zum Neuen Testament 7/1. Zürich: Benziger; Neukirchen-Vluyn: Neukirchener, 1991.

Schreiner, Thomas R. *The Law and Its Fulfillment.* Grand Rapids: Baker, 1993.

Schröter, Jens. "Gerechtigkeit und Barmherzigkeit: Das Gottesbild der Psalmen Salomos in seinem Verhältnis zu Qumran und Paulus." *New Testament Studies* 44 (1998): 557-77.

Schürmann, Heinz. "'Das Gesetz des Christs' (Gal 6,2): Jesu Verhalten und Wort als letztgültige sittliche Norm nach Paulus." Pages 282-300 in *Neue Testament und Kirche.* Edited by J. Gnilka. Freiburg: Herder, 1974.

Schütz, John H. *Paul and the Anatomy of Apostolic Authority.* Society for New Testament Studies Monograph Series. Cambridge: Cambridge University Press, 1975.

Schweizer, Edward. "1. Korinther 15,20-28 als Zeugnis paulinischer Eschatologie und ihrer Verwandtschaft mit der Verkündigung Jesu." Pages 301-14 in *Jesus und Paulus:*

Festschrift für Werner Georg Kümmel zum 70. Geburtstag. Edited by E. Earle Ellis and Erich Grässer. Göttingen: Vandenhoeck & Ruprecht, 1975.

―――. "ὁ υἱὸς τοῦ θεοῦ." Pages 363-92 in *Theological Dictionary of the New Testament.* Edited by Gerhard Friedrich. Volume 8.

Scott, James M. "'For as Many as Are of Works of the Law Are under a Curse' (Galatians 3.10)." Pages 187-221 in *Paul and the Scriptures of Israel.* Edited by Craig A. Evans and James A. Sanders. Sheffield: JSOT Press, 1993.

―――. *Paul and the Nations: The Old Testament and Jewish Background of Paul's Mission to the Nations with Special Reference to the Destination of Galatians.* Wissenschaftliche Untersuchungen zum Neuen Testament 84. Tübingen: Mohr-Siebeck, 1995.

―――. "The Triumph of God in 2 Cor 2:14: Additional Evidence of Merkabah Mysticism in Paul." *New Testament Studies* 42 (1996): 260-81.

―――. "Throne-Chariot Mysticism in Qumran and in Paul." Pages 101-19 in *Eschatology, Messianism, and the Dead Sea Scrolls.* Edited by Craig A. Evans and Peter W. Flint. Grand Rapids: Eerdmans, 1997.

Seebass, Horst. בחר, Columns 592-608 in *Theologisches Wörterbuch zum Alten Testament.* Edited by G. Johannes Botterweck and Helmer Ringgren. Vol. 1.

Segal, Alan F. *Paul the Convert: The Apostolate and Apostasy of Saul the Pharisee.* New Haven: Yale University Press, 1990.

―――. "Paul and the Beginning of Jewish Mysticism." Pages 95-122 in *Death, Ecstasy, and Other Worldly Journeys.* Edited by John J. Collins and Michael Fishbane. Albany: State University of New York Press, 1995.

―――. "Paul's Thinking about Resurrection in Its Jewish Context." *New Testament Studies* 44 (1998): 400-19.

―――. *Two Powers in Heaven: Early Rabbinic Reports about Christianity and Gnosticism.* Studies in Judaism in Late Antiquity 25. Leiden: E. J. Brill, 1977.

Seifrid, Mark A. "Blind Alleys in the Controversy over the Paul of History." *Tyndale Bulletin* 45 (1994): 73-95.

―――. *Justification by Faith: The Origin and Development of a Central Pauline Theme.* Supplements to Novum Testamentum 68. Leiden: E. J. Brill, 1992.

Silva, Moisés. "The Law and Christianity: Dunn's New Synthesis." *Westminster Theological Journal* 53 (1991): 339-53.

Sjöberg, Erik. *Gott und die Sünder im palästinischen Judentum.* Stuttgart: Kohlhammer, 1939.

Smalley, Stephen S. *1, 2, 3 John.* Word Biblical Commentary 51. Waco: Word, 1984.

Snodgrass, Klyne R. "Justification by Grace — To the Doers: An Analysis of the Place of Romans 2 in the Theology of Paul." *New Testament Studies* 32 (1986): 72-93.

Stanley, Christopher D. "'Under a Curse': A Fresh Reading of Galatians 3.10-14." *New Testament Studies* 36 (1990): 481-511.

Stanton, Graham N. "The Law of Moses and the Law of Christ: Galatians 3:1–6:2." Pages 99-116 in *Paul and the Mosaic Law.* Edited by James D. G. Dunn. Wissenschaftliche Untersuchungen zum Neuen Testament 89. Tübingen: Mohr-Siebeck, 1996.

Stendahl, Krister. "The Apostle Paul and the Introspective Conscience of the West." *Harvard Theological Review* 56 (1963): 199-215. Repr. in *Paul among Jews and Gentiles.* London: SCM, 1973.

Stenger, Werner. "Biographisches und Idealbiographisches in Gal 1,11–2,14." Pages 123-40 in *Kontinuität und Einheit,* F. Mussner FS. Edited by Paul-Gerhard Müller and Werner Stenger. Freiburg: Herder, 1981.

Stockhausen, Carol K. *Moses' Veil and the Glory of the New Covenant.* Analecta biblica 116. Rome: Editrice Pontificio Istituto Biblico, 1989.

Strachan, Robert H. *The Second Epistle of Paul to the Corinthians.* London: Hodder, 1935.

Strecker, Christian. *Die liminale Theologie des Paulus: Zugänge zur paulinischen Theologie aus kultuanthropologischer Perspektive.* Forschungen zur Religion und Literatur des Alten und Neuen Testaments 185. Göttingen: Vandenhoeck & Ruprecht, 1999.

Strecker, Georg. *Das Judenchristentum in den Pseudoklementinen.* Berlin: Akademie, 1981.

Stroumsa, Gedaliahu G. "Form(s) of God: Some Notes on Metatron and Christ." *Harvard Theological Review* 76 (1983): 269-88.

Stuhlmacher, Peter. *Biblische Theologie des Neuen Testaments,* vol. I. *Grundlegung von Jesus und Paulus.* Göttingen: Vandenhoeck & Ruprecht, 1992.

———. "'Das Ende des Gesetzes': Über Ursprung und Ansatz der paulinischen Theologie." *Zeitschrift für die Theologie und Kirche* 67 (1970): 14-39.

———. "Erwägungen zum ontologischen Charakter der καινὴ κτίσις bei Paulus." *Evangelische Theologie* 27 (1967): 1-35.

———. "Erwägungen zum Problem von Gegenwart und Zukunft in der paulinischen Eschatologie." *Zeitschrift für Theologie und Kirche* 64 (1967): 423-50.

———. *Gerechtigkeit Gottes bei Paulus.* Forschungen zur Religion und Literatur des Alten und Neuen Testaments 87. Göttingen: Vandenhoeck, 1966.

———. "The Hermeneutic Significance of 1 Cor 2:6-16." Pages 328-47 in *Tradition and Interpretation in the New Testament: Essays in Honor of E. Earle Ellis for His Sixtieth Birthday.* Edited by Gerald F. Hawthorne and Otto Betz. Grand Rapids: Eerdmans; Tübingen: Mohr-Siebeck, 1987.

———. "Jesustradition im Römerbrief?" *Theologische Beiträge* 14 (1983): 240-50.

———. *Das paulinische Evangelium,* vol. 1, *Vorgeschichte.* Forschungen zur Religion und Literatur des Alten und Neuen Testaments 95. Göttingen: Vandenhoeck & Ruprecht, 1968.

———. *Paul's Letter to the Romans.* Louisville: Westminster, 1994.

Thielman, Frank. *From Plight to Solution.* Novum Testamentum Supplement 61. Leiden: E. J. Brill, 1989.

———. *Paul and the Law.* Downers Grove: InterVarsity Press, 1994.

Thompson, Michael B. *Clothed with Christ: The Example and Teaching of Jesus in Romans 12.1–15.13.* Journal for the Study of the New Testament Supplement 59. Sheffield: JSOT Press, 1991.

Thrall, Margaret E. *A Critical and Exegetical Commentary on the Second Epistle to the*

Corinthians. Vol. 1. *Introduction and Commentary on II Corinthians I–VII*. International Critical Commentary. Edinburgh: T & T Clark, 1994.

———. "Super-Apostles, Servants of Christ, and Servants of Satan." *Journal for the Study of the New Testament* 6 (1980): 42-57.

Turner, Max. *The Holy Spirit and Spiritual Gifts*. Rev. ed. Peabody: Hendrickson, 1998.

Tyson, John B. "'Works of the Law' in Galatians." *Journal of Biblical Literature* 92 (1973): 423-31.

van Unnik, W. "The Christian's Freedom of Speech in the NT." Pages 269-289 in *Sparsa Collecta*, Part II. Leiden: Brill, 1980.

Wagner, J. Ross. "The Heralds of Isaiah and the Mission of Paul: An Investigation of Paul's Use of Isaiah 51-55 in Romans." Pages 193-222 in *Jesus and the Suffering Servant: Isaiah 53 and Christian Origins*. Edited by William H. Bellinger, Jr., and William R. Farmer. Harrisburg: Trinity, 1998.

Walter, Nikolaus. "Paul and the Early Christian Jesus-Tradition." Pages 51-80 in *Paul and Jesus: Colleted Essays*. Edited by Alexander J. M. Wedderburn and Christian Wolff. Journal for the Study of the New Testament Supplement 37. Sheffield: JSOT Press, 1989.

Wanamaker, Charles A. *The Epistles to the Thessalonians: A Commentary on the Greek Text*. New International Greek Testament Commentary. Grand Rapids: Eerdmans, 1990.

Wedderburn, Alexander J. M. "Paul and Jesus: The Problem of Continuity." Pages 99-115 in *Paul and Jesus*. Edited by Alexander J. M. Wedderburn and Christian Wolff. Sheffield: JSOT Press, 1989.

———. "Paul and Jesus: Similarity and Continuity." Pages 117-43 in *Paul and Jesus*.

Wenham, David. *Paul: Follower of Jesus or Founder of Christianity?* Grand Rapids: Eerdmans, 1995.

———. "Paul's Use of the Jesus Tradition: Three Samples." Pages 7-37 in *The Jesus Tradition outside the Gospels*. Vol. 5 of *Gospel Perspectives*. Sheffield: JSOT Press, 1989.

———. *The Rediscovery of Jesus' Eschatological Discourse*. Vol. 4 of *Gospel Perspectives*. Sheffield: JSOT Press, 1984.

Westerholm, Stephen. *Israel's Law and the Church's Faith: Paul and His Recent Interpreters*. Grand Rapids: Eerdmans, 1988.

———. "Sinai as Viewed from Damascus: Paul's Reevaluation of the Mosaic Law." Pages 147-65 in *The Road from Damascus: The Impact of Paul's Conversion on His Life, Thought, and Ministry*. Edited by Richard N. Longenecker. Grand Rapids: Eerdmans, 1997.

Westermann, Claus. *Das Buch Jesaja: Kapitel 40–66*. Das Alte Testament Deutsch. Göttingen: Vandenhoeck & Ruprecht, 1966.

Wilckens, Ulrich. *Der Brief an die Römer (Röm 1–5)*. Evangelisch-katholischer Kommentar zum Neuen Testament. Zürich: Benziger; Neukirchen-Vluyn: Neukirchener, 1978.

———. *Der Brief an die Römer (6-11)*. Zürich: Benziger; Neukirchen: Neukirchener, 1980.

————. "Der Ursprung der Überlieferung der Erscheinung des Auferstandenen: Zur traditionsgeschichtlichen Analyse von 1 Kor 15,1-11." Pages 56-95 in *Dogma und Denkstrukturen*, E. Schlink FS. Edited by Wilfried Joest and Wolfhart Pannenberg. Göttingen: Vandenhoeck & Ruprecht, 1963.

————. *Die Missionsreden der Apostelgeschichte*. Wissenschaftliche Monographien zum Alten und Neuen Testament. Neukirchen-Vluyn: Neukirchener, 1974.

Wildberger, Hans. *Jesaja*. Biblischer Kommentar: Altes Testament. 2 vols. Neukirchen-Vluyn: Neukirchener, 1972-1982.

Williams, Sam K. "Justification and the Spirit in Galatians." *Journal for the Study of the New Testament* 29 (1987): 91-100.

Witherington, Ben. *Grace in Galatia: A Commentary on Paul's Letter to the Galatians*. Edinburgh: T & T Clark, 1998.

Wolff, Christian. "Humility and Self-Denial in Jesus' Life and Message and in the Apostolic Existence of Paul." Pages 145-60 in *Paul and Jesus: Collected Essays*. Edited by Alexander J. M. Wedderburn and Christian Wolff. Journal for the Study of the New Testament Supplement 37. Sheffield: JSOT Press, 1989.

————. "True Apostolic Knowledge of Christ: Exegetical Reflections on 2 Corinthians 5.14ff." Pages 81-98 in *Paul and Jesus: Collected Essays*.

————. *Der zweite Brief des Paulus an die Korinther*. Berlin: Evangelische Verlagsanstalt, 1989.

Wood, Herbert G. "The Conversion of Paul: Its Nature, Antecedents and Consequences," *New Testament Studies* 1 (1954-55): 276-82.

Wrede, William. *Paul*. London: Philip Green, 1907.

Wright, Nicholas T. "Adam, Israel and the Messiah." Pages 18-40 in *The Climax of the Covenant: Christ and the Law in Pauline Theology*. Edinburgh: T & T Clark, 1991; Minneapolis: Fortress, 1992.

————. "Curse and Covenant: Galatians 3.10-14." Pages 137-56 in *The Climax of the Covenant: Christ and the Law in Pauline Theology*.

————. "The Paul of History and the Apostle of Faith." *Tyndale Bulletin* 29 (1978): 61-88.

————. *What Saint Paul Really Said*. Grand Rapids: Eerdmans; Cincinnati: Forward Movement Publications, 1997.

Wright, Robert B. "Psalms of Solomon." Pages 639-70 in *The Old Testament Pseudepigrapha*. Vol. 2. *Expansions of the "Old Testament" and Legends, Wisdom and Philosophical Literature, Prayers, Psalms, and Odes, Fragments of Lost Judeo-Hellenistic Works*. Edited by James H. Charlesworth. Garden City: Doubleday, 1985.

Young, Norman H. "Who's Cursed — and Why? (Galatians 3:10-14)." *Journal of Biblical Literature* 117 (1998): 79-92.

Zeller, Dieter. *Juden und Heiden in der Mission des Paulus*. Stuttgart: Katholisches Bibelwerk, 1975.

Zimmerli, Walther. *Ezechiel 1*. Biblischer Kommentar: Altes Testament. Neukirchen-Vluyn: Neukirchener, 1969.

317

Index of Modern Authors

Index of Scripture and Other Ancient Texts